# The New York Times
## Guide To

# Hotels In
# *New York City*

## By Charles Suisman

and the staff of Manhattan User's Guide

# The New York Times
New York, New York

**Please send all comments to:**

The New York Times Guide to Hotels
122 E. 42d St., 14th Floor
New York, NY 10168

**Published by:**
**The New York Times**
229 W. 43d St.
New York, NY 10036

ISBN 0-9668659-3-6
Printed in the United States of America
First Printing 1999
10   9   8   7   6   5   4   3   2   1

**For the New York Times:** Mitchel Levitas, Editorial Director, Book Development; Thomas K. Carley, President, News Services Division; Nancy Lee, Director of Business Development. Elliott Rebhun and the staff of nytoday.com provided essential help and cooperation.

**Design and Production:** G&H SOHO, Hoboken, N.J.; Jim Harris, Gerry Burstein, Ian Wright, Alan Joyce, Mary Jo Rhodes, Gerald Wolfe.

**Cover Design:** Tim Oliver

Distributed by Publishers Group West

# Acknowledgments

This book wouldn't exist without the hard work of two people.

Carol Molesworth, the backbone of *Manhattan User's Guide,* not only kept the newsletter together while I was frequently AWOL visiting hotel after hotel, she made substantial contributions to this book. She wrote the introductory sections to each neighborhood and used her sharp editorial skills in honing the book's evaluations.

David Yantorno sifted through a blizzard of information, reconciling the often contradictory or occasionally dubious "facts" provided by the hotels. He also arranged every site inspection I made—and that was far more difficult than it sounds. That he did all of it patiently and with good humor made the project far more pleasurable than it would otherwise have been.

I'd also like to thank the Times's Web site, www.nytoday.com, for coming up with the idea of a hotel guide and for trusting me to do it. In particular, thanks to Elliott Rebhun, Rich Meislin and especially Howard Sherman. He not only edited the evaluations with enormous care, he has been supportive well beyond the call of duty. Thanks to Mike Levitas, head of Book Development at the Times, for his enthusiastic support of the project.

Linda DeVito, Sharone Yarone and Maggie Suisman did great work fact checking, and doing it graciously, even for the second, third and fourth times.

For updated information on hotels, as well as
reviews and directions
by car or mass transit, check online at
New York Today (www.nytoday.com/hotels)

# Introduction

## WHAT'S NEW

New York's good fortunes at the close of the century means it welcomes millions of visitors every year, touching off a scramble to offer fresh accommodations. Every hotel, it seems, is redecorating. There are more and better hotels in New York than there have ever been.

Following the usual high-demand, limited space pattern of the city, though, New York has its own unwritten rules about hospitality. Room size is almost invariably smaller here than in most other places, including bathrooms and closets. New York is more expensive than most other places. Paying more for less space is a familiar New York routine.

It is easy to spend hundreds of dollars a night to sleep in Manhattan, but it's not necessary to do so. In this book there are many places to stay for (relatively) reasonable rates—inns, guest houses, bed and breakfasts, extended stay properties and hostels—that can offer a special way of experiencing New York.

This is the era of the boutique hotel in New York. You'll know you're in one because there are usually only a couple of hundred rooms, instead of a couple of thousand, and the design is likely to be distinctive—doing whatever it can to let you know you're in *this* hotel, rather than in any old hotel. Boutique hotels offer distinctive or unusual amenities to get your attention, if nothing else. Sometimes these are comfort-oriented, such as the pillow menu at the Benjamin; sometimes they're more fanciful— the bottle of scent at the Time comes to mind. Many of these hotels have a developed a hip reputation, attracting visitors and natives to their bars, lounges and restaurants.

## STRATEGIES

Some things to know when you're planning a stay in New York. If you're a light sleeper, hotels midblock are generally quieter than hotels on an avenue, and you should ask for a room in the back of the hotel. It may be darker, but you'll be awakened to fewer sirens.

A good shower is important to us at a hotel—it's important to a lot of people, usually simultaneously at 7:30 A.M. Older hotels, even highly rated ones, may have plumbing troubles. The higher floors often have the weakest pressure.

Many hotels have their published "rack rates," which they then discount six ways (or more) from Sunday. Don't accept the first rate you're quoted. It used to be the case that New York hotels offered serious discounts on the weekends, but you'll find less of that than there used to be. The hotel tax has been reduced to a somewhat more reasonable 13.25 percent (plus a $2 per night room charge)—keep it in mind when you're calculating the real cost of a visit.

Hotels left and right claim to have "concierges," but a front desk person isn't a concierge—not in our book. A concierge is a staff member whose sole job it is to make arrangements for you and otherwise enhance your stay. When an evaluation says the concierge has the "Clefs d'Or designation," you know that such concierges have been so honored because they are distinguished at what they do.

New hotels are opening with regularity, and older ones are renovating feverishly. Ask when you reserve if the hotel is renovating when you plan to visit. Even if the renovation isn't taking place on the floor you're staying on, it can be disruptive.

## RATINGS AND WRITTEN EVALUATIONS

The ratings and evaluations were prepared following announced inspections of each property in this book.

I visited a variety of room types, paying special attention to what the hotel identifies as its "standard" accommodation. I look, first and foremost, at the fundamentals of a room: Is it clean and well lit? Are the bed and bedding comfortable? Is the room noisy or quiet? How comfortable is the furniture and how spacious are the surroundings? Is the water pressure strong?

Next, I check the amenities: What does the hotel offer to enhance a guest's comfort, convenience and pleasure? These would include a VCR, CD player, clock radio, hair dryer, bathrobe, wooden clothes hangers (rather than plastic) and whether the rooms have views, terraces or other distinctive features.

Finally, I look at the rest of the hotel: on-site restaurants and bars, business and fitness centers, the concierge, the hotel's commitment to service, its location and any other noteworthy features.

In determining a rating, the quality of the rooms is weighted most heavily. Simply, what level of accommodation and comfort does the hotel offer? Factored in are value for the dollar, hotel features outside of the guest rooms, service and style.

You'll get the best sense of a hotel if you look at the rating in conjunction with its evaluation, rather than relying solely on the rating. Some hotels may be in the lower or higher end of the category; the nuances and rationale for the ratings should be apparent in the evaluation.

Below are brief descriptions of the ratings, designed to further explain each one.

**Extraordinary:** One of the best hotels in New York and probably one of the most expensive. The comfort, design, ambience, amenities and service add up to a hotel that is pleasurable and memorable.

**Excellent:** Strong in rooms, service and ambience—consistently reliable lodging with a broad range of features throughout the hotel's public spaces and in the rooms.

**Very Good:** A comfortable hotel, strong in many areas. Greater attention may be paid to amenities and/or design, or the hotel may have some appealing features that lend it distinction.

**Good:** A solid and reasonably appointed hotel with respectable services and basic amenities. It may lack the style and flair of higher rated spots or fall short in a number of areas.

**Basic:** You shouldn't assume this is a "bad" hotel—a basic rating often means simply that there is a limited level of service and amenities. The hotel may have its own charm and offer visitors reasonable accommodations, but lacks several standard hotel features. Check the evaluation carefully.

**Poor:** Serious failings prevent us from recommending the property as a place to stay.

## RATES

Since there can be so much variation in rates at a hotel, we have calculated the average room price or "standard rack rate" for a double-occupancy room over the course of a year. That price is then placed in one (or more) of the following rate ranges.

under $75
$75–$149
$150–$249
$250–$349
$350–$449
$450 & over

When more than one rate range is indicated for a hotel, it means that the degree of fluctuation in room prices at that hotel is especially high for a standard double and the rates can fall anywhere in the ranges shown.

## HOSTELS

Staying at a hostel is different from staying at a hotel. In most cases, rooms are shared, sometimes up to a dozen or so people in the same room. Hostelers tend to be younger. There is usually a communal kitchen but otherwise minimal amenities. Bedbugs are a frequent problem for hostels since the pests can travel along with a sleeping bag or backpack. Even the cleanest hostels can't claim they never have bedbugs. Hostels that emphasize cleanliness, have foam mattresses, plastic mattress coverings, and don't allow sleeping bags onto guest room floors are likely to have the fewest problems.

## BED AND BREAKFASTS

There are many alternatives in New York to standard hotel accommodations, including some charming bed and breakfasts. Some are hosted in the traditional way, and some are unhosted and therefore more like renting an apartment.

## WHEELCHAIR ACCESS

Since the passage of the 1990 Americans with Disabilities Act, wheelchair access to New York hotels has improved significantly. Larger hotels are more likely to be accessible than others, but if you are concerned about access at a particular hotel, it is best to call ahead and inquire about the accommodations.

"Accessibility" is a broad term. When a hotel indicates that it is wheelchair accessible, that can mean a number of things about both the rooms and public areas. In the public areas, there may be sidewalk ramps, wide doors and aisles, accessible public restrooms and telephones. In the guest rooms, there may be specially designed rooms for wheelchair maneuverability, grab bars in the shower, roll-in showers, features for the hearing impaired or any combination of these.

## NEW YORK TODAY

At *The New York Times* Web site, New York Today, www.nytoday.com/hotels, you can find information on newly opened hotels, ongoing updates and directions to each hotel by car or mass transit.

## MANHATTAN USER'S GUIDE

*Manhattan User's Guide* has been an essential resource for New Yorkers since 1992 and has been called "the best insider's guide." Every month the newsletter offers useful and entertaining information about dining, shopping, special events, the arts, sports and where to find the best deals. For subscription information, call (212) 645-8025 or visit our Web site, www.manhattanusersguide.com.

I hope this hotel guide helps you have a wonderful stay in this wonderful city. I welcome your feedback on any aspect of this book at mugoffice@mindspring.com.

Charlie Suisman

# Table of Contents

# Downtown

## LOWER MANHATTAN/LOWER EAST SIDE

| Hotel | Price Range | Rating |
|---|---|---|
| Best Western Seaport Inn | $150–$249 | Good |
| Fulton Plaza | $250–$349 | Good |
| Holiday Inn Downtown | $150–$249 | Basic |
| Holiday Inn Wall St. | $150–$249 | Very Good |
| Manhattan Seaport Suites | $75–$249 | Good |
| Millenium Hilton | $150–$349 | Very Good |
| New York Marriott Financial Center Hotel | $150–$349 | Very Good |
| New York Marriott World Trade Center | $150–$349 | Very Good |
| Off SoHo Suites Hotel | $75–$249 | Basic |
| The Regent Wall St. | $450 and over | Unrated |
| Wall St. Inn | $150–$249 | Very Good |

## NEIGHBORHOOD BOUNDARIES

### Lower Manhattan
South — The Battery, West — Hudson River, North — Vesey St. east of Broadway, Worth St. west of Broadway, East — East River

### Lower East Side
South — Brooklyn Bridge, West — St. James Place/ Bowery, North — Grand St., East — East River

## ABOUT THE NEIGHBORHOOD

The agglomeration of skyscrapers tells you this is both the financial and the governmental heart of the city. Wall Street and City Hall are a short walk apart. By contrast, the architecture associated with the Lower East Side is that of the tenement — this is the neighborhood where many immigrants settled. Many of the tenements today are being renovated to accommodate new residents. There is a thriving bar and hip music scene in the area of Ludlow, Rivington and Orchard Streets in the late evening hours.

## TRANSPORTATION

Many subway trains pass through lower Manhattan. The 1, 9, N and R will take you close to the Staten Island Ferry terminal; the J, M, Z Broad St. stop puts you near the Wall St. Heliport. The Bowling Green stop on the 4 and 5 train makes a tour of Battery Park easy, and the 2 and 3 will put you right on Wall St. At various points on the Battery you can get ferries to Liberty and Ellis Islands as well as Weehawken, Port Liberty and Jersey City, all in New Jersey. At the South Street Seaport you can access ferries to La Guardia Airport, and both Yankee and Shea Stadiums. Ferries to Hoboken and Liberty Science Center leave from North Cove at the World Financial Center.

## LANDMARKS

The new and the old jostle each other in lower Manhattan. Fraunces Tavern (1719), famous as the site where George Washington said farewell to his soldiers (1783), is in the shadow of the 1960 Skidmore, Owings and Merrill Chase Manhattan Bank, complete with outdoor sculptures by Isamu Noguchi and Jean Dubuffet. The South Street Seaport Museum celebrates the days when New York Harbor was home to ships' chandlers and suppliers. The Bowne and Co. Stationers on Front St. is a relic of that era. The South Street Market celebrates commerce with a mall-like structure on Pier 18. The World Trade Towers do tower over all. They are filled with stores and shops on their concourses, office spaces up to their tops. At the very top you will find an observation deck and a restaurant, Windows on the World, 1 World Trade Center 524-7000, with an only-in-New-York view.

## SHOPPING

For all of the bustle in lower Manhattan, it is not a key shopping area. But there are some high points. Century 21, 22 Cortland St. 227-9092, is a department store that sells top designer goods at man-in-the-street prices. Other bargains for women can be found at Anbar Shoes, 60 Reade St. 227-0253, a bi-level shoe store where shoes are stocked by color and at Designer's Promise, 93 Nassau St. 513-1532, a crammed shop selling top label clothing at discounted prices. At South Street Seaport, look for the gadget-filled Brookestone, 18 Fulton St. 344-8108, and the Yankee Clubhouse Shop, 8 Fulton St. 514-7182. J & R, 23 Park Row 238-9000, is one of the best places in the city to check out computers and electronics.

## EATING AND DRINKING

Besides Windows on the World, new to New York is Roy's New York, 130 Washington St. 266-6262, which features pan-Pacific cuisine and the Bridge Cafe, 279 Water St. 227-3344, which is a tavern serving good and modestly priced American cuisine since

1794. 14 Wall Street Restaurant, 233-2780, and American Park at the Battery, Battery Park 809-5508, make the most of their settings, the first a beautiful interior and the second the vista of New York Harbor.

For information on new hotels, ongoing updates, and directions to each hotel by car or mass transit, check online at New York Today, www.nytoday.com/hotels.

## THE HOTELS

### Best Western Seaport Inn

| | |
|---|---|
| Extraordinary | $450 and over |
| Excellent | $350–$449 |
| Very Good | $250–$349 |
| **Good** | **$150–$249** |
| Basic | $75–$149 |
| Poor | under $75 |

Although this hotel is a stone's throw from the South Street Seaport, it still feels out of the way. The southeastern part of Manhattan isn't a usual choice for visitors, but that's exactly why we like this spot — it offers a different perspective, rich with historical sites.

The Seaport Inn is pleasant and modestly priced. The traditional rooms, done in green and beige, don't deviate much from designs at other Best Western hotels. Closet space is fairly limited; some are simply indentations into the wall and have no doors. Rooms come with a small refrigerator, hair dryer, safe, VCR (you can rent videos from a vending machine in the lobby), but no full-length mirror. Bathrooms have good water pressure, and some have oval-shaped tubs with a whirlpool.

The guest rooms with a terrace are especially desirable. You can lounge and soak in views of the South Street Seaport, the Fulton Fish Market and, best of all, the Brooklyn Bridge. The proximity to the fish market, though, not known for its soothing ambience or aromatherapy, may not be desirable to some.

In all, conventional lodging in an unconventional location.

**Best Western Seaport Inn,** 33 Peck Slip, New York NY 10038
**cross streets:** at Front Street
**phone:** (212) 766-6600, (800) 468-3569
**fax:** (212) 766-6615
**email:** bwseaportinn@usa.net
**website:** www.bestwestern.com/seaportinn
**number of rooms:** 72
**number of floors:** 7
**smoking policy:** designated nonsmoking rooms
**restaurants:** none
**bars:** none
**room service:** none

**hotel amenities:** none
**room amenities:** air-conditioning, VCR, safe, mini-fridge, iron and board
**parking:** none
**cancellation:** 4 P.M. day of arrival
**wheelchair accessibility:** public areas — yes, rooms — yes. ADA compliant

## Fulton Plaza

| | |
|---|---|
| Extraordinary | $450 and over |
| Excellent | $350–$449 |
| Very Good | **$250–$349** |
| **Good** | $150–$249 |
| Basic | $75–$149 |
| Poor | under $75 |

"Soft goods" is hotel lingo for things like curtains and draperies. When a hotel undergoes a renovation, it could be structural, it could be a major redesign, or it could be just the soft goods.

The Fulton Plaza is a downtown hotel with potential not fully realized. The new General Manager, Peter Jaques, impresses us as capable of getting the hotel to bloom, and he's started with a soft goods makeover. This is a property with very large Americana-styled rooms, a fair number of amenities, but without a bruising price tag. With a little work, the hotel could jump up a rating category.

From some rooms, you get a view of the World Trade Center and the Woolworth Building. They're currently the most atmospheric asset of the guest rooms. As things stand, acceptable, if unlovely suites (some standard rooms, too) with single-line phones, voice mail, clock radio, iron and ironing board, Gilchrist and Soames bath products and hair dryer. Some rooms have T1 Internet access. At a minimum, rooms have a mini-fridge and coffeepot. Larger suites have a full kitchen that includes microwave, toaster, stove, dishwasher, pots and pans and utensils. It makes the Fulton a smart choice for an extended stay.

There is a big continental breakfast on the second floor of the hotel for $4.95. Daily maid service is provided for short-term guests. Those staying longer can make an arrangement for housekeeping service.

It wouldn't surprise us, on our next visit to the Fulton, to discover it delivering the goods.

**Fulton Plaza,** 106 Fulton St., New York, NY 10038
**cross streets:** between William and Dutch Streets
**phone:** (212) 835-8600, (888) 212-2345
**fax:** (212) 748-7913
**email:** info@fultonex.com
**website:** www.fultonplaza.com
**number of rooms:** 84 (includes 72 suites)
**number of floors:** 15

**smoking policy:** designated nonsmoking floors
**restaurants:** yes
**bars:** none
**room service:** yes
**hotel amenities:** business center, meeting rooms, function room, concierge
**room amenities:** air-conditioning, kitchen, VCR and fax on request, modem line, mini-fridge
**parking:** none
**cancellation:** 4 P.M. day of arrival
**wheelchair accessibility:** public areas — no, rooms — no

## Holiday Inn Downtown

| | |
|---|---|
| Extraordinary | $450 and over |
| Excellent | $350–$449 |
| Very Good | $250–$349 |
| Good | **$150–$249** |
| **Basic** | $75–$149 |
| Poor | under $75 |

Think of a sweet bed and breakfast in the country, chirping birds outside your window and the smell of warm muffins baking in the morning. That's not the Holiday Inn Downtown. As much as we like the hurly-burly of this part of town, it's a tough sell — you might as well know what you're in for.

The area of New York around Canal Street is not the most prepossessing. Visitors not used to this bustling neighborhood might find its littered streets and noisy main arteries off-putting. If noise is an important consideration for you, be sure to ask for a room at the back of the hotel. Otherwise, be prepared for the garbage truck concerto in the early morning hours. If this has you bouncing off the walls, at least there isn't much room to bounce — some accommodations are extremely small, closet space is minimal (one room had only four hangers, the unre-movable kind), both mattresses and water pressure are variable throughout the hotel, from firm and strong to soft and weak. Windows were in sore need of a cleaning.

Before it was a Holiday Inn, it was a hotel geared toward the Asian community, since it is located in Chinatown. Now, visitors from Asia make up about 25 percent of the hotel's guests, the rest being government employees (visiting the nearby govern-ment offices farther downtown) and tourists.

One bright spot — the hotel's proximity to Chinatown's inter-esting restaurants and some of the city's fashionable neighbor-hoods such as SoHo. We'll look in again after the hotel gets a multimillion-dollar renovation, scheduled for 1999.

**Holiday Inn Downtown,** 138 Lafayette St., New York, NY 10013
**cross streets:** between Canal and Howard Streets
**phone:** (212) 966-8898, (800) 465-4329 (HOLIDAY)
**fax:** (212) 966-3933

**email:** holinnsoho@aol.com
**website:** www.holiday-inn.com/hotels/nycdt/welcome.html
**number of rooms:** 227 (includes12 suites)
**number of floors:** 14
**smoking policy:** designated nonsmoking floors
**restaurants:** yes
**bars:** yes
**room service:** yes
**hotel amenities:** concierge, valet dry cleaning
**room amenities:** air-conditioning, modem line
**parking:** valet
**cancellation:** 6 P.M. day of arrival
**wheelchair accessibility:** public areas — yes, rooms — yes

## Holiday Inn Wall St.

| | |
|---|---|
| Extraordinary | $450 and over |
| Excellent | $350–$449 |
| **Very Good** | $250–$349 |
| Good | **$150–$249** |
| Basic | $75–$149 |
| Poor | under $75 |

Eight feet of desk space may be all you need to know about this
Holiday Inn. It's actually located close by, rather than on, Wall
Street. Still, everything about the hotel has been designed with
the business traveler in mind.

Line at the front desk? Swipe your credit card into a kiosk,
you're checked in, receiving directions to your room. Once
you're there, you'll be well served on many fronts. There are
two-line phones with dataport, direct inward dial, and voice
mail. Ignore the pokey 56K modem in your laptop by plugging in
to their live T1 Internet connection. Sit in the swivel chair at
your eight feet of desk space, outfitted with a dictionary, pencils,
mini calculator, Liquid Paper and paper clips. Get to work.

When it's time to get to sleep, the Holiday Inn has 800 coil
count bedding (excellent), and the neighborhood cooperates by
being peaceful during the wee hours. Amenities are in good supply. They include mini-fridge, clock radio, CD player (there's a
complimentary CD library as well as a periodical library),
bathrobe, safe, iron and ironing board, makeup mirror, coffee
maker and hair dryer. There are Gilchrist and Soames bath products in the marble bathrooms. Rooms aren't huge, but 40 percent of the accommodations have 14-foot ceilings, which gives
the feeling of space. Closets are an open rack.

A business area contains a computer, printer, fax and copier.
Laptops and cell phones are available for rent. The fitness room
has bikes and stairmasters — if you want one in your room, the
hotel will put one in for no additional charge. The hotel has
made arrangements with some area restaurants so that you can
simply sign the check and have the meal billed to your hotel

account. In fact, this Holiday Inn is coming into the neighborhood with many fresh ideas, ready to do business. That's Wall Street style.

**Holiday Inn Wall St.,** 15 Gold St., New York, NY 10038
**cross streets:** at Platt St.
**phone:** (212) 232-7700, (800) 465-4329 (HOLIDAY)
**fax:** (212) 425-0330
**email:** hiwsd@aol.com
**website:** www.holidayinnwsd.com
**number of rooms:** 138 (includes 15 suites)
**number of floors:** 17
**smoking policy:** designated nonsmoking floors
**restaurants:** yes
**bars:** yes
**room service:** yes
**hotel amenities:** fitness equipment, business center, meeting and function rooms, laundry and dry cleaning, cell phone on request
**room amenities:** air-conditioning, VCR on request, safe, fax on request, modem line (T1), mini-bar, multiline phone, TV Internet browser, CD player
**parking:** valet
**cancellation:** 3 P.M. day prior to arrival
**wheelchair accessibility:** public areas — yes, rooms — yes. ADA compliant
**notes:** pets allowed with advance approval

## Manhattan Seaport Suites

| | |
|---|---|
| Extraordinary | $450 and over |
| Excellent | $350–$449 |
| Very Good | $250–$349 |
| **Good** | **$150–$249** |
| Basic | **$75–$149** |
| Poor | under $75 |

You've been asked to do consultant work with a Wall Street firm for a couple of months. You're not in town to soak up atmosphere. Your housing options downtown are few, but the Seaport Suites fits the bill.

It doesn't have the atmosphere you don't need anyway, but it does have rooms of reasonably large dimensions, one-line phones, some with dataport, clock radio, safe, hair dryer and VCRs. Some of the larger suites have full kitchens, including stove, microwave, dishwasher, pots and pans and utensils. Bedding checks out well, and windows are double-paned (though you shouldn't be troubled in this part of town by too much noise at night).

Guests get complimentary passes to the New York Sports Club two blocks away, and there is a complimentary continental breakfast (even the omelet station is gratis). There's no getting around the plainness of the rooms, but weekend visitors (who may pay less than $125 per night) and visitors here for an extended stay will probably overlook the looks for location and value. When we visited, one consultant who came for "a couple of months," was still at the hotel a year later.

**Manhattan Seaport Suites,** 129 Front St., New York, NY 10005
**cross streets:** between Wall Street and Maiden Lane
**phone:** (212) 742-0003, (877) 777-8483
**fax:** (212) 742-0124
**email:** none
**website:** www.seaportny.com
**number of rooms:** 55 (includes 40 suites)
**number of floors:**8
**smoking policy:** designated nonsmoking floors
**restaurants:** none
**bars:** none
**room service:** none
**hotel amenities:** business services, laundry and dry cleaning
**room amenities:** air-conditioning, kitchen, VCR, safe, modem line
**parking:** none
**cancellation:** 3 P.M. 1 day prior to arrival
**wheelchair accessibility:** public areas — no, rooms — no

## Millenium Hilton

| | |
|---|---|
| Extraordinary | $450 and over |
| Excellent | $350–$449 |
| **Very Good** | **$250–$349** |
| Good | **$150–$249** |
| Basic | $75–$149 |
| Poor | under $75 |

You feel the Millenium's corporate focus when you enter the double-story lobby, which has the modern, dark-wood ambience of a board room, albeit on a large scale. The elevators up to the guest floors are as fast and efficient as an ambitious administrative assistant. (On the way down, the elevators are just as whizzingly fast, but there's a somewhat disconcerting rumble). Hallways are modern, bright and, at the elevator banks, there are delightful views to the east, overlooking Brooklyn.

Guest rooms are contemporary in design using warm beige colors and lots of curly maple wood. They tend to be on the small side. Beds have particularly sturdy and comfortable mattresses, windows are double-paned and rooms come equipped with a good number of drawers, iron and ironing board, umbrella, hair dryer, scale, phone in the bathroom and movies on demand. The prints of old New York on the walls offer a nice contrasting flavor to the resolutely modern feel of the hotel.

The business center is surprisingly basic for a hotel with this orientation, but who would spend time there, anyway, when they could be in the fitness center? It has a full range of machines, a sauna and a swimming pool enclosed by glass —

the views of St. Paul's Chapel are a delight. In fact, views are among the Millenium's prime assets: guest rooms rise up 55 floors, and few Manhattan hotels can compete with these thrilling views of downtown Manhattan and the Hudson.

**Millenium Hilton,** 55 Church St., New York, NY 10007
**cross streets:** between Fulton and Dey Streets
**phone:** (212) 693-2001, (800) 752-0014
**fax:** (212) 571-2316
**email:** none
**website:** www.newyorkmillenium.hilton.com
**number of rooms:** 561 (includes 98 suites)
**number of floors:** 55
**smoking policy:** designated nonsmoking rooms
**restaurants:** 2
**bars:** 2
**room service:** yes
**hotel amenities:** health club, swimming pool, concierge, laundry and dry cleaning, business center, meeting and function rooms
**room amenities:** air-conditioning, mini-bar, VCR on request, modem line, safe
**parking:** valet
**cancellation:** 4 P.M. day prior to arrival
**wheelchair accessibility:** public areas — yes, rooms — yes. ADA compliant

## New York Marriott Financial Center Hotel

| | |
|---|---|
| Extraordinary | $450 and over |
| Excellent | $350–$449 |
| **Very Good** | **$250–$349** |
| Good | **$150–$249** |
| Basic | $75–$149 |
| Poor | under $75 |

Marriott has two hotels in close proximity to each other in Manhattan's downtown business district. This hotel is smaller than the one at the World Trade Center, with much less hubbub. Rooms are traditional in design. Fall colors predominate — green, brown, rust — and the look is familiar, though a bit drab. Mattresses are extra firm, water pressure is fine, ceilings are low (which makes the rooms feel smaller), and there are armoires instead of closets. Some rooms have appealing views of the southern tip of the island, including the Statue of Liberty.

As with the World Trade Center property just to the north along West Street, there is a Concierge Lounge for "Concierge Level" guests. The telescope in the lounge would certainly yield some interesting sights.

The Marriott Financial Center houses Roy's New York, one of the growing chain of chef Roy Yamaguchi's restaurants and the first in New York. Yamaguchi's Hawaiian-fusion cooking has made him one of the country's more highly regarded chefs.

The hotel also has a business center that consists of two computers, a copy machine and a fax machine (you might expect a more robust business center), a modest fitness room and a 50-foot by 20-foot pool.

For the business traveler who wants to be in the center of the action but at a peaceful remove, the Marriott Financial Center would be a good choice.

**New York Marriott Financial Center Hotel,** 85 West St., New York, NY 10006
**cross streets:** between Carlisle and Albany Streets
**phone:** (212) 385-4900, (800) 242-8685
**fax:** (212) 227-8414
**email:** none
**website:** www.marriott.com/marriott/nycws
**number of rooms:** 504 (includes 13 suites)
**number of floors:** 38
**smoking policy:** designated nonsmoking rooms
**restaurants:** Roy's New York
**bars:** yes
**room service:** yes
**hotel amenities:** health club, swimming pool, meeting rooms, concierge, laundry and dry cleaning
**room amenities:** air-conditioning, safe, modem line, mini-bar
**parking:** valet
**cancellation:** 6 P.M. day of arrival
**wheelchair accessibility:** public areas — yes, rooms — yes. ADA compliant

## New York Marriott World Trade Center

| | |
|---|---|
| Extraordinary | $450 and over |
| Excellent | $350–$449 |
| **Very Good** | **$250–$349** |
| Good | **$150–$249** |
| Basic | $75–$149 |
| Poor | under $75 |

Marriott took over this hotel in 1995, giving them two properties a very short stroll from each other in the heart of New York's downtown financial and business center.

The Marriott WTC does, in fact, connect to one of the World Trade Center concourses, offering guests easy access to things like airline ticket desks, car rental counters, a discount theater ticket booth, the WTC observation deck and an indoor shopping mall. The other Marriott, called the Marriott Financial Center, is smaller, quieter and has a somewhat more "boutique hotel" feeling.

The WTC has more bells and whistles. One of the most attractive amenities is the full-service health club near the top of the building. Besides a range of machines, there is a running track and lap pool, all with views over the Hudson into New Jersey. Health club access is complimentary to hotel guests. Massage and personal trainers are available at additional cost.

For $40 over the regular rates, the "Concierge Level" guest rooms allow you into the Concierge Lounge (with a variety of business amenities), and your room is slightly upgraded in style. All rooms feature a more contemporary design than you'll find at other Marriotts. Room amenities include clock radio, voice mail, complimentary newspaper, iron and ironing board and coffee maker. Closet space and water pressure check out well, windows are double-paned, bathroom lighting is on the harsh side, and ceilings tend to be low throughout the hotel.

The hotel has a small but nicely designed and perfectly adequate business center, a concierge and 24-hour room service. In all, the business traveler should be well served and even the tourist can take advantage of the hotel's proximity to neighborhoods like TriBeCa and SoHo.

**New York Marriott World Trade Center,** 3 World Trade Center, New York, NY 10048
**cross streets:** between Liberty and Barclay Streets
**phone:** (212) 938-9100, (800) 550-2344
**reservations fax:** (212) 444-4094, guest fax: (212) 444-3444
**email:** none
**website:** www.marriott.com
**number of rooms:** 818 (includes 17 suites)
**number of floors:** 21
**smoking policy:** designated nonsmoking rooms
**restaurants:** 2
**bars:** yes
**room service:** yes, 24-hour
**hotel amenities:** health club, swimming pool, business center, meeting rooms, concierge, laundry and dry cleaning
**room amenities:** air-conditioning, VCR on request, safe, minibar, multiple phone lines
**parking:** valet
**cancellation:** 6 P.M. 1 day prior to arrival
**wheelchair accessibility:** public areas — yes, rooms — yes. ADA compliant

## Off SoHo Suites Hotel

| | |
|---|---|
| Extraordinary | $450 and over |
| Excellent | $350–$449 |
| Very Good | $250–$349 |
| Good | **$150–$249** |
| **Basic** | **$75–$149** |
| Poor | under $75 |

The name of this hotel is somewhat misleading. Not-too-far-from SoHo Suites would be more accurate. It's not just a technicality: this is not a neighborhood that all visitors will be comfortable with, since the Bowery is still the Bowery and it's only a block away.

With that understanding, the hotel can be recommended for adventurous families on a budget or for three or four adults who want to share an apartment-like accommodation to save some money.

Some of the suites, though, have one bedroom and one fold-out sofa and a few of those sofa beds looked as if they had been opened once too often — it didn't look as if they would offer the most cushioned night's sleep.

Noise, too, could affect your slumber, filtering through the windows even though they are double-paned. Window gates are also on these windows, unusual for a hotel, but a reminder that this hasn't been the most secure of neighborhoods. Bathrooms are pine-smelling clean and generally have at least a small window and a full-size closet with shelves. The bedrooms aren't great: soft mattresses, closets with only five plastic hangers, no bedside lamps and very few drawers.

There are full kitchens in each suite: gas ovens, microwaves and enough pots, pans and dishes for you to prepare a simple meal. Given the money you save by staying here, you could almost afford to shop for groceries at Dean and Deluca.

**Off SoHo Suites Hotel,** 11 Rivington St., New York, NY 10002
**cross streets:** between Chrystie Street and the Bowery
**phone:** (212) 353-0860, (800) 633-7646
**fax:** (212) 979-9801
**email:** info@offsoho.com
**website:** www.offsoho.com
**number of rooms:** 38 (all suites)
**number of floors:** 6
**smoking policy:** designated nonsmoking rooms
**restaurants:** yes
**bars:** no
**room service:** yes
**hotel amenities:** fitness equipment, self-service laundry
**room amenities:** kitchen, mini-fridge, modem line
**parking:** none
**cancellation:** 2 days prior to arrival
**wheelchair accessibility:** public areas — yes, rooms — yes.

## The Regent Wall St.

| | |
|---|---|
| Extraordinary | **$450 and over** |
| Excellent | $350–$449 |
| Very Good | $250–$349 |
| Good | $150–$249 |
| Basic | $75–$149 |
| Poor | under $75 |

When we visited the Regent Wall Street, it was still a construction site, which is why it has no rating. It's scheduled to open in late fall 1999. We did see some model rooms, renderings and the architectural gem they are inhabiting. From all signs, this looks to be a serious entry into the luxury hotel market, and its location downtown means it has virtually has the field to itself.

The Greek Revival building dates to 1842, replacing an earlier building destroyed by fire, and housing the Merchant's Exchange. It also served as the New York Custom House, and place of employment for Herman Melville. McKim, Mead, and White added four stories in 1907.

The smallest guest rooms are 525 square feet, which gives you an idea of how generously sized these accommodations are. Chenille, silks and velvets are the fabric choices. Amenities are to include two-line phones, dataport, voice mail, fax/copier /printer, 24-hour room service, marble baths, bathrobes and slippers. Expect a concierge staff, a fitness facility and spa. The 12,000-square-foot Grand Ballroom has a dome with 16 Wedgwood panels — no other hotel in the city has a ballroom anything like it. The Regent's restaurant will be called 55 Wall Street.

We do evaluations, not forecasts, but it's hard not to be bullish about the Regent Wall Street.

**The Regent Wall St.,** 55 Wall St. New York, NY 10005
**cross streets:** William St. and Exchange Pl.
**phone:** (212) 845-8600, (800) 545-4000
**fax:** (212) 845-8601
**email:** none
**website:** www.rih.com
**number of rooms:** 144 (includes 46 suites)
**number of floors:** 4
**smoking policy:** designated nonsmoking rooms
**restaurants:** 55 Wall Street
**bars:** 1
**room service:** yes, 24 hours
**hotel amenities:** fitness equipment and spa, business center, meeting and function rooms, concierge, laundry and dry cleaning
**room amenities:** air-conditioning, VCR, safe, mini-bar, multi line phones, TV Internet browser, modem line
**parking:** valet
**cancellation:** 1 day prior to arrival
**wheelchair accessibility:** public areas — yes, rooms — yes. ADA compliant

## Wall St. Inn

| | |
|---|---|
| Extraordinary | $450 and over |
| Excellent | $350–$449 |
| **Very Good** | $250–$349 |
| Good | **$150–$249** |
| Basic | $75–$149 |
| Poor | under $75 |

The best deal downtown and a very nice place to stay.

On this site around 1660, a house was built for Asser Levy, a Jewish butcher and moneylender. A synagogue was later on the property. A fire destroyed the buildings in 1835 after which various commercial buildings and businesses occupied the block. Lehman Brothers, the investment banking firm that dates back to before the Civil War, moved to South William Street in 1928 and had its annex here.

This new inn, which opened in June, 1999, has been four years in the making as the existing structure was renovated from top to bottom. It seems safe to say that their 46 rooms will be booked for a long time to come.

They appear to have done everything right at this hotel, paying close attention to the fundamentals and staying away from showier but less useful gimmicks. The basics start with bedding — high-quality mattresses and 200-thread count sheets. Windows are not only double-paned, they are filled with argon gas. One step more to insure quiet: the panes are of different thicknesses, which is another noise baffler. Nobody books a hotel based on the basement, but the owners have gone to the expense of installing a four-pipe system, which means you can have a choice of heat or air-conditioning all year round (in two-pipe hotels, you can have heat when the hotel has the heat on but not a.c. and vice versa). Water pressure is also strong. Rooms are not large, but don't feel cramped relative to the rest of the city's rooms.

Amenities include clock radio, three two-line phones (one in the bathroom) with dataport and voice mail, a safe large enough to hold a laptop and a mini-bar chosen because it runs quietly (you don't have to listen to the compressor turn on and off all night). In the bathroom, a hair dryer, makeup mirror, plush towels and Caswell-Massey bath products. The bathroom has two additional switches of note — one to hear the television and another that sets a low level "night light" so you can get there in the middle of the night. The iron and ironing board have also been cleverly stowed behind a custom-built, wood-framed mirror.

The newly opened Regent Wall Street has the luxury end of the downtown market in its sights. The Wall Street Inn's ambitions are more modest, but, from everything we could see during a pre-opening visit, its initial public offerings should be most agreeable.

**Wall St. Inn,** 9 S. William St., New York, NY 10005
**cross streets:** between Broad and Beaver Streets
**phone:** (212) 747-1500
**fax:** (212) 747-1900
**email:** none
**website:** www.wallstinn.com
**number of rooms:** 46 (includes 10 suites)
**number of floors:** 7
**smoking policy:** designated nonsmoking floor
**restaurants:** none
**bars:** none
**room service:** yes
**hotel amenities:** health club, business center, meeting and function rooms, concierge, laundry and dry cleaning
**room amenities:** air-conditioning, VCR, safe, fax on request, multiline phone, modem line, mini-bar
**parking:** none
**cancellation:** 4 P.M. 1 day prior to arrival
**wheelchair accessibility:** public areas — yes, rooms — yes. ADA compliant

# TRIBECA/SOHO

| Hotel | Price Range | Rating |
| --- | --- | --- |
| Cosmopolitan Hotel | $75–$149 | Basic |
| The Mercer Hotel | $350–$449 | Excellent |
| Pioneer Hotel | $75–$149 | Basic |
| SoHo Bed and Breakfast | $75–$149 | Very Good |
| SoHo Grand Hotel | $350–$449 | Very Good |

## NEIGHBORHOOD BOUNDARIES

### SoHo
South — Canal St., West — Hudson River, North — Houston St.,
East — Bowery

### TriBeCa
South — Vesey St., West — Hudson River, North — Canal St.,
East — Broadway

## ABOUT THE NEIGHBORHOOD

Not so long ago SoHo was a light manufacturing neighborhood,
filled with lofts where people were sewing and shipping goods.
When the factories began to close up, artists decided they liked
working in the big spaces left behind. Galleries flooded into
SoHo to show the work of the artists, followed by restaurants
and shops. Soon the loft studios became dwelling spaces,
spawning a whole style of interior architecture and apartment
design. Now the words "SoHo style" are used to mean a cool,
clean, contemporary look in clothing and interior design. Today,
many galleries have decamped to West Chelsea and other neighborhoods, chased out, they said, by the proliferation of shops
and raising of their rents. While there are fewer galleries, there
are restaurants and shops in abundance. In TriBeCa, the triangle
below Canal, you may see cast-iron on the ground floor of a
building which is brickwork above. The grand size of some of
the buildings indicates their original use as factories, ware-
houses and cold storage for food. Many butter and egg businesses were located here. Today, the only butter and eggs you'll
find are in the clutch of fine restaurants that have settled in what
is fast becoming a residential neighborhood.

## TRANSPORTATION

It's easy to get to points in SoHo on the 1, 9, C, E, N, R, B, D or
F trains. Once there, it's an on-foot neighborhood.

## LANDMARKS

Cast-iron architecture is typical of the buildings here. Interior columns, supporting the weight of the floors above, were what made the big open spaces possible. You can see many columns on the outside of the buildings, and many of the shops and galleries work their displays around them. Not all of the art has left. The Guggenheim SoHo, 578 Broadway 423-3500, New Museum, 583 Broadway 219-1222, The Drawing Center, 35 Wooster St. 219-2166, and Dieu Donne Papermill, 433 Broome St. 226-0573, can be relied on for engaging exhibitions. Film Forum, 209 W. Houston 727-8110, is a good place to see movies. The Knitting Factory, 75 Leonard St. 219-3055, has four performance spaces on three floors for live music every night.

## SHOPPING

The blocks in the section from Broadway to Avenue of the Americas, from Grand to W. Houston are chock-ablock with stores, and it seems as if there are more coming all the time. The French-based Sephora, 555 Broadway 625-1309, gives you a worldwide overview of cosmetics and scents; Armani Exchange, 568 Broadway 431-6000, shows off the lower-priced line of the famous designer. Other designers in the area are Todd Oldham, Agnes B, Yohji Yamamoto, Betsey Johnson, Anna Sui, and Helmut Lang. Dean & Deluca, 560 Broadway 226-6800, can be visited for a cup of espresso at the stand-up bar at front or to load up on all manner of foodstuffs — artisanal pastas or Thai sauces. Gourmet Garage, 453 Broome St. 941-5850, doesn't pretend to be as encyclopedic, but they are less expensive. Moss, 146 Greene St. 226-2190, Troy, 138 Greene 941-4777 and Ad Hoc Softwares, 410 W. Broadway 925-2652, make much of the SoHo esthetic in their housewares and furniture displays. Broadway Panhandler, 477 Broome St. 966-3434, used to be on Broadway long before SoHo was a household word. The store is a great source for kitchen and bakeware. Canal Surplus, 363 Canal St. 966-3275, is a mad hodgepodge where artists like to poke around for odd materials. Pearl Paint, 308 Canal St. 431-7932, sells standard art supplies in a five-floor setting. Ceramica, 59 Thompson 941-1307, is stocked with hand-painted Italian dishes and serving pieces. Kate's Paperie, 561 Broadway 941-9816, is a large shop selling all manner of wrapping and writing papers. A Photographer's Place, 133 Mercer St. 431-9358, serves up vintage photography books and some vintage photographs. Ted Muehling's jewelry is deservedly popular, 47 Greene St. 431-3825.

## EATING AND DRINKING

Some of the city's best restaurants are in these two neighborhoods. Chanterelle, 2 Harrison St. 966-6960, is one of the most civilized restaurants anywhere and has four stars from the *New*

*York Times.* Nobu, 105 Hudson St. 219-0500, has high-style, eclectic Japanese food. Bouley Bakery, 120 W. Broadway 964-2525, gastronomic temple of chef David Bouley, has enlarged the restaurant, so reservations should be slightly easier to get. Blue Ribbon, 97 Sullivan St. 274-0404, is a favorite of chefs, so you know the food is good. Zoë, 90 Prince St. 966-6722, is as accommodating as can be — a festive place with food and wine to match. At Honmura An, 170 Mercer St. 334-5253, you'll find a peaceful place for Japanese noodles. There's plenty of buzz surrounding The Mercer Kitchen in the Mercer Hotel, 99 Prince St. 966-5454, under the direction of Jean-Georges Vongerichten. Balthazar, 80 Spring St. 965-1414, has done everything by way of decor, service and menu choices to make you feel as if you are in a French brasserie. If nightlife is what you came for, visit one of the many bars in the area — Bar 89, 89 Mercer St. 274-0989, Merc Bar, 151 Mercer St. 966-2727, Bubble Lounge, 228 W. Broadway 431-3433, or Fanelli's, 94 Prince St. 226-9412 and the nearby Ñ, 33 Crosby St. 219-8856, or Pravda, 281 Lafayette St. 226-4696.

For information on new hotels, ongoing updates, and directions to each hotel by car or mass transit, check online at New York Today, www.nytoday.com/hotels.

## THE HOTELS

### Cosmopolitan Hotel

| | |
|---|---|
| Extraordinary | $450 and over |
| Excellent | $350–$449 |
| Very Good | $250–$349 |
| Good | $150–$249 |
| **Basic** | **$75–$149** |
| Poor | under $75 |

The Cosmopolitan can trace its ancestry back to the 1850s, which allows it to claim being the longest, continuously operating hotel in New York. Abraham Lincoln, before he was president, slept here. Don't come for the history, though: the owners did a gut renovation in 1997 that left only the exterior walls intact.

What you should come for are rooms priced at less than $150 in lower Manhattan. As you'd expect after such an overhaul, the rooms are perfectly clean, and, understandably at these prices, amenities are few. You'll find a one-line phone with dataport, double-paned windows, clock radio, TV, air-conditioning and ceiling fan. Iron, ironing board and hair dryer are available on request.

Furnishings are simple — most have gray wallpaper and burgundy color carpeting. Rooms in the back are quieter but darker.

The "22" line of rooms up to the sixth floor is especially appealing. They are corner rooms that include the building's original brickwork for the fireplace (now bricked up). From one window, you look uptown to see the Empire State Building. If you poke your head out of another window, you can see the nearby World Trade towers. We particularly like these rooms, but they can be chilly in winter. Another room type is the "loft" — they're small but have the bed up a narrow set of stairs (it's the kind of loft you can sleep in but not stand up in). These loft rooms have built-in furniture downstairs with a generous number of drawers and a pleasant workspace.

Drawbacks are a deodorized smell in many rooms (smoking is allowed throughout so this is a necessity), closets that may simply be a tiny rack with a few hangers, and the size of the rooms themselves. There is no food and beverage service in the hotel, but TriBeCa has a wonderful range of restaurants and bars. The location itself might have been a drawback a few years ago, but lower Manhattan has become increasingly popular. A Starbucks is even set to open on the hotel's ground floor.

The Cosmopolitan offers very fair value for your dollar.

**Cosmopolitan Hotel,** 95 West Broadway, New York, NY 10007
**cross streets:** at Chambers St.
**phone:** (212) 566-1900, (888) 895-9400
**fax:** (212) 566-6909
**email:** chnyc95@aol.com
**website:** www.cosmohotel.com
**number of rooms:** 104
**number of floors:** 7
**smoking policy:** all smoking rooms
**restaurants:** none
**bars:** none
**room service:** none
**hotel amenities:** laundry and dry cleaning
**room amenities:** air-conditioning, modem line
**parking:** none
**cancellation:** noon 1 day prior to arrival
**wheelchair accessibility:** public areas — no, rooms — no

## The Mercer Hotel

| Extraordinary | $450 and over |
| **Excellent** | **$350–$449** |
| Very Good | $250–$349 |
| Good | $150–$249 |
| Basic | $75–$149 |
| Poor | under $75 |

Memorable hotels have personalities quite apart from the furniture, paint and towels. It is in this category that this genuinely individual hotel belongs. With owner Andre Balazs, designer Christian Liaigre has created an environment with a cool, modern, downtown ambience — clean, elegant, comfortable, unshowy and secure enough for flowers on the windowsills.

The rooms have ample space, the bathrooms especially. There is 24-hour room service from the Mercer Kitchen (the restaurant is overseen by Jean-Georges Vongerichten, whose uptown French restaurant Jean-Georges has four stars). Each room includes a cordless phone, bathroom freebies from the cosmetics company FACE Stockholm, cable, VCR and a CD player. There are also guest passes to the nearby David Barton gym.

One of the nicest details: Check-in takes place in your room. The hotel reflects the neighborhood's mix of classic and cutting-edge, but isn't insistent that you pay attention to it at every turn. In other words, the Mercer has style *and* character.

**The Mercer Hotel,** 147 Mercer St., New York, NY 10012
**cross streets:** at Prince Street
**phone:** (212) 966-6060, (888) 918-6060
**fax:** (212) 965-3838
**email:** none
**website:** www.themercer.com
**number of rooms:** 75 (includes 5 suites)
**number of floors:** 6
**smoking policy:** all smoking rooms
**restaurants:** The Mercer Kitchen
**bars:** yes
**room service:** yes
**hotel amenities:** laundry and dry cleaning, business services
**room amenities:** air-conditioning, mini-bar, VCR, fax on request, modem line, safe
**parking:** none
**cancellation:** 2 days prior to arrival
**wheelchair accessibility:** public areas — yes, rooms — yes

## Pioneer Hotel

| | |
|---|---|
| Extraordinary | $450 and over |
| Excellent | $350–$449 |
| Very Good | $250–$349 |
| Good | $150–$249 |
| **Basic** | **$75–$149** |
| Poor | under $75 |

A small step up from most hostels, but a budget hotel of the most basic sort. Something about the peculiar atmosphere suggests a ward or reformatory — hospitality is not the thing that comes to mind from its near-the-Bowery location and a room that contains, say, three single beds, linoleum floor, pressed tin ceiling, a few pieces of wood furniture.

The furnishings are certainly eclectic. A rolltop desk in one room, lampshades with plastic on them in another, as if someone was just back from a jumble sale and hadn't had time to organize their van load. Rooms have a sink in them, AC, ceiling fan and TV but little else. Windows are double-paned, but noise from the street can be heard. Closets are likely to be a small rack in the room. Many rooms do not have a bath en suite — the ones that do are quite small. The hall bathrooms aren't clean enough for surgery, but are fine for a shave. Considering the prices, younger budget travelers may find the Pioneer just fine. The fact that they're near the East Village, as well as TriBeCa and SoHo, is also likely to be a plus.

**Pioneer Hotel,** 341 Broome St., New York, NY 10013
**cross streets:** between Elizabeth Street and the Bowery
**phone:** (212) 226-1482, (800) 737-0702
**fax:** (212) 226-3525
**email:** pioneer_hotel@worldnet.att.net
**website:** www.pioneer-hotel.com
**number of rooms:** 125
**number of floors:** 4 in a walk-up building
**smoking policy:** all smoking rooms
**restaurants:** none
**bars:** none
**room service:** none
**hotel amenities:** none
**room amenities:** some shared baths, air-conditioning
**parking:** none
**cancellation:** 6 P.M. day of arrival
**wheelchair accessibility:** public areas — no, rooms — no

## SoHo Bed and Breakfast

| | |
|---|---|
| Extraordinary | $450 and over |
| Excellent | $350–$449 |
| **Very Good** | $250–$349 |
| Good | $150–$249 |
| Basic | **$75–$149** |
| Poor | under $75 |

This B & B, located on the back-street-feeling Crosby St., has no exterior profile. You could pass a thousand times and never know it's there. The building dates from 1792. Rent one of the two available spaces, though, and you could get hooked. It doesn't have a sparkling, paper-strip-over-the-toilet-seat quality — it's a quirky and lived-in feeling.

Two parts. The first is the large loft over a live-in studio of the artist/owner. It's a genuine SoHo loft — a big open space — though the bedroom is separate. Artifacts collected from Africa, the South Seas and Mexico adorn the brick walls. A large (full) kitchen area with a breakfast table is next to a large dining room table. Walk farther to the back and there's a living room area, with TV, VCR, couches. The bedroom is comfortable but note it's the only area with an air conditioner. Ceilings fans do a good job on all days but New York's worst. This loft, connected as it is to the artist's studio, is considered a "hosted" accommodation, which means he'll be a discreet part of your vacation. It will only enhance your stay.

Part two is the adjoining carriage house, considered "unhosted." It's much smaller than the loft, but it has its own charms and some history, as well. Billie Holiday lived here for a time. The three skylights add plenty of light.

Amenities include one-line phones, answering machine, clock radio, iron and ironing board, and umbrella. We'd have to include the well-informed and amiable host as an amenity, too.

**SoHo Bed and Breakfast,** 167 Crosby St., New York, NY 10012
**cross streets:** at Bleecker Street
**phone:** (212) 925-1034
**fax:** (212) 226-9081
**email:** crosby3@juno.com
**website:** none
**number of rooms:** 2 apartments
**number of floors:** 2
**smoking policy:** all smoking rooms
**restaurants:** none
**bars:** none
**room service:** none
**hotel amenities:** bike rental
**room amenities:** air-conditioning, VCR, kitchen, iron and board, laundry, fax on request, modem line
**parking:** none
**cancellation:** forfeit 20% deposit
**wheelchair accessibility:** public areas — no, rooms — no
**notes:** does not accept credit cards

## SoHo Grand Hotel

| | |
|---|---|
| Extraordinary | $450 and over |
| Excellent | **$350–$449** |
| **Very Good** | $250–$349 |
| Good | $150–$249 |
| Basic | $75–$149 |
| Poor | under $75 |

David Paul Helpern and William Sofield, the SoHo Grand's architect and interior designer, are the stars of this new hotel.

You can't beat the sheer effect of ascending the staircase from the ground floor to the hotel's lobby, in which bold, industrial, urban elements give way to 24-foot ceilings and two-story windows. The SoHo Grand is full of allusions to SoHo present (cool, understated design), to SoHo past (cast-iron architectural elements) and even to the Colonial era (the lanterns outside guests' doors). The rooms are mostly celadon green, some with gray accents. There are saddle stitch leather headboards, pedestal sinks and honeycomb-pattern tile floors. The eye here is unassailable.

Touches of comfort include 300-count Frette linens, superbly firm mattresses, Kiehl's products in the bathrooms and a dozen wooden hangers in the closets (including skirt hangers). Water pressure is so strong that after we quickly turned a faucet, water sprayed out, necessitating a call to housekeeping to clean up. Many rooms boast entrancing views, including one north to midtown that is worth the price of admission. There are some drawbacks, however. Rooms, bathrooms and closets are spatially challenged. There are no in-room fax machines, CD or video players, irons or ironing boards, no business center and no night turndown service.

To the extent that clothes make the man, this hotel has it made. We'd like to see, though, the same passion brought to the look of the place focused on some hospitality fundamentals.

**SoHo Grand Hotel,** 310 W. Broadway, New York, NY 10013
**cross streets:** between Grand and Canal Streets
**phone:** (212) 965-3000, (800) 965-3000
**reservations fax:** (212) 965-3244, guest fax: (212) 965-3200
**email:** none
**website:** www.sohogrand.com
**number of rooms:** 369 (includes 4 suites)
**number of floors:** 17
**smoking policy:** designated nonsmoking rooms
**restaurants:** yes
**bars:** yes
**room service:** yes
**hotel amenities:** fitness equipment, concierge, laundry and dry cleaning, meeting and function rooms
**room amenities:** air-conditioning, mini-bar, modem line, safe
**parking:** valet
**cancellation:** 4 P.M. day of arrival
**wheelchair accessibility:** public areas — yes, rooms — yes

# WEST VILLAGE/EAST VILLAGE

| Hotel | Price Range | Rating |
|---|---|---|
| Abingdon Guest House | $150–$249 | Good |
| East Village Bed & Coffee | under $75 | Basic |
| Incentra Village House | $75–$149 | Good |
| Larchmont Hotel | $75–$149 | Good |
| Riverview Hotel | under $75 | Poor |
| Rooms to Let | $75–$249 | Good |
| Second Home on Second Ave. | $75–$149 | Good |
| Washington Square Hotel | $150–$249 | Good |

## NEIGHBORHOOD BOUNDARIES

### West Village:
South — W. Houston St., West — Hudson River, North — W. 14th St., East — Fifth Ave.

### East Village:
South — E. Houston St., West — Fifth Ave., North — E. 14th St., East — East River

## ABOUT THE NEIGHBORHOOD

A list of former residents of the Village reads like a Who's Who of American literature — the neighborhood was at one time home to e.e. cummings, Edna St. Vincent Millay, Marianne Moore, Willa Cather, Sherwood Anderson, Allen Ginsberg, Djuna Barnes and many others. The words "Greenwich Village" came to define a kind of bohemian lifestyle of the Auntie Mame variety. In fact, the model for that character, Marion Tanner, lived at 72 Bedford St. Today, you will find shady, residential streets with a loud strip of shops on W. 8th St. Christopher St., which runs diagonally from 6th Ave. to West St., contains many small interesting shops and some gay bars. The Stonewall Inn, at number 53, is the site at which, in 1969, resistance by gays to police harassment led to the Gay Pride movement. St. Mark's Place, one of the main drags in the East Village, is lined with often-changing shops and is a magnet for the young and unconventional.

## TRANSPORTATION

The W. 4th St. subway stop is a large, two-level subway station where you can access the A, B, C, D, E, F and Q lines. At Sheridan Square you can pick up the 1 and 9 trains, which run along Manhattan's west side, and at Astor Place you will find the 6 train, which runs along the east side of Manhattan. Nearby, the N and R Broadway locals are at W. 8th St.

## LANDMARKS

Washington Square Park, at the foot of Fifth Ave., is the gateway to the West Village. New York University fills many of the buildings around and near to the park. The East Village begins at Astor Place, a traffic intersection formed by the meeting of Lafayette St., Fourth Ave., W. 8th St. and Astor Place. The resulting central place is an irregular piece of concrete containing a black iron sculpture, *Alamo* by Bernard Rosenthal. It's common to hear people say they will meet "by the cube in Astor Place." The Joseph Papp Public Theater, 425 Lafayette St. 539-8500, is located nearby. Many famous jazz clubs have been part of the village's history. The Village Vanguard, 178 7th Ave. South 255-4037 and the Blue Note, 131 W. 3rd St. 475-8592 remain, bringing in major acts each week. The Amato Opera Company, 319 Bowery 228-8200, puts on enthusiastic productions in their intimate theater. Anthology Film Archives, 32 2nd Ave. 505-5181, and Cinema Village, 22 E. 12th St. (212) 924-3363, are movie theatres committed to screenings of retrospectives and non-commercial releases.

## SHOPPING

You will find small specialty shops in both the East and West Village. Papivore, 117 Perry St. 627-6055, sells hand-made stationery, Burgundy Wine Co., 323 W. 11th St. 691-9092, specializes in only the best of this famous wine, Love Saves the Day, 119 2nd Ave. 228-3802, is a vintage shop made famous by Madonna in the movie, *Desperately Seeking Susan.* Mxyplyzyk, 125 Greenwich Ave. 989-4300 and Amalgamated Home, 19 Christopher St. 255-4160, are well known for classy housewares, and the recently opened Flight 001, 96 Greenwich Ave. 691-1001, sells travel products. Both Kiehl's, 109 3rd Ave. 677-3171, and Bigelow Pharmacy, 414 Ave. of the Americas 533-2700, are famous for their range of skin care products. Stop at Aedes De Venustas, 15 Christopher St. 206-8674, for extravagant fragrances. Dinosaur Hill, 306 E. 9th St. 473-5850, Classic Toys, 218 Sullivan St. 674-4434, and Chess Forum, 219 Thompson St. 475-2369, are well stocked with toys and games. Have a pair of sandals made at Barbara Shaum Leather, 60 E. 4th St. 254-4250. Food shops abound — Murray's Cheese, 257 Bleecker St. 243-3289, ships their worldwide selection; Bespeckled Trout, 422 Hudson St. 255-1421, sells candies you remember from your childhood; Myers of Keswick, 634 Hudson St. 691-4194, specializes in English foods — groceries and freshly made sausages and meat pies; Balducci's, 426 Ave. of the Americas 673-2600, is one of the best-loved gourmet markets in the city. First Ave. Pierogi, 130 1st Ave. 420-9690 and Kurowycky Meats, 124 1st Ave. 477-0344, sell fresh-smoked sausages and hand-made pierogis.

## EATING AND DRINKING

Restaurants tend to be small, and, in general, are on the less expensive side. There are quiet tea shops like Anglers and Writers, 420 Hudson St. 675-0810, that serve a proper 4:00 P.M. meal and busy ones like Tea & Sympathy, 108 Greenwich Ave. 807-8329, which is an outpost of England for the lines of people that form outside in all weathers. 'ino, 21 Bedford St. 989-5769, specializes in Italian snacks and sandwiches, and Blue Ribbon Bakery, 33 Bedford St. 337-0404, is a place where you can have a snack or a full meal with a glass or a bottle of wine. Danal, 90 E. 10th St. 982-6930, is a bit of New England in New York. John's Pizza, 278 Bleecker St. 243-1680, has sold innumerable pies to the famous and not-so. On Cornelia St. an informal restaurant row has developed — Mario Batali's Pó, 31 Cornelia St. 645-2189, and David Page's Home, 20 Cornelia St. 243-9579, have become destination restaurants. Little Havana, 30 Cornelia St. 255-2212, Cornelia Street Cafe, 29 Cornelia St. 989-9319, and Le Gigot, 18 Cornelia St. 627-3737, round out the selection of cuisines. Babbo, 110 Waverly Pl. 777-0303, brings high dining to the neighborhood. The bohemians passed some time in the bars in the area. Today, the ambience varies considerably from place to place. The recently opened Joe's Pub, in the Public Theater, 425 Lafayette St. 539-8500, features cabaret acts. Kettle of Fish, 130 W. 3rd 533-4790, more decidedly down-scale, is a place where darts are taken seriously. Chumley's, 86 Bedford St. 675-4449 does more than nod in the direction of the neighborhood history. A former speakeasy, it still sports no signage or name on the door. In the East Village, McSorley's Old Ale House, 15 E. 7th 473-9148, has been around since 1854. They brew their own ale, and, yes, this is the bar that did not admit women until 1970, after a court case. Vasac's, aka 7B because of its location at the corner of E. 7th St and Avenue B 473-8840, is the site of the best pinball games in town.

For information on new hotels, ongoing updates, and directions to each hotel by car or mass transit, check online at New York Today, www.nytoday.com/hotels.

# THE HOTELS

## Abingdon Guest House

| | |
|---|---|
| Extraordinary | $450 and over |
| Excellent | $350–$449 |
| Very Good | $250–$349 |
| **Good** | **$150–$249** |
| Basic | $75–$149 |
| Poor | under $75 |

The two West Village townhouses that make up the Abingdon Guest House are over 140 years old. They have wonderfully creaky staircases, and many rooms have wood floors, brick walls and tin ceilings. Much care has been take to create an inviting, residential feel that is authentically "Village." Staying here is like staying with a friend — one with a good eye for detail.

What you may notice first are the guest-room and hallway walls: They've been treated to a rich coat of paint (Ralph Lauren "Lantern Light" is one of the attractive colors). Rooms come with a clock radio, a private phone (free local calls), answering machine, Gilchrist and Soames bath products, a hair dryer and a dish of candies. Plastic hangers in the armoires are an off note. It is the relative lack of in-room amenities (wooden hangers, a fax, iron and ironing board, VCR, CD player, etc.) that keeps the Abingdon from getting a "Very Good" rating.

Other things you should know about the Abingdon: Two rooms share a bath, there is no elevator (there are as many as four flights of stairs), and while the windows are double-paned, Eighth Avenue has its noisy moments. This is a gay-friendly guest house, though by no means exclusively gay.

The Abingdon is appealing for its decor and tranquil aura.

**Abingdon Guest House,** 13 Eighth Ave., New York, NY 10014
**cross streets:** between W. 12th and Jane Streets
**phone:** (212) 243-5384
**fax:** (212) 807-7473
**email:** abingdon@msn.com
**website:** www.abingdonguesthouse.com
**number of rooms:** 9
**number of floors:** 4
**smoking policy:** all nonsmoking rooms
**restaurants:** none
**bars:** none
**room service:** none
**hotel amenities:**
**room amenities:** air-conditioning, some shared baths, hair dryer, iron and ironing board, answering machine
**parking:** none
**cancellation:** 2 P.M. 4 days prior to arrival
**wheelchair accessibility:** public areas — no, rooms — yes
**notes:** no children

## East Village Bed & Coffee

| | |
|---|---|
| Extraordinary | $450 and over |
| Excellent | $350–$449 |
| Very Good | $250–$349 |
| Good | $150–$249 |
| **Basic** | $75–$149 |
| Poor | **under $75** |

For some New Yorkers, Avenue C (a street in the East Village area known as Alphabet City) was, until recently, a gritty spot too far on the periphery to be considered safe. While the restaurants, shops, clubs and housing renovation in Alphabet City have created a more welcoming environment these days, people unfamiliar with New York might still consider it a marginal area in many ways. Having said that, the East Village Bed and Coffee is a find.

You won't think so from the outside, which is graffiti-strewn and suggests an abandoned building. The inside, however, is another matter. The owner, Carlos Delfin, lives here with his dog, Fang (a German shepherd mixed breed), in a large loft space. Some floors may be plywood planks, but the furnishings are comfortable. There are a total of five rooms in a separate area of the loft and on the building's second floor.

There is a communal feel to all this; indeed you share Mr. Delfin's kitchen and living area. With congenial groups, dinner may be taken together at the kitchen table. There is also a second kitchen and living room on the second floor. Rooms are quite simple, and standard hotel amenities are quite obviously not in abundance. The rooms in the loft area do not have air-conditioning.

There are plenty of people who are looking for a place to stay in New York that will be an experience in itself — which this is. It offers inexpensive lodging in an edgy part of town and instant camaraderie.

We asked Mr. Delfin about the bikes lying around near the front of the loft space. "Sometimes I rent them, but usually I just let people borrow them." That's what this place is about.

**East Village Bed and Coffee,** 110 Avenue C, New York, NY 10009
**cross streets:** between Seventh and Eighth Streets
**phone:** (212) 533-4175
**fax:** (212) 533-4175
**email:** evbandc@aol.com
**website:** www.citysearch.com/nyc/eastvillagebed
**number of rooms:** 6
**number of floors:** 2
**smoking policy:** all smoking rooms
**restaurants:** none
**bars:** none
**room service:** none
**hotel amenities:** all shared baths, common kitchen, living room, air-conditioning, VCR

**room amenities:** none
**parking:** none
**cancellation:** 7 days prior to arrival
**wheelchair accessibility:** public areas — no, rooms — no

## Incentra Village House

| | |
|---|---|
| Extraordinary | $450 and over |
| Excellent | $350–$449 |
| Very Good | $250–$349 |
| **Good** | $150–$249 |
| Basic | **$75–$149** |
| Poor | under $75 |

In spite of its somewhat corporate-sounding name, the Incentra is an inviting guest house geared for gay or lesbian visitors but welcoming all. Two adjacent 1841 townhouses have twelve rooms. In one of the houses, the Victorian double parlor is the common room, and it has two fireplaces, a piano (which guests can play) and daily papers.

Each room is named for a place or thing that figured prominently in the life of Gaylord Hoftiezer, the man who started the Incentra. When he passed away, he left the house as a trust. The Maine room has a dresser and a four-poster bed from a farmhouse in Maine. The Washington room has a flag, a picture of GW and patriotic colors. It is popular with Europeans. The Stable room is on the ground floor, where the building's stable was located in the 19th century. It features double Dutch doors, a wagon wheel and stone walls. One room has access to a small garden, ten have working fireplaces.

Amenities include a two-line phone with dataport, coffee maker and mini-fridge. Many have a kitchenette. Windows are double-paned, helping to reduce the noise from Eighth Avenue. Light sleepers, though, should request a room in the back.

The Incentra wins you over with its West Village ambience and friendly staff.

**Incentra Village House,** 32 Eighth Ave., New York, NY 10014
**cross streets:** between W. 12th and Jane Streets
**phone:** (212) 206-0007
**fax:** (212) 604-0625
**email:** none
**website:** none
**number of rooms:** 12 (includes 1 suite)
**number of floors:** 3
**smoking policy:** all smoking rooms
**restaurants:** none
**bars:** none
**room service:** none
**hotel amenities:** none
**room amenities:** air-conditioning, kitchen, fireplace
**parking:** none

**cancellation:** 3 days prior to arrival, 3 night minimum stay for weekends. For holidays 4 night minimum stay with a nonrefundable one night charge.
**wheelchair accessibility:** public areas — no, rooms — no
**notes:** no children under 10

## Larchmont Hotel

| | |
|---|---|
| Extraordinary | $450 and over |
| Excellent | $350–$449 |
| Very Good | $250–$349 |
| **Good** | $150–$249 |
| Basic | **$75–$149** |
| Poor | under $75 |

Downtown could use a dozen more Larchmonts. The West Village is short on hotels and the Larchmont is not only a cheerful, small lodging, it's a value.

Stop right here if you can't handle shared bathrooms; that's all the Larchmont has, located down narrow, winding hallways. The rooms, though, come equipped with a TV, some books, air-conditioning, a writing desk, a ceiling fan, as well as slippers and a robe for getting back and forth to the bathroom. The design scheme runs to light pink walls and gray-green carpets, along with animal and floral prints on the walls (and in the hallways). It is done with a light and pleasing touch. However, you won't find full-length mirrors, and there are only about half a dozen plastic hangers in the closets.

The highest-priced rooms ($99) are worth the few extra dollars for the additional space they buy. Each floor has a shared kitchen, where you can make a full meal (it would be nice if the hotel would consider providing plates and utensils), but with only one table, it may be a tight squeeze if other guests are hungry when you are. Complimentary breakfast is offered in the basement breakfast room.

Clean, comfortable and modest, the Larchmont is a great choice for people who want to stay in the West Village and not spend a lot of money on their hotel.

**Larchmont Hotel,** 27 W. 11th St., New York, NY 10011
**cross streets:** between Fifth Avenue and Avenue of the Americas.
**phone:** (212) 989-9333
**fax:** (212) 989-9496
**email:** none
**website:** www.larchmonthotel.citysearch.com
**number of rooms:** 57
**number of floors:** 6
**smoking policy:** all smoking rooms
**restaurants:** none
**bars:** none
**room service:** none

**hotel amenities:** business services, shared kitchens
**room amenities:** all shared baths, air-conditioning, slippers and bathrobes
**parking:** none
**cancellation:** 2 days prior to arrival
**wheelchair accessibility:** public areas — no, rooms — no

## Riverview Hotel

| | |
|---|---|
| Extraordinary | $450 and over |
| Excellent | $350–$449 |
| Very Good | $250–$349 |
| Good | $150–$249 |
| Basic | $75–$149 |
| **Poor** | **under $75** |

The sorriest of over 250 hotels we have visited in New York. Management wouldn't show us rooms for reasons that became abundantly clear. Thus, we wait on line as two people in front of us check in. Each guest is asked if they have stayed at the Riverview before. If the answer is no, you are brought up to a room and shown it before they will check you in. This procedure surely came about as a result of too many guests who had already checked in, gone to their room, and demanded their money back.

The first thing you notice is that the guest room floors look like a prison. Then you notice that the doors are unusually narrow. When you enter the room, you realize that this is because the rooms are this narrow. They are small and barren and awful. The walls are filthy, the floor is cement, the mirror has a large taped-over crack, there are a few hangers on a nail. Besides the saggy bed, there is a small table with an ashtray and a bar of soap. The bathrooms smell of urine and mildew. In one of them, a homeless person is cleaning himself up at the sink. He deserves better.

**Riverview Hotel,** 113 Jane St., New York, NY 10014
**cross streets:** between Washington and West Streets
**phone:** (212) 929-0060
**fax:** (212) 675-8581
**email:** hriverview@aol.com
**website:** none
**number of rooms:** 211
**number of floors:** 10
**restaurants:** none
**bars:** none
**room service:** none
**hotel amenities:** all shared baths, laundry
**cancellation:** 7 P.M. day of arrival
**wheelchair accessibility:** public areas — no, rooms — no
**notes:** no guests under 18 years of age

## Rooms to Let

| | |
|---|---|
| Extraordinary | $450 and over |
| Excellent | $350–$449 |
| Very Good | $250–$349 |
| **Good** | **$150–$249** |
| Basic | **$75–$149** |
| Poor | under $75 |

In many ways, this bed and breakfast offers a genuine West Village experience in the way people imagine it to be. The charming mid-19th-century house where the owner raised her family has a sitting room with a fireplace, a pretty garden, and rooms with brick walls and antiques. Two rooms share a phone, there are some shared baths, and two do not have air-conditioning.

One deserves special mention — the attic room. Even though it has a very low ceiling (a six-foot person would be scraping it), it is enormously appealing. You'll find wood floors, wood beams, two skylights, garret windows and a clawfoot tub in the bath area, which is only separated from the sleeping area by furniture. It is the coziest of hideaways.

Rooms to Let not only has many repeat guests, but also many who stay for months at a time. This is the kind of place we generally respond to with enthusiasm, tempered in this case by the owner. We do hope she treats guests with more warmth than we were accorded.

**Rooms to Let,** 83 Horatio St., New York, NY 10014
**cross streets:** between Washington and Greenwich Streets
**phone:** (212) 675-5481
**fax:** (212) 675-9432
**email:** margecolt@aol.com
**website:** www.roomstolet.net
**number of rooms:** 4
**number of floors:** 4½
**smoking policy:** all nonsmoking rooms
**restaurants:** none
**bars:** none
**room service:** none
**hotel amenities:** some shared baths
**room amenities:** air conditioing in some rooms
**parking:** none
**cancellation:** 10 days prior to arrival
**wheelchair accessibility:** public areas — no, rooms — no
**notes:** no credit cards, 4-night minimum stay

## Second Home on Second Ave.

| | |
|---|---|
| Extraordinary | $450 and over |
| Excellent | $350–$449 |
| Very Good | $250–$349 |
| **Good** | $150–$249 |
| Basic | **$75–$149** |
| Poor | under $75 |

This small, attractive lodging has the same owner as East Village Bed and Coffee on Avenue C. As with that property, the exterior promises little. But after you walk up the flight of stairs to the first level of guest rooms, it's immediately obvious that you have stumbled onto a nifty secret.

The seven bedrooms are done in different themes (tribal, modern and Caribbean, for instance), and they are tastefully, if not luxuriously, executed. The rooms are large, as are the closets (plastic hangers, though). There are wooden floors with area rugs, TV's, VCR's, two full-size beds and mostly shared bathrooms.

It wouldn't be a second home without a kitchen, and this one is stocked with the basic pots, pans, dishes and silverware. It might be a tight squeeze, though, fitting more than a couple of people at the kitchen table while someone is trying to cook. It's a four-flight climb from the ground level to the top guest floor room, with no elevator. But even with its drawbacks, Second Home is well done.

**Second Home on Second Ave.,** 221 Second Ave., New York, NY 10003
**cross streets:** between E. 13th and E.14th Streets
**phone:** (212) 677-3161
**fax:** (212) 677-3161
**email:** secondh@aol.com
**website:** www.citysearch.com/nyc/secondhome
**number of rooms:** 7 (includes 1 suite)
**number of floors:** 4
**smoking policy:** all smoking rooms
**restaurants:** none
**bars:** none
**room service:** none
**hotel amenities:** common kitchen
**room amenities:** air-conditioning, VCR
**parking:** none
**cancellation:** 3 days prior to arrival
**wheelchair accessibility:** public areas — no, rooms — no

## Washington Square Hotel

| Extraordinary | $450 and over |
| Excellent | $350–$449 |
| Very Good | $250–$349 |
| **Good** | **$150–$249** |
| Basic | $75–$149 |
| Poor | under $75 |

The family that runs this inexpensive hotel in the West Village keeps making slow and steady improvements. Rooms are more attractive now than when we visited in 1993, featuring sea-green sponged walls and new furniture. The mostly leisure travelers who come to the Washington Square appreciate the clean rooms, firm mattresses, double-glazed windows and high ceilings.

On the down side, many rooms have extremely limited closet space, and the lighting throughout could do with some softening. If you want a room with good natural light, ask for one facing the front.

There is a small fitness room, a restaurant, C3, and a lounge featuring jazz on Tuesday nights and during Sunday brunch. The hotel has been in the Paul family for more than two decades. Judy Paul oversees the restaurant, her father handled construction work on the property, and her mother has done some of the design as well as the tile art in the hallways and lounge. This family effort must account for some of the hotel's character, which, along with modest prices and downtown location, keeps it full year round.

**Washington Square Hotel,** 103 Waverly Place, New York, NY 10011
**cross streets:** between MacDougal and Waverly Streets
**phone:** (212) 777-9515, (800) 222-0418
**fax:** (212) 979-8373
**email:** wshotel@ix.netcom.com
**website:** www.wshotel.com
**number of rooms:** 170
**number of floors:** 3 and 9 floors in two connecting buildings
**smoking policy:** all smoking rooms
**restaurants:** yes
**bars:** none
**room service:** none
**hotel amenities:** fitness equipment, meeting room and function room
**room amenities:** air-conditioning, modem line, safe
**parking:** none
**cancellation:** noon 1 day prior to arrival
**wheelchair accessibility:** public areas — no, rooms — no

# CHELSEA

| Hotel | Price Range | Rating |
|---|---|---|
| The Chelsea Hotel | $150–$349 | Good |
| Chelsea International Hostel | under $75 | Basic |
| Chelsea Pines Inn | $75–$149 | Good |
| Chelsea Savoy Hotel | $75–$149 | Good |
| The Inn on 23rd St. | $150–$249 | Very Good |

## NEIGHBORHOOD BOUNDARIES

South — W. 14th St., West — Hudson River, North — W. 28th
St., East — Avenue of the Americas

## ABOUT THE NEIGHBORHOOD

The streets between 7th Avenue and 9th Avenue here are largely
residential — houses have high stoops, small gardens and window boxes. The avenues are commercial, often with the kind of
small, sometimes quirky, businesses that are needed to run the
city. From 10th Avenue to 12th Avenue, art galleries are redefin-
ing the former warehouse landscape. Chelsea in the '90's
replaced the West Village as the gay center of the city, with
shops, bars and restaurants concentrated along 8th Avenue from
14th Street to 23rd Street.

## TRANSPORTATION

The A, C, E, F, 1 and 9 trains run north/south (in this area)
with 14th St. being a major stop. The L train runs across 14th
St. and into Brooklyn. There are crosstown buses on both 14th
and 23rd Sts.

## LANDMARKS

The General Theological Seminary of the Episcopal Church, 179
Ninth Avenue 243-5150, fills the block between 9th and 10th
Avenues and W. 20th and W. 21st Sts. The courtyard can be visited Monday-Friday noon-3 P.M. and Saturday 11 A.M.-3 P.M.
Clement Clarke Moore Park at W. 22nd and 10th Avenue is
named in honor of the author of *A Visit from St. Nicholas*, an
early resident of the area. The Fashion Institute of Technology
runs from W. 26th to W. 28th Sts. fronting along 7th Avenue. Its
graduates supply the garment and fashion industry with fresh
talent each year. You can visit its gallery when exhibitions are on
display. To reach the gallery call 217-5970. The DIA Center for
the Arts, 548 W. 22nd Street 229-2744, at the corner of 11th

Avenue is an anchor for the many galleries clustered on the blocks from W. 19th St. to W. 26th St. Chelsea Piers, at W. 23rd St. and the Hudson River 336-6666, is a huge sports complex, housing a golf driving range, two ice rinks, a bowling alley and much else. There you will also find dockside access to the dinner cruise boats run by Bateaux New York, 352-2022.

## SHOPPING

Saturday and Sunday mornings bring flea markets to the area around W. 25th St. and Avenue of the Americas. For serious hunting, get there early. The Garage, a two level indoor flea market, operates on weekends next door to the Chelsea Antiques Building at 110 W. 25th St. 929-0909, itself a 12-story building containing many small shops open weekdays as well. Dress up your home with finds from the charming Paris-in-New York shop, La Maison Moderne, 144 W. 19th 691-9603, and Desiron, 139 W. 22nd. 414-4070, a maker of iron furniture. Bright, modern designs in stationery is what you will find at IS, 136 W. 17th St. 620-0300, a shop typical of new small shops turning up in Chelsea.

## EATING AND DRINKING

Restaurants tend to be smaller than the midtown eateries and with a little more personal character. Alley's End, 311 W. 17th St. 627-8899, serves American food in a casual atmosphere; Bottino, 246 10th Ave. 206-6766, has Italian food and a pleasant garden; Bright Food Shop, 216 8th Ave. 243-4433, splits their menu between Mexican and Asian dishes; Chelsea Bistro & Bar, 358 W. 23rd Street 727-2026, is reliable for French food; the Empire Diner, 210 10th Ave. 243-2736, is a neighborhood institution. O Padeiro, 641 6th Ave. 414-9661, sells Portuguese takeout during the day and serves modest sit-down dinners in the evening. Royal Siam, 240 8th Ave. 741-1732, has the best Thai food in the area.

For information on new hotels, ongoing updates, and directions to each hotel by car or mass transit, check online at New York Today, www.nytoday.com/hotels.

## THE HOTELS

### The Chelsea Hotel

| | |
|---|---|
| Extraordinary | $450 and over |
| Excellent | $350–$449 |
| Very Good | **$250–$349** |
| **Good** | **$150–$249** |
| Basic | $75–$149 |
| Poor | under $75 |

Dylan Thomas, Arthur Miller, Eugene O'Neill, Tennessee Williams, Bob Dylan, O. Henry, Sid Vicious, Mark Twain, Thomas Wolfe, Virgil Thomson and survivors of the Titanic . . . have we missed anyone?

Yes, dozen, hundreds, of authors, artists, actors and other creative types have stayed at or lived in the Chelsea Hotel. As a place to stay, the Chelsea, built in 1884, is unlike any in the city. As a building, as a crucible of creative forces, as an idea, the Chelsea is unique. In the lobby, artwork from tenants covers the walls and hangs from the ceiling, enlivening every available space. In true Chelsea Hotel style, the lovely, undulating Italian Carrera marble on the lobby floor was forgotten until about two years ago when the carpeting and padding covering it were pulled up.

The Chelsea is largely residential today, but has about 70 hotel rooms as well. You get more space than in most New York hotels; most rooms have good light and walls are famously thick. Some have nonworking fireplaces made of hand-carved marble. Windows in the front are single-paned (any kind of exterior alternation is difficult given that the Chelsea is an historic landmark), but double-paned in the back. Closets tend to be roomy, bathrooms are old-fashioned and soap is the amenity.

About half the hotel rooms have kitchenettes that include a full oven and a mini-fridge. Although well-kept, the ghosts hovering in every corner of this landmark see to it that nothing is obsessively clean. A stay at the Chelsea may not be an indulgence in creature comforts, but it is a window into a remarkable artistic heritage.

**The Chelsea Hotel,** 222 W. 23d St., New York, NY 10011
**cross streets:** between Seventh and Eighth Avenues
**phone:** (212) 243-3700
**fax:** (212) 675-5531
**email:** none
**website:** www.chelseahotel.com
**number of rooms:** 400
**number of floors:** 12
**smoking policy:** all smoking rooms
**restaurants:** yes
**bars:** yes
**room service:** yes
**hotel amenities:** laundry and dry cleaning

**room amenities:** air-conditioning, mini-fridge, kitchen
**parking:** valet
**cancellation:** 3 days prior to arrival
**wheelchair accessibility:** public areas — yes, rooms — yes.
ADA compliant

## Chelsea International Hostel

| | |
|---|---|
| Extraordinary | $450 and over |
| Excellent | $350–$449 |
| Very Good | $250–$349 |
| Good | $150–$249 |
| **Basic** | **$75–$149** |
| Poor | **under $75** |

Dutch visitors will feel at home when they climb the steep, narrow stairs that lead to the warren of rooms that make up the Chelsea International Hostel.

The property has its share of chips, scuffs and flakes, but keep in mind that students and other travelers used to hostels won't be bothered when they're paying $23 for a bed in one of the bunk bed rooms (up to six people) or $55 for a private room.

What you'll find in each room is . . . not much. A mirror, a sink, a small closet, the bedding (linen and blankets). You won't get towels, a phone or air-conditioning.

Two kitchen areas are set up with a fridge, electric burners, and microwave; in two lounges you can eat, watch TV or get on the Net (there are two machines). There are also several barbecues and picnic tables in the backyard court area. A laundry room has four dryers and three washers. The hostel has a security guard at night, and there is a police station virtually across the street.

**Chelsea International Hostel,** 251 W. 20th St., New York, NY 10011
**cross streets:** between Seventh and Eighth Avenues
**phone:** (212) 647-0010, (800)720-5086
**fax:** (212) 727-7289
**email:** email@chelseahostel.com
**website:** www.chelseahostel.com
**number of rooms:** 340 beds, includes 60 private rooms
**number of floors:** 4
**smoking policy:** designated nonsmoking rooms
**restaurants:** none
**bars:** none
**room service:** none
**hotel amenities:** Internet access, laundry, all shared baths, two common kitchens and dining rooms
**room amenities:** limited air-conditioning, lockers in dorms, sinks
**parking:** none

**cancellation:** 9 P.M. 1 day prior to arrival
**wheelchair accessibility:** public areas — no, rooms — no
**notes:** guests under 18 must be chaperoned

## Chelsea Pines Inn

| | |
|---|---|
| Extraordinary | $450 and over |
| Excellent | $350–$449 |
| Very Good | $250–$349 |
| **Good** | $150–$249 |
| Basic | **$75–$149** |
| Poor | under $75 |

Since 1985, the Chelsea Pines Inn has been offering modest
accommodations, mostly to the gay and lesbian community. The
rooms here have been decorated with a sense of humor — each
is named for a film star, from Susan Hayward to Rock Hudson.
The inn is a five-floor walkup without an elevator. Some rooms
share a bath. It is clean, though, and the staff is friendly.

Rooms have high ceilings, which keeps them from feeling
cramped. There aren't a large number of amenities; some rooms
have a hair dryer, some have an iron, ironing board and mini-
fridge. A few rooms even have canopy beds. All rooms have
voice mail, double-paned windows and a supply of condoms.

A complimentary continental breakfast includes home-baked
bread and Krispy Kreme doughnuts. In warm weather, guests
can eat breakfast in the backyard outdoor garden. Charlie, the
hotel cat, tends to sleep around a lot (with favored guests) —
he's quite popular.

The Chelsea Pines was a single room occupancy hotel in a
bad state of neglect before it was transformed into what is now a
thriving inn. That's something Susan Hayward would like.

**Chelsea Pines Inn,** 317 W. 14th St., New York, NY 10014
**cross streets:** between Eighth and Ninth Avenues
**phone:** (212) 929-1023
**fax:** (212) 620-5646
**email:** cpiny@aol.com
**website:** www.q-net.com/chelseapines
**number of rooms:** 23
**number of floors:** 5
**smoking policy:** all smoking rooms
**restaurants:** none
**bars:** none
**room service:** none
**hotel amenities:** some shared baths
**room amenities:** air-conditioning, microwave, refrigerators,
hairdryer
**parking:** none
**cancellation:** $50–$100 cancellation fee
**wheelchair accessibility:** public areas — no, rooms — no

## Chelsea Savoy Hotel

| | |
|---|---|
| Extraordinary | $450 and over |
| Excellent | $350–$449 |
| Very Good | $250–$349 |
| **Good** | $150–$249 |
| Basic | **$75–$149** |
| Poor | under $75 |

Over the last 10 years, Chelsea has been transformed from a
sleepy backwater neighborhood to one of the city's liveliest. The
hotel situation, though, still reflects the bygone days, and the
choices are few. One sign of a changing hotel scene is the
Chelsea Savoy, which opened in March, 1997. If only it were
more attractive.

From the outside, the new brick building looks less like a
hotel and more like a place where you might be doing a maximum of 10 to 20. The lobby is sterile — how about a little music
or more greenery, or softer light, or a conversation nook, or a
comfortable cranny? And the sign by the elevator reads "No visitors after 10 P.M." You don't see that very often in hotels.

The rooms are traditional in decor although not as bad as
you'd fear from the exterior or the lobby. No surprises either —
each includes a TV, a clock radio, an iron and ironing board and
voice mail. Mattresses are firm, windows are double-paned,
water pressure is acceptable, though you would expect the pressure to be quite strong from a small, new building. Telephones
are single-line.

Looking for charm? Move on. But given the relative lack of
choices in the neighborhood and the modest rates, the Chelsea
Savoy may fit the bill.

**Chelsea Savoy Hotel,** 204 W. 23rd St., New York, NY 10011
**cross streets:** at Seventh Avenue
**phone:** (212) 929-9353
**fax:** (212) 741-6309
**email:** none
**website:** www.citysearch.com
**number of rooms:** 90
**number of floors:** 6
**smoking policy:** designated nonsmoking floors
**restaurants:** none
**bars:** none
**room service:** none
**hotel amenities:** laundry and dry cleaning
**room amenities:** air-conditioning, modem line, safe
**parking:** none
**cancellation:** 3 P.M. 1 day prior to arrival
**wheelchair accessibility:** public areas — yes, rooms — yes

## The Inn on 23rd St.

| Extraordinary | $450 and over |
| Excellent | $350–$449 |
| **Very Good** | $250–$349 |
| Good | **$150–$249** |
| Basic | $75–$149 |
| Poor | under $75 |

The Inn on 23rd Street, which hadn't opened its doors when we visited in May, 1999, looks to be a marvelous bed and breakfast at modest prices in a neighborhood that has few choices for lodging. It's the right place at the right time.

Owner Annette Fisherman and her husband loved staying at bed and breakfasts on their travels, so, when they sold their Victorian house in Port Washington, they decided to move into the city, open a B & B and furnish it with the contents of their former home. Ms. Fisherman says she chose Chelsea because she likes the neighborhood — "it fits who I am."

Each room is themed. There is the Victorian Room with a canopy bed, a '40's room with a genuine Haywood-Wakefield furniture set, a Quilt Room with Mr. Fisherman's grandmother's quilt hanging on the wall. In the Rosewood room, the furniture hangs from rosewood panels (you have to see it . . .). There are 11 rooms in all on five floors (with an elevator).

Amenities include a two-line phone with dataport, TV, a king — or queen-size bed, hair dryer and "pillowtop" mattresses, which make for a most comfortable night's sleep. Iron and ironing board are available on request. Windows are double-paned, and bathrooms aren't large but they're brand new. While the bathrooms may be small, the rooms are quite large by New York standards. There is much exposed brick throughout, adding to the charm, and rooms on the top floor have large skylights. The Loft Room has the bed on a loft at the skylight level. You climb up via a ship's ladder.

On the second floor of the Inn is a library where guests can relax, read a book or play cards. On the ground floor, there is a front parlor, kitchen and dining room table where Ms. Fisherman will serve breakfast. It won't be a "New England" breakfast, she says, but she expects to serve Danish or muffins, fruits, yogurt, cereal, coffee and juice. If someone wanted to entertain clients, say, the professional kitchen could be used with a caterer.

Rates start under $200, which makes the Inn on 23rd Street one of the nicest surprises in the New York hospitality market.

**The Inn on 23rd St.**, 131 W. 23rd St., New York, NY 10011
**cross streets:** between Avenue of the Americas and Seventh Avenue
**phone:** (212) 463-0330, (877) 387-2323
**fax:** (212) 463-0302
**email:** innon23rd@aol.com

**website:** none
**number of rooms:** 11 (includes 1 suite)
**number of floors:** 5
**smoking policy:** all nonsmoking rooms
**restaurants:** none
**bars:** none
**room service:** none
**hotel amenities:** library, function room
**room amenities:** air-conditioning, TV, multiline phone, fax on request, copier on request, hairdryer, iron and board on request
**parking:** none
**cancellation:** one week prior to arrival or forfeit one night's rent
**wheelchair accessibility:** public areas — yes, rooms — yes

# FLATIRON/GRAMERCY PARK

| Hotel | Price Range | Rating |
|---|---|---|
| Arlington Hotel | $75–$149 | Basic |
| Carlton Arms Hotel | $75–$149 | Basic |
| Chelsea Inn | $150–$249 | Good |
| The Gershwin Hotel | $75–149 | Basic |
| Gramercy Park Hotel | $150–$249 | Good |
| Hotel 17 | $75–$149 | Basic |
| The Inn at Irving Place | $350–$449 | Very Good |
| La Semana Inn | $75–$149 | Basic |
| Madison Hotel | 75–$149 | Basic |
| The Marcel | $150–$249 | Basic |

## NEIGHBORHOOD BOUNDARIES

South — 14th St., West  — Avenue of the Americas, North — 28th St., East  — East River

## ABOUT THE NEIGHBORHOOD

The Flatiron area takes its name from the distinctive Flatiron Building at 23rd Street where 5th Avenue and Broadway cross. It is one of the liveliest neighborhoods in the city, offering great dining, shopping and the revitalized Union Square Park. The area around Gramercy Park, with its low architecture and tree-lined streets, offers a sense of seclusion from the city at large. Madison Square Park, site of the original Madison Square Garden, now sports some dynamic new restaurants nearby. The former shopping district, known as Ladies Mile, ran along Broadway from Union Square to Madison Square. Looking up along those blocks will reveal some of the turn-of-the-century architecture.

## TRANSPORTATION

The transportation hub in the area is the subway station at Union Square where the L, N, R, 4, 5 and 6 trains converge.

## LANDMARKS

The Flatiron Building has been much photographed, notably by Steichen, since its completion in 1902. The MetLife Building nearby at 23rd and Madison, beautiful as its Cass Gilbert design is, has never provoked the same affection. Union Square Park breaks up the traffic grid where Broadway angles east after crossing Fifth Ave. in the blocks between 14th and 17th Streets.

New Yorkers flock there to go to a farmer's market that partly
rings the park four days a week. Theodore Roosevelt, the only U.
S. President to be born in New York City, is remembered in this
neighborhood at the Theodore Roosevelt Birthplace, 28 E. 20th
St. 260-1616.

## SHOPPING

Many major retailers have an outpost here — Barnes and Noble,
Banana Republic, Virgin Records, to name a few. There are a few
unusual shops in the area. Abracadabra Magic & Costumes at 19
W. 21st St. 627-5194, is a source for magic tricks, jokester materials and costumes. You can find fun vintage togs at The Fan Club,
22 W. 19th St. 929-3349, and across the street at Darrow Vintage,
7 W. 19th St. 255-1550. T Salon, 11 E. 20th St. 358-0506, is not
only a place to take a cup but a place that sells a big variety of
teas and everything needed to brew a cup. ABC Carpet and
Home, 888 Broadway 473-3000, sells rugs, furniture, bed and
bath linens and many gift items. Paragon Sporting Goods, 867
Broadway 255-8036, can outfit you for just about any outdoor
activity.

## EATING AND DRINKING

Follonico, 6 W. 24th St. 691-6359, is noted for its fine Tuscan cuisine, and Cal's, 55 W. 21st St. 929-0740 is admired for its bar
menu. Take a step back in time in the Victorian parlors at Lady
Mendl's, 56 Irving Pl. 533-4466, for tea. Gramercy Tavern, 42 E.
20th St. 477-0777, and Union Square Cafe, 21 E. 16th 243-4020,
both offer remarkably reliable fine dining. City Bakery, 22 E.
17th St. 366-1414, is renowned for its tarts, cookies, croissants
and hot chocolate. Bolo, 23 E. 22nd St. 228-2200, and Patria, 250
Park Ave. S. 777-6211, are two chef-driven restaurants (Bobby
Flay and Douglas Rodriguez) where you can taste Spanish and
Nuevo Latino dishes respectively. Union Pacific, 111 E. 22nd St.
995-8500, has exceptional food. Veritas, 43 E. 20th St. 353-3700,
is a wine lover's paradise; the list is long, not over-priced and
the food is a tasty foil. 27 Standard, 116 E. 27th St. 447-7733,
offers a light menu to go with some hot jazz. Eleven Madison
Park, 11 Madison Ave. 889-0905 and Tabla, 11 Madison Ave. 889-
0667, two adjoining restaurants owned by restaurateur Danny
Meyer, offer contemporary American and Indian fusion food
respectively. I Trulli, 122 E. 27th St. 481-7372, has delicious Apu-
lian food, a fireplace for the winter and an outdoor garden for
the summer.

For information on new hotels, ongoing updates and directions to each hotel by car or mass transit, check online at New
York Today, www.nytoday.com/hotels.

## THE HOTELS

### Arlington Hotel

| | |
|---|---|
| Extraordinary | $450 and over |
| Excellent | $350–$449 |
| Very Good | $250–$349 |
| Good | $150–$249 |
| **Basic** | **$75–$149** |
| Poor | under $75 |

Renovations of this former single-room occupancy hotel (15 percent of the place still operates as such) have been ongoing since 1997. It is now up to a level possibly suitable for budget travel, but keep your expectations low — very low.

Rooms come equipped with a one-line phone and voice mail, air-conditioning and an old TV without cable. Windows have thin double panes, there are cheap drop ceilings, many rooms are dark and virtually none has anything like a view unless air shafts are your thing.

The dark blue carpeting is new but is already showing heavy use. Some bathrooms have bathtubs with cigarette burns. The mattresses are the biggest problem of all — they're poor and one actually tipped downward when we sat on it.

Note that the hotel does not accept reservations for one night only on the weekends.

**Arlington Hotel,** 18 W. 25th St., New York, NY 10010
**cross streets:** between Broadway and Avenue of the Americas
**phone:** (212) 645-3990
**fax:** (212) 633-8952
**email:** none
**website:** www.citysearch.com
**number of rooms:** 95 (includes 2 suites)
**number of floors:** 11
**smoking policy:** all smoking rooms
**restaurants:** yes
**bars:** yes
**room service:** yes
**hotel amenities:** none
**room amenities:** air-conditioning, TV
**parking:** none
**cancellation:** 2 days prior to arrival
**wheelchair accessibility:** public areas — no, rooms — no

## Carlton Arms Hotel

| | |
|---|---|
| Extraordinary | $450 and over |
| Excellent | $350–$449 |
| Very Good | $250–$349 |
| Good | $150–$249 |
| **Basic** | **$75–$149** |
| Poor | under $75 |

"It Ain't No Holiday Inn," say the back of the Carlton Arms T-shirts, and that is certainly the case. This is a bohemian crash pad in a non-bohemian neighborhood. What makes the Carlton Arms far from ordinary are the leaps and swoops of various artists' imaginations; they have transformed the rooms into three-dimensional art installations. One room has a pastoral mural, another a brightly colored cartoon, most have a trippy, sensual ambience.

Amenities? Little rectangles of soap. Be prepared to schlep your luggage since there's no elevator (and nothing remotely like a bellman), to sweat in the summer (no air-conditioning) and to share a bathroom (though some rooms do have their own bath). The Carlton Arms isn't like any hotel in the city, and even at its budget rate it's obviously not for everyone. It's low on creature comforts but high on creative energy.

**Carlton Arms Hotel,** 160 E. 25th St., New York, NY 10010
**cross streets:** between Third and Lexington Avenues
**phone:** (212) 679-0680
**fax:** none
**email:** none
**website:** www.carltonarms.com
**number of rooms:** 54
**number of floors:** 4
**smoking policy:** all smoking rooms
**restaurants:** none
**bars:** none
**room service:** none
**hotel amenities:** some shared baths
**room amenities:** fans
**parking:** none
**cancellation:** "it's nice if they cancel"
**wheelchair accessibility:** public areas — no, rooms — no

# Chelsea Inn

| | |
|---|---|
| Extraordinary | $450 and over |
| Excellent | $350–$449 |
| Very Good | $250–$349 |
| **Good** | **$150–$249** |
| Basic | $75–$149 |
| Poor | under $75 |

A hotel with a lot of heart and a lot of stairs.

In spite of its name, it falls into our Flatiron boundaries. The five-floor, elevator-less property has been upgraded over time and has shed its formerly Spartan look. There is now carpeting in the rooms and cheerful murals of, say, tulips in the old-fashioned bathrooms. The ceilings are remarkably high, which adds to the ambience, but fluorescent lights in the hallways and bathrooms detract.

The beds are passable but not great, the closets could use a few more hangers and while all rooms have curtains, they don't all have shades. The kitchenettes have two gas burners each — you won't whip up major meals here, though you could scramble eggs. Even with double-glazed windows, noise can still be a bit of a problem. The front desk isn't staffed 24 hours — guests are given keys to the front door, and callers can leave a voice mail message for a guest at all times. The Chelsea Inn offers friendly, simple and spotlessly clean lodging.

**Chelsea Inn,** 46 W. 17th St., New York, NY 10011
**cross streets:** between Fifth and Sixth Avenues
**phone:** (212) 645-8989, (800) 640-6469
**fax:** (212) 645-1903
**email:** chelseainn@earthlink.net
**website:** www.chelseainn.com
**number of rooms:** 25 (includes 16 suites)
**number of floors:** 5
**smoking policy:** all smoking rooms
**restaurants:** none
**bars:** none
**room service:** none
**hotel amenities:** business services, some shared baths
**room amenities:** air-conditioning, kitchens, safe
**parking:** none
**cancellation:** 2 days prior to arrival
**wheelchair accessibility:** public areas — no, rooms — no

## The Gershwin Hotel

| | |
|---|---|
| Extraordinary | $450 and over |
| Excellent | $350–$449 |
| Very Good | $250–$349 |
| Good | $150–$249 |
| **Basic** | **$75–$149** |
| Poor | under $75 |

"New York's newest museum of contemporary art is also a hotel" says one of the promotional brochures from the Gershwin, which gives you an idea of the management's ambitions.

There is contemporary art work in the hotel's gallery space and throughout the property. The Gershwin also hosts a variety of parties, with the one in the fall of 1998 for Joe Dallesandro, a Warhol star, being typical.

The basic facility is decidedly modest, though they have made steady improvements since the hotel opened. The rooms are simply furnished with "Philippe Starck-like" furniture. Rooms have televisions and voice mail, but only some have air-conditioning. Prices are modest, which helps attract the young, hip crowd that the Gershwin targets.

There's even a floor specifically reserved for models — reservations for those rooms have to be made by a modeling agency. For those on an especially tight budget, there are bunk-bed dorm rooms. This hotel is patently not for the traveler who needs extensive service or amenities. The accommodations may be basic, but the atmosphere is charged.

**The Gershwin Hotel,** 7 E. 27th St., New York, NY 10016
**cross streets:** between Fifth and Madison Avenues
**phone:** (212) 545-8000
**fax:** (212) 684-5546
**email:** reservations@gershwinhotel.com
**website:** www.gershwinhotel.com
**number of rooms:** 134 (includes 24 dormitory style rooms)
**number of floors:** 13
**smoking policy:** all nonsmoking rooms
**restaurants:** none
**bars:** yes
**room service:** none
**hotel amenities:** concierge, dry cleaning, business services, meeting room, Internet kiosk
**room amenities:** voice mail
**parking:** valet
**cancellation:** 2 days prior to arrival
**wheelchair accessibility:** public areas — no, rooms — no

## Gramercy Park Hotel

| | |
|---|---|
| Extraordinary | $450 and over |
| Excellent | $350–$449 |
| Very Good | $250–$349 |
| **Good** | **$150–$249** |
| Basic | $75–$149 |
| Poor | under $75 |

Pinky is missed. This hotel's bellhop was a familiar figure to guests and to residents of the Gramercy Park neighborhood. His small frame lugged huge suitcases for 51 years, starting in 1945. Pinky died, but the hotel soldiers on, one foot in the past and the other foot in the old days.

The Gramercy has changed hands over the years, but nothing seems to affect its character. One of its owners liked yellow, so the lobby got a good coating of it. Subsequent owners found a chemical that got rid of all that yellow paint, restoring the original wood until it looked like new, or at least like old. Walk into the lobby today and it could be opening day — in 1924.

Babe Ruth and Humphrey Bogart stayed here, but guest rooms now have more history to them than design sense. The solid doors open into rooms with a faded air. The rooms do have a mini-fridge, a safe, a one-line phone with voice mail and good-size closets. The old bathrooms have no amenities except soap. Water pressure is better, as you might expect, on the lower floors than the upper ones. Mattresses lack spring.

One of the perks of the hotel is that guests get a key to the idyllic Gramercy Park, a privilege otherwise given only to residents of buildings that face the park. The hotel also has a terrific outdoor space on the roof (used for parties) with great views of the city to the north and south.

Pinky may be gone, but the Gramercy Park Hotel he knew is now as it always was, with just a few more wrinkles.

**Gramercy Park Hotel,** 2 Lexington Ave., New York, NY 10010
**cross streets:** at E. 21st Street
**phone:** (212) 475-4320, (800) 221-4083
**fax:** (212) 505-0535
**email:** none
**website:** none
**number of rooms:** 356 (includes 157 suites)
**number of floors:** 17
**smoking policy:** designated nonsmoking rooms
**restaurants:** yes
**bars:** yes
**room service:** yes
**hotel amenities:** laundry and dry cleaning, meeting and function rooms

**room amenities:** air-conditioning, safe
**parking:** valet
**cancellation:** 6 P.M. 3 days prior to arrival
**wheelchair accessibility:** public areas — yes, rooms — yes.
ADA compliant

# Hotel 17

| | |
|---|---|
| Extraordinary | $450 and over |
| Excellent | $350–$449 |
| Very Good | $250–$349 |
| Good | $150–$249 |
| **Basic** | **$75–$149** |
| Poor | under $75 |

The Hotel 17 — like its sister property, Hotel 31 — offers basic
accommodations with few amenities. While the numbers 17 and
31 refer to the streets on which the hotels are located, they are
probably good indicators of the age range of their guests, as well.

The mattresses vary in quality: Some seem fine, others have a
crunch — not a sound you want from a mattress. The rooms are
bare bones (nothing on the walls) with the closet consisting of a
small rack in the room. There is minimal furniture — a dresser
or a desk but not much else. Windows are double-paned, and
the water pressure is okay. Most rooms do not have a private
bath in the suite, but the hall bathrooms are reasonably clean,
though the fixtures are well worn.

Double rooms come with a TV, clock radio, and hair dryer
(single rooms do not have these amenities). Not all rooms have
air-conditioning — those that do are considered deluxe and fetch
a higher rate. Smoking is permitted in all rooms.

The Hotel 17 has something of a hip reputation, as it is used
for magazine shoots, among other things. But looking at the surroundings, you may have a hard time determining exactly why.

**Hotel 17,** 225 E. 17th St., New York, NY 10003
**cross streets:** between Second and Third Avenues
**phone:** (212) 475-2845
**fax:** (212) 677-8178
**email:** hotel17@worldnet.att.net
**website:** hotel17.citysearch.com
**number of rooms:** 130
**number of floors:** 8
**smoking policy:** all smoking rooms
**restaurants:** none
**bars:** none
**room service:** none
**hotel amenities:** laundry
**room amenities:** some rooms have air-conditioning
**parking:** none
**cancellation:** 1 P.M. 1 day prior to arrival
**wheelchair accessibility:** public areas — no, rooms — no

# The Inn at Irving Place

| | |
|---|---|
| Extraordinary | $450 and over |
| Excellent | **$350–$449** |
| **Very Good** | $250–$349 |
| Good | $150–$249 |
| Basic | $75–$149 |
| Poor | under $75 |

The Inn at Irving Place is an unconventional hotel: No conventions, no groups, no business orientation, not even a sign out front to distinguish it from the other town houses in the fashionable, historic Gramercy Park neighborhood.

You walk up the front steps into a 19th-century parlor on the ground floor. Each guest room has a different layout and design. The antique or antique-style furniture, queen-size beds, non-working fireplaces, wood floors and oriental rugs make it feel like a hideaway-away-from-home.

There are nice touches everywhere, but a drawback that must be noted is the single-glazed windows. While the area isn't among the city's rowdiest, the noise might be a problem for some. The adjacent two-star restaurant, Verbena, supplies room service, which is certainly an added value. But some rooms are right over the restaurant's uncovered and sometimes noisy back garden. The three-story inn doesn't have elevators. There are hotels in the city with more amenities, but not many with more charm.

**The Inn at Irving Place,** 56 Irving Pl., New York, NY 10003
**cross streets:** between E. 17th and E. 18th Streets
**phone:** (212) 533-4600, (800) 685-1447
**fax:** (212) 533-4611
**email:** inn@innatirving.com
**website:** www.innatirving.com
**number of rooms:** 12 (includes 6 suites)
**number of floors:** 3
**smoking policy:** all smoking rooms
**restaurants:** yes
**bars:** yes
**room service:** yes
**hotel amenities:** laundry and dry cleaning, business services, function rooms
**room amenities:** mini-bar, air-conditioning, modem line, VCR
**parking:** valet
**cancellation:** 2 days prior to arrival
**wheelchair accessibility:** public areas — no, rooms — no
**notes:** no children under 12

## La Semana Inn

| | |
|---|---|
| Extraordinary | $450 and over |
| Excellent | $350–$449 |
| Very Good | $250–$349 |
| Good | $150–$249 |
| **Basic** | **$75–$149** |
| Poor | under $75 |

The general premise of restaurants is that you're there to eat; the premise of hotels is that you're there to sleep. At La Semana Inn, your mind may be elsewhere.

All those Jacuzzis in the room is one clue. Another is the three-hour "refresher" room rate. You can use the large mirror facing the bed as you refresh. The rooms have light tangerine-colored walls, zebra-patterned carpeting, one-line phones and double-paned windows. Each room has a mini-fridge, hair dryer and air-conditioner. Closets consist of a few shelves behind a curtain.

Some of the rooms could use a freshening up themselves — one has wallpaper peeling and a phone number written on the wall. The rooms with a shared bath are the least desirable — walls are dirty and cigarette burns act as a leitmotif.

Our rating system breaks down a bit when it comes to a place like La Semana. In this case, we'd prefer to borrow from the system used to rate films.

**La Semana Inn,** 25 W. 24th St,. New York, NY 10010
**cross streets:** between Broadway and Avenue of the Americas
**phone:** (212) 255-5944
**fax:** (212) 675-3830
**email:** none
**website:** www.citysearch.com/nyc/lasemana
**number of rooms:** 44 (includes 1 suite)
**number of floors:** 5
**smoking policy:** all smoking rooms
**restaurants:** none
**bars:** none
**room service:** none
**hotel amenities:** none
**room amenities:** air-conditioning, Jacuzzis in 10 rooms, mini-fridge
**parking:** none
**cancellation:** 6 P.M. 2 days prior to arrival
**wheelchair accessibility:** public areas — no, rooms — no

## Madison Hotel

| | |
|---|---|
| Extraordinary | $450 and over |
| Excellent | $350–$449 |
| Very Good | $250–$349 |
| Good | $150–$249 |
| **Basic** | **$75–$149** |
| Poor | under $75 |

Madison Square Park and the surrounding area is undergoing a renaissance. The same cannot be said for the Madison Hotel.

A slow elevator drops you off on a hallway with stained carpets and pink guest room doors. We're still wondering why, in the guest room, there are two identical framed prints on the wall. One would have been enough. There are one-line phones, double-paned windows and an old TV. The TV has frequently doubled as an ashtray. Most rooms have an unstocked minifridge. Mattresses, some of which are foam, are definitely newer than the TV. One room has an armoire, another has three hooks in the wall. The Madison offers a voucher for three or four items at a coffee shop next door. We wonder if the coffee shop offers closet space, too.

**Madison Hotel,** 21 E. 27th St., New York, NY 10016
**cross streets:** at Madison Avenue
**phone:** (212) 532-7373, (800) 962-3476 (MADISON)
**fax:** (212) 686-0092
**email:** madihotel@aol.com
**website:** www.madison-hotel.com
**number of rooms:** 74
**number of floors:** 12
**smoking policy:** all smoking rooms
**restaurants:** none
**bars:** none
**room service:** none
**hotel amenities:** none
**room amenities:** air-conditioning
**parking:** none
**cancellation:** 2 days prior to arrival
**wheelchair accessibility:** public areas — no, rooms — no

# The Marcel

| Extraordinary | $450 and over |
|---|---|
| Excellent | $350–$449 |
| Very Good | $250–$349 |
| Good | **$150–$249** |
| **Basic** | $75–$149 |
| Poor | under $75 |

The front of this hotel is so promising — a jaunty black-and-white-striped awning and a trim, modern glass facade. Inside, the lobby has a few pieces of stylish furniture.

The hotel is undergoing renovations (as of March, 1999). But here's where the trouble starts. Even the revamped rooms still have so many little flaws that they detract from the attempt to offer style for less. It's the stains on the carpet in the hallways and in the guest rooms, the nicks on the furniture and the cigarette burns on the blankets that are the biggest problems.

Headboards have wood-framed black-and-white photos of various flowers. That's nice. Windows are double-paned. That's nice, too. So are the room amenities which include a VCR, a clock radio, an iron and ironing board, a hair dryer and a phone in the bathroom. There is also a complimentary continental breakfast. Phones have one line, and the tiny room closet has a small rack with four plastic hangers.

If the guest rooms looked as good as the outside of the hotel, you'd have a jewel.

**The Marcel,** 201 E. 24th St., New York, NY 10010
**cross streets:** between Second and Third Avenues
**phone:** (212) 696-3800
**fax:** (212) 696-0077
**email:** none
**website:** none
**number of rooms:** 41
**number of floors:** 4
**smoking policy:** designated nonsmoking rooms
**restaurants:** under renovation
**bars:** under renovation
**room service:** none
**hotel amenities:** laundry and dry cleaning
**room amenities:** air-conditioning, mini-fridge on request, VCR, modem line
**parking:** none
**cancellation:** 3 P.M. 1 day prior to arrival
**wheelchair accessibility:** public areas — yes, rooms — no

# Midtown

## MURRAY HILL

| Hotel | Rate Range | Rating |
|---|---|---|
| The Avalon | $150–$349 | Good |
| The Carlton Hotel | $150–$249 | Good |
| Clarion Fifth Avenue | $150–$249 | Good |
| Deauville Hotel | $75–$149 | Basic |
| Doral Park Avenue | $250–$449 | Good |
| Dumont Plaza | $250–$349 | Very Good |
| Eastgate Tower | $250–$349 | Very Good |
| The Envoy Club | $150–$349 | Excellent |
| Grand Union Hotel | $75–$149 | Basic |
| Hotel Bedford | $150–$249 | Good |
| Hotel 31 | $75–$149 | Basic |
| Howard Johnson on Park Ave. | $150–$249 | Basic |
| Jolly Madison Towers Hotel | $150–$249 | Good |
| The Kitano New York | $350–$449 | Excellent |
| Martha Washington | NA | Unrated |
| Morgans | $250–$349 | Very Good |
| Murray Hill East Suites | $150–$249 | Good |
| Murray Hill Inn | $75–$149 | Basic |
| Murray Hill Suites | $150–$249 | Very Good |
| New York Helmsley | $250–$349 | Very Good |
| Quality Hotel Eastside | $150–$249 | Good |
| The Roger Williams | $150–$349 | Very Good |
| Seton Hotel | $75–$149 | Poor |
| Shelburne Murray Hill | 150–$349 | Very Good |
| Sheraton Russell Hotel | $350–$449 | Very Good |
| W New York, The Court | $250–$349 | Very Good |
| W New York, The Tuscany | $250–$449 | Very Good |

## NEIGHBORHOOD BOUNDARIES

South — E. 28th St., West — Fifth Ave., North — E. 42nd St.,
East — East River

## ABOUT THE NEIGHBORHOOD

Murray Hill is one of New York's quieter and more pleasant
neighborhoods in spite of its central location. It was named for
Robert Murray, whose 25-acre farm, Inclenberg, was at Park and
37th. It included a corn field where Grand Central is located.
While it doesn't have a great number of cultural institutions,
major restaurants or active nightlife, it is nevertheless a good
choice for a home base when you're visiting the city since it is
easy to get everywhere from this neighborhood.

## TRANSPORTATION

The so-called Lexington Ave. lines, the 4, 5, and 6 trains, have
their subway stations on Park Ave. South in Murray Hill. The 6
local train stops at 28th St. and 33rd St., and all three make
stops at Grand Central Terminal at 42nd St. where you can also
get the crosstown 7 and the shuttle train to Times Square.

## LANDMARKS

The Pierpont Morgan Library, 29 E. 36th St., 685-0610, is interesting, civilized and restorative — you can't ask more than that
of a cultural institution. The special exhibitions of drawings,
prints, books, or manuscripts are invariably worth seeing, and
their permanent collection includes a Gutenberg Bible. Don't
miss Mr. Morgan's library and study. Otherwise, there are not a
lot of large or flashy landmarks in this neighborhood. But there
are many architectural beauties that will reward a self-guided
walking tour. At 233 Madison is the De Lamar Mansion, a landmarked French Empire chateau (a wonderfully extravagant
building) by C. P. H. Gilbert, now used as the Polish consulate.
Murray Hill still has a number of its original carriage houses —
they're at 158 E. 35th St., 148 E. 40th St. and a Dutch style one
at 149 E. 38th St. The first home of Franklin and Eleanor Roosevelt was at 125 E. 36th St. Sniffen Court at 150-158 E. 36th St.,
was built in the 1850's by John Sniffen as a series of small coach
houses and stables. In the '20's, they became houses. Sculptress
Malvina Hoffman had her studio at the back of the court. The
Greek horsemen plaques at the back are her work. At the FDR
and 37th, the East River Esplanade has a rather nice view of the
East River and Queens, once you get through its creepy
entrance. The newest addition to Murray Hill is the fairly aston-
ishing Science, Industry and Business Library, 188 Madison Ave.
592-7000, formerly B. Altman's department store. Designed by
Gwathmey Siegel, the place is beautiful to look at, and there are
1.2 million volumes in the research collection (31 miles of shelv-

ing), 110,000 periodical titles, 69 computers with Internet access, 1 million items on microform and a free training center with 26 computers. Stop in the Church of the Incarnation and Parish House, 205-209 Madison Ave. opened in 1864 as an uptown chapel of Grace Church. After a fire in 1882, the new church installed stained glass windows by Tiffany, Burne-Jones, Henry Holiday and LaFarge.

## SHOPPING

Pantry and Hearth, 121 E. 35th St. 532-0535, sells 18th-century Americana. Call ahead for an appointment. The Complete Traveller, 199 Madison Ave. 685-9007, is a great resource, especially for their out-of-print travel books. Alberene Scottish Cashmeres, 435 Fifth Ave. 689-0151, has superb Scottish cashmere sweaters at good prices. T. O. Dey, 9 E. 38th St. 683-6300, has been making custom shoes since 1926, in any style with over 300 colors of leather. Shoes start at $650 and take 6-7 weeks.

## EATING AND DRINKING

One hot spot in the neighborhood is Asia de Cuba in Morgans Hotel, 237 Madison Ave., 726-7755. The Ginger Man, 11 E. 36th St. 532-3740, is midtown's king of beers: over 60 draft beers, and about 100 in bottles (including 40 Belgian brews). Le Totof, 163 E. 33rd St. 684-3799, is a neighborhood bistro. The Water Club, 500 E. 30th St. 683-3333, has views out over the East River. Chef Larry Forgione has opened The Coach House in the Avalon Hotel, 16 E. 32nd St. 696-1800, serving traditional American dishes.

For information on new hotels, ongoing updates, and directions to each hotel by car or mass transit, check online at New York Today, www.nytoday.com/hotels.

## THE HOTELS

## The Avalon

| Extraordinary | $450 and over |
|---|---|
| Excellent | $350–$449 |
| Very Good | **$250–$349** |
| **Good** | **$150–$249** |
| Basic | $75–$149 |
| Poor | under $75 |

The Avalon is located in a former commercial building that was extensively renovated to create a practically brand-new hotel. This gives the place an unmistakable freshness and means that everything "under the hood" is in top working order — things like water pressure, heat and air-conditioning.

One drawback, however, is that in renovating the hotel, developers had to contend with the proportions of commercial spaces — so most guest rooms are long and narrow. There has been an attempt to turn this into an asset by dividing the rooms with things like shoji screens and calling them suites, though that's a stretch.

The Avalon rises above the space problems with appealing features like pleasant, old-world-style hallways and impressive, in-your-face views of the Empire State Building from some rooms.

There are also smart amenities: good-quality cotton sheets, body pillows and custom-designed desk chairs that swivel and tilt. The new restaurant from well-respected chef Larry Forgione, The Coach House, is also an asset.

This is a solid, mid-range hotel for leisure and business travelers who are willing to forgo some services for a break on price.

**The Avalon,** 16 E. 32nd St., New York, NY 10016
**cross streets:** between Madison and Fifth Avenues
**phone** 212-299-7000, 888-(442-8256) HI AVALON
**fax:** 212-299-7001
**email:** rooms@theavalonny.com
**website:** www.theavalonny.com
**number of rooms:** 100 (includes 80 suites)
**number of floors:** 12
**smoking policy:** designated nonsmoking rooms
**restaurants:** The Coach House
**bars:** yes
**room service:** yes
**hotel amenities:** business services, laundry and dry cleaning, concierge, meeting and function rooms
**room amenities:** mini-bar, VCR on request, fax, modem line, safe
**parking:** none
**cancellation:** 6 P.M. 1 day prior to arrival
**wheelchair accessibility:** public areas — yes, rooms — yes. ADA compliant

## The Carlton Hotel

| | |
|---|---|
| Extraordinary | $450 and over |
| Excellent | $350–$449 |
| Very Good | $250–$349 |
| **Good** | **$150–$249** |
| Basic | $75–$149 |
| Poor | under $75 |

As *Variety* might say, Zzzs Tease, Nix Ritz. In other words, the Carlton isn't the Ritz.

It is, though, getting an upgrade — renovations continue throughout 1999. The hallways are now looking neat and trim, the traditional rooms are small but pleasant enough. What we like most are the new mattresses — they are especially comfortable. There are one-line phones with dataport and voice mail, clock radio, iron and ironing board. Closets are large, at least in proportion to the room size. In the bathroom, adequate water pressure, a hair dryer, and Gilchrist and Soames bath products. A few off-notes: even in renovated rooms we found a peeling ceiling, some enamel off of a tub, dirty windows.

We'll visit again after renovations, which will include the lobby, are complete. When rates are around $200, we'd say the Carlton is a reasonable choice. If the rate spikes up, we'd look elsewhere.

**The Carlton Hotel,** 22 E. 29th St., New York, NY 10016
**cross streets:** between Madison and Fifth Avenues
**phone:** (212) 532-4100, (800) 542-1502
**reservations fax:** (212) 889-8683, guest fax: (212) 696-9758
**email:** none
**website:** www.carltonhotelny.com
**number of rooms:** 308 (includes 14 suites)
**number of floors:** 12
**smoking policy:** designated nonsmoking floors
**restaurants:** yes
**bars:** yes
**room service:** yes
**hotel amenities:** laundry and dry cleaning, concierge, meeting rooms
**room amenities:** modem line, voice mail
**parking:** valet
**cancellation:** 1 day prior to arrival
**wheelchair accessibility:** public areas — no, rooms — no

## Clarion Fifth Avenue

| | |
|---|---|
| Extraordinary | $450 and over |
| Excellent | $350–$449 |
| Very Good | $250–$349 |
| **Good** | **$150–$249** |
| Basic | $75–$149 |
| Poor | under $75 |

A renovation that was going on when we visited looks to be pulling the former Quality Inn up by its bootstraps.

They're not designer bootstraps — the guest rooms have standard issue written all over them. New Serta mattresses seem of good quality, there are two-line phones, dataport, voice mail, clock radio, iron and ironing board, hair dryer, coffee maker, and double-paned windows. Bathrooms are now outfitted in marble, but water pressure is not commanding. Low ceilings and very small closets are structural drawbacks. All rooms have a smoke detector and sprinklers.

A restaurant is planned for the ground floor, but as of now, there are no food services. Guests can use the Bally health club four blocks away for $15 a day.

The Clarion, centrally located at 5th Avenue and 40th Street is a reasonable choice for low maintenance visitors.

**Clarion Fifth Avenue,** 3 E. 40th St., New York, NY 10016
**cross streets:** between Fifth and Madison Avenues
**phone:** (212) 447-1500, (800) 228-5151
**fax:** (212) 685-5214
**email:** hotelon5th@aol.com
**website:** www.qualityinn.com
**number of rooms:** 189
**number of floors:** 30
**smoking policy:** designated nonsmoking rooms
**restaurants:** none
**bars:** none
**room service:** none
**hotel amenities:** laundry and dry cleaning,
**room amenities:** air-conditioning, modem line, coffee maker, iron and board
**parking:** no
**cancellation:** 6 P.M. 1 day prior to arrival
**wheelchair accessibility:** public areas — yes, rooms — yes

## Deauville Hotel

| | |
|---|---|
| Extraordinary | $450 and over |
| Excellent | $350–$449 |
| Very Good | $250–$349 |
| Good | $150–$249 |
| **Basic** | **$75–$149** |
| Poor | under $75 |

The ten rooms with purple bathtubs are the most distinctive thing about the Deauville, a friendly relic of a hotel.

An old-fashioned elevator cab takes you to clean hallways, rooms with old furniture, one-line phones, TV with cable. Closets mostly consist of a rack in the room with a few hangers. Windows are double-paned, rooms are generally clean but look gray, thanks to the dim overhead light. Much of the hotel is booked out to German tourists through a German tour company. Assuming they get a break off the rack rate of $125, they probably won't complain.

**Deauville Hotel,** 103 E. 29th St., New York, NY 10016
**cross streets:** between Park and Lexington Avenues
**phone:** (212) 683-0990
**fax:** (212) 689-5921
**email:** no
**website:** no
**number of rooms:** 58 (includes 7 suites)
**number of floors:** 7
**smoking policy:** all smoking rooms
**restaurants:** no
**bars:** no
**room service:** yes, 24 hours
**hotel amenities:** none
**room amenities:** none
**parking:** no
**cancellation:** 2 days prior to arrival
**wheelchair accessibility:** public areas — no, rooms — no

## Doral Park Avenue

| Extraordinary | $450 and over |
|---|---|
| Excellent | **$350–$449** |
| Very Good | **$250–$349** |
| **Good** | $150–$249 |
| Basic | $75–$149 |
| Poor | under $75 |

This hotel had a $4.5 million renovation in 1997, but what seems lacking here is a continuity of vision. The contemporary furniture in the lobby sitting area feels stuffy, while the music over the loudspeakers ("I Want to Know What Love Is"), seems too informal. The windows onto Park Avenue give the sitting area a cheerful aspect, but the mood is quickly dashed as you make your way upstairs through the dingy guest-room hallways, where little of the renovation money and even less thought seems to have been spent.

The rooms are done in earth tones — olive green, pumpkin and burnt sienna — and there is a modern Italian look to them. Many bathrooms are tiny and some have better water pressure than others. The rooms do feature a generous number of amenities: iron and ironing board, real hangers, umbrella, safe, hair dryer, a makeup mirror and a daily copy of *The New York Times*. Windows, though, have been unaccountably neglected: they're single-glazed.

The Doral Fitness Center, next door to the hotel, is a full-service health club that charges hotel guests $10 a day. Doral Park Avenue has a very New York-sounding name, but it lacks personality, which isn't very New York after all.

**Doral Park Avenue,** 70 Park Avenue, New York, NY 10016
**cross streets:** at E. 38th Street
**phone:** (212) 687-7050
**reservations fax:** (212) 973-2447, guest fax: (212) 808-9029
**email:** doralpark@aol.com
**website:** www.doralparkavenue.com
**number of rooms:** 188 (includes 9 suites)
**number of floors:** 17
**smoking policy:** designated nonsmoking rooms
**restaurants:** yes
**bars:** yes
**room service:** yes
**hotel amenities:** laundry and dry cleaning, business services, concierge
**room amenities:** mini-bar, modem line, safe, iron and board
**parking:** valet
**cancellation:** 4 P.M. 1 day prior to arrival
**wheelchair accessibility:** public areas — yes, rooms — yes. ADA compliant

## Dumont Plaza

| | |
|---|---|
| Extraordinary | $450 and over |
| Excellent | $350–$449 |
| **Very Good** | **$250–$349** |
| Good | $150–$249 |
| Basic | $75–$149 |
| Poor | under $75 |

The Dumont Plaza is one of ten hotels in the Manhattan East Suite Hotels chain. The group shares a number of features. Not only are they all-suites hotels, each offers somewhat-spacious-to-very-spacious accommodations, kitchen or kitchenette, fitness room and a good number of amenities. They divide things up as studio suites (which are the smallest and really like a standard hotel room), junior suites, one-bedroom suites and two-bedroom suites. None is a design award-winner, but they are quality hotels at a fair price.

The Dumont has a more modern tilt, with a cool, all-marble lobby and room designs that fall between traditional and contemporary. The hallways are the least appealing part of the property: the fluorescent lighting is a downer. Once inside the room, though guests will find restful olive green and beige colors, two-line phones with dataport, fax, clock radio, iron and ironing board, hair dryer and kitchen or kitchenette. The kitchens consist of microwave, range, toaster, coffee maker and coffee, refrigerator. Some have a dishwasher, though the housekeeping staff will do your dishes for you as well as your grocery shopping. On the "D" line of rooms, the studio suites get views of the Empire State Building. Those on the "E" line are corner rooms and get lots of light plus views east to the East River. On the "F" line, the studio suites have wonderful southern exposures. Windows are double-paned.

The fitness room has several treadmills, stairsteppers, bikes, free weights and men and women's saunas. There is a small, 24-hour business center operated by debit card, and a laundry room. The hotel now has the relocated Sonia Rose restaurant — one that has many longtime fans but maintains its low profile. One nice thing about the restaurant's new quarters is the outdoor terrace open in warm weather.

The Dumont is a relatively new building (1986) and hasn't got either old-style charm or new-style style. It's a safe bet, though — a hotel that is comfortable and accommodating.

**Dumont Plaza,** 150 E. 34th St., New York, NY 10016
**cross streets:** between Lexington and Third Avenues
**phone:** (212) 481-7600
**fax:** (212) 889-8856
**email:** info@mesuite.com
**website:** www.mesuite.com
**number of rooms:** 248 (all suites)
**number of floors:** 37

**smoking policy:** designated nonsmoking rooms
**restaurants:** Sonia Rose
**bars:** yes
**room service:** yes
**hotel amenities:** health club, laundry and dry cleaning, business center, meeting and function rooms
**room amenities:** fax, modem line, kitchen or kitchenette
**parking:** valet
**cancellation:** 3 P.M. day of arrival
**wheelchair accessibility:** public areas — yes, rooms — yes. ADA compliant

## Eastgate Tower

| | |
|---|---|
| Extraordinary | $450 and over |
| Excellent | $350–$449 |
| **Very Good** | **$250–$349** |
| Good | $150–$249 |
| Basic | $75–$149 |
| Poor | under $75 |

The Eastgate Tower is one of 10 hotels in the Manhattan East Suite Hotels chain. This group of hotels shares a number of features. Not only are they all-suites hotels, but each offers somewhat-spacious-to-very-spacious accommodations, a kitchen or kitchenette, a fitness room and a fair number of amenities. These hotels classify their various rooms as studio suites (which are the smallest and really like a standard hotel room), junior suites, one-bedroom suites and two-bedroom suites.

The lobby of the Eastgate isn't unpleasant, but it is totally nondescript — more like an anonymous office building than a hotel. The hallways, though, are cast in depressing fluorescent light. The rooms have a much more cheerful look: a contemporary design with purple and beige figuring prominently.

Standard amenities include a two-line phone with a dataport and voice mail, an iron and ironing board, a clock radio and a safe. All accommodations have a kitchen or kitchenette that is fully stocked (down to the dishes and silverware). The housekeeping staff will do the dishes for you as well as your grocery shopping.

**Eastgate Tower,** 222 E. 39th Street, New York, NY 10016
**cross streets:** between Second and Third Avenues
**phone:** (212) 687-8000, (800) 637-8483
**fax:** (212) 490-2634
**email:** info@mesuite.com
**website:** www.mesuite.com
**number of rooms:** 188 (all suites)
**number of floors:** 25
**smoking policy:** designated nonsmoking rooms
**restaurants:** yes

**bars:** yes
**room service:** yes
**hotel amenities:** health club, laundry and dry cleaning, grocery shopping, meeting and function rooms
**room amenities:** kitchen or kitchenette, iron and ironing board
**parking:** valet
**cancellation:** 3 P.M. day of arrival
**wheelchair accessibility:** public areas — yes, rooms — yes.
ADA compliant

## The Envoy Club

| | |
|---|---|
| Extraordinary | $450 and over |
| **Excellent** | $350–$449 |
| Very Good | **$250–$349 \*** |
| Good | **$150–$249** |
| Basic | $75–$149 |
| Poor | under $75 |

Across the street from NYU Medical Center on 1st and 33rd, a dozen blocks from the U.N., and practically a straight shot downtown to Wall Street, the Envoy Club is an extended stay property (one-month minimum) that seems to have every amenity you can think of and some that wouldn't occur to you.

This new building, which opened in December, 1998, has studios, one-bedrooms and two-bedrooms that range from 500 to 1200 square feet. The look is contemporary, textured and warm, with a predominance of earth tones. You won't love the Envoy Club for spaciousness because, except for the largest quarters, they are somewhat tight. But get ready for the amenities: two-line phones, high-speed Internet access, voice mail, clock radio, safe, bathrobe and slippers, Frette bed linens, Molton Brown bath products, makeup mirror, hair dryer, daily delivery of *The New York Times*, umbrella, iron and ironing board, VCR, CD and fax. Each guest gets personalized business cards that includes the direct dial number and fax number.

Kitchens are more than large enough to turn around in and include a stove, microwave, dishwasher, coffeepot, Christofle flatware and Royal Doulton china. The housekeeper will wash your dishes for you. There is no room service, but the Envoy provides a packet of menus from local restaurants that will deliver. Grocery shopping can be arranged through the nearby, excellent Todaro Brothers. Gas and electricity are included, local calls are 50 cents each. Windows are double-paned. The Envoy has smoke alarms but no sprinklers, which seems like an error in judgment.

An extensive array of hotel amenities also distinguishes the Envoy Club. A smart-looking business center offers teleconferencing, a conference room and computers (no Macs). There is a coin-operated washer and dryer, a fitness room with resistance machines, the usual treadmills, stairsteppers and bikes, free weights, sauna and steam. Just off the fitness area, a children's play area. It's BYOT (bring your own toys) but kids should enjoy playing underneath the (artificial) tree that takes up much of the room. A roof deck has chaises for sunbathing.

Two unusual features. One is a 14-seat cinema room, which can show videotapes, DVD or cable. Microwaved popcorn is available. The other is their Suddenly Single program, created to help divorced or separated people through the stressful period. Amenities include a sound machine, an aromatherapy candle, a book called The *New Creative Divorce,* and a list of attorneys and therapists. On call are people who will give you a massage or a psychic reading.

You don't have to be psychic to get the message — the Envoy is a welcome addition to the extended stay properties in New York.

**The Envoy Club,** 377 E. 33rd St., New York, NY 10016
**cross streets:** at First Ave.
**phone:** (212) 481-4600
**reservations fax:** (212) 402-1070, guest fax: (212) 481-8600
**email:** envoyclub@aol.com
**website:** none
**number of rooms:** 57 (all suites)
**number of floors:** 5 floors
**smoking policy:** designated nonsmoking rooms
**restaurants:** none
**bars:** none
**room service:** none
**hotel amenities:** health club, business center, meeting room and function room, laundry and dry cleaning, concierge, meeting and function rooms
**room amenities:** air-conditioning, kitchen, CD player, multiline phones, hairdryer, iron and board
**parking:** valet
**cancellation:** full prepayment required
**wheelchair accessibility:** public areas — yes, rooms — no
**\*notes:** minimum stay 30 days

## Grand Union Hotel

| Extraordinary | $450 and over |
|---|---|
| Excellent | $350–$449 |
| Very Good | $250–$349 |
| Good | $150–$249 |
| **Basic** | **$75–$149** |
| Poor | under $75 |

Old habits die hard. The Grand Union, which has been around since 1978, remodeled their lobby in the early '90's but left the front desk protected by Plexiglas. The rooms are in the dictionary under "drab."

The white light of the guest room hallways gives everyone a five o'clock shadow. The rooms are no more cheerful, with their drop ceilings and floral bedspreads that do no favors for the plant kingdom. There are one-line phones with dataport and voice mail, thin, double-paned windows that need a squeegee and acceptable bedding (though some mattresses are on the soft side). There are no closets, just a rack in the room plus a chest of drawers. Water pressure is variable — we have our doubts about a 7 A.M. shower on an upper floor. Amenities include a mini-fridge, TV, soap and shampoo. That's it. The most attractive feature here is price — four people can stay in one of their quad rooms (one double bed and two singles) for $150.

**Grand Union Hotel,** 34 E. 32nd St., New York, NY 10016
**cross streets:** between Madison and Park Avenues
**phone:** (212) 683-5890
**fax:** (212) 689-7397
**email:** none
**website:** none
**number of rooms:** 96
**number of floors:** 10
**smoking policy:** all smoking rooms
**restaurants:** yes
**bars:** none
**room service:** none
**hotel amenities:** none
**room amenities:** mini-fridge
**parking:** none
**cancellation:** 6 P.M. day of arrival
**wheelchair accessibility:** public areas — no, rooms — no

## Hotel Bedford

| | |
|---|---|
| Extraordinary | $450 and over |
| Excellent | $350–$449 |
| Very Good | $250–$349 |
| **Good** | **$150–$249** |
| Basic | $75–$149 |
| Poor | under $75 |

As with its sister property, the San Carlos, the Bedford offers comfortable, low-to-no-style lodging at modest prices. If the blah, old-fashioned design doesn't matter to you, you may be pleasantly surprised by the rest.

There are spacious rooms with amenities including a trouser press, hair dryer, safe and a complimentary continental buffet breakfast. Other features, not necessarily expected at a lower-priced hotel, include room service and both laundry and dry cleaning. The doubles and suites have a kitchen that consists of a range, coffee maker, unstocked mini-fridge, pots, pans and silverware. Even those rooms without a kitchen have a mini-fridge, microwave and coffee maker. Rooms facing south get plenty of light. Some suites have balconies.

Windows are single-paned, but since the hotel is in the middle of the block rather than on an avenue, this is not quite as serious a problem as it could be at other hotels. There are one-line phones only, and water pressure isn't the greatest.

Still, in a city where some hoteliers think nothing of charging a lot and offering little, it's nice to visit a hotel where the equation is reversed.

**Hotel Bedford,** 118 E. 40th St., New York, NY 10016
**cross streets:** between Park and Lexington Avenues
**phone:** (212) 697-4800, (800) 221-6881
**fax:** (212) 697-1093
**email:** bedford@cosmoweb.net
**website:** www.bedfordhotelbox.com
**number of rooms:** 136 (includes 60 suites)
**number of floors:** 17
**smoking policy:** designated nonsmoking rooms
**restaurants:** yes
**bars:** yes
**room service:** yes
**hotel amenities:** laundry and dry cleaning
**room amenities:** kitchens, modem line, safe
**parking:** none
**cancellation:** 1 day prior to arrival
**wheelchair accessibility:** public areas — no, rooms — no

## Hotel 31

| Extraordinary | $450 and over |
| Excellent | $350–$449 |
| Very Good | $250–$349 |
| Good | $150–$249 |
| **Basic** | **$75–$149** |
| Poor | under $75 |

A similar profile to its sister hotel, Hotel 17, the 31 is a tad nicer, if not as hip.

Most of the rooms have a private bath and tend to be more spacious than the rooms with a shared bath. Windows are double-paned and some have a view of the Empire State Building. The mattresses, though, are inconsistent: some have considerably better support than others. The water comes out of the bathroom faucet rather slowly. "Closets" consist of a rack in the room.

While there are few hotel services, all rooms here have air-conditioning, a clock radio, a hair dryer, one-line phone and voice mail. Many of the rooms tend to be done in dark colors and are clean but no great shakes.

This is very modest lodging at fairly reasonable rates.

**Hotel 31,** 120 E. 31st St., New York, NY 10016
**cross streets:** between Park and Lexington Avenues
**phone:** (212) 685-3060
**fax:** (212) 532-1232
**email:** hotel31@worldnet.att.net
**website:** www.citysearch.com
**number of rooms:** 60
**number of floors:** 8
**smoking policy:** all smoking rooms
**restaurants:** none
**bars:** none
**room service:** none
**hotel amenities:** some shared baths
**room amenities:** air-conditioning, modem line
**parking:** none
**cancellation:** 3 P.M. 1 day prior to arrival
**wheelchair accessibility:** public areas — no, rooms — no

## Howard Johnson on Park Avenue

| Extraordinary | $450 and over |
|---|---|
| Excellent | $350–$449 |
| Very Good | $250–$349 |
| Good | **$150–$249** |
| **Basic** | $75–$149 |
| Poor | under $75 |

Do you mind if we run down the brochure of the HoJo Park Avenue with you?

"A European Hideaway in the Heart of New York City." This is a matter of opinion, of course, and words are so often imprecise. Nevertheless, we'd favor something along the lines of A Hackensack-style Motor Lodge as more generally descriptive. "Reminiscent of the gracious country inns of Europe" might be stretching things *just a little.*

"Each of our 55 guest rooms and suites . . ." (there are 53) ". . . have been newly renovated . . ." (the last renovation was in 1993). "Our front desk personnel will greet you by name . . ." (not observed). "The bartender knows your favorite beverage . . ." (no bartender; no bar, actually). "Our concierge is on call to grant any request . . ." (no concierge) "Our guests may take full advantage of the health and exercise center adjacent to the hotel . . ." ($15 a day, two blocks away). The Javits Center, listed as being close to the hotel, is indeed "minutes away", it being an open point just how many minutes that might be.

Somehow omitted from this imaginative brochure are these facts and observations: one-line phones with dataport, no voice mail, no clock radio, or hair dryer. There are faded carpets, very small rooms and suites, peeling wallpaper, bad caulking work, and quite a hodgepodge of mattresses.

The HoJo on Park Avenue is "known by discerning travelers the world over"? Proof of that might be hard to come by.

**Howard Johnson on Park Avenue,** 429 Park Ave. S., New York, NY 10016
**cross streets:** between E. 29th and E. 30th Streets
**phone:** (212) 532-4860, (800) 258-4290
**fax:** (212) 545-9727
**email:** hojopark@juno.com
**website:** www.bestnyhotels.com/hojo
**number of rooms:** 53 (includes 13 suites)
**number of floors:** 7
**smoking policy:** designated nonsmoking rooms
**restaurants:** none
**bars:** none
**room service:** none
**hotel amenities:** business services, laundry and dry cleaning
**room amenities:** air-conditioning, modem line, mini bar, coffee maker
**parking:** valet
**cancellation:** 4 P.M. 1 day prior to arrival
**wheelchair accessibility:** public areas — no, rooms — no

# Jolly Madison Towers Hotel

| Extraordinary | $450 and over |
| Excellent | $350–$449 |
| Very Good | $250–$349 |
| **Good** | **$150–$249** |
| Basic | $75–$149 |
| Poor | under $75 |

Money and effort have gone into the ongoing renovations at the Jolly Madison Towers. While we have given the Jolly Madison a "good" rating, it is on the borderline of "very good," and we'll look in again after the renovations are done.

The biggest downside of the hotel is the size of the rooms — most are fairly small. Even so, the Italian company that owns it (it's a well-known chain in Europe) has brought in Italian fabrics for the bedspreads, Italian marble for the bathrooms and Italian flair in general. There are two-line phones with dataport and voice mail (in Italian and English), a desk with a comfortable swivel chair, clock radio, hair dryer and a phone in the bathroom. Guests can control heat and air conditioning in the room. Bedding is very good, there are double-paned windows and fair water pressure. Room service is available for breakfast only.

Given the effort that has been put into upgrading the rooms, a few more amenities might go a long way — missing are an iron and ironing board, fax, CD player, makeup mirror, umbrella, in-room safe or arrangement with any health club. Perhaps they'd reconsider the plastic hangers, too.

The hotel connects to Cinque Terre, an admirable Italian restaurant. The Jolly Madison Towers has a concierge, and everyone at the front desk speaks at least two languages, English and Italian.

**Jolly Madison Towers Hotel,** 22 E. 38th St., New York, NY 10016
**cross streets:** at Madison Avenue and E. 38th Street
**phone:** (212) 802-0600
**fax:** (212) 447-0747
**email:** jollymadison@worldnet.att.net
**website:** none
**number of rooms:** 252 (includes 6 suites)
**number of floors:** 18
**smoking policy:** designated nonsmoking rooms
**restaurants:** yes
**bars:** yes
**room service:** yes
**hotel amenities:** concierge, laundry and dry cleaning
**room amenities:** mini-bar, modem line
**parking:** valet
**cancellation:** 1 day prior to arrival
**wheelchair accessibility:** public areas — yes, rooms — yes

## The Kitano New York

| Extraordinary | $450 and over |
|---|---|
| **Excellent** | **$350–$449** |
| Very Good | $250–$349 |
| Good | $150–$249 |
| Basic | $75–$149 |
| Poor | under $75 |

In the middle of the Kitano's lobby sits a bronze dog by the sculptor Botero. He seems to be sitting there quietly, listening to the classical music that is playing, among the rich woods, green suede couches and Japanese flourishes. It's a peaceful tableau and a fitting one, given this Japanese-owned hotel's general feeling of repose.

The hotel was built in 1995 and the most notable feature of its modern, understated guest rooms is an absence of noise — though the windows do open, they seem to hermetically seal each room. You're on Park Avenue, a few blocks from Grand Central, but a good night's sleep is practically guaranteed. The beds have duvets instead of blankets and there are plenty of amenities that should keep you relaxed. These include bathrobe, fax, clock radio, umbrella, safe, hair dryer, a phone in the bathroom, Neutrogena bath products, heated towel rack. You can also make a cup of soothing green tea. Phones are two-line with dataport, and there is voice mail. Many rooms have appealing views, which could be of Grand Central, the Empire State Building or of Park Avenue.

The hotel has a concierge, a restaurant, Nadaman Hakubai, that is an exceptional excursion into haute Japanese cooking, and a business center is in the works. Guest receive complimentary passes to a New York Sports Club three blocks away.

You have the feeling at the Kitano that even if the dog in the lobby were real, he'd be sitting there peacefully, too.

**The Kitano New York,** 66 Park Ave., New York, NY 10016
**cross streets:** at E. 38th Street
**phone:** (212) 885-7000
**fax:** (212) 885-7100
**email:** reservations@kitano.com
**website:** www.kitano.com
**number of rooms:** 150 (includes 18 suites)
**number of floors:** 18
**smoking policy:** designated nonsmoking rooms
**restaurants:** Nadaman Hakubai
**bars:** yes
**room service:** yes
**hotel amenities:** concierge, laundry and dry cleaning, meeting and function rooms
**room amenities:** fax, bathrobe, safe, hair dryer
**parking:** valet
**cancellation:** 4 P.M. 1 day prior to arrival
**wheelchair accessibility:** public areas — yes, rooms — yes. ADA compliant

## Martha Washington

*"We've learned what women want,"* said the Smithsonian-worthy, earnestly unfashionable brochure of the old Martha. The women-only hotel has long been an odd throwback, frequented of late by young European women in possession of more humor than cash. The Martha has been closed throughout much of 1999 for renovation, reopening, at the earliest, in the fall. It probably makes sense to renovate the place, but a quirky patch of the city is sure to be lost forever.

**Martha Washington,** 30 E. 29th St., New York, NY 10016
**cross streets:** between Madison and Park Avenues
**phone:** (212) 689-1900
**fax:** (212) 689-0023

## Morgans

| | |
|---|---|
| Extraordinary | $450 and over |
| Excellent | $350–$449 |
| **Very Good** | **$250–$349** |
| Good | $150–$249 |
| Basic | $75–$149 |
| Poor | under $75 |

When they were installing new televisions in the rooms at Morgans, hotelier Ian Schrager lay on a guest room bed while his staff adjusted the TV (up, down, back and forth) until finally Mr. Schrager said, "That's the perfect angle." This attention to detail is a primary reason why Schrager is a successful hotelier. In addition to Morgans, Schrager's other hotels include the Royalton and the Paramount in New York, the Delano in Miami and the Mondrian in L.A.

In the case of Morgans, designer Andrée Putman's stylish rooms don't hurt, either. The modern design has been warmed up (a bit) since the hotel first opened in 1984 — where there was black and white there is now taupe and ivory. Rooms aren't spacious, but everything in them is low — 18 inches off the ground. This trick of the eye makes the rooms feel larger than they are. Fabrics are not typical of other hotel rooms: Ultrasuede is used on window seats, throw pillows are covered in silk and the window shades are done with corduroy.

Most hotels don't have signed Mapplethorpe prints on the walls, either. Amenities include excellent bedding, a clock radio, a 27-inch television (and the angle is perfect), a VCR, a safe, an iron and ironing board, direct-to-room dial, voice mail, a dataport for computers and a single flower. The bathrooms are quite small, but Putman has made the most of them, using black-and-white tile as well as glass shower stalls that seem to take their inspiration from New York City bus shelters.

The most requested room in the hotel is number 1902, called the Cathedral Room because of its vaulted ceiling. It's not like most hotel rooms you've seen — few rooms in New York have the bathtub in the entry way.

The hotel also has an unlobby-like lobby — it's small, quiet and no one lounges for longer than it takes to call a car service. It is a distinct contrast to Mr. Schrager's Royalton, where the lobby is full of life. The restaurant, Asia de Cuba, is adjacent to the hotel and provides room service; there is a complimentary continental breakfast and Morgans Bar is in the basement.

Morgans may be too coolly contemporary for some, too quiet for others. For many, though, it's a hotel at a perfect angle.

**Morgans,** 237 Madison Ave., New York, NY 10016
**cross streets:** between E. 37th and E. 38th Streets
**phone:** (212) 686-0300, (800) 334-3408
**fax:** (212) 779-8352
**email:** morgansale@aol.com
**website:** none
**number of rooms:** 113 (includes 27 suites)
**number of floors:** 15
**smoking policy:** designated nonsmoking rooms
**restaurants:** Asia de Cuba
**bars:** yes
**room service:** yes
**hotel amenities:** business services
**room amenities:** mini-bar, VCR, safe, fax on request
**parking:** valet
**cancellation:** 3 P.M. 1 day prior to arrival
**wheelchair accessibility:** public areas — yes, rooms — no

## Murray Hill East Suites

| | |
|---|---|
| Extraordinary | $450 and over |
| Excellent | $350–$449 |
| Very Good | $250–$349 |
| **Good** | **$150–$249** |
| Basic | $75–$149 |
| Poor | under $75 |

The Murray Hill East is one of ten hotels in the Manhattan East Suite Hotels chain. The group shares a number of features. Not only are they all-suites hotels, each offers somewhat-spacious-to-very-spacious accommodations, kitchen or kitchenette, fitness room, and a good number of amenities. They divide things up as studio suites (which are the smallest and really like a standard hotel room), junior suites, one-bedroom suites and two-bedroom suites. None is a design award-winner but they are quality hotels at a fair price.

When you walk into the Murray Hill East, it doesn't feel like a hotel at all — the lobby seems far more like an apartment building. New York hallways are notoriously unattractive, and the ones here run true to form. In the large guest rooms, you'll find green or blue carpeting, paisley bedspreads, but not much else in the way of decor. There are double-paned windows and plenty of closet space. Clock radio, safe, iron and ironing board, hair dryer and Gilchrist and Soames bath products are standard. Phones are one-line only.

Each suite has a kitchen or kitchenette, full or mini-fridge, and full service of plates, pots and pans and silverware. There may be a dishwasher, but if there's not, housekeeping will take care of it. Unlike most other Manhattan East hotels, there is no grocery shopping service.

**Murray Hill East Suites,** 149 E. 39th St., New York, NY 10016
**cross streets:** between Lexington and Third Avenues
**phone:** (212) 661-2100, (800) 248-9999
**fax:** (212) 818-0724
**email:** info@mesuite.com
**website:** www.mesuite.com
**number of rooms:** 125 (all suites)
**number of floors:** 14
**smoking policy:** designated nonsmoking rooms
**restaurants:** none
**bars:** none
**room service:** none
**hotel amenities:** business services, laundry and dry cleaning, meeting and function room
**room amenities:** kitchen or kitchenette, modem, safe, iron and ironing board
**parking:** none
**cancellation:** noon day of arrival
**wheelchair accessibility:** public areas — no, rooms — no

## Murray Hill Inn

| | |
|---|---|
| Extraordinary | $450 and over |
| Excellent | $350–$449 |
| Very Good | $250–$349 |
| Good | $150–$249 |
| **Basic** | **$75–$149** |
| Poor | under $75 |

The Murray Hill Inn was supposed to have been a hostel, but the hotel market has been sliding upscale since work on the Inn began in 1997. As a result, the owners decided to make it a hotel, losing the "s" and charging a few bucks more per room. It's still modest in scope and price.

Dark green carpeting is the most distinctive thing about the simple decor. Windows are double-paned, but beds vary in quality, so ask for a room with a new mattress. There are one-line phones and air-conditioning, but no other room amenities or hotel services. Closets consist of a small rack in the room with about five plastic hangers. Some rooms get no direct natural light.

Most of the rooms share bathrooms, in which everything is

clean and well kept. Hallways are extremely narrow, so a wide suitcase might be difficult to navigate. The hotel is also a walk-up (there are five floors). Rooms without a bath are around $85.

While there are some inconveniences, you won't pay a lot of money for safe (everyone must get buzzed in) and clean, if basic, accommodations.

**Murray Hill Inn,** 143 E. 30th St., New York, NY 10016
**cross streets:** between Lexington and Third Avenues
**phone:** (212) 683-6900
**fax:** (212) 545-0103
**email:** murrhillinn@aol.com
**website:** www.murrayhillinn.com
**number of rooms:** 50
**number of floors:** 5
**smoking policy:** designated nonsmoking rooms
**restaurants:** none
**bars:** none
**room service:** none
**hotel amenities:** none
**room amenities:** air-conditioning, cable TV
**parking:** none
**cancellation:** 2 days prior to arrival
**wheelchair accessibility:** public areas — no, rooms — no
**notes:** accepts payment in cash and traveler's check only

## Murray Hill Suites

| | |
|---|---|
| Extraordinary | $450 and over |
| Excellent | $350–$449 |
| **Very Good** | $250–$349 |
| Good | **$150–$249** |
| Basic | $75–$149 |
| Poor | under $75 |

There are three apartments available for transient use in this otherwise regular apartment building. It's a pre-war building, which means the walls are thick and solid, so noise is not likely to be a problem.

It's a nice setup here. High beamed ceilings, wood floors with rugs, marble bathroom, and some touches that give it a homey feel — knickknacks — but nice ones. There are one-line phones with an answering machine, iron and ironing board, TV, VCR and full kitchen — stove, dishwasher, microwave and fridge. Plenty of closet space, powerful air conditioner and coin-op laundry in the basement round out the picture. One apartment has a small terrace where you can laze around on the chaise or sit at the table enjoying your breakfast. Maid service isn't standard but can be arranged. The only downside is how few accommodations are available here — so keep it under your hat.

**Murray Hill Suites,** E. 31st St. New York, NY 10016
**cross streets:** between Park and Lexington Avenues
**phone:** (212) 472-200, (800) 835-8880
**fax:** none
**email:** none
**website:** www.abodenyc.com
**number of rooms:** 3 apartments
**number of floors:** 3
**smoking policy:** all nonsmoking
**restaurants:** none
**bars:** none
**room service:** none
**hotel amenities:** self-service laundry
**room amenities:** air-conditioning, VCR, kitchen, modem line, CD player
**parking:** none
**cancellation:** 14 days prior to arrival
**wheelchair accessibility:** public areas — no, rooms — no

## New York Helmsley

| | |
|---|---|
| Extraordinary | $450 and over |
| Excellent | **$350–$449** |
| **Very Good** | $250–$349 |
| Good | $150–$249 |
| Basic | $75–$149 |
| Poor | under $75 |

"Say what you will, she runs a helluva hotel" went the advertising slogan for the Helmsley hotels. What we will say is, at the New York Helmsley, she runs a very good hotel.

Wide hallways, with mellow lighting, lead to the sort of ornate French designs that Mrs. Helmsley favors, here emphasizing beige and cream colors. Black-and-white photos of old New York add a bit of atmosphere. The bedding is in top shape, there are two-line phones with dataport, but no voice mail. Amenities include clock radio, hair dryer, makeup mirror, and Neutrogena bath products.

The hotel's restaurant is Mindy's, which provides room service. There are three people on the concierge staff, one of whom has the Clefs d'Or designation. A tiny business center offers a full range of services.

**New York Helmsley,** 212 E. 42nd St., New York, NY 10017
**cross streets:** between Second and Third Avenues
**phone:** (212) 490-8900
**reservations fax:** (212) 490-8909, guest fax: (212) 986-4792
**email:** none
**website:** www.helmsleyhotel.com
**number of rooms:** 788 (including 10 suites)
**number of floors:** 41

**smoking policy:** designated nonsmoking rooms
**restaurants:** yes
**bars:** yes
**room service:** yes
**hotel amenities:** concierge, laundry and dry cleaning, business
services, meeting and function rooms
**room amenities:** multiline phones, dataport
**parking:** valet
**cancellation:** 4 P.M. day of arrival
**wheelchair accessibility:** public areas — yes, rooms — yes.
ADA compliant

## Quality Hotel Eastside

| | |
|---|---|
| Extraordinary | $450 and over |
| Excellent | $350–$449 |
| Very Good | $250–$349 |
| **Good** | **$150–$249** |
| Basic | $75–$149 |
| Poor | under $75 |

Overlook the nicks and scratches and the Quality Hotel Eastside
is a good value. The lobby has flagstone floors, brick walls and
bookshelves, which makes it feel a bit like a Montana lodge. The
books, though, appear hastily arranged, listing to one side or the
other. That's a fair summary of the rest of the place.

The guest rooms have an early Americana theme — some of
them have a border of ducks along the top of the walls — not
particularly New York but good for counting to make you sleepy.
The bedding seems fine, windows are double-paned, telephones
are only one-line, but have a dataport, and there is voice mail.
Other room amenities like a clock radio, an iron and ironing
board, a hair dryer, a coffee maker and coffee are all standard.

When we visited, renovations were ongoing. But just as the
books in the lobby are askew, some of the rooms have dirty windows, smudged mirrors, peeling paint and wallpaper and
assorted scuff marks — and these are in the "renovated rooms."

In the business center, a credit card will activate the computer, printer and fax. The fitness room, open 24 hours, has a
bike, a stairstepper, a treadmill and a cross-country ski machine.
If this hotel actually was a Montana lodge, you'd be able to do
some real cross-country skiing — not recommended on the
streets of Murray Hill.

**Quality Hotel Eastside,** 161 Lexington Ave., New York, NY 10016
**cross streets:** at E. 30th Street
**phone:** (212) 545-1800, (800) 567-7720
**reservations fax:** (212) 790-2760, guest fax: (212) 481-7270
**email:** neal@applecorehotels.com
**website:** www.applecorehotels.com
**number of rooms:** 90
**number of floors:** 9

**smoking policy:** designated nonsmoking rooms
**restaurants:** none
**bars:** none
**room service:** none
**hotel amenities:** fitness room, business center
**room amenities:** modem line, iron and ironing board, coffee maker
**parking:** valet
**cancellation:** 3 P.M. 1 day prior to arrival.
**wheelchair accessibility:** public areas — yes, rooms — yes. ADA compliant

## The Roger Williams

| | |
|---|---|
| Extraordinary | $450 and over |
| Excellent | $350–$449 |
| **Very Good** | **$250–$349** |
| Good | **$150–$249** |
| Basic | $75–$149 |
| Poor | under $75 |

A mid-priced hotel that has been enhanced with a lot of style and a fair number of amenities. The rooms are on the small side, but Rafael Viñoly, the architect, has wrangled use out of every bit of space. The layout is as interlocking as an ocean liner cabin. The style is sleek and contemporary but not cold: beige and taupe colors soothe and there are interesting touches, such as shoji screens, covering some windows, with far more interesting prints on the wall than the usual.

Amenities include two-line phones with a dataport and direct inward dialing, safe, VCR, CD player, and hair dryer. You can borrow a CD or videotape from the hotel's library. Belgian cotton is used for the bed linen. On the penthouse level, rooms have semi-private terraces with memorable views of midtown.

Room service is provided by the restaurant Mad 28, the hotel serves a complimentary European breakfast and a dessert buffet, and there's a 24-hour coffee and tea service on the mezzanine.

There's much to like about this hotel.

**The Roger Williams,** 131 Madison Ave., New York, NY 10016
**cross streets:** at E. 31st Street
**phone:** (212) 448-7000, (888) 448-7788, (877) 847-4444
**fax:** (212) 448-7007
**email:** info@rogerwilliams.com
**website:** www.uniquehotels.com
**number of rooms:** 185 (includes 2 suites)
**number of floors:** 16
**smoking policy:** designated nonsmoking rooms
**restaurants:** none
**bars:** none
**room service:** yes
**hotel amenities:** laundry, dry cleaning, concierge, spa services

**room amenities:** Belgian linens and down comforters
**parking:** valet
**cancellation:** 1 day prior to arrival
**wheelchair accessibility:** public areas — yes, rooms — yes.
ADA compliant

## Seton Hotel

| | |
|---|---|
| Extraordinary | $450 and over |
| Excellent | $350–$449 |
| Very Good | $250–$349 |
| Good | $150–$249 |
| Basic | **$75–$149** |
| **Poor** | under $75 |

Among the most depressing hotels in the city. The details of this
property summon up a Dickensian gloom: the lobby consists of
a Plexiglas window and an elevator. Please, sir, could we have a
chair. Guest room doors are painted brown. Is brown paint actually cheaper than something less dreary? Perhaps it helps hide
the cigarette burns that seem to be everywhere. In the room: a
fluorescent ring overhead, pinkish walls, one shade to keep out
daylight, a sink, mini–fridge and an old TV. Most, but not all
rooms, have AC; none is equipped with phone. A small rack
serves as a closet, but one room had just one hanger, another
had none at all. Some rooms have private baths, some are
shared. The shared baths are worst of all: peeling paint, tubs in
bad shape, pull-down tissues instead of toilet paper. Avoid.

**Seton Hotel,** 144 E. 40th St., New York, NY 10016
**cross streets:** between Lexington and Third Avenues
**phone:** (212) 889-5301, (888) 879-2132
**fax:** (212) 889-5302
**email:** setonhotel@aol.com
**website:** www.hotelseton.citysearch.com
**number of rooms:** 70
**number of floors:** 6
**smoking policy:** all smoking rooms
**restaurants:** none
**bars:** none
**room service:** none
**hotel amenities:** none
**room amenities:** some shared baths, mini-fridge
**parking:** none
**cancellation:** 4 P.M. 2 days prior to arrival
**wheelchair accessibility:** public areas — no, rooms — no

## Shelburne Murray Hill

| Extraordinary | $450 and over |
|---|---|
| Excellent | $350–$449 |
| **Very Good** | **$250–$349** |
| Good | **$150–$249** |
| Basic | $75–$149 |
| Poor | under $75 |

The Shelburne Murray Hill is one of ten hotels in the Manhattan East Suite Hotels chain. The group shares a number of features. Not only are they all-suites hotels, each offers somewhat-spacious-to-very-spacious accommodations, kitchen or kitchenette, fitness room, and a fair number of amenities. They divide things up as studio suites (the smallest and really like a standard hotel room), junior suites, one-bedroom suites and two-bedroom suites. None is a design award-winner, but they are all quality hotels at a fair price.

The Shelburne was built in 1926 as a hotel and befitting its years, the lobby maintains an old-world aura with chandeliers, wallpaper, and oriental rugs. Unlike some of the other Manhattan East hotels, the hallways here are quite pleasant in a traditional hotel way, with the addition of atmospheric black-and white photos of New York.

Guest rooms are traditionally designed with brown predominating and plenty of dark, hardwood furniture. Standard are two-line phones with dataport, voice mail, clock radio, iron and ironing board, safe and kitchen or kitchenette. The latter are fully stocked (down to the dishes and silverware) plus housekeeping will do the dishes for you as well as your grocery shopping.

Floors twelve and above are considered "deluxe" suites — which means they are a bit larger, have bathrobes, and night turndown. In addition, rooms on floors 12, 13 and 15 have terraces. One unusual feature of the hotel is the five suites that are accessed only by going outside on the roof and then entering your front door from there. When you're on the roof, you get great views of the Empire State Building, the Chrysler Building and the East River. In the morning, there couldn't be a more delightfully New York place to have your coffee.

The Shelburne has a small fitness room with adequate cardio machines, universal and free weights, though the equipment isn't exactly state of the art. It's open 24 hours, and there are men's and women's saunas. There is no business center but there is a coin-operated laundry room.

**Shelburne Murray Hill**, 303 Lexington Ave., New York, NY 10016
**cross streets:** between E. 37th and E. 38th Streets
**phone:** (212) 689-5200, (800) 637-8483
**fax:** (212) 779-7068

**email:** info@mesuite.com
**website:** www.mesuite.com
**number of rooms:** 270 (all suites)
**number of floors:** 16
**smoking policy:** designated nonsmoking rooms
**restaurants:** yes
**bars:** yes
**room service:** yes
**hotel amenities:** fitness room, laundry and dry cleaning, meeting and function room
**room amenities:** kitchen or kitchenette, safe
**parking:** valet
**cancellation:** 3 P.M. 1 day prior to arrival
**wheelchair accessibility:** public areas — yes, rooms — yes.
ADA compliant

## Sheraton Russell Hotel

| Extraordinary | $450 and over |
| --- | --- |
| Excellent | **$350–$449** |
| **Very Good** | $250–$349 |
| Good | $150–$249 |
| Basic | $75–$149 |
| Poor | under $75 |

This hotel hums: it is pleasant in the extreme and very well run. The lounge in the lobby, which they call the "living room," does look more like a living room than a lounge, with comfortable couches set in a room with bookshelves and a gas fireplace. On your way to your room, you pass the concierge desk, staffed by one of two concierges, both of whom have the Clefs d'Or designation. When you step into the elevator, you'll probably notice the wood paneling.

Entering your room, you first hear music coming from a Bose Wave Radio. You find a traditionally designed room in many respects, but the tones are light (yellow and blue in one scheme, coral and green in another) and the atmosphere inviting.

You may be surprised when you sit in the desk chair to note that it is an ergonomically designed swivel chair and that the desk has an under-desk that pulls out for more work space. There is also a Hewlett Packard fax/printer/copier in each room. Beds are comfortable, and the television offers movies on demand, Nintendo video games and hotel check-out. There are two phones in each room and a third in the bathroom. Bathrooms are small and water pressure seems adequate but not forceful.

As you walk around the room, you may notice that the floors creak — underneath the carpeting, they have left the original wood floors. It adds an atmospheric note not found in most hotels. Guests have use of a fitness room with treadmills, bikes, weights and a seasonal sun deck. A complimentary breakfast is served in a lounge near the "living room." Check-in and check-

out are unusually liberal — check-in can be as early as 9 A.M.
and check-out as late as 5 P.M. That's almost unheard of and just
one more thoughtful touch in a hotel that seems to be doing
everything right.

**Sheraton Russell Hotel,** 45 Park Ave., New York, NY 10016
**cross streets:** between E. 36th and E. 37th Streets
**phone:** (212) 685-7676, (800) 325-3535
**reservations fax:** (212) 315-4265, guest fax: (212) 889-3193
**email:** none
**website:** www.sheraton.com
**number of rooms:** 146 (includes 26 suites)
**number of floors:** 10
**smoking policy:** designated nonsmoking rooms
**restaurants:** yes
**bar:** yes
**room service:** yes
**hotel amenities:** fitness room, laundry and dry cleaning,
concierge, meeting and function room
**room amenities:** fax, safe, mini-bar
**parking:** valet
**cancellation:** 6 P.M. 1 day prior to arrival
**wheelchair accessibility:** public areas — yes, rooms — yes.
ADA compliant

## W New York, The Court

| | |
|---|---|
| Extraordinary | $450 and over |
| Excellent | $350–$449 |
| **Very Good** | **$250–$349** |
| Good | $150–$249 |
| Basic | $75–$149 |
| Poor | under $75 |

## W New York, The Tuscany

| | |
|---|---|
| Extraordinary | $450 and over |
| Excellent | **$350–$449** |
| **Very Good** | **$250–$349** |
| Good | $150–$249 |
| Basic | $75–$149 |
| Poor | under $75 |

The Court and the Tuscany, formerly Dorals, now W hotels, are
still only a few doors down from each other. Just about everything else has changed.

Once staid, gently disheveled properties have been unstaid
and sheveled by the Starwood Design Group. Unlike the W New
York farther uptown, the designer has the advantage of larger
rooms to work with — and handsome they are.

The modern, understated rooms are mostly black, white,
brown and gray, with red accents. The rooms are quiet, speaking

metaphorically and literally — the double-paned windows keep most of the city noise out.

Bedding is exceptionally comfortable — including quality mattresses, feather bedding, chenille throws. Amenities include two-line phones (one is a portable) with dataport and voice mail, clock radio, CD player, iron and ironing board, bathrobe, hair dryer and Aveda bath products. Bathrooms aren't generously spaced as many of the rooms are, and water pressure isn't impressive.

On the walls, black framed black-and-white photos of New York. In virtually all of the suites, there is a desk, making it possible and comfortable to do some work in your room.

The differences between the Court and the Tuscany are these: the Tuscany is smaller, but the rooms are a bit larger, and there is a bit less activity at the Tuscany. The Court will have a restaurant called Icon New York from Drew Nieporent's Myriad Group, and the bar will be called Wet Bar. The Tuscany will have a spa.

**W New York, The Court,** 130 E. 39th St., New York, NY 10016
**cross streets:** at Lexington Ave.
**phone:** (212) 685-1100, (877) 946-8357 (W HOTELS)
**reservations fax:** (212) 770-0148, guest fax: (212) 889-0287
**email:** none
**website:** www.whotels.com
**number of rooms:** 199 (includes 49 suites)
**number of floors:** 16
**smoking policy:** designated nonsmoking rooms
**restaurants:** yes
**bars:** yes
**room service:** none
**hotel amenities:** health club, laundry, concierge, meeting and function rooms
**room amenities:** multiline phone, modem line, safe, VCR, minibar, CD player, coffee maker
**parking:** none
**cancellation:** 4 P.M. 1 day prior to arrival
**wheelchair accessibility:** public areas — yes, rooms — yes. ADA compliant

**W New York, The Tuscany,** 120 E. 39th St., New York, NY 10016
**cross streets:** between Lexington and Park Avenues
**phone:** (212) 686-1600, (877) 946-8357 (W HOTELS)
**reservations fax:** (212) 779-0148, guest fax: (212) 779-7822
**email:** none
**website:** www.whotels.com
**number of rooms:** 122 (includes 12 suites)
**number of floors:** 16
**smoking policy:** designated nonsmoking floors
**restaurants:** none
**bars:** none
**room service:** none

**hotel amenities:** health club, spa, laundry
**room amenities:** modem line, multiline phone, safe, VCR, mini-bar, CD player, coffee maker
**parking:** none
**cancellation:** 4 P.M. 1 day prior to arrival
**wheelchair accessibility:** public areas — yes, rooms — yes. ADA compliant

# MIDTOWN WEST

| Hotel | Price Range | Rating |
| --- | --- | --- |
| Aladdin Hotel | $75–$149 | Basic |
| The Algonquin | $250–$349 | Very Good |
| Americana Inn | $75–$149 | Basic |
| Ameritania | $150–$249 | Good |
| Amsterdam Court Hotel | $150–$249 | Basic |
| Belvedere Hotel | $150–$249 | Good |
| Best Western Ambassador | $150–$249 | Good |
| Best Western Manhattan | $75–$249 | Good |
| Best Western President Hotel | $75–$249 | Good |
| Best Western Woodward | $150–$349 | Good |
| Big Apple Hostel | under $75 | Basic |
| Broadway Inn | $75–$149 | Good |
| Carnegie Hotel | $250–$349 | Good |
| Central Park Inter-Continental | $350 and over | Excellent |
| Comfort Inn Manhattan | $75–$249 | Good |
| Comfort Inn Midtown | $75–$249 | Good |
| Courtyard by Marriott | $150–$349 | Good |
| Crowne Plaza Manhattan | $250–$449 | Very Good |
| Days Hotel | $150–$249 | Good |
| Doubletree Guest Suites | $250–$449 | Very Good |
| Essex House, A Westin Hotel | $350 and over | Excellent |
| Flatotel | $350–$449 | Very Good |
| The Gorham New York | $150–$349 | Good |
| Hampshire Hotel & Suites | $150–$249 | Poor |
| Helmsley Park Lane | $350–$449 | Very Good |
| Helmsley Windsor | $150–$249 | Good |
| Herald Square Hotel | $75–$149 | Basic |
| Holiday Inn Broadway | $150–$249 | Good |
| Holiday Inn Midtown | $250–$349 | Good |
| Hotel Carter | $75–$149 | Poor |
| Hotel Casablanca | $250–$349 | Good |
| Hotel Edison | $75–$149 | Basic |
| Hotel Metro | $150–$249 | Good |
| Hotel Pennsylvania | $150–$249 | Basic |
| Hotel St. James | $75–$149 | Poor |
| The Hotel Wolcott | $75–$149 | Basic |
| Howard Johnson on 34th | $75–$249 | Poor |
| Howard Johnson Plaza Hotel | $150–$349 | Good |
| The Iroquois New York | $250–$449 | Very Good |
| The Mansfield | $150–$349 | Good |
| Mayfair New York | $150–$249 | Good |

| | | |
|---|---|---|
| The Michelangelo | $350–$449 | Very Good |
| Milford Plaza | $75–$249 | Basic |
| Millennium Broadway | $250–$349 | Very Good |
| Millennium Premier | $350–$449 | Very Good |
| The Moderne | $75–$249 | Good |
| New York Hilton & Towers | $250–$449 | Good |
| New York Inn | $75–$150 | Poor |
| New York Marriott Marquis | $150–$349 | Very Good |
| The New Yorker Hotel | $150–$249 | Good |
| Novotel New York | $150–$349 | Good |
| Paramount | $250–$349 | Good |
| The Park Central Hotel | $150–$349 | Very Good |
| The Park Savoy Hotel | $75–$249 | Basic |
| Le Parker Meridien | $350–$449 | Excellent |
| The Peninsula New York | $450 and over | Excellent |
| The Plaza | $150–$349 | Very Good |
| Portland Square | $75–$149 | Basic |
| Quality Hotel & Suites Midtown | $75–$249 | Good |
| Radio City Apartments | $75–$149 | Basic |
| Renaissance New York Hotel | $350–$449 | Very Good |
| RIHGA Royal | $450 and over | Excellent |
| Royalton | $350–$449 | Excellent |
| St. Moritz | $150–$349 | Good |
| Salisbury Hotel | $150–$249 | Good |
| Sheraton Manhattan | $150–$249 | Very Good |
| Sheraton NY Hotel & Towers | $150–$349 | Very Good |
| The Shoreham | $250–$349 | Very Good |
| Skyline Hotel | $75–$149 | Basic |
| Southgate Tower | $250–$349 | Good |
| Stanford Hotel | $75–$149 | Good |
| The Time | $150–$349 | Very Good |
| Travel Inn Hotel | $150–$249 | Good |
| The Warwick | $250–$349 | Very Good |
| Washington Jefferson Hotel | $75–$149 | Basic |
| Wellington Hotel | $150–$249 | Basic |
| Westpark | $75–$149 | Basic |
| Wyndham | $150–$249 | Very Good |

## NEIGHBORHOOD BOUNDARIES

South — W. 28th St., West — Hudson River, North — W. 59th St., East — Fifth Ave.

## ABOUT THE NEIGHBORHOOD

If bustle is what you're after, this is your neighborhood. The concentration of skyscrapers, theaters and shops keeps the sidewalks and streets filled with hurrying people and yellow taxis.

Many publishing houses are located here — Time Life, McGraw Hill and Warner Books are housed in the cluster of tall buildings around Ave. of the Americas and 53rd St. There is no tour of CBS in the tall black building at 52nd St., but you can visit NBC located in 30 Rockefeller Center. Call 664-4444 for information on the one-hour tour. The Municipal Art Society, 935-3960, offers scheduled guided architectural tours of Rockefeller Center and Fifth Ave. from 42nd to 59th. Times Square, at the intersection of Seventh Ave. and Broadway, is more than the center for New Year's Eve festivities. Much cleaned up and restored, it has become once again, a place for entertainment in the form of cabaret, comedy and jazz clubs.

## TRANSPORTATION

The western-most trains are the A, C, and E running along Eighth Ave., the B, D, and F trains run along Avenue of the Americas and the 1, 2, 3 and 9 run along Broadway. The 7 train goes crosstown on 42nd St. Major subway stations are located at 34th St., 42nd St. and 59th St.

## LANDMARKS

A list of the landmarks in this area requires no explanation: The Empire State Building, 5th Ave. at 34th St. 736-3100; Madison Square Garden, 465-6741, and Penn Station are both located at 33rd St. and Seventh Ave. Here you will also find the Jacob Javits Convention Center, 655 W. 34th St. 216-2000, Port Authority Bus Terminal, 41st St. and Eighth Ave. 564-8484. You can see free exhibitions (featuring books, naturally) at the 42nd St. branch of the New York Public Library 42nd St. and Fifth Ave. 340-0849. Rockefeller Center, Fifth Ave. and 49th St., 332-6868, is a complex of buildings that features some gardens leading to the below-street-level ice rink. There are many theaters, cabarets and clubs here and the TKTS booth in Times Square at 47th St. is the place for reduced price tickets for today's shows. Go to The Museum of Modern Art, 11 W. 53rd St. 708-9400, for their world-class collection, special exhibitions and daily movie screenings — all for the price of admission. You can see screenings of another sort at The Museum of Television and Radio, 25 W. 52nd St. 621-6800. The American Craft Museum, 40 W. 53rd St. 956-3535, keeps you abreast of the best artisans working today. Carnegie Hall, at the corner of W. 57th St. and 7th Ave. 247-7800, has a full schedule of mostly classical music performances. A new Times Square Visitor Center, filled with helpful information about subway and bus transportation and events, is located at 1560 Broadway between 46th and 47th Sts.

## SHOPPING

There is something in this neighborhood for every taste and budget. Macy's covers a city block from W. 34th St. to W. 35th St. and from Avenue of the Americas to 7th Ave. 695-4400, with clothing, accessories, luggage, toys and foodstuffs. Lord & Taylor, 424 Fifth Ave. 391-3344, Henri Bendel, 712 Fifth Ave. 247-1100, and Felissimo, 10 W. 56th St. 247-5656, tempt with fine clothes and household goods. The Museum of Modern Art Design Store, 44 W. 53rd St. 767-1050, is a good stop for classy housewares, toys and desktop items. The windows at Aaron Faber, 666 Fifth Ave. 586-8411, are filled with hand-worked jewelry; you will find a selection of classic vintage watches inside. Much more jewelry can be ogled at and purchased on the block of W. 47th St. between Fifth Ave. and Avenue of the Americas that makes up the Diamond District. The Gotham Book Mart, 41 W. 47th St. 719-4448, nestled among the diamond dealers, specializes in both new and used literary books. Shop for fancy goods at Manolo Blahnik, 15 W. 55th St. 582-3007 (women's shoes), Tuscan Square, 16 W. 51st St. 977-7777 (luxury Italian products), and Brookstone, 620 Fifth Ave. 262-3237 (gadgets).

## EATING AND DRINKING

Try upscale Scandinavian food at Christer's, 145 W. 55th St. 974-7224, and Aquavit, 13 W. 54th St. 307-7311, well-prepared American fare at Judson Grill, 152 W. 52nd St. 582-5252, over-stuffed sandwiches at the Carnegie Deli, 854 7th Ave. 757-2245. The Brooklyn Diner USA, 212 W. 57th St. 581-8900, serves American staples like hot dogs and macaroni and cheese, while Petrossian, 182 W. 58th St. 245-2214, specializes in meals featuring caviar. "21" Club, 21 W. 52nd St. 582-7200, made its reputation during Prohibition. It sticks now because of the cooking of Erik Blauberg. Firebird, 365 W. 46th St. 586-0244, serves Russian food, steps away from the Moroccan restaurant, Lotfi's, 358 W. 46th St. 582-5850. For a good breakfast, go to Norma's in the Parker Meridien Hotel, 118 W. 57th St. 708-7460. Before or after the theater, try Orso, 322 W. 46th St. 489-7212. If you love Asian cuisines, Pongsri Thai, 244 W. 48th St. 582-3392, and Wu Liang Ye, 36 W. 48th St. 398-2308, offer inexpensive, tasty Thai and Chinese food, respectively. Virgil's Real BBQ, 152 W. 44th St. 921-9494, is a big, bustling place with plenty of strategically located TVs tuned to sports events. Ninth Avenue offers an array of international and mostly modestly priced restaurants.

For information on new hotels, ongoing updates, and directions to each hotel by car or mass transit, check online at New York Today, www.nytoday.com/hotels.

## THE HOTELS

### Aladdin Hotel

| | |
|---|---|
| Extraordinary | $450 and over |
| Excellent | $350–$449 |
| Very Good | $250–$349 |
| Good | $150–$249 |
| **Basic** | **$75–$149** |
| Poor | under $75 |

The Aladdin is more a hostel than a hotel. The lobby has a raff-ish appeal that doesn't extend to the sleeping quarters. The most popular (cheapest) sleeping arrangements are the dorm rooms, each with two bunk beds, which cost $28 per person. The private rooms have a bed, a desk, a chair and a small, walk-in closet. One room, though, has no closet at all, no rack and no drawers. The Aladdin is clean enough — by hostel standards.

There are no phones and no private baths. Carpets are stained, windows are single-paned and mattresses are saggy. In one bunk-bed room, the person on the bottom bunk would have a few very warm toes in winter, since their left foot would be within inches of the radiator. Towels are provided for groups only. That's not unusual for a hostel but it is for a hotel.

This spot is fine for students or budget travelers, but not for people interested in even the most standard hotel accommodations.

**Aladdin Hotel,** 317 W. 45th St., New York, NY 10036
**cross streets:** between Eighth and Ninth Avenues
**phone:** (212) 977-5700
**fax:** (212) 246-6036
**email:** aladdinhot@aol.com
**website:** www.aladdinhotel.com
**number of rooms:** 125, (30 dormitory, 95 private)
**number of floors:** 9 floors
**smoking policy:** all nonsmoking
**restaurants:** none
**bars:** none
**room service:** none
**hotel amenities:** all shared baths, self-service laundry, Internet access
**room amenities:** none
**parking:** none
**cancellation:** 1 day prior to arrival
**wheelchair accessibility:** public areas — no, rooms — no

# The Algonquin

| Extraordinary | $450 and over |
| Excellent | $350–$449 |
| **Very Good** | **$250–$349** |
| Good | $150–$249 |
| Basic | $75–$149 |
| Poor | under $75 |

If Lerner and Loewe had written *My Fair Lady* in your hotel, that would be your calling card, your claim to fame. You'd probably have an Eliza Doolittle breakfast room and an 'enry 'iggins bar with a Rain in Spain cocktail. When you consider that Lerner and Loewe wrote *My Fair Lady* at the Algonquin, and that it's only one of the hotel's many bragging rights, a stay at this hotel feels like a cultural immersion.

The Algonquin is even more closely identified with the regular gathering of 1920's literary luminaries known as the Round Table, and as the setting for the birth of *The New Yorker* magazine. It has played host to scores of writers and actors, and continues to book top singing talent in the Oak Room cabaret. It is, not surprisingly, an official New York City landmark. The Algonquin's popovers were legendary, too, but they have sadly passed into culinary history.

Today, the hotel is looking refreshed from a 1998 overhaul. The lobby is inviting, cozied up with oak paneling, a grandfather clock, murals, delicately painted frescoes and clusters of velvety furniture. The guest floor hallways have gotten new wallpaper — it's composed of *New Yorker* cartoons that were selected by its cartoon editor Robert Mankoff — the perfect diversion when you're waiting for an elevator. The hotel cat, (there have been a numer of them) is always named Hamlet, except when it's named Matilda.

Guest rooms are small — you pay for history here, not elbow room. The new color schemes are a becoming celery and a pale butter yellow — all traditionally furnished (of course). The rooms with window seats set into bay windows are especially charming. Since space is at a premium, many rooms forgo minibars, fax machines and VCRs. The new mattresses are very good. Bathrooms and closets are also on the small side, and while the hot water pressure has been improved during the renovation, it's not exactly roaring.

The hotel does have some themed suites (walls are adorned with posters, photos, and magazine covers) focused around Algonquin legends, such as Lerner and Loewe, James Thurber, Dorothy Parker and Al Hirschfeld. For some reason, the popovers don't get a suite.

**The Algonquin,** 59 W. 44th St., New York, NY 10036
**cross streets:** between Fifth Avenue and Avenue of the Americas
**phone:** (212) 840-6800, (800) 555-8000

**reservations fax:** (212) 944-1618, guest fax: (212) 944-1419
**email:** none
**website:** www.camberleyhotels.com
**number of rooms:** 165 (includes 23 suites)
**number of floors:** 12
**smoking policy:** designated nonsmoking floors
**restaurants:** 2
**bars:** yes
**room service:** yes
**hotel amenities:** health club, laundry and dry cleaning, business center, meeting and function rooms
**room amenities:** air-conditioning, VCR on request, modem line, safe
**parking:** valet
**cancellation:** 1 day prior to arrival, September-December 3 days prior to arrival
**wheelchair accessibility:** public areas — yes, rooms — yes. ADA compliant

## Americana Inn

| | |
|---|---|
| Extraordinary | $450 and over |
| Excellent | $350–$449 |
| Very Good | $250–$349 |
| Good | $150–$249 |
| **Basic** | **$75–$149** |
| Poor | under $75 |

The locked ground-floor entrance is monitored by video from a second-floor office that serves as the front desk. Guest rooms are devoid of personality, but they are quite clean. So are the bathrooms, which are shared. There are five baths to a floor, so you're not likely to have to wait. Each floor shares one kitchen as well, which has a small fridge, microwave and burners but no utensils or pots and pans, reducing the usefulness of the kitchen. The closets aren't overly small, but they could use some extra hangers — three seems to be the average. Even though the rooms' square footage isn't especially small, it can get crowded — one room had a dresser nearly blocking access to a closet. There are no guest room phones. Your chances of a good night's sleep are abetted by the adequate bedding but undermined by the thinness of the double-paned windows, which allows noise from Sixth Avenue to be heard.

The Americana's starkness make it a place you wouldn't warm to but rates are low, so it might do in a pinch.

**Americana Inn,** 69 W. 38th St., New York NY 10018
**cross streets:** between Fifth Avenue and Avenue of the Americas
**phone:** (212) 840-2019, (888) 468-3558 (HOTEL 58)
**fax:** (212) 840-1830
**email:** travel@superlink.net

**website:** www.newyorkhotel.com
**number of rooms:** 50
**number of floors:** 5
**smoking policy:** designated nonsmoking rooms
**restaurants:** none
**bars:** none
**room service:** none
**hotel amenities:** all shared baths
**room amenities:** none
**parking:** none
**cancellation:** noon 1 day prior to arrival
**wheelchair accessibility:** public areas — yes, rooms — no

## Ameritania

| | |
|---|---|
| Extraordinary | $450 and over |
| Excellent | $350–$449 |
| Very Good | $250–$349 |
| **Good** | **$150–$249** |
| Basic | $75–$149 |
| Poor | under $75 |

Every new modern hotel these days inevitably gets compared to the hotels designed by Frenchman Philippe Starck, such as the Royalton. At the Ameritania (which was not designed by Starck), the homage is earnest, even if it doesn't have that Starck *je ne sais quoi*. We do know that the lite-FM lobby music is not the *"quoi."* Still, this hotel offers reasonably priced lodging with some flair.

We especially like the newly redecorated rooms, with bold, checkerboard-pattern carpets and solid armoires. There aren't many amenities, but mattresses are good, hangers are real wood (though there aren't many of them) and windows are double-glazed. Given the location in the busy theater district, however, ask for a room on a higher floor if you're sensitive to noise.

Room 1105 is a two-bedroom suite with a Jacuzzi. It typically goes for $350 and is a nice way for four adults to have a little bit of style and a good soak.

**Ameritania,** 230 W. 54th St., New York NY 10019
**cross streets:** at Broadway
**phone:** (212) 247-5000, (800) 922-0330
**reservations fax:** (212) 247-3316, guest fax: (212) 247-3313
**email:** none
**website:** www.nycityhotels.net
**number of rooms:** 207 (includes 13 suites)
**number of floors:** 12
**smoking policy:** designated nonsmoking rooms
**restaurants:** yes
**bars:** yes
**room service:** yes
**hotel amenities:** laundry and dry cleaning

**room amenities:** air-conditioning, modem line
**parking:** none
**cancellation:** 3 P.M. 1 day prior to arrival
**wheelchair accessibility:** public areas — no, rooms — no

## Amsterdam Court Hotel

| | |
|---|---|
| Extraordinary | $450 and over |
| Excellent | $350–$449 |
| Very Good | $250–$349 |
| Good | **$150–$249** |
| **Basic** | $75–$149 |
| Poor | under $75 |

We have our doubts about the hospitality and the maintenance
here.

The brochure for the hotel is most attractive, and you'd feel
confident booking a room here. The brochure doesn't show you
the stained room carpets, the filthy windows, the blankets that
have rips and cigarette burns, the bathtub with cracking enamel,
the bathroom that smelled of mildew, the small rack in the room
for you to hang your clothes (there are no drawers, either), and
the fact that many rooms are dark.

Hotels with, shall we say, physical imperfections, can make
up for a lot by pouring on the charm. The gum-chewing desk
clerk and the bellman we encountered did no pouring. This
behavior was repeated, we observed, when the desk clerk,
speaking on the phone to a future guest, was trying to find a
reservation. The guest clearly did not speak English well, and
the desk clerk responded by repeating himself, more slowly but
with obvious irritation. It is no way to run a hotel (and spit the
gum out).

The look of the place is modest modern. Rooms feature much
black and white, with a recurring stripe motif throughout. Windows are double-paned (though it can still be noisy), and the
one-line phones come with dataport and voice mail. Most of the
rooms have a CD player. Bathrooms are attractive, hair dryers
are standard, and water pressure is robust. There is a complimentary continental breakfast.

For the relatively modest rates the hotel charges, we could
overlook some of the shortcomings. Were they to retrain the
staff and replace the blankets (et al.), they might have something here.

**Amsterdam Court Hotel,** 226 W. 50th St., New York NY 10019
**cross streets:** between Broadway and Eighth Avenue
**phone:** (212) 459-1000, (800) 341-9889
**fax:** (212) 265-5070
**email:** leonor@worldnet.att.net
**website:** www.citysearch.com/nyc/nychotels
**number of rooms:** 117 (includes 2 suites),
**number of floors:** 7

**smoking policy:** designated nonsmoking floors
**restaurants:** yes
**bars:** yes
**room service:** yes
**hotel amenities:** business services, some shared baths, laundry and dry cleaning
**room amenities:** air-conditioning, VCR on request, modem line
**parking:** none
**cancellation:** 1 day prior to arrival
**wheelchair accessibility:** public areas — no, rooms — no

## Belvedere Hotel

| | |
|---|---|
| Extraordinary | $450 and over |
| Excellent | $350–$449 |
| Very Good | $250–$349 |
| Good | **$150–$249** |
| **Basic** | $75–$149 |
| Poor | under $75 |

Built in 1926 to offer lodging to those in town visiting Madison Square Garden, at that time across the street, the Belvedere has mostly completed a major renovation in 1999. It is one of a number of septugenarian, octogenarian and nonagenarian hotels that have lately undergone reconstructive and cosmetic surgery. It's a success with one exception, which keeps its rating down.

The Belvedere is located just west of Eighth Avenue in the theater district. You may recall from visits to New York that this area had its share of nocturnal activities unrelated to theater-going, but the area is transforming rapidly as the 42nd Street and Times Square regeneration spikes off in many directions.

The lobby is stylishly attractive, featuring a multicolored terrazzo marble floor. Guest rooms are not large, but they are pleasingly outfitted in traditional-looking dark woods and maroon accents. Bedding is mostly double-doubles, and the mattresses are comfortable. There are one-line phones with dataport and voice mail, unstocked mini-fridges, clock radio, hair dryer, a phone in the bathroom and Gilchrist and Soames bath products.

No room service is available at the moment, though they are planning to introduce it. Guests can eat at Churrascaria Plataforma, the Brazilian restaurant that connects to the hotel. A washer and dryer is on the premises as is a fax machine that works with a credit card. A unique feature scheduled for completion in 1999 is a locker and dressing room area on the ground floor. It's intended for guests who have checked out but whose flight is late in the day — you can leave your luggage, have a last spin around the city, come back and freshen up (no shower, though) and then be on your way to the airport. That's a wonderful amenity and another indicator of the thought that has gone into rejuvenating this hotel.

The major drawback of the Belvedere is a cockroach problem. When that is solved, consider it a "good" hotel.

**Belvedere Hotel,** 319 W. 48th St., New York NY 10036
**cross streets:** between Eighth Avenue and Ninth Avenue
**phone:** 212-245-7000, (888) 468-3558 (HOTEL 58)
**reservations fax:** (212)-245-4455, guest fax: (212) 265-7778
**email:** travel@superlink.net
**website:** www.newyorkhotel.com
**number of rooms:** 300 (includes 1 suite)
**number of floors:** 17
**smoking policy:** designated nonsmoking floors
**restaurants:** yes
**bars:** yes
**room service:** none
**hotel amenities:** concierge, laundry and dry cleaning
**room amenities:** air-conditioning, microwave, mini-fridge, multiline phone
**parking:** none
**cancellation:** 5 P.M. 1 day prior to arrival
**wheelchair accessibility:** public areas — yes, rooms — yes. ADA compliant

## Best Western Ambassador

| | |
|---|---|
| Extraordinary | $450 and over |
| Excellent | $350–$449 |
| Very Good | $250–$349 |
| **Good** | **$150–$249** |
| Basic | $75–$149 |
| Poor | under $75 |

A low "good." This hotel is due for some renovation work, which it is getting in the public areas, and it could use it in the guest rooms, which is not planned. Nothing is terribly awry, but when rooms are small, as they are here, and the range of amenities the hotel offers is limited, it helps if the rooms are in pristine condition — that carpets don't seem faded, that doors don't stick.

There are, however, a number of things in the hotel's favor. Mattresses are in good condition, water pressure is zesty and the amenity package is fair enough. These include one-line phones with dataport and voice mail, clock radio, hair dryer, makeup mirror, and coffee maker. Mini-fridges are available on request at no extra charge as are cribs. Closets are quite small. Windows are double-paned, and perhaps as it is mid-block, the rooms are reasonably quiet, given the busy location.

Elsewhere, not much. There is one slow elevator to the guest rooms. The lobby is small and a tight squeeze. The plan is to expand into spaces next door to offer a fitness room and a more comfortable lobby. A complimentary continental breakfast is offered, heavy on the carbs (croissants, muffins, bagels) but also fruit, juice and coffee.

At $200 a night, it's not exactly a bargain, but it's passably good lodging at the doorstep to the theater district.

**Best Western Ambassador,** 132 W. 45th St., New York, NY 10036
**cross streets:** between Avenue of the Americas and Broadway
**phone:** (212) 921-7600, (800) 242-8935
**fax:** (212) 719-0171
**email:** ambassadorny@juno.com
**website:** www.bestnyhotels.com
**number of rooms:** 70
**number of floors:** 8
**smoking policy:** designated nonsmoking floors
**restaurants:** none
**bars:** none
**room service:** none
**hotel amenities:** business services, laundry and dry cleaning
**room amenities:** air-conditioning, mini-fridge on request, crib on request, modem line, coffee makers with coffee
**parking:** none
**cancellation:** 4 P.M. 1 day prior to arrival
**wheelchair accessibility:** public areas — no rooms — no

## Best Western Manhattan

| | |
|---|---|
| Extraordinary | $450 and over |
| Excellent | $350–$449 |
| Very Good | $250–$349 |
| **Good** | **$150–$249** |
| Basic | **$75–$149** |
| Poor | under $75 |

The Best Western Manhattan has a checkered past. For many years it was a down-on-its-luck lodging with a Beaux Arts facade. After getting a new lease on life as a modestly stylish hotel called The Manhattan, it's now part of the Best Western chain. The lobby is distinctive: black and white with contemporary, clean lines. The rooms, though, are far more predictable: traditional decor without much finesse. This duality runs throughout — there's a "concierge," but she also runs the gift shop, and the hotel has a business center, but it's run by an outside company (it's unstaffed, open 24 hours and everything is done with a credit card).

Rooms are generally adequate, certainly for the price range, which means things are clean and in good working order. Drawbacks: limited drawer space, small bathrooms with no amenities to speak of and closets that won't hold a large suitcase-load of clothes. On the plus side there are a fair number of extras, especially for a budget-conscious hotel. Each room has an iron and ironing board, hair dryer, coffee maker and coffee. The hotel has, besides the previously noted business center, a four-machine fitness room.

We particularly like the Sky Bar, an open-air rooftop bar that operates during the warmer weather months under the looming Empire State Building. Comedy and music are featured some nights, but it's best with just a grilled burger, a beer and the Empire, straight up.

**Best Western Manhattan,** 17 W. 32nd St., New York NY 10001
**cross streets:** between Fifth Ave. and Broadway
**phone:** (212) 736-1600, (800) 567-7720
**reservations fax:** (212) 790-2760, guest fax: (212) 563-4007
**email:** reservations@applecorehotels.com
**website:** www.applecorehotels.com
**number of rooms:** 176 (includes 35 suites)
**number of floors:** 13
**smoking policy:** designated nonsmoking rooms
**restaurants:** yes
**bars:** yes
**room service:** yes
**hotel amenities:** fitness equipment, laundry and dry cleaning, business center
**room amenities:** air-conditioning
**parking:** valet
**cancellation:** 3 P.M. 1 day prior to arrival
**wheelchair accessibility:** public areas — yes, rooms — yes

## Best Western President Hotel

| | |
|---|---|
| Extraordinary | $450 and over |
| Excellent | $350–$449 |
| Very Good | $250–$349 |
| **Good** | **$150–$249** |
| Basic | **$75–$149** |
| Poor | under $75 |

This hotel in the theater district has been around since 1906, but Best Western, which took over in 1992, has polished up the place. The design of the guest rooms is attractive in a traditional way — with the deep red carpets adding a note of richness — although ceilings are low.

The beds here are particularly comfortable, windows are double-paned and phones have two lines with a dataport and voice mail. Some of the marble bathrooms have whirlpools and some have steam showers. They also come equipped with hair dryers, but the bath amenities are only generic, the water pressure isn't impressive and the bathtubs can be tiny.

The grand piano in the lobby has been rigged as a player piano: it's a big statement for a small area, and the concierge, who teaches piano in her off hours, must wish it would take five now and then. But this is a quirky touch to what is otherwise conventional but rather nice lodging.

**Best Western President Hotel,** 234 W. 48th St., New York, NY 10036
**cross streets:** between Eighth Avenue and Broadway

**phone:** (212) 246-8800, (800) 826-4667
**reservations fax:** (212) 265-6727, guest fax: (212) 974-3922
**email:** reshhr@aol.com
**website:** www.bestnyhotels.com
**number of rooms:** 327 (includes 47 suites)
**number of floors:** 16
**smoking policy:** designated nonsmoking rooms
**restaurants:** 2
**bars:** yes
**room service:** none
**hotel amenities:** concierge, laundry, dry cleaning
**room amenities:** air-conditioning, VCR
**parking:** none
**cancellation:** 2 days prior to arrival
**wheelchair accessibility:** public areas — yes, rooms — yes.
ADA compliant

## Best Western Woodward

| | |
|---|---|
| Extraordinary | $450 and over |
| Excellent | $350–$449 |
| Very Good | **$250–$349** |
| **Good** | **$150–$249** |
| Basic | $75–$149 |
| Poor | under $75 |

This hotel's location on the northern end of the theater district,
as well its relatively modest prices, make it a good choice for
visitors loading up on Broadway.

The lobby is pleasant enough, if not entirely successful in its
mix of old and new, plaster work on the ceiling, modern lights
and sconces. We wish the bedding were not a mixed bag —
some of the mattresses seem in prime shape but not all. There
are quite a few amenities in the contemporary-style rooms: iron
and ironing board, hair dryer, most rooms have a makeup mirror, coffee maker and coffee, complimentary *USA Today,* one-line
phone with dataport, voice mail, and individually controlled air-
conditioning. The showers have temperature control although
water pressure isn't vigorous. Noise may still make its way
through from Broadway through the double-paned windows.
There are sprinklers and smoke detectors in every room.

The hotel has no fitness or business room, but there is a
concierge, room service is provided by the Carnegie Deli and
guests get a free pass to Prescriptive Fitness around the corner,
where six months on the treadmill might undo one of the
Carnegie's hot pastramis.

**Best Western Woodward,** 210 W. 55th St., New York, NY 10019
**cross streets:** between Broadway and Seventh Avenue
**phone:** (212) 247-2000, (800) 336-4110
**fax:** (212) 581-2248
**email:** none
**website:** www.bestwestern.com/woodward

**number of rooms:** 150 (includes 40 suites)
**number of floors:** 14
**smoking policy:** designated nonsmoking rooms
**restaurants:** yes
**bars:** none
**room service:** yes
**hotel amenities:** concierge, meeting rooms, laundry and dry cleaning
**room amenities:** air-conditioning
**parking:** valet parking
**cancellation:** 6 P.M. 1 day prior to arrival
**wheelchair accessibility:** public areas — no, rooms — no

## Big Apple Hostel

| | |
|---|---|
| Extraordinary | $450 and over |
| Excellent | $350–$449 |
| Very Good | $250–$349 |
| Good | $150–$249 |
| **Basic** | $75–$149 |
| Poor | **under $75** |

A beauty it's not; centrally located, cheap sleeps it is.

The building is old, but it is kept clean. The paint is flaking in a few places, though that's not likely to be of much concern to the hostel crowd. The fluorescent lighting goes without saying. The windows are double-paned, and the mattresses are "good, for a hostel" as a hotel staff person said to us, accurately enough. The bunk-bed rooms sleep four. There are some private rooms (single and double), which come equipped with a phone and clock radio, but not much else. Note that there is no air-conditioning.

Everyone shares the bathrooms and a spacious kitchen area, which has a refrigerator, pots and pans, silverware and a microwave, but no oven. While there is no place to eat indoors (other than in your room), there is an outdoor terrace where people hang out and barbecue during the warm weather. A washer, dryer, iron and ironing board are located in the basement.

It's hard to sleep for less in the Times Square area, which makes this spot particularly attractive for students and other young visitors.

**Big Apple Hostel,** 119 W. 45th St., New York, NY 10036
**cross streets:** between Avenue of the Americas and Seventh Avenue
**phone:** (212) 302-2603
**fax:** (212) 302-2605
**email:** bigapple@concentric.net
**website:** www.concentric.net/~ bigapple
**number of rooms:** 24 (includes 11 private rooms and 100 dorm beds)

**number of floors:** 7
**smoking policy:** designated nonsmoking floors
**restaurants:** cafe
**bars:** none
**room service:** none
**hotel amenities:** laundry, common room and kitchen
**room amenities:** none
**parking:** none
**cancellation:** 7 days prior to arrival
**wheelchair accessibility:** public areas — no, rooms — no

## Broadway Inn

| | |
|---|---|
| Extraordinary | $450 and over |
| Excellent | $350–$449 |
| Very Good | $250–$349 |
| **Good** | $150–$249 |
| Basic | **$75–$149** |
| Poor | under $75 |

The frenetic pace of the theater district dissipates as you walk
up the flight of stairs into the lobby of this bed-and-breakfast
inn. The stocked bookshelves, newspapers and magazines
strewn around, geraniums in the windowsill and classical
music in the background create a casual, peaceful and homey
impression. The personable staff does much to accentuate this
feeling.

The rooms are far from the most glamorous in the city, but
they're impeccably clean and the prices are certainly fair, given
the location. You would expect noise to be a problem here, busy
as the area is, but the windows are triple-glazed to keep out
the din.

Most of the clientele are international visitors; many are avid
theatergoers attracted by the proximity to Broadway theaters.
The biggest drawback might be the lack of elevators throughout
the four-story structure, but if this isn't a problem, the Broadway
Inn offers modest, pleasant accommodations at reasonable
prices.

**Broadway Inn,** 264 W. 46th St., New York, NY 10036
**cross streets:** between Broadway and Eighth Avenue
**phone:** (212) 997-9200, (800) 826-6300
**fax:** (212) 768-2807
**email:** broadwayinn@att.net
**website:** www.broadwayinn.com
**number of rooms:** 41 (includes 12 suites)
**number of floors:** 3 floors
**smoking policy:** designated nonsmoking rooms
**restaurants:** none
**bars:** none
**room service:** none
**hotel amenities:** none

**room amenities:** air-conditioning
**parking:** none
**cancellation:** 3 P.M. 1 day prior to arrival
**wheelchair accessibility:** public areas — no, rooms — no

## Carnegie Hotel

| | |
|---|---|
| Extraordinary | $450 and over |
| Excellent | $350–$449 |
| Very Good | **$250–$349** |
| **Good** | $150–$249 |
| Basic | $75–$149 |
| Poor | under $75 |

For about $200 a night, visitors to the city get a reasonably comfortable, if not especially charming, hotel near Central Park and many prime tourist spots. The pattern-on-pattern lobby has large, low candles on the tables in the seating areas. Befitting the name, classical music is playing.

The semblance of atmosphere created in the lobby is dispensed with in the guest rooms. The usual dark furniture prevails, along with green carpet and pink and green bedspreads. There are one-line phones with dataport, fake plants, clock radio and safe. Some rooms have an armoire instead of a closet; there are three clothes drawers. In the bathroom are Gilchrist and Soames products, hair dryer, and a phone. Each room has a kitchen that includes a range, kettle, coffee maker, microwave, mini-fridge but no pots and pans, no plates except a couple of plastic ones, no silverware except two spoons. This curious configuration would make a Stouffer's dinner and a cup of tea possible. If the Carnegie keeps the prices low and you keep your expectations low too, all should be well.

**Carnegie Hotel,** 229 W. 58th St., New York, NY 10019
**cross streets:** between Broadway and Seventh Avenue
**phone:** (212) 245-4000, (888) 468-3558 (HOTEL 58)
**fax:** (212) 245-6199
**email:** none
**website:** www.newyorkhotel.com
**number of rooms:** 20 (all suites)
**number of floors:** 5
**smoking policy:** all smoking
**restaurants:** none
**bars:** none
**room service:** none
**hotel amenities:** none
**room amenities:** air-conditioning, kitchen, modem line, safe
**parking:** none
**cancellation:** 5 P.M. 1 day prior to arrival
**wheelchair accessibility:** public areas — yes, rooms — no

# Central Park Inter-Continental New York

| Extraordinary | **$450 and over** |
|---|---|
| **Excellent** | **$350–$449** |
| Very Good | $250–$349 |
| Good | $150–$249 |
| Basic | $75–$149 |
| Poor | under $75 |

This hotel has been changing owners lately almost as frequently as bed linen. Since none of the owners could do anything to improve the views over Central Park, they have instead insured that everything within the place is gleaming.

As guests step into the lobby, we suspect that the elegant old-world atmosphere will come closer to their image of a New York hotel than many of the newer kids on this and other blocks. This impression continues through the guest room hallways into the rooms themselves, which nearly beg you to describe them as tastefully appointed. They're tastefully appointed.

Rooms with a view are the jewels (some even have terraces), but view or not, there's plenty of creature comfort. Two-line phones, dataport, voice mail, VCR, clock radio, iron and ironing board, mini-bar, makeup mirror, bathrobe, umbrella, phone in the bathroom and comfortable bedding and double-paned windows. The upper floors (which means deluxe and park view rooms, as opposed to standard ones) get Molton Brown bath products. Room service is available 24 hours, and night turndown is standard.

The hotel has the requisite fitness room with views over the park. You can enjoy them from a stairstepper, bike or treadmill. There are some resistance machines and free weights and a sauna for afterward. The business center is a small room with a copier, computer with Internet access and typewriter. The hotel also has a concierge staff.

**Central Park Inter-Continental New York,** 112 Central Park South, New York, NY 10019
**cross streets:** between Avenue of the Americas and Seventh Avenue
**phone:** (212) 757-1900, (800) 327-0200
**fax:** (212) 757-9620
**email:** centralpark@interconti.com
**website:** www.new-york.interconti.com
**number of rooms:** 208 (includes 16 suites)
**number of floors:** 25
**smoking policy:** designated nonsmoking floors
**restaurants:** yes
**bars:** yes
**room service:** yes, 24 hours
**hotel amenities:** fitness equipment, concierge, laundry and dry cleaning, meeting and function rooms, business center

**room amenities:** air-conditioning, mini-bar, VCR on request, fax on request, modem line
**parking:** valet
**cancellation:** 4 P.M. 1 day prior to arrival
**wheelchair accessibility:** public areas — yes, rooms — yes. ADA compliant

## Comfort Inn Manhattan

| | |
|---|---|
| Extraordinary | $450 and over |
| Excellent | $350–$449 |
| Very Good | $250–$349 |
| **Good** | **$150–$249** |
| Basic | **$75–$149** |
| Poor | under $75 |

The West 35th Street location of this Comfort Inn, while not the city's most bucolic area, makes sense for some visitors, many of whom are international, because it's possible to walk to many midtown and downtown locations with ease. The theater district and the garment center are short strolls.

The rooms have an extra inch or two of elbow room, compared to many other hotels in this range. The look is traditional, with fresh wallpaper and carpet as of March, 1999. Ceilings are high, adding to the sense of openness. Closets are also good-sized, and each room has a dresser with six drawers for clothes. Room amenities include clock radio, safe, iron and ironing board, and a hair dryer. The one-line phone has a dataport and voice mail. Rooms on the "3" line come with a mini-fridge and a microwave at no extra cost.

A complimentary continental breakfast is served in the adjoining restaurant, and coffee and tea are available in the lobby all the time (in winter, there's hot chocolate, too).

On the down side, you'll find a few chips here and there, not all windows are double-paned, some bathtubs are quite small, the bubblegum pink paint color in the hallways could use a rethink, and there are no temperature controls in the guest rooms. The heat in the winters can be stifling.

In all, acceptable budget lodging with few frills.

**Comfort Inn Manhattan,** 42 W. 35th St., New York, NY 10001
**cross streets:** between Fifth Avenue and Avenue of the Americas
**phone:** (212) 947-0200, (800) 228-5150
**fax:** (212) 594-3047
**email:** mur75a@aol.com
**website:** www.comfortinnmanhattan.com
**number of rooms:** 131
**number of floors:** 12
**smoking policy:** designated nonsmoking rooms
**restaurants:** none

**bars:** none
**room service:** none
**hotel amenities:** laundry and dry cleaning
**room amenities:** air-conditioning, modem line, safe
**parking:** none
**cancellation:** 1 day prior to arrival
**wheelchair accessibility:** public areas — yes, rooms — no

## Comfort Inn Midtown

| | |
|---|---|
| Extraordinary | $450 and over |
| Excellent | $350–$449 |
| Very Good | $250–$349 |
| **Good** | **$150–$249** |
| **Basic** | **$75–$149** |
| Poor | under $75 |

The same company that owns the Quality Hotel and Suites down the street owns this smaller hotel. The lobby here is considerably more attractive, with some of the feeling that the designer intended: a 5th Avenue mansion at the turn of the 20th century. The hallways have none of that theme but they are much more comely than the ones at the Quality Inn. Guest rooms veer toward country Americana. There are double-paned windows, one-line phone with dataport and voice mail. Amenities include clock radio, hair dryer and coffee maker. Closets are small, bedding adequate. A workout room has three machines: a treadmill, a stairstepper, and a bike. Lodging plain and simple.

**Comfort Inn Midtown,** 129 W. 46th St., New York, NY 10036
**cross streets:** between Avenue of the Americas and Broadway
**phone:** (212) 221-2600, (800) 567-7720
**reservations fax:** (212) 790-2760, guest fax: (212) 790-7481
**email:** none
**website:** www.applecorehotels.com
**number of rooms:** 80
**number of floors:** 7
**smoking policy:** designated nonsmoking floors
**restaurants:** none
**bars:** none
**room service:** none
**hotel amenities:** fitness equipment, business center, meeting room, laundry and dry cleaning
**room amenities:** air-conditioning, modem line
**parking:** valet
**cancellation:** 3 P.M. 1 day prior to arrival
**wheelchair accessibility:** public areas — yes, rooms — no

# Courtyard by Marriott-Manhattan Times Square South

| | |
|---|---|
| Extraordinary | $450 and over |
| Excellent | $350–$449 |
| Very Good | **$250–$349** |
| **Good** | **$150–$249** |
| Basic | $75–$149 |
| Poor | under $75 |

The general manager's "office" at this Courtyard by Marriott is in the lobby, opposite the front desk. It's not a gimmick — that's his only desk. It's the only one of its kind that we have seen, and it's a tip-off that this Courtyard takes its hospitality mandate seriously. It does not have much of a New York personality, and rooms are very small — 200 square feet, bathroom included. Still, it offers visitors who want to be in midtown, near the theater district and the garment center, comfortable and predictable lodging.

The hotel opened in December, 1998, so everything is in excellent condition. Browns and greens predominate in the classic contemporary look. There are two-line phones with dataport and voice mail, clock radio, double-paned windows that open, 25-inch television with HBO, on command movies, and individually-controlled AC and heat. The Courtyard chain is designed to be corporate-traveler-friendly so you'll always find a desk and ergonomically designed swivel chair as well as conveniently placed dataport access. There are Marriott-standard foam mattresses. Other amenities include iron and ironing board, coffee maker and coffee, hair dryer and a Shower Massage. Rooms have smoke detectors and a sprinkler system.

There is no room service, but local restaurants will deliver. The hotel has a washer and dryer available for guests, a small fitness room, valet parking and an $11.95 all-you-can-eat breakfast buffet, though other breakfast options are available. Thirteen rooms are designed for people with disabilities, including three with roll-in showers.

One other notable feature of the Courtyard is its pricing structure. Unlike most hotels, it doesn't have one. The rate is the rate — they don't have a high "rack" rate and then discount heavily. It's one more sensible feature of this carefully thought out hotel.

**Courtyard by Marriott-Manhattan Times Square South,** 114 W. 40th St., New York NY 10018
**cross streets:** between Avenue of the Americas and Broadway
**phone:** (212) 391-0088, (800) 321-2211
**fax:** (212) 391-6023
**email:** none
**website:** www.courtyard.com/nycmd
**number of rooms:** 244 rooms (includes 4 suites)
**number of floors:** 32
**smoking policy:** designated nonsmoking rooms
**restaurants:** yes
**bars:** yes

**room service:** none
**hotel amenities:** fitness equipment, business services, laundry and dry cleaning, concierge, meeting room
**room amenities:** air-conditioning, multiple phone lines, voice mail, modem line, mini-fridge on request, coffee maker, hairdryer, iron and board
**parking:** valet
**cancellation:** 6 P.M. day of arrival
**wheelchair accessibility:** public areas — yes, rooms — yes. ADA compliant
**notes:** pets permitted with advance approval

## Crowne Plaza Manhattan

| | |
|---|---|
| Extraordinary | $450 and over |
| Excellent | **$350–$449** |
| **Very Good** | **$250–$349** |
| Good | $150–$249 |
| Basic | $75–$149 |
| Poor | under $75 |

The pink neon lights on the lower facade of the Crowne Plaza were no doubt intended to reflect the garish excitement of Times Square, but were they to be replaced with something just a bit less garish and less exciting, no one would mind a bit.

The taste for pink neon, fortunately, doesn't extend to the interior. The Crowne Plaza is actually quite a pleasant hotel as things stand, although they have begun a multimillion-dollar renovation featuring an Adam Tihany design. Mr. Tihany is best known for his work on the restaurants Le Cirque 2000 and Jean Georges, and he will likely add a more dramatic luster to this mainstream-style hotel. Some of the more winning assets will remain the same. The views, for example, start in the hallways, where single, square windows are cut out at various points, giving guests a connection to the city below. The city is "below" because there are no hotel rooms below the 16th floor; the panoramas from the hallways and many guest rooms are energizing.

Each room has a generous number of amenities — safe, iron and ironing board, makeup mirror, coffee maker and clock radio. "Club" level rooms are not significantly different than other rooms in the hotel but guests in these rooms get private check-in and the use of a special lounge on the 46th floor for $30 more per night. The hotel also has an excellent 29,000-square-foot New York Sports Club that boasts an attractive 50-foot swimming pool. We'll look in again after Mr. Tihany is done.

**Crowne Plaza Manhattan,** 1605 Broadway, New York, NY 10019
**cross streets:** between W. 48th and W. 49th Streets
**phone:** (212) 977-4000, (800) 243-6969 (NYNY)
**reservations fax:** (212) 315-6164, guest fax: (212) 333-7393
**email:** none

**website:** www.crowneplaza.com
**number of rooms:** 770 (includes 19 suites)
**number of floors:** 46
**smoking policy:** designated nonsmoking rooms
**restaurants:** 3
**bars:** 2
**room service:** yes, 24 hours
**hotel amenities:** concierge, meeting and function rooms, health club, swimming pool, business center, laundry and dry cleaning
**room amenities:** air-conditioning, kitchens, mini-bar, VCR on request, modem line, safe
**parking:** valet
**cancellation:** 6 P.M. day of arrival
**wheelchair accessibility:** public areas — yes, rooms — yes. ADA compliant

## Days Hotel

| | |
|---|---|
| Extraordinary | $450 and over |
| Excellent | $350–$449 |
| Very Good | $250–$349 |
| **Good** | **$150–$249** |
| Basic | $75–$149 |
| Poor | under $75 |

The Days Hotel is a virtual twin of the Howard Johnson a few blocks up Eighth Avenue. They're owned by the same company, run in tandem, and it is difficult to tell the difference between the rooms of the two properties.

Dark hallways lead into traditional guest rooms with beige-striped wallpaper. Dusty rose and green coordinate among the carpet, bedspread and curtains. Closets are reasonable in size, windows are double-paned (some noise from the street is likely, though). A safe is standard in all rooms, as is cable TV and on command movies. Room service is from the Metro Deli.

There is a business level, which gets you some additional amenities. These include a coffee maker, iron and ironing board, hair dryer and dataport.

Nothing fancy here — the Days Hotel and the Hojo fill their niche competently.

**Days Hotel,** 790 Eighth Avenue, New York, NY 10019
**cross streets:** at W. 48th Street
**phone:** (212) 581-7000, (800) 572-6232
**fax:** (212) 974-0291
**email:** none
**website:** none
**number of rooms:** 367
**number of floors:** 15
**smoking policy:** designated nonsmoking floors
**restaurants:** yes
**bars:** yes

**room service:** none
**hotel amenities:** laundry and dry cleaning
**room amenities:** air-conditioning, safe
**parking:** valet
**cancellation:** 4 P.M. 1 day prior to arrival
**wheelchair accessibility:** public areas — yes, rooms — yes.
ADA compliant

## Doubletree Guest Suites

| | |
|---|---|
| Extraordinary | $450 and over |
| Excellent | **$350–$449** |
| **Very Good** | **$250–$349** |
| Good | $150–$249 |
| Basic | $75–$149 |
| Poor | under $75 |

Walk out the front door of the Doubletree, (which opened in
1990 as Embassy Suites and became a Doubletree in 1994), and
you're across the street from the TKTS booth, the much-loved
discount ticket center for Broadway and off-Broadway. The
hotel's in-the-heart-of-the-theater-district location makes it ideal
for a catching up with the fabulous invalid (*Aida* is playing at
the Palace downstairs), but Doubletree's amenities also make it
a good choice for families or people on business.

Everyone should be comfortable in the attractive, contemporary suites. There are three phones, two lines, dataport and voice
mail. Clock radio, safe, hair dryer, coffee maker and coffee,
microwave, iron and ironing board are also standard. The ceilings are low but, as these are suites, you don't feel cramped.
There are armoires in lieu of closets and a separate bureau of
three drawers for clothes. Water pressure is good, as are the mattresses, and the rooms are remarkably quiet, given the location.
There is 23-hour room service.

Theater-lovers will appreciate the concierge in the lobby to
help with tickets, as well as the million-dollar views over Times
Square. There are 28 rooms that look out over 1 Times Square,
where the New Year's ball drops.

Business people will appreciate the attention given to the
meeting rooms in the hotel and the "conference suite" guest
rooms. Each of these contains a conference table that can seat
up to eight instead of a more traditional sitting area.

Families will like the attention paid to kids. The hotel offers
them a welcome pack and a "club" — it's a room (unsuper-
vised) with Nintendo, stuffed animals, toys and books. Parents
will appreciate that children 17 and under are free.

There is a small fitness room with a few pieces of equipment,
a Universal-type machine and free weights. The lobby, located
on the third floor of the hotel, has been designed so that the
front desk and some of the seating area get natural light. It's one
more surprising touch in a hotel that has many of them.

**Doubletree Guest Suites,** 1568 Broadway, New York, NY 10036
**cross streets:** at W. 47th Street
**phone:** (212) 719-1600, (800) 325-9033
**reservations fax:** (212) 403-6340, guest fax: (212) 921-5212
**email:** none
**website:** ww.nyc.doubltreehotels.com
**number of rooms:** 460 (all suites)
**number of floors:** 44
**smoking policy:** designated nonsmoking rooms
**restaurants:** yes
**bars:** yes
**room service:** yes
**hotel amenities:** health club, concierge, business center, meeting and function rooms, laundry and dry cleaning
**room amenities:** air-conditioning, mini-bar, VCR on request, modem line, safe
**parking:** valet
**cancellation:** 6 P.M. day of arrival
**wheelchair accessibility:** public areas — yes, rooms — yes. ADA compliant

## Essex House, A Westin Hotel

| | |
|---|---|
| Extraordinary | **$450 and over** |
| **Excellent** | **$350–$449** |
| Very Good | $250–$349 |
| Good | $150–$249 |
| Basic | $75–$149 |
| Poor | under $75 |

The Essex House, over 60 years old, got a makeover in 1990 and now reflects a glamorous, romanticized version of the city's past. The gorgeous Art Deco lobby, where the black marble gleams almost as much as the gold leaf, is instantly transporting to a time when the hotel hosted celebrity-filled parties, Hollywood premieres and big bands broadcasting over the radio.

The hotel is located across from Central Park, and rooms from the eighth floor and up on the front side of the hotel get the views. The Park View Suites are small but popular. It's hard to say exactly what style of room you will get because the Essex House has 28 different types, but you can expect traditional design, high-quality mattresses and decent-sized bathrooms. However, you may also get some street noise and a room of modest if not downright small proportions. If you need a lot of space, the Essex House may not be the ideal choice. The rooms, though, have solid amenities including two-line phones with dataport and a third phone in the bathroom, voice mail, a fax/printer, VCR, safe, scale, hair dryer, bathrobe, 24-hour room service, night turndown and free shoeshine.

There are four concierges employed by the hotel, three of whom have the designation Clefs d'Or. The hotel has a pleasant and well-equipped business center, a fitness center that features ten or so machines along with a sauna, tanning bed and spa services. You can get a massage, facial and many other treatments. Given the hotel's proximity to Central Park, a stroll through this historic bit of greenery, followed by the complimentary foot bath at the spa, may be just the way to end a day in Manhattan.

**Essex House, A Westin Hotel,** 160 Central Park South, New York, NY 10019
**cross streets:** between Avenue of the Americas and Seventh Avenue
**phone:** (212) 247-0300, (800) 937-8461 (WESTIN1)
**reservations fax:** (212) 484-4602, guest fax: (212) 315-1839
**email:** none
**website:** www.essexhouse.com
**number of rooms:** 597 (includes 79 suites)
**number of floors:** 39
**smoking policy:** designated nonsmoking floors
**restaurants:** yes
**bars:** yes
**room service:** yes, 24 hours
**hotel amenities:** health center, concierge, laundry and dry cleaning, business center, meeting and function rooms
**room amenities:** air-conditioning, mini-bar, VCR, fax, modem line, safe
**parking:** valet
**cancellation:** 3 P.M. 1 day prior to arrival
**wheelchair accessibility:** public areas — yes, rooms — yes. ADA compliant
**notes:** pets permitted with advance approval

## Flatotel

| | |
|---|---|
| Extraordinary | $450 and over |
| Excellent | **$350–$449** |
| **Very Good** | $250–$349 |
| Good | $150–$249 |
| Basic | $75–$149 |
| Poor | under $75 |

You can't have everything, and that goes for the Flatotel. But this spot does give you an awful lot — especially space. Their smallest rooms are 750 square feet, and there is more closet space in this hotel's guest quarters than you might find in an entire Upper West Side brownstone.

Flatotel started out as a condo development but became a hotel in 1994 when not enough units were sold. That explains why its rooms are so big and why the contemporary beige-colored furnishings are a bit on the unattractive side — they were an afterthought. Of course, the design is a matter of taste, but what's indisputable (in addition to all the space) is the stack of amenities.

Each room comes with a fully-equipped kitchen (and that means everything: range, dishwasher, fridge, microwave, pots and pans and dinnerware), iron and ironing board and a two-line phone with dataport, voicemail and direct inward dial. "Executive Level" rooms also come with VCR, CD player and bathrobe. The bathrooms are roomy and each has a hair dryer, a scale, ProTerra bath products and a whirlpool bath.

There is a 24-hour fitness room, but although reasonably outfitted, the equipment doesn't look very new. The hotel offers business services as well. Unfortunately, there's also a lobby — with low ceilings, reflective surfaces and plastic plants — that is ugly, ugly, ugly. Fortunately, you won't be sleeping in the lobby, and the Flatotel offers enough leg room to satisfy an extended family.

**Flatotel,** 135 W. 52nd St., New York, NY 10019
**cross streets:** between Avenue of the Americas and Seventh Avenue
**phone:** (212) 887-9400, (800) 352-8683 (FLATOTE)
**reservations fax:** (212) 887-9838, guest fax (212) 887-9795
**email:** none
**website:** www.flathotel-intl.com
**number of rooms:** 169 (all suites)
**number of floors:** 46
**smoking policy:** designated nonsmoking rooms
**restaurants:** none
**bars:** none
**room service:** none
**hotel amenities:** fitness center, business center
**room amenities:** air-conditioning, kitchen, VCR on request, modem line
**parking:** valet
**cancellation:** 6 P.M. 1 day prior to arrival
**wheelchair accessibility:** public areas — yes, rooms — yes

## The Gorham New York

| | |
|---|---|
| Extraordinary | $450 and over |
| Excellent | $350–$449 |
| Very Good | **$250–$349** |
| **Good** | **$150–$249** |
| Basic | $75–$149 |
| Poor | under $75 |

Unpretentious and quirky are attributes that go well with small hotels, and the Gorham is both.

Entering a narrow lobby, you find potted palms, a sofa and racks of brochures. Nothing unusual here, but then you notice the artwork on the walls, painted by the owner's wife, and the mirrored ceiling. Upstairs, a taste for bright colors is at work. There are modern art prints in the hallways, motley bedspreads and bright red lacquer dressers in the rooms. You'll also find 27-inch TVs, Nintendo games, real hangers, excellent water pressure and two-line phones. Bathrooms are small but thoughtfully outfitted, including hair dryers and digital thermostats for shower and bath water. Small kitchenettes have microwaves, baby fridges, coffee makers and coffee.

The rooms on the 54th Street side may get a little symphony from the Hilton's garbage facility across the way. The fitness room has just a few machines but would do in a pinch.

There is something quite likable about the Gorham. Perhaps it's simply that the hotel is run by people, not by the numbers.

**The Gorham New York,** 136 W. 55th St., New York, NY 10019
**cross streets:** between Avenue of the Americas and Seventh Avenue
**phone:** (212) 245-1800, (800) 735-0710
**fax:** (212) 582-8332
**email:** reservations@gorhamhotel.com
**website:** www.gorhamhotel.com
**number of rooms:** 115 (includes 44 suites)
**number of floors:** 17
**smoking policy:** designated nonsmoking floors
**restaurants:** yes
**bars:** yes
**room service:** yes
**hotel amenities:** fitness equipment, concierge, laundry and dry cleaning, meeting room
**room amenities:** kitchenette, air-conditioning, VCR on request, modem line, safe
**parking:** none
**cancellation:** 6 P.M. 1 day prior to arrival
**wheelchair accessibility:** public areas — yes, rooms — yes. ADA compliant

## Hampshire Hotel & Suites

| | |
|---|---|
| Extraordinary | $450 and over |
| Excellent | $350–$449 |
| Very Good | $250–$349 |
| Good | **$150–$249** |
| Basic | $75–$149 |
| **Poor** | under $75 |

The 1999 Basil Fawlty Award for Inhospitability goes to . . . the manager of the Hampshire Hotel and Suites.

We can only reflect on how richly the manager deserves her award, having been accorded the shabbiest treatment by her from over 250 hotels in the five boroughs. Our first correspondence with the hotel was on November 4, 1998 and it wasn't until June 1, 1999 that we finally were allowed in to see it. The manager here hung up on our staff quite a few times during that eight month period. After we finally complained to the owner of the hotel, the manager failed to show for a scheduled site inspection. When we rescheduled, she arrived half an hour late for this second attempt, Sbarro bag in hand, no apology on her lips. We'll spare you further details, but it's our contention that if on an announced evaluation of the hotel the welcome is inhospitable, woe to the guest who needs more than his or her room key card.

There's nothing wrong with this property that a coup d'hotel couldn't fix. True, phones are only one line, there are no views, no room service, no fitness room, no restaurant or bar, no business center, no wheelchair access, stained hall carpet, other carpeting that doesn't quite line up with the door, some tubs have enamel worn off, and the lobby is dingy. Even so, the mattresses and the water pressure are both firm, there is a complimentary continental breakfast, and there are far less appealing properties in town that charge more money.

Would we stay here? No. Frankly, if we were walking on the same side of the block as this hotel, we'd make a point to cross the street.

**Hampshire Hotel and Suites,** 157 W. 47th St., New York, NY 10036
**cross streets:** between Avenue of the Americas and Seventh Avenue
**phone:** (212) 768-3700, (800) 334-4667
**reservations fax: (212) 768-7573,** guest fax: (212) 768-3403
**email:** none
**website:** www.bestnyhotels.com
**number of rooms:** 154 (includes 52 suites)
**number of floors:** 10 Floors
**smoking policy:** designated nonsmoking rooms
**restaurants:** none
**bars:** none
**room service:** none
**hotel amenities:** concierge, meeting room, laundry and dry cleaning
**room amenities:** air-conditioning, mini-fridge on request, modem line
**parking:** none
**cancellation:** 1 day prior to arrival
**wheelchair accessibility:** public areas — yes, rooms — no

## Helmsley Park Lane

| | |
|---|---|
| Extraordinary | $450 and over |
| Excellent | **$350–$449** |
| **Very Good** | $250–$349 |
| Good | $150–$249 |
| Basic | $75–$149 |
| Poor | under $75 |

You'll supply your own adjective for the Helmsley Park Lane's park views but it's going to be along the lines of "thrilling."

Nothing about the rest of the Park Lane is as memorable, but everything about the hotel seems to run smoothly. In the lobby, pure Helmsley — plenty of brown-jacketed staff, marble, red and gold rugs, chandeliers, electric candle sconces, an American flag.

The hallways have low ceilings but are brightly lit and have a cheerful enough aspect. Rooms have the old French style you expect, are good-sized and have two or three closets per room. Many travelers favor the hotel because of the generous closet space. Bathrooms are mid-sized to compact. Amenities include two-line phones with dataport, clock radio, bathrobe, hair dryer, makeup mirror, scale, shoeshine machine, phone in bath and video checkout. There is 24-hour room service. You should be able to get a good night's sleep here — beds are firm and the rooms are quiet.

The hotel has a concierge staff, two of which have the Clefs d'Or designation. There is a small business center with computers you can use there, a color copier, Internet access, and cell phone rental. A 24-hour fitness room for guests only has brand new Cybex, Tectrix and Trotter (all excellent brand names) equipment and free weights. On the second floor, Harry's Bar leads into the dining room called Room with a View for its double-height windows overlooking Central Park. On the dessert menu for the Room With A View restaurant, there is listed "Mrs. Helmsley's Key lime pie." We have our doubts about that one.

**Helmsley Park Lane,** 36 Central Park South, New York, NY 10019
**cross streets:** between Fifth Avenue and Avenue of the Americas
**phone:** (212) 371-4000, (800) 221-4982
**reservations:** 212 682-6299, guest fax: (212) 521-6666
**email:** sales@helmsleyparklane.com
**website:** www.helmsleyhotels.com
**number of rooms:** 630 (includes 39 suites)
**number of floors:** 46
**smoking policy:** designated nonsmoking rooms
**restaurants:** yes
**bars:** yes
**room service:** yes
**hotel amenities:** fitness center, laundry and dry cleaning, business center, meeting and function rooms
**room amenities:** air-conditioning, modem line
**parking:** valet
**cancellation:** 4 P.M. day of arrival
**wheelchair accessibility:** public areas — yes, rooms — yes

## Helmsley Windsor

| | |
|---|---|
| Extraordinary | $450 and over |
| Excellent | $350–$449 |
| Very Good | $250–$349 |
| **Good** | **$150–$249** |
| Basic | $75–$149 |
| Poor | under $75 |

The Helmsley Windsor is low on amenities but keeps the price modest and the rooms in fighting form. "We refurbish, we don't renovate," our guide tells us, and that becomes evident — it's old-style innkeeping all the way. That's not a bad thing.

What this means is you walk into a wood-paneled lobby, with red-patterned carpeting, a hunting print, a nonworking fireplace. The staff at all the Helmsley properties are on their toes, which means there shouldn't be any nonsense between check-in and check-out.

Rooms are traditional with plenty of florals, some Chinoiserie or other touches of the Far East, and framed prints of old New York. The bedding is comfortable enough but beware the single-paned windows throughout the hotel. If you live in a place where it's actually quiet at night (however peculiar a concept to New Yorkers) be sure to ask for a room in the back. It's darker but you'll sleep better.

Standard amenities are one-line phones, clock radio, mini-fridge, a desk, plenty of drawer space. The brochure promises a makeup mirror in every room but that is not the case. There are at least two closets in every room, a popular feature of the Windsor. The hotel has no restaurant or room service, no fitness room or concierge. As doubles are in the $200 range, it seems a fair trade-off.

**Helmsley Windsor,** 100 W. 58th St., New York, NY 10019
**cross streets:** at Avenue of the Americas
**phone:** (212) 265-2100, (800) 221-4982
**reservations fax:** (212) 581-1382, guest fax: (212) 315-0371
**email:** none
**website:** none
**number of rooms:** 244 (includes 53 suites)
**number of floors:** 16
**smoking policy:** designated nonsmoking rooms
**restaurants:** none
**bars:** none
**room service:** none
**hotel amenities:** laundry and dry cleaning
**room amenities:** air-conditioning, VCR on request, mini-fridge on request, iron and board on request
**parking:** valet
**cancellation:** 4 P.M. day of arrival
**wheelchair accessibility:** public areas — yes, rooms — yes

## Herald Square Hotel

| Extraordinary | $450 and over |
| --- | --- |
| Excellent | $350–$449 |
| Very Good | $250–$349 |
| Good | $150–$249 |
| **Basic** | **$75–$149** |
| Poor | under $75 |

This hotel has been regularly cited in guidebooks as one of Manhattan's better value hotels. But, while it's still modestly priced, the Herald Square has always been more appealing on the outside than within. It also has more competition these days.

The owners lovingly restored the exterior of what was once the Life Building (*Life* was originally a humor magazine before the name was bought in the 1930's by Time, Inc.). As you approach, you'll see well-maintained shrubbery and a gold cherub hovering over the entrance. There is a distinct letdown, though, when you walk in. First, you must be buzzed in to enter. That lets you into a tacky, low-ceilinged area where the front desk is behind two glass partitions. It all reinforces the dated stereotype that every moment of New York life is dangerous.

The plain, clean rooms have been kept in fairly good shape since our last visit in 1996, and indeed there have even been some improvements. Some of the smallest rooms have been enlarged, some of the harsh white lighting has been softened, there is now voice mail and most (though not all) rooms have double-glazed windows. But only three small drawers are available for your clothes, mattresses are only in fair condition, the bathroom has few amenities and the hinged closet doors are hard to open.

Perhaps someday the Herald Square's rooms will live up to the building itself. For now, it's an option for budget-minded travelers for whom price is of far more interest than charm.

**Herald Square Hotel,** 19 W. 31st St., New York, NY 10001
**cross streets:** between Fifth Ave. and Broadway
**phone:** (212) 279-4017, (800) 727-1888
**fax:** (212) 643-9208
**email:** info@heraldsquarehotel.com
**website:** www.heraldsquarehotel.com
**number of rooms:** 120
**number of floors:** 9
**smoking policy:** none
**restaurants:** none
**bars:** none
**room service:** none
**hotel amenities:** some shared baths
**room amenities:** air-conditioning
**parking:** none
**cancellation:** 1 day prior to arrival
**wheelchair accessibility:** public areas — yes, rooms — yes

## Holiday Inn Broadway

| | |
|---|---|
| Extraordinary | $450 and over |
| Excellent | $350–$449 |
| Very Good | $250–$349 |
| **Good** | **$150–$249** |
| Basic | $75–$149 |
| Poor | under $75 |

Originally the infamous Martinique Hotel, this spot has seen very good times and very bad. Built in 1891, it was, for a time, quite fashionable. But its fortunes declined in recent decades, becoming a rundown welfare hotel in such dire condition that the city finally closed it in 1988. It was reborn in 1998 as a Holiday Inn.

Still in place are the original mosaics and the marble and iron spiral staircase that offers startling perspectives up and down the building's 18 floors — Hitchcock could have used it to great effect. Just about everything else is new. The single best decision was probably the pale yellow paint on guest-room walls. It is such a good shade that it gives great cheer to each room. The rest of the decorating is surprisingly pleasant, especially if you don't usually equate Holiday Inn with aesthetics. Even the brown-and-red carpet looks like a smart decision. Rooms are adequate in size.

Amenities include an iron and ironing board, a hair dryer, a coffee maker, a two-line phone (with direct inward dial), a clock radio and voice mail. Upper floors have rooms with safes and mini-bars. Windows are double-paned, bedding is solid, but there are no closets — just a rack in the room.

The fitness room is made up of a handful of machines and free weights, while the business center consists of two computers and a copier. The two "concierge-level" floors get complimentary continental breakfast, night turn-down service, a newspaper and use of a lounge on the 17th floor.

The combination of building details left intact from the Martinique and the Holiday Inn's clean sweep make for a pleasant physical plant. In two recent visits, though, we spent some time observing the less-than-friendly clerks at the front desk (we didn't see one crack a smile). Although the hotel has done a good job putting on a new face, not seeing a smiling face at check-in gives us pause.

**Holiday Inn Broadway,** 49 W. 32d St., New York, NY 10001
**cross streets:** between Broadway and Fifth Avenue
**phone:** (212) 736-3800, (888) 694-6543
**reservations fax:** 277-2702, guest fax: (212) 277-2681
**email:** none
**website:** www.holidayinnbroadway.com
**number of rooms:** 532 (includes 5 suites)
**number of floors:** 18
**smoking policy:** designated nonsmoking floors

**restaurants:** 2
**bars:** yes
**room service:** yes
**hotel amenities:** fitness center, concierge, laundry and dry cleaning, business center, meeting and function rooms
**room amenities:** air-conditioning, modem line
**parking:** valet
**cancellation:** 6 P.M. day of arrival
**wheelchair accessibility:** public areas — yes, rooms — yes. ADA compliant

## Holiday Inn Midtown

| | |
|---|---|
| Extraordinary | $450 and over |
| Excellent | $350–$449 |
| Very Good | **$250–$349** |
| **Good** | $150–$249 |
| Basic | $75–$149 |
| Poor | under $75 |

This Holiday Inn opened in 1963, the first time the chain ventured into Manhattan, lured by the draw of the 1964 World's Fair. Since then, this property has changed hands a number of times but it's back to being a Holiday Inn and a newly renovated one at that.

Two identical towers make up the hotel. Room have surprisingly contemporary flourishes in rusts and greens, including a more-attractive-than-it-sounds gold star motif on the walls. There are one-line phones with dataport and voice mail, clock radio, iron and ironing board (curiously stowed in the bathroom), hair dryer, coffee maker and coffee. Basics are well covered: there are dressers with four drawers, a full-length mirror, decent water pressure.

Guests have use of a small but adequate fitness center and one of the few outdoor hotel pools in the city, located on the roof. This includes a spacious deck area with views facing midtown. It's a great perk. (It's also open to city residents for a daily or seasonal fee).

Holiday Inn has completely redone the lobby. If you stayed here in the past few years, you couldn't help noticing the lobby's resemblance to a parking garage. Not anymore — it's moderned up, lit well, and features a 30-foot skylight in the bar area. A currency exchange and an ATM machine in the lobby are added conveniences. On-site valet parking for $11.75 a day (no in and out, no trucks or vans) is a deal.

The hotel's location may be a bit far west for some, but the hotel is solid.

**Holiday Inn Midtown,** 440 W. 57th St., New York, NY 10019
**cross streets:** between Ninth and Tenth Avenues
**phone:** (212) 581-8100, (800) 231-0405

**fax:** (212) 581-7739
**email:** nyholidayinn@email.com
**website:** www.citysearch.com/nyc/holidayinnmid57
**number of rooms:** 600
**number of floors:** south tower — 18, north tower — 10
**smoking policy:** designated nonsmoking floors
**restaurants:** 2
**bars:** yes
**room service:** yes
**hotel amenities:** health club, outdoor swimming pool, laundry
and dry cleaning, business services, meeting and function
rooms
**room amenities:** air-conditioning, modem line, coffee maker,
iron and board
**parking:** valet
**cancellation:** 4 P.M. day of arrival
**wheelchair accessibility:** public areas — yes, rooms — no

# Hotel Carter

| | |
|---|---|
| Extraordinary | $450 and over |
| Excellent | $350–$449 |
| Very Good | $250–$349 |
| Good | $150–$249 |
| **Basic** | **$75–$149** |
| **Poor** | under $75 |

We have no details on this hotel because the owner, understand-
ably enough, keeps slamming down the phone when we ask
questions. There isn't much to know except the 24 floors of this
hotel are fiendishly bad. We checked in to have a look at a
room.

The mattress looked at least 20 years old, the cigarette burn
in the linen looked much newer. The wallpaper is peeling, electric cords run over the carpet, the mustard yellow-striped walls
look hung over, and there's plenty of street noise. There are no
shades, just flimsy curtains, so the natural light highlights every
sad square inch.

**Hotel Carter,** 250 W. 43rd St., New York, NY 10036
**cross streets:** between Seventh and Eighth Avenues
**phone:** (212) 944-6000
**number of rooms:** 700
**number of floors:** 24
**restaurants:** none
**bars:** none
**room service:** none
**parking:** none
**cancellation:** no policy

## Hotel Casablanca

| Extraordinary | $450 and over |
| --- | --- |
| Excellent | $350–$449 |
| **Very Good** | **$250–$349** |
| Good | $150–$249 |
| Basic | $75–$149 |
| Poor | under $75 |

This Moroccan-spiced hotel avoids the kitsch pitfall — the theme is done with a light hand. More to the point, the Casablanca feels like a surprise. You may be shocked, shocked to find such a welcoming, charming, peaceful spot in the eye of the Times Square storm.

The Casablanca does not earn its "very good" rating primarily based on guest rooms. Let's say that they are on the lower end of this category. The rooms are more comfortable and solid than luxurious. There is not extensive closet space, bathtubs are undersized. What distinguishes the hotel are the thoughtful touches — and there are many of them — and the service.

In the rooms, you'll find bathrobes, complimentary bottled water, Ghirardelli chocolate and a bottle of wine. Over 150 movies are available at no charge for your VCR. Design flourishes include modern Murano glass sconces and framed Berber pillowcases in the hallways. On the second floor there is an extremely inviting lounge with books, newspapers, coffee, leather chairs and laptops with free Internet access. Classical music plays softly in the background. In warm weather months, the lounge opens out onto a small outdoor space where you can have breakfast.

We haven't encountered many warmer hotel staffs. Observing two front-desk clerks help foreign guests with their questions was an object lesson in hospitality. The Casablanca is an oasis.

**Hotel Casablanca,** 147 W. 43rd St., New York, NY 10036
**cross streets:** between Broadway and Avenue of the Americas
**phone:** (212) 869-1212, (888) 922-7225
**fax:** (212) 391-7585
**email:** casahotel@aol.com
**website:** www.casablancahotel.com
**number of rooms:** 48 (includes 5 suites)
**number of floors:** 6
**smoking policy:** designated nonsmoking floors
**restaurants:** yes
**bars:** yes
**room service:** yes
**hotel amenities:** laundry and dry cleaning, business services, meeting and function rooms
**room amenities:** air-conditioning, mini-bar, VCR, fax on request
**parking:** none
**cancellation:** 3 P.M. 1 day prior to arrival
**wheelchair accessibility:** public areas — yes, rooms — yes. ADA compliant

# Hotel Edison

| | |
|---|---|
| Extraordinary | $450 and over |
| Excellent | $350–$449 |
| Very Good | $250–$349 |
| Good | $150–$249 |
| **Basic** | **$75–$149** |
| Poor | under $75 |

The Edison, located in the heart of the theater district since it opened in 1931, has been, along with the Broadway community it serves, through good times and bum times. It's seen them all and it's still here.

At its opening, instead of cutting a ribbon, the hotel had Thomas Edison turn on the lights by remote control from his home in Menlo Park. The Hotel Edison may have been a symbol for the cutting edge then, but it has long since become a symbol of Broadway's "fabulous invalid" status. To put it plainly, it's fairly dingy upstairs. Hallways have the quiet gloom of a Broadway show that is about to close; many rooms are dark and get little cheer from the faded, floral-print bedspreads. The hotel could use some of the same bounce that the mattresses have.

The popular Cafe Edison is a de facto canteen, however humble, for people in the theater, and it's a good place to eavesdrop on showbiz gossip. The Supper Club is also located here, a popular nightclub with many types of musical artists booked into it.

Given what's happened to the neighborhood, the Edison is a hotel that has seen better days but one that could yet stage its own revival.

**Hotel Edison,** 228 W. 47th St., New York, NY 10036
**cross streets:** between Broadway and Eighth Avenue
**phone:** (212) 840-5000, (800) 637-7070
**reservations fax:** (212) 596-6850, guest fax: (212) 596-6868
**email:** edisonnyc@aol.com
**website:** www.edisonhotelnyc.com
**number of rooms:** 900 (includes 30 suites)
**number of floors:** 22
**smoking policy:** designated nonsmoking rooms
**restaurants:** 2
**bars:** yes
**room service:** none
**hotel amenities:** laundry and dry cleaning
**room amenities:** air-conditioning
**parking:** yes
**cancellation:** 2 P.M. 1 day prior to arrival
**wheelchair accessibility:** public areas — yes, rooms — yes

## Hotel Metro

| | |
|---|---|
| Extraordinary | $450 and over |
| Excellent | $350–$449 |
| Very Good | $250–$349 |
| **Good** | **$150–$249** |
| Basic | $75–$149 |
| Poor | under $75 |

They buried the old Collingwood Hotel and not a moment too soon. The Metro has risen in the same physical plant, but it now has a bright and jaunty Art Deco ambience. The lobby lounge is especially comfortable and roomy for a small hotel. The back room, called the library, could give you the illusion of having your own living room in the city. Guest rooms all have the same Deco design, beige wallpaper that looks as if it's sponged-painted and olive green carpets. Up on the roof, there is a public area where you can relax and soak in the Empire State Building, which looms dramatically. The hotel makes especially good sense for people in the fashion and garment industries — this is isn't a high luxe property, but coming back here after a long day would be cheering: the Metro is spotless, peaceful, and well designed.

**Hotel Metro,** 45 W. 35th St., New York, NY 10001
**cross streets:** between Fifth Avenue and Avenue of the Americas
**phone:** (212) 947-2500, (800) 356-3870
**fax:** (212) 279-1310
**email:** none
**website:** www.hotelmetronyc.com
**number of rooms:** 175 (includes 21 suites)
**number of floors:** 14
**smoking policy:** designated nonsmoking rooms
**restaurants:** yes
**bars:** yes
**room service:** yes
**hotel amenities:** health club, laundry and dry cleaning, meeting room, business services
**room amenities:** air-conditioning, mini-fridge, modem line
**parking:** none
**cancellation:** 4 P.M. 1 day prior to arrival
**wheelchair accessibility:** public areas — yes, rooms — no

# Hotel Pennsylvania

| | |
|---|---|
| Extraordinary | $450 and over |
| Excellent | $350–$449 |
| Very Good | $250–$349 |
| Good | **$150–$249** |
| **Basic** | $75–$149 |
| Poor | under $75 |

The lobby is awash in groups of people sitting on the floor (chairs are in short supply), piles of luggage dot the room and luggage carts swerve through any free space. The noise is constant, punctuated by the ringing of a telephone. A guard is stationed at the roped-in elevator banks to stop unsavory characters. Upstairs, the 1700 rooms are exhausted.

"It's going to change. Everything's going to change," says, the person giving us a tour of the hotel. It could use a change. The hallways, despite bright lighting and maroon carpets, looked gray. Throughout the hotel, paint was cracked, doors were scuffed, bulbs were out, wallpaper was banged up and carpets didn't align with the walls.

The rooms aren't God-awful — they're just tired. Mattresses have a bit of wobble, but windows are double-paned and water pressure is acceptable. Rooms come with clock radios, but not much else. The best amenity of the hotel is the large, well-equipped Bally Total Fitness (which includes a good swimming pool), to which guests get a discounted rate ($12 a day instead of $25).

Currently, the hotel is 90 percent international tourists but, "that's going to change," with plans to cater to business travelers. The hotel has been sold and a renovation is on the boards. We'll look in again if and when it's near completion.

During its heyday, the Hotel Pennsylvania, whose telephone number (Pennsylvania 6-5000) was immortalized by Glenn Miller, featured many Big Band orchestras in its ballroom. When we asked what year the hotel first opened, the representative for the hotel said, "I want to say it's, like, 19-something." For the record, it was 1919.

**Hotel Pennsylvania,** 401 Seventh Ave., New York, NY 10001
**cross streets:** between W. 32nd and W. 33rd Streets
**phone:** (212) 736-5000, (800) 223-8585
**reservations fax:** (212) 502-8712, guest fax: (212) 502-8799
**email:** sales@hotelpennsylvania.com
**website:** www.hotelpennsylvania.com
**number of rooms:** 1705 (includes 23 suites)
**number of floors:** 16
**smoking policy:** designated nonsmoking rooms
**restaurants:** 3
**bars:** 2
**room service:** none

**hotel amenities:** concierge, laundry and dry cleaning, business center, meeting and function rooms
**room amenities:** air-conditioning, modem line
**parking:** valet
**cancellation:** 6 P.M. day of arrival
**wheelchair accessibility:** public areas — yes, rooms — yes. ADA compliant

# Hotel St. James

| | |
|---|---|
| Extraordinary | $450 and over |
| Excellent | $350–$449 |
| Very Good | $250–$349 |
| Good | $150–$249 |
| Basic | **$75–$149** |
| **Poor** | under $75 |

There's a line that came to mind from Lanford Wilson's *Hot L Baltimore,* a play set in a hotel that has seen better days. The resident hooker is complaining about the water and says, "Last night it was cold. Today it's cold — and it's *orange!*" That's the St. James in a nutshell, a decrepit hotel with orange in its plumbing veins and a drag queen soaking in the lobby's atmosphere. It is not clear, however, if the St. James ever *had* better days.

"Are you coming back?" asks the small, bantamweight proprietress, who looks to have been stationed behind the Plexiglas at the front desk since groundbreaking began at this hotel or at least since Plexiglas was invented. We have checked in 15 minutes previously and returned the key to the front desk on our way out when she asks the question. She must ask it a lot. The answer must be no a lot.

The proprietress has a mean right hook. She uses it to slam down the receiver every time we've called the hotel asking for information. So we've checked in only to have our life flash before our eyes as we step onto the plywood floor of the elevator and it lurches upward. (It is sufficiently spooky that we walk back down). Room numbers are scrawled by hand on the door. Our room has no air-conditioning, broken Venetian blinds, a TV with no cable, a one-line phone, four plastic hangers to hang your clothes and a bathroom with a smell suggesting a thriving microbial population.

As we leave the St. James, the drag queen is talking quietly with a gentleman. She may be coming back — but not us.

**Hotel St. James,** 109 W. 45th St., New York, NY 10019
**cross streets:** between Broadway and Sixth Avenue
**phone:** (212) 221-3600, (888) 311-2978
**fax:** (212) 391-6216
**number of rooms:** 173
**number of floors:** 14

**smoking policy:** all nonsmoking
**restaurants:** none
**bars:** none
**room service:** none
**parking:** none
**cancellation:** forfeit 25 percent deposit

## The Hotel Wolcott

| | |
|---|---|
| Extraordinary | $450 and over |
| Excellent | $350–$449 |
| Very Good | $250–$349 |
| Good | $150–$249 |
| **Basic** | **$75–$149** |
| Poor | under $75 |

The faded glory of this 1905 hotel's ornate lobby has been restored, somewhat, but the Wolcott remains a budget hotel that hasn't aged particularly gracefully.

Slow elevators take you to guest floors, where the rooms are fairly small, often dark, and, despite double-paned windows, street noise may be heard. Bedding varies between scrunchy and adequate; there are one-line phones with voice mail, a mini-fridge and safe. Bathrooms are generally closet-sized, with a tiny sink, bar of soap and rough-feeling towels. The water pressure should be enough for an acceptable shower.

There is a fitness room with treadmills, stairstepper, and bikes. The Wolcott also has, somewhat surprisingly, a concierge. We say surprising because it seems out of keeping with the rudimentary appurtenances of the rest of the hotel.

**The Hotel Wolcott,** 4 W. 31st St., New York, NY 10001
**cross streets:** between Broadway and Fifth Avenue
**phone:** (212) 268-2900
**fax:** (212) 563-0096
**email:** sales@wolcott.com
**website:** www.wolcott.com
**number of rooms:** 165 (includes 23 suites)
**number of floors:** 14
**smoking policy:** none
**restaurants:** none
**bars:** none
**room service:** none
**hotel amenities:** concierge, laundry and dry cleaning, business services
**room amenities:** air-conditioning, mini-fridge, safe
**parking:** none
**cancellation:** 6 P.M. 1 day prior to arrival
**wheelchair accessibility:** public areas — yes, rooms — yes

## Howard Johnson on 34th

| | |
|---|---|
| Extraordinary | $450 and over |
| Excellent | $350–$449 |
| Very Good | $250–$349 |
| Good | **$150–$249** |
| Basic | **$75–$149** |
| **Poor** | under $75 |

Howard Johnson eased so many road trips for us way back when (specifically, mocha chip ice cream) that we hate to pick on them as an adult. Nevertheless, any reservoir of affection cannot excuse the shabbiness of this hotel.

The walls and windows are dirty, the doors filthy, the carpets stained, and there is paint peeling. Purple paint was spilled on a bathroom door and floor and was left to dry as it was. Radiators have peeling paint, wallpaper is peeling, walls have chips and scuffs. Some shower curtains are mildewed, and the shower stalls smell musty. One bathroom ceiling had a leak and was chipping and moldy. A number of tubs have cigarette burns and chipped enamel. Another guest room had a lamp next to a bed with a shade missing. The beds are in terrible shape. Most rooms are dark.

For the record, rooms have a one-line phone, some have a dataport, and there is voice mail. The hotel offers free continental breakfast in a second-floor lounge.

In all, a disgrace.

**Howard Johnson on 34th,** 215 W. 34th St., New York, NY 10001
**cross streets**: between Seventh and Eighth Avenues
**phone:** (212) 947-5050, (888) 651-6111
**fax:** (212) 268-4829
**email:** none
**website:** www.hojo.com
**number of rooms:** 145 (includes 10 suites)
**number of floors:** 7
**smoking policy:** designated nonsmoking rooms
**restaurants:** none
**bars:** none
**room service:** none
**hotel amenities:** none
**room amenities:** air-conditioning, modem line
**parking:** valet
**cancellation:** 5 P.M. 1 day prior arrival
**wheelchair accessibility:** public areas — yes, rooms — no

## Howard Johnson Plaza Hotel

| Extraordinary | $450 and over |
|---|---|
| Excellent | $350–$449 |
| Very Good | **$250–$349** |
| **Good** | **$150–$249** |
| Basic | $75–$149 |
| Poor | under $75 |

The Howard Johnson Plaza is a virtual twin with the Days Hotel a few blocks down Eighth Avenue. They're owned by the same company, run in tandem, and it is difficult to tell the difference between the rooms of the two properties.

Dark hallways lead into traditional guest rooms with beige-striped wallpaper. Dusty rose and green coordinate among the carpet, bedspread and curtains. Closets are reasonable in size, windows are double-paned (some noise from the street is likely, though). A safe is standard in all rooms, as is cable TV and on-command movies. Room service is from Beefsteak Charlie's.

There is a business level, which gets you additional amenities. These include a coffee maker, iron and ironing board, hair dryer, and dataport.

Nothing fancy here — the Hojo and the Days fill their niche competently.

**Howard Johnson Plaza Hotel,** 851 Eighth Ave., New York, NY 10019
**cross streets:** between W. 51st and W. 52nd Streets
**phone:** (212) 581-4100, (800) 654-2000
**fax:** (212) 974-7502
**email:** none
**website:** none
**number of rooms:** 300
**number of floors:** 14
**smoking policy:** designated nonsmoking floors
**restaurants:** yes
**bars:** yes
**room service:** yes
**hotel amenities:** dry cleaning
**room amenities:** air-conditioning, safe
**parking:** valet
**cancellation:** 4 P.M. 1 day prior to arrival
**wheelchair accessibility:** public areas — yes, rooms — yes. ADA compliant

## The Iroquois New York

| Extraordinary | $450 and over |
|---|---|
| Excellent | **$350–$449** |
| **Very Good** | **$250–$349** |
| Good | $150–$249 |
| Basic | $75–$149 |
| Poor | under $75 |

"What happened here!?" was our first question to the new owner of this hotel. A once sleepy old hotel has gotten a remarkable wake-up call.

The Iroquois was built in 1923, and, except for the fact that James Dean lived here from 1951 to 1953, it faded into the landscape without much notice. The new owner, 25-year-old Shimmie Horn, had other ideas, remodeling it from top to bottom.

Guest rooms, while not large, have been redone attractively in traditional style with light olive-green tones and a fair number of amenities. There are two-line phones with direct inward dial, a bathroom phone, a clock radio with a CD player, a VCR (the hotel has a complimentary video library), a safe, a hair dryer, complimentary mineral water and Frette linens. Suites have whirlpool tubs. Windows are double-glazed. One drawback is that water pressure is only fair.

The hotel is also planning to launch a restaurant with well-respected chef Troy Dupuy, who comes from Lespinasse in Washington, D.C. The restaurant is scheduled to open late in 1999.

It's hard to say what's more surprising: a 76-year-old hotel that feels so young, or an owner that *is* so young. Either way, a cheering turn of events for the Iroquois.

**The Iroquois New York,** 49 W. 44th St., New York, NY 10036
**cross streets:** between Fifth Avenue and Avenue of the Americas
**phone:** (212) 840-3080, (800) 332-7220
**fax:** (212) 398-1754
**email:** none
**website:** www.iroquoisny.com
**number of rooms:** 114 (includes 9 suites)
**number of floors:** 12
**smoking policy:** designated nonsmoking floors
**restaurants:** yes
**bars:** yes
**room service:** yes, 24 hours
**hotel amenities:** laundry and dry cleaning, business center, meeting and function rooms, concierge
**room amenities:** air-conditioning, VCR, fax, modem line, safe
**parking:** valet
**cancellation:** 6 P.M. 1 day prior to arrival
**wheelchair accessibility:** public areas — yes, rooms — yes. ADA compliant

# The Mansfield

| | |
|---|---|
| Extraordinary | $450 and over |
| Excellent | $350–$449 |
| Very Good | **$250–$349** |
| **Good** | **$150–$249** |
| Basic | $75–$149 |
| Poor | under $75 |

Small rooms. Don't write to us and say we didn't specify the Mansfield has small rooms. It has small rooms. Just east of the theater district, in the heart of the city, you can get great style at relatively affordable rates.

It also has much else to recommend it. The renovation of this 1904 property was done in 1996. The original terrazzo floors and mahogany balustrades in the hallways are the link to old New York. Once you're in the room, it's mostly modern, in tones of beige, pale green and yellow. The walls have appealing framed prints with a nostalgic cast.

Each room has a sleigh bed with a black mesh headboard, Belgian bed linen, VCR, CD player, (there's a free video and CD library in the lobby), safe, hair dryer, complimentary bottled water, and a copy of *Time Out*. Phones are two-line with dataport and voice mail. The small bathrooms have a phone and Neutrogena bath products. Some of the rooms have cedar closets; others have "voting booth" closets in the room with a pull curtain.

We're sorry to see that the owners who bought the hotel in 1998 have dropped some of the previous owner's touches such as free parking and after-theater dessert in the lobby lounge. They have kept the complimentary continental breakfast.

Even if the rooms are small (there, we've said it again), the Mansfield is an object lesson in how distinctive a small hotel can be.

**The Mansfield,** 12 W. 44th St., New York, NY 10036
**cross streets:** between Fifth Avenue and Avenue of the Americas
**phone:** (212) 944-6050, (877) 847-4444
**fax:** (212) 764-4477
**email:** mansfieldhotel@mindspring.com
**website:** www.uniquehotels.com
**number of rooms:** 124 (includes 20 suites)
**number of floors:** 12
**smoking policy:** designated nonsmoking floors
**restaurants:** none
**bars:** yes
**room service:** yes
**hotel amenities:** laundry and dry cleaning, business services, meeting and function rooms, concierge
**room amenities:** air-conditioning, VCR, modem line, safe
**parking:** yes
**cancellation:** 1 day prior to arrival
**wheelchair accessibility:** public areas — yes, rooms — yes. ADA compliant

# Mayfair New York

| | |
|---|---|
| Extraordinary | $450 and over |
| Excellent | $350–$449 |
| Very Good | $250–$349 |
| **Good** | **$150–$249** |
| Basic | $75–$149 |
| Poor | under $75 |

The Mayfair is one of the nicest budget hotels in the city. It is located in the theater district, a few doors from the more stylish but also more expensive Time Hotel.

Rooms here are small, so if you need a lot of lounging space, the Mayfair isn't for you. They are stylish without calling much attention to themselves with furniture, such as night tables, custom-designed to fit the small space. Continuing a theme from the lobby, rooms have black-and-white historic photos of New York and other subjects.

The hotel has focused on the basics, something we heartily endorse. The bedding is exceptionally comfortable, with good mattresses and Irish linen. Note that all rooms are one-bedded king or queen, and all are nonsmoking. They are in the process of triple-paning the windows.

Amenities include a two-line phone with dataport and voice mail, clock radio, safe, ironing board (irons are available on request), luggage rack, and individual thermostats. Bathrooms feature a hair dryer, phone, temperature gauge in the shower, and some have vanity mirrors. Deluxe rooms, which don't cost much more than standard rooms, are somewhat larger, have marble baths and glassed-in showers.

There is a complimentary continental buffet breakfast served in the hotel's restaurant called the Garrick. The lobby's wood-paneled walls feature black-and-white photos of many Broadway and Hollywood stars, including Fred Astaire, Zero Mostel, Jolson and Dietrich.

**Mayfair New York,** 242 W. 49th St., New York, NY 10019
**cross streets:** between Eighth Avenue and Broadway
**phone:** (212) 586-0300, (800) 556-2932
**fax:** (212) 307-5226
**email:** mayfairny@prodigy.net
**website:** www.mayfairnewyork.com
**number of rooms:** 77
**number of floors:** 7
**smoking policy:** all rooms are nonsmoking
**restaurants:** yes
**bars:** none
**room service:** none
**hotel amenities:** laundry and dry cleaning
**room amenities:** air-conditioning, safe, modem line
**parking:** none
**cancellation:** 3 P.M. 1 day prior to arrival
**wheelchair accessibility:** public areas — yes, rooms — yes

## The Michelangelo

| Extraordinary | $450 and over |
|---|---|
| Excellent | **$350–$449** |
| **Very Good** | $250–$349 |
| Good | $150–$249 |
| Basic | $75–$149 |
| Poor | under $75 |

The Michelangelo may not live up to its namesake in terms of beauty (one section of the lobby is so cluttered with furniture that it looks like the furniture department at Bloomingdale's), but the hotel makes up for it by being surprisingly peaceful (the hallways are notably attractive and calming) given its high-traffic location.

There are four styles of rooms — contemporary, neo-Classic, Art Deco and French country — with French country the most popular. Nice touches include a dressing area in "Executive" rooms, large bathtubs, a mini-TV in every bathroom and Frette terrycloth bathrobes. The fitness room is fairly basic, but for $15 guests can use the excellent Equitable Fitness Center around the corner.

On the downside, you do get some street noise in the rooms, and ceilings can be low. As with many hotels, there are more corporate travelers during the week and leisure travelers on the weekend. The hotel serves both well.

**The Michelangelo,** 152 W. 51st St., New York, NY 10019
**cross streets:** at Seventh Avenue
**phone:** (212) 765-1900, (800)237-0990
**fax:** (212) 541-6604
**email:** reservations@michelangelohotel.com
**website:** www.michelangelohotel.com
**number of rooms:** 178 (includes 52 suites)
**number of floors:** 7
**smoking policy:** designated nonsmoking floors
**restaurants:** 2
**bars:** yes
**room service:** yes, 24 hours
**hotel amenities:** fitness room, concierge, laundry and dry cleaning, meeting and function rooms
**room amenities:** air-conditioning, VCR on request, CD player on request, fax, printer, copier, modem line, mini-bar
**parking:** valet
**cancellation:** 6 P.M. 1 day prior to arrival
**wheelchair accessibility:** public areas — yes, rooms — yes. ADA compliant

## Milford Plaza

| | |
|---|---|
| Extraordinary | $450 and over |
| Excellent | $350–$449 |
| Very Good | $250–$349 |
| Good | **$150–$249** |
| **Basic** | **$75–$149** |
| Poor | under $75 |

After years of languishing, the new Times Square has material-
ized with a big bang. The Milford Plaza, however, recalls a time
in the 1970's, when *Oh, Calcutta!* was a long-running show, people packed the Gaiety delicatessen for a hot pastrami and sex
shops lined Eighth Avenue. Memories of those days came flood-
ing back after a visit to the Milford Plaza, which appears to have
no idea that Times Square is a-changin'.

The lobby is garish in a particularly 1970's way, the hallways
have fluorescent lighting and the rooms have single-paned windows. Some bathrooms smelled of mildew, the TVs we saw look
to have been manufactured when The Mod Squad was a hit
show. Dusty rose, the color hotels love because it helps hide dirt,
is pervasive here. The fluorescent lighting in the rooms, though,
is glaring and exposes some of the heavy use on the carpets.

Is it a complete disaster? No. Mattresses and water pressure
are good, there are two-line phones and voice mail in each
room. Closet space is adequate. Guests have access to airline–
and theater-ticket desks in the lobby. The Milford is fine as a
time machine, depressing as a hotel.

**Milford Plaza,** 700 Eighth Ave., New York, NY 10036
**cross streets:** between W. 44th and W. 45th Streets
**phone:** (212) 869-3600, (800) 221-2690
**fax:** (212) 944-8357
**email:** none
**website:** none
**number of rooms:** 1300 (includes 16 suites)
**number of floors:** 29
**smoking policy:** designated nonsmoking floors
**restaurants:** 2
**bars:** yes
**room service:** none
**hotel amenities:** fitness equipment, laundry and dry cleaning,
meeting rooms
**room amenities:** air-conditioning, modem line
**parking:** valet
**cancellation:** 6 P.M. day of arrival
**wheelchair accessibility:** public areas — yes, rooms — no

## Millennium Broadway

| | |
|---|---|
| Extraordinary | $450 and over |
| Excellent | $350–$449 |
| **Very Good** | **$250–$349** |
| Good | $150–$249 |
| Basic | $75–$149 |
| Poor | under $75 |

## Millennium Premier

| | |
|---|---|
| Extraordinary | $450 and over |
| Excellent | **$350–$449** |
| **Very Good** | $250–$349 |
| Good | $150–$249 |
| Basic | $75–$149 |
| Poor | under $75 |

The Millennium is built for business, but suitable for any visitor wanting a sleek hotel in the theater district.

There are three levels of accommodations here. The basic Millennium hotel rooms are contemporary in design. Many have views to the south and the west — you know you're in New York. The fundamentals are good: mattresses, double-glazed windows, water pressure and room amenities. Guests on the ten "Club" floors have use of the appealing lounge on the 52d floor with sweeping views west over midtown. There are some additional amenities to the club rooms, including a fax machine and complimentary bottled water. These rooms run $50 over the standard rate.

For $100 more than the standard rate, you can stay at The Premier, an annex to the Millennium, which opened in November, 1998. There is no lobby here to speak of, just two desks, which give a more residential, if somewhat sterile, feel. The rooms here are, in most ways, handsome and inviting. White sycamore veneer predominates, making the rooms feel cool and light. Amenities include a CD player, a clock radio, a fax, a throw blanket, exceptionally comfortable bedding and three two-line phones. Bathrooms have attractive, green-glass counter tops and Aveda products. The Premier is not as tall a building as the Millennium, so the views are not as good, and some of the closets at the Premier are simply too small.

The Millennium has 33 meeting rooms spread out over several floors, and they are well equipped and good-looking. For visitors on business, the Millennium offers a flexible range of options for meetings. For everybody else, it's an attractive place to stay.

**Millennium Broadway,** 145 W. 44th St., New York, NY 10036
**cross streets:** between Broadway and Avenue of the Americas
**phone:** (212) 768-4400, (800) 622-5569
**reservations fax:** (212) 789-7688, **guest fax:** (212) 768-0847
**email:** none
**website:** www.millbdwy.com
**number of rooms:** 627 (includes 10 suites)
**number of floors:** 52
**smoking policy:** designated nonsmoking floors
**restaurants:** yes
**bars:** yes
**room service:** yes, 24 hours
**hotel amenities:** concierge, health club, laundry and dry cleaning, business center, meeting and function rooms
**room amenities:** mini-bar, air-conditioning, modem line, safe
**parking:** valet
**cancellation:** 4 P.M. day of arrival
**wheelchair accessibility:** public areas — yes, rooms — yes. ADA compliant

**Millennium Premier,** 133 W. 44th St., New York, NY 10036
**cross streets:** between Avenue of the Americas and Broadway
**phone:** (212) 768-4400, (800) 622-5569
**reservations fax:** (212) 789-7688, **guest fax:** (212) 768-0847
**email:** none
**website:** www.millbdwy.com
**number of rooms:** 125
**number of floors:** 21
**smoking policy:** designated nonsmoking floors
**restaurants:** none
**bars:** none
**room service:** yes, 24 hours
**hotel amenities:** health club, business center, meeting rooms, concierge, laundry and dry cleaning
**room amenities:** air-conditioning, VCR on request, safe, fax, modem line, mini-bar, CD player
**parking:** valet
**cancellation:** 6 P.M. 1 day prior to arrival
**wheelchair accessibility:** public areas — yes, rooms — yes. ADA compliant

## The Moderne

| | |
|---|---|
| Extraordinary | $450 and over |
| Excellent | $350–$449 |
| Very Good | $250–$349 |
| **Good** | **$150–$249** |
| Basic | **$75–$149** |
| Poor | under $75 |

The Amsterdam Hospitality Group has one hotel we like unre-
servedly — the Bentley — and a number of others about which we
have some concerns, having to do generally with maintenance.

The Moderne opened in October 1998 after a total gut renovation, even adding two floors to the building. In terms of
design, it's playful and winsome, using forms (lamps, chairs)
from the '50's and '60's to good effect, including a Warhol image
of Marilyn Monroe as a framed print. There are two-line phones
with dataport and voice mail, clock radio, CD player, ironing
board, hair dryer and a phone in the bathroom. Water pressure
is good. The brochure says rooms have VCRs, but this is not the
case. Some rooms can be quite dark. There is a lovely little
breakfast room with windows over 55th Street and complimentary copies of *USA Today*. For those who want a great lunch, the
Soup Man, immortalized on *Seinfeld,* is down the block (though
he closes up shop during the warm weather months).

What troubles us is the fact that despite being a new hotel
there are so many visible flaws. A chunk of wall is missing from
a light switch, marble is chipped in the bathroom, walls have
chips and scuffs, and the enamel is in terrible shape in one bathtub. One duvet has a big, black smudgy stain in it. Plaster is
crumbling by a window. And one armoire has an ironing board
stationed in it so that you wouldn't be able to hang clothes without removing the board.

That makes no sense to us just as it makes no sense to go to
the trouble of adding a glossy design to your hotel but not pay
for the upkeep.

**The Moderne,** 243 W. 55th St., New York, NY 10019
**cross streets:** between Broadway and Eighth Avenue
**phone:** (212) 397-6767
**fax:** (212) 397-8787
**email:** none
**website:** www.nycityhotels.net
**number of rooms:** 39 (includes 4 suites)
**number of floors:** 8
**smoking policy:** designated nonsmoking floors
**restaurants:** none
**bars:** none
**room service:** none
**hotel amenities:** laundry and dry cleaning
**room amenities:** air-conditioning, VCR on request, modem line
**parking:** valet
**cancellation:** 1 day prior to arrival
**wheelchair accessibility:** public areas — yes, rooms — no

# New York Hilton & Towers

| | |
|---|---|
| Extraordinary | $450 and over |
| Excellent | **$350–$449** |
| Very Good | **$250–$349** |
| **Good** | $150–$249 |
| Basic | $75–$149 |
| Poor | under $75 |

The largest hotel in New York is a virtual city, with huge amounts of traffic in the lobby, guests from all over the planet, a staff that speaks 30 languages and a 24-hour foreign currency exchange office. Visitors come for the Hilton name, which guarantees a certain level of quality. Rooms are small, as are bathrooms. The design isn't at all distinguished, but most of the things Hilton guests want are here.

The Towers section of the hotel is a slightly upscale hotel-within-a-hotel. These rooms are virtually the same size as the hotel's other accommodations but have a more handsome, contemporary style and a few (but only a few) more amenities. You do get the Tower Lounge, though, with complimentary breakfast, tea, nice views of midtown and a place to work or meet with people. The Towers have their own manager, staff and private check-in on the 39th floor.

The hotel's hallways are incredibly long — *amazingly* long — and it can be a hike from your room to the nearest elevator. The hotel plays host to countless conferences, meetings, charity events and weddings in a number of function rooms, including the largest grand ballroom in New York. While the Hilton offers a dependable experience and a wide range of services, it has the flavor of Hilton rather than of New York.

**New York Hilton & Towers,** 1335 Avenue of the Americas, New York, NY 10019
**cross streets:** between W. 53rd and W. 54th Streets
**phone:** (212) 586-7000, (800) 445-8667 (HILTONS)
**reservations fax:** (570) 450-1590, guest fax: (212) 315-1374
**email:** none
**website:** www.newyorktowers.hilton.com
**number of rooms:** 2,041 (includes 95 suites)
**number of floors:** 46 floors
**smoking policy:** designated nonsmoking rooms
**restaurants:** 3
**bars:** 2
**room service:** yes
**hotel amenities:** concierge, health club, business center, meeting and function rooms, laundry and dry cleaning
**room amenities:** air-conditioning, mini-bar, fax, safe
**parking:** valet
**cancellation:** 2 days prior to arrival
**wheelchair accessibility:** public areas — yes , rooms — yes. ADA compliant

# New York Inn

| | |
|---|---|
| Extraordinary | $450 and over |
| Excellent | $350–$449 |
| Very Good | $250–$349 |
| Good | $150–$249 |
| Basic | **$75–$149** |
| **Poor** | under $75 |

The New York Inn is an unhappy reminder of the Eighth Avenue that used to be. We cannot recommend this hotel — it's just too skeevy. Carpets are stained, shower curtains are mildewed and the whole thing dispiriting. Look elsewhere.

**New York Inn,** 765 Eighth Ave., New York, NY 10036
**cross streets:** between W. 46th and W. 47th Streets
**phone:** (212) 247-5400, (888) 450-5555
**fax:** (212) 586-6201
**email:** none
**website:** none
**number of rooms:** 40
**number of floors:** 4
**smoking policy:** all smoking
**restaurants:** yes
**bars:** none
**room service:** none
**hotel amenities:** none
**room amenities:** air-conditioning
**parking:** none
**cancellation:** 4 P.M. 1 day prior to arrival
**wheelchair accessibility:** public areas — no, rooms — no

# New York Marriott Marquis

| | |
|---|---|
| Extraordinary | $450 and over |
| Excellent | $350–$449 |
| **Very Good** | **$250–$349** |
| Good | **$150–$249** |
| Basic | $75–$149 |
| Poor | under $75 |

If they were breaking ground for the Marriott Marquis today, the hotel would likely have turned out very differently. When construction on the hotel began in the 1980's, even the thought of a renaissance in Times Square seemed fantastical. The hotel put eight floors between the pavement and its lobby (which may have helped improve security) and did everything else it could to make you forget you were in Times Square. It was a laudable step in the redevelopment of the area, but Marriott took the step while holding its nose.

   The insular nature of the hotel is now a drawback. The 37-story atrium lobby with its glass-capsule elevators, Marriott tricks, is pale energy compared to what's outside its doors. The look is somewhere between a convention hall and a parking garage. The plastic plants seem like an admission of defeat.

The reasonably-sized rooms are completely tolerable, done in greens and rusts with cherry wood accents. The bedding seems comfortable; there is a two-line phone with dataport and voice mail, a clock radio, a mini-fridge, an iron and ironing board, pay-per-view movies, a safe, a hair dryer and a coffee maker. What the hotel calls "Workstation 2000" you will call a rolling desk with wheels and useful workspace. The water pressure is very good. Although the ceilings are low, you get a sense of space in those rooms with views over Broadway or the Hudson River.

With a large hotel such as this, you get a lot of extras, including a small business center and a basic fitness room as well as a number of bars and restaurants. The Encore is the busiest restaurant in Marriott's chain worldwide; there is Katen, a sushi bar with a chef formerly of Nobu, and the revolving restaurant called The View on the 47th through 49th floors, which looks out at everything from Bryant Park and the New York Public Library to the Chrysler Building, the Hudson River and Central Park. The hotel also has a concierge desk, an American Express desk and a desk for theater tickets.

When we visited the hotel not long after it opened in 1985, there were long lines to check in. During our latest visit we asked if this problem had been addressed; in fact, it has. The hotel now gives beepers to anyone who wants to be alerted that their room is ready. So if you arrive at the hotel at 9 A.M. and have to rush off to a meeting, the hotel will beep you anywhere in the tri-state area during the day. That's a good touch.

We'll never warm up to the Marriott Marquis, but it does serve its purpose as a reliable place to stay. It may be most usefully thought of as a lodging component of the Jacob K. Javits Convention Center, a fifteen minute walk away. For conventioneers, the Marriott makes sense, as it does for large groups.

**New York Marriott Marquis,** 1535 Broadway, New York, NY 10036
**cross streets:** between W. 45th and W. 46th Streets
**phone:** (212) 398-1900, (800) 843-4898
**reservations fax:** (212) 704-8966, guest fax: (212) 704-8930
**email:** none
**website:** www.marriot.com
**number of rooms:** 1919 (includes 57 suites)
**number of floors:** 35
**smoking policy:** designated nonsmoking floors
**restaurants:** 3
**bars:** 2
**room service:** yes, 24 hours
**hotel amenities:** health club, concierge, laundry and dry cleaning, business center, meeting and function rooms
**room amenities:** air-conditioning, mini-bar, VCR on request, modem line, safe
**parking:** valet

**cancellation:** 6 P.M. day of arrival
**wheelchair accessibility:** public areas — yes, rooms — yes.
ADA compliant
**notes:** small pets permitted with advance approval

## The New Yorker Hotel

| | |
|---|---|
| Extraordinary | $450 and over |
| Excellent | $350–$449 |
| Very Good | $250–$349 |
| **Good** | **$150–$249** |
| Basic | $75–$149 |
| Poor | under $75 |

The New Yorker Hotel has, for many years, been a sleeping
giant. It is now stirring. After a glittering start (it opened in
1930), the 1,000-room hotel had fallen on hard times in the
intervening years and the Unification Church bought it in 1976.
It fell off the hotel map as the Rev. Sun Myung Moon and his fol-
lowers made it their headquarters.

The New Yorker has begun a new and promising chapter in
its life as it undergoes renovations begun in 1998. (It is still
owned by the Unification Church.) The rooms are small and traditional in design. The ones done in lighter colors are the most
appealing as are the rooms on the upper floors. Many have
priceless views — to the west over the Hudson, to the south
with views of the World Trade Center and the Statue of Liberty
and to the east into the heart of Manhattan.

Standard rooms don't come loaded up with amenities, but
the mattresses are new and so are the boilers that the hotel has
installed to enhance water pressure. You'll get a clock radio, just
enough closet space and double-paned windows. If you want
more amenities, "Tower" rooms have them (at higher rates).
These rooms are snappier looking than the standard New Yorker
accommodation and have fax machines, two-line phones (the
phones in other rooms are only one-line), hair dryers, irons and
ironing boards and coffee makers. Room rates in general are
decidedly moderate and a small tower room like #3904, with
great views to the south, is a steal at $185 (as of early 1999).
Some Tower rooms have terraces.

The hotel's elevators are noticeably swift and will whisk you
down from your room to the fitness room, a coin-operated laundry or the Tick Tock Diner, (which is open 24 hours and also
provides room service).

The New Yorker is in the process of reinventing itself, and we
will follow its progress with interest.

**The New Yorker Hotel,** 481 Eighth Ave., New York, NY 10001
**cross streets:** at W. 34th Street
**phone:** (212) 971-0101, (800) 764-4680
**reservations fax:** (212) 563-6136, guest fax: (212) 629-6536
**email:** info@nyhotel.com
**website:** none

**number of rooms:** 1000 (includes 100 suites)
**number of floors:** 40
**smoking policy:** designated nonsmoking floors
**restaurants:** 2
**bars:** yes
**room service:** none
**hotel amenities:** fitness equipment, laundry and dry cleaning, meeting and function rooms
**room amenities:** air-conditioning, mini-fridge, modem line
**parking:** valet
**cancellation:** 6 P.M. day of arrival
**wheelchair accessibility:** public areas — yes, rooms — yes. ADA compliant

## Novotel New York

| | |
|---|---|
| Extraordinary | $450 and over |
| Excellent | $350–$449 |
| Very Good | **$250–$349** |
| **Good** | **$150–$249** |
| Basic | $75–$149 |
| Poor | under $75 |

The Novotel is acceptable lodging in the theater district, though not an especially good value in high season: When rates hover around $200, rooms look much better than they do when they cost over $300 a night.

The hallways are carpeted in bright orange and blue with pale orange walls; they are jaunty enough that guest rooms are a bit of a letdown. The rooms have low ceilings and are furnished in a simple, contemporary design with more orange and blue (and some beige thrown in), but the furniture, bedspreads and curtains look like they're from the bargain basement.

Standard room amenities include a mini-bar, a clock radio, an iron and ironing board, safe, two-line phone with dataport and voice mail and in-room video checkout. Bathrooms are small but well lit and clean. A fitness room has a handful of aerobics machines and a few free weights.

Guests may get a good view from their room of the Hudson River or down Broadway to Times Square, but this is a theater district hotel without any of the Great White Way's razzle-dazzle.

**Novotel New York,** 226 W. 52nd St., New York, NY 10019
**cross streets:** between Broadway and Eighth Avenue
**phone:** (212) 315-0100, (800) 221-3185
**reservations fax:** (212) 765-5365, guest fax: (212) 765-5369
**email:** newymail@aol.com
**website:** www.accor.com
**number of rooms:** 479
**number of floors:** 33
**smoking policy:** designated nonsmoking floors
**restaurants:** yes
**bars:** yes

**room service:** yes
**hotel amenities:** fitness equipment, concierge, meeting and function rooms, laundry and dry cleaning
**room amenities:** air-conditioning, mini-bar, modem line, safe
**parking:** none
**cancellation:** 4 P.M. 1 day prior to arrival
**wheelchair accessibility:** public areas — yes, rooms — yes. ADA compliant

## Paramount

| | |
|---|---|
| Extraordinary | $450 and over |
| Excellent | $350–$449 |
| Very Good | **$250–$349** |
| **Good** | $150–$249 |
| Basic | $75–$149 |
| Poor | under $75 |

Style over square footage — that's what this Ian Schrager-owned and Philippe Starck-designed hotel offers, and there are plenty of takers.

The hallways leading to guest rooms are narrow but Zen-like, thanks to pale walls, chocolate brown carpet and soft, low-wattage lighting. Your blood pressure will stay low if you know what to expect, which means very small, very white rooms. Some rooms have large blowups of a Vermeer painting over the bed, others have a bright white canvas in a large frame where Vermeer blowups used to be. The all-white themes bring the hotel in line with another Schrager/Starck property, the Delano in Miami.

The Paramount's amenities — alarm clocks, hair dryers, TV/VCRs, mini-bars with food, T-shirts and disposable cameras — may compensate for some of the hotel's drawbacks. Besides the square-foot squeeze, windows are single-glazed, and closet space is tiny with only three teensy drawers.

Much of the appeal of the Paramount is outside of the rooms: a newly redone lobby that's still great for people-watching; the Whiskey Bar; the newer, loungey Library Bar off the second floor balcony; the Italian restaurant Coco Pazzo Teatro, and a Dean and Deluca gourmet snack shop (with the world's slowest moving line). The fitness room has also had a makeover. It is now stylish (of course), with a handful of machines (a small TV attached to each), along with a stack of white towels and a bowl of fruit that wait invitingly. The hotel also has a small, whimsical playroom for young children, created by the designer of the television show *Peewee's Playhouse*.

**Paramount,** 235 W. 46th St., New York, NY 10036
**cross streets:** between Broadway and Eighth Avenue
**phone:** (212) 764-5500, (800) 225-7474
**reservations fax:** (212) 575-4892, guest fax: (212) 354-5237
**email:** none

**website:** none
**number of rooms:** 602 (includes 12 suites)
**number of floors:** 19
**smoking policy:** designated nonsmoking floors
**restaurants:** 2
**bars:** 2
**room service:** yes, 24 hours
**hotel amenities:** fitness equipment, concierge, laundry and dry cleaning, business services, meeting room
**room amenities:** air-conditioning, VCR, mini-bar, modem line, fax on request
**parking:** none
**cancellation:** 4 P.M. day of arrival
**wheelchair accessibility:** public areas — yes, rooms — yes

## The Park Central Hotel

| | |
|---|---|
| Extraordinary | $450 and over |
| Excellent | $350–$449 |
| **Very Good** | **$250–$349** |
| Good | **$150–$249** |
| Basic | $75–$149 |
| Poor | under $75 |

You want a hotel to offer a good night's sleep, not induce somnolence from sheer boredom. Until recently, the Park Central, which opened in 1928, was a barely stifled yawn. It's amazing how a $60 million dollar overhaul can put the spring back in your step.

Image Design of Atlanta has done excellent rehabilitative work. An attractive palette of browns, blacks and golds gives the rooms a handsome look. Amenities of standard rooms include two-line phones with dataport and voice mail, safe, hair dryer, iron and ironing board, and movies on demand.

The Executive Club level rooms on the upper floors, more than one fourth of the hotel, costs $25 over the regular rate. These include the additional amenities of a fax machine, desk and ergonomic chair, mini-bar and coffee maker, bathrobe, additional phone in the bathroom, as well as access to the Executive Club lounge. In that lounge, complimentary continental buffet breakfast is available as are evening hors d'oeuvres. An especially attractive feature of the lounge is its three terraces — so you can grab some coffee, walk outside and soak in the city.

The bedding throughout is comfortable, and most of the windows are double-paned, but not all. That should be fixed without delay. A small point, but it would be nice if the bedside lights had different brightness levels. A fitness room has a Universal machine, treadmill, bike, stairstepper and free weights. There was no room service or hotel restaurant when we visited, but both are on the way.

We can't resist mentioning one unique feature of the Park Central, found in its presidential suite, called here the Carnegie

Suite. Located on the 20th floor, it is the only two-bedroom suite in the hotel. It's the bathtub we love — the one with the southern view — the one where you could sit and soak while watching the ball drop in Times Square.

**The Park Central Hotel,** 870 Seventh Ave., New York, NY 10019
**cross streets:** between W. 55th and W. 56th Streets
**phone:** (212) 247-8000, (800) 346-1359
**reservations fax:** (212) 707-4500, guest fax: (212) 707-5557
**email:** none
**website:** none
**number of rooms:** 935 (includes 21 suites)
**number of floors:** 25
**smoking policy:** designated nonsmoking floors
**restaurants:** yes
**bars:** yes
**room service:** yes
**hotel amenities:** meeting rooms, laundry and dry cleaning, fitness equipment
**room amenities:** air-conditioning, VCR on request, safe, modem line, multiline phone, iron and board
**parking:** valet
**cancellation:** 4 P.M. day of arrival
**wheelchair accessibility:** public areas — yes, rooms — yes. ADA compliant

## The Park Savoy Hotel

| | |
|---|---|
| Extraordinary | $450 and over |
| Excellent | $350–$449 |
| Very Good | $250–$349 |
| Good | **$150–$249** |
| **Basic** | **$75–$149** |
| Poor | under $75 |

As plain as it can be, the Park Savoy nevertheless offers clean and very inexpensive lodging in midtown. In terms of services and amenities, expect little, though the staff seems cordial enough. There isn't even a lobby per se — you walk in off of West 58th Street down a hallway to the front desk.

Four adults could share a room with two double beds for $145, including tax. That's hard to beat. The carpets may have some stains and the walls some scuffs, but the bathrooms, with their black and white tiles, are well maintained. Both the bedding and the water pressure are soft. Some rooms have armoires instead of closets. All have private baths, with soap and towels but nothing else in the way of bath products. The windows are double-paned, but you may still get noise from the street.

The attraction of the Park Savoy is clearly not either in the rooms or the services. You do get a roof over your head for not much money just a block from Central Park, a short walk down to the theater district or up to the East Side's museums.

**The Park Savoy Hotel,** 158 W. 58th St., New York, NY 10019
**cross streets:** between Avenue of the Americas and Seventh Avenue
**phone:** (212) 245-5755
**fax:** (212) 765-0668
**email:** none
**website:** none
**number of rooms:** 67
**number of floors:** 9
**smoking policy:** all smoking rooms
**restaurants:** none
**bars:** none
**room service:** none
**hotel amenities:** none
**room amenities:** air-conditioning
**parking:** none
**cancellation:** 2 days prior to arrival
**wheelchair accessibility:** public areas — no, rooms — no

## Le Parker Meridien

| | |
|---|---|
| Extraordinary | $450 and over |
| **Excellent** | **$350–$449** |
| Very Good | $250–$349 |
| Good | $150–$249 |
| Basic | $75–$149 |
| Poor | under $75 |

The new Do Not Disturb signs at the Parker Meridien do not say "Do Not Disturb," they say "Go Away." A hotel that is thinking about its Do Not Disturb signs in fresh ways (a hotel spokesman says management thought it was funny and New York in attitude) is a hotel with no grass growing under its feet. Le Parker Meridien is, in fact, emerging from a slump and has an unmistakable new energy and look.

Renovations have been ongoing since 1998, and the gussying up has been top to bottom. The new lobby wasn't finished when we visited, but you sense a forward-looking mandate — signaled by the Damien Hirst painting and all new restaurants. There is Seppi's, the French bistro run by the same people who have run Raoul's in SoHo for many years. The bar, Jack's, is named for hotel owner Jack Parker, and there is Norma's, named for Mrs. Parker, which, in its bright, modern setting, serves one of the city's best breakfasts.

Guests have use of the first-class, 15,000-square-foot health club, which includes two racquetball courts, a squash court and a spa. Up at the top of the building, there is a glass-enclosed swimming pool. You can have a light lunch by the pool or play some Ping-Pong. There is an outdoor jogging track and a sundeck on the roof as well. The pool and the jogging track have great city views. Le Parker Meridien has a basic business center (one IBM computer, one Mac, a printer and fax) as well as a concierge staff. One of the concierges holds the Clefs d'Or designation.

Guest rooms are looking gussied up, too. The look is classic contemporary, making elegant use of ivory, beige and black. Amenities include a hair dryer, safe, iron and ironing board, makeup mirror, a tie rack, dataport, voice mail, phone in bathroom, a scale, CD player, clock radio, and a fax machine. There is ample closet space; the marble bathrooms are small but pleasant. Most suites have kitchens or kitchenettes (pots and pans are available on request). Night turndown is standard. Rooms with a south view tend not to look out onto much except rooftop machinery, but those with a north view look toward Central Park. One off-note: while two-line phones are said to be standard, in reality they are not. If it's important to you, be sure to ask.

Gleaming new hotels are rolling off the line in New York, and many existing hotels are working through their mid-life crises with a complete rejuvenation regime. Le Parker Meridien falls into the latter category and is one of the best such examples.

**Le Parker Meridien,** 118 W. 57th St., New York, NY 10019
**cross streets:** between Avenue of the Americas and Seventh Avenue
**phone:** (212) 245-5000, (800) 543-4300
**reservations:** 212 708-7471, guest fax: (212) 307-1776
**email:** reservations@parkermeridien.com
**website:** www.parkermeridien.com
**number of rooms:** 700 (includes 100 suites)
**number of floors:** 42
**smoking policy:** designated nonsmoking floors
**restaurants:** 2
**bars:** yes
**room service:** yes, 24 hours
**hotel amenities:** health club, swimming pool, concierge, laundry and dry cleaning, business center, meeting and function rooms
**room amenities:** air-conditioning, mini-bar, VCR, fax, modem line, safe, CD player
**parking:** valet
**cancellation:** 4 P.M. day of arrival
**wheelchair accessibility:** public areas — yes, rooms — yes. ADA compliant

# The Peninsula New York

| Extraordinary | **$450 and over** |
|---|---|
| **Excellent** | $350–$449 |
| Very Good | $250–$349 |
| Good | $150–$249 |
| Basic | $75–$149 |
| Poor | under $75 |

The Peninsula doesn't have the large gestures or expansive views of the Four Seasons, nor the grand-luxe look and reputation for service that distinguishes the St. Regis. Nevertheless, a $45 million renovation, during which the hotel was closed (and this in a very rosy period for hotels), has turned the Peninsula into a top contender. Having just reopened when we visited, it is too early to say whether the hotel deserves an "extraordinary" rating, but the ingredients seem to be there.

Not a great deal of the money spent refurbishing the Peninsula was earmarked for the lobby, which retains its slightly curious configuration of an entrance on the ground floor, its main floor one flight up. The guest rooms, though, have had a total structural and cosmetic makeover. They are exquisitely done in a classic contemporary style.

Every possible high and low-tech amenity seems to have been included. There are mini-bars and TVs built in behind doors, along with a bedside electronics console that controls the lights, room temperature and does everything but tuck you in. Many of the bathrooms have a TV and radio built into the wall so you can watch or listen while you bathe (or even have a conversation over a nearby speakerphone). About $17,000 was spent on each guest room for technology alone.

There are Molton Brown products in the bathrooms, flowers in every room, Art Nouveau wooden headboards and attractive paintings and prints on the walls. The new windows seem to do great work keeping out the noise of Fifth Avenue. We're not convinced about the space given to stowing your luggage; suites, for instance, have a specially designed area in the room's hallway where you're supposed to lay your suitcases. We'd rather store them out of sight.

The hotel's spa is a big asset, offering a full range of services, a complete health club and a swimming pool with lovely views.

It remains to be seen how the Peninsula will stack up in terms of service and how guests will react to the handsome, understated rooms (which whisper, rather than shout, "luxury"). Neither a Grande Dame nor a Master of the Universe, the Peninsula's personality will undoubtedly unfold with time.

**The Peninsula New York,** 700 Fifth Ave., New York, NY 10019
**cross streets:** at W. 55th Street
**phone:** (212) 956-2888, (800) 262-9467
**reservations fax:** (212) 903-3943, guest fax: (212) 903-3949
**email:** pny@peninsula.com

**website:** www.peninsula.com
**number of rooms:** 241 (includes 55 suites)
**number of floors:** 23
**smoking policy:** designated nonsmoking rooms
**restaurants:** 2
**bars:** 2
**room service:** yes
**hotel amenities:** health club, swimming pool, concierge, laundry and dry cleaning, business center, meeting and function rooms
**room amenities:** air-conditioning, mini-bar, fax, modem line, safe
**parking:** valet
**cancellation:** 6 P.M. 1 day prior to arrival, 2-3 days during peak seasons
**wheelchair accessibility:** public areas — yes, rooms — yes. ADA compliant
**notes:** small pets permitted with advance approval

## The Plaza

| | |
|---|---|
| Extraordinary | $450 and over |
| Excellent | $350–$449 |
| **Very Good** | **$250–$349** |
| Good | **$150–$249** |
| Basic | $75–$149 |
| Poor | under $75 |

If ever a hotel has earned the right to be called a landmark, it is The Plaza. At the 1907 French Renaissance building, designed by famed architect Henry J. Hardenbergh, people from all worlds have crossed paths. The first guest book was signed by Alfred G. Vanderbilt, Mark Twain and "Diamond" Jim Brady, and it has been ever thus at The Plaza. Kings and movie stars have been frequent guests, and the hotel itself has starred in many movies. The 19-story building was declared a New York City landmark in 1969 and a National Historic Landmark in 1986. How is the Grande Dame of New York hotels doing? There is a dance in the old dame yet.

"They just shot a rap video in the Baroque Room," says our guide, which gives you a fair idea of both the ability of The Plaza to keep pace with the times and the pace of the hotel itself. This is not a hotel for those who don't like lively. The Palm Court, where brunch and afternoon tea are served, the Oak Bar, various movie and television crews, and 805 guest rooms, keep The Plaza on its toes.

The guest rooms got a $60 million sprucing up in 1998 and look good, though there is a wide variety of rooms here both in terms of size and design. Inevitably, some are better than others. Following the renovation, the look has been toned down compared to the Ivana Trump regime. The brochure boasts of "fine period details," which is accurate enough, but the design reflects an amalgam of periods, emphasizing its Edwardian heritage. Standard amenities include two-line phones, dataport, voice mail, fax, clock radio, iron and ironing board. The majority have VCRs, too. Closets are large and bathrooms are equipped with a robe, scale, hair dryer and phone. Some rooms get a view as well — especially coveted are the ones facing north over Central Park.

You'd expect The Plaza to have a wealth of services, and they do. There is 24-hour room service, a concierge staff that includes a member with the Clefs d'Or designation, and a business center has computers, copiers, fax machines. A small fitness room would suffice for the basics, but guests have use of the NY Health and Racquet Club for $25 a day at 56th between Sixth and Seventh Avenues. As in hotels of old, there are many shops on site: a florist, a salon, a chocolate shop, and jewelers.

Inevitably with The Plaza, there is more. In the Oak Room, a plaque commemorates the "Cohan Corner," where George M. Cohan would regularly meet with friends and where he is said to have written some of his songs. Fitzgerald and Hemingway spent a great deal of time there as well. There is the beloved character of Eloise, whose portrait by Hilary Knight hangs near the Palm Court.

You may be familiar with The Plaza from movies where it is featured, such as *Plaza Suite, North by Northwest, Funny Girl* and *Crocodile Dundee*. All this fame has its down side — The Plaza can be unpleasantly overcrowded, and so many people can cause service to be uneven. So, too, the rooms, which run rather too large a gamut. You might be delighted with yours — or not.

**The Plaza,** Fifth Ave. at Central Park South, New York, NY 10019
**cross streets:** at W. 59th Street
**phone:** (212) 759-3000, (800) 759-3000
**reservations fax:** (212) 546-5324, guest fax: (212) 759-3167
**email:** none
**website:** www.fairmont.com
**number of rooms:** 805 (includes 96 suites)
**number of floors:** 18 floors
**smoking policy:** designated nonsmoking rooms
**restaurants:** 3
**bars:** yes
**room service:** yes, 24 hours
**hotel amenities:** fitness equipment, concierge, laundry and dry cleaning, business services, meeting and function rooms
**room amenities:** air-conditioning, mini-bar, fax, modem line, safe
**parking:** valet
**cancellation:** 4 P.M. 1 day prior to arrival
**wheelchair accessibility:** public areas — yes, rooms — yes. ADA compliant

## Portland Square

| | |
|---|---|
| Extraordinary | $450 and over |
| Excellent | $350–$449 |
| Very Good | $250–$349 |
| Good | $150–$249 |
| **Basic** | **$75–$149** |
| Poor | under $75 |

From the outside, the all-white columned facade makes the Portland Square look like a cozy London hotel, promising equal measures of chintz and cheer. Not quite.

First, you must get buzzed in. Then you check in with the staff, who are behind glass (it's the same scenario at the hotel's sister property, the Herald Square). The lobby is painted pink, as are the hallways, but that's about as cheerful as it gets.

Rooms tend to be dark, with harsh lights, small closets, basic furniture and mattresses that crunch when you sit on them, an indicator that they're not exactly top of the line. The cleanliness quotient is acceptable, but no Cockney charwoman has been scrubbing until things gleam. That's the bad news.

The good news is that prices are still under $100, and the hotel is ideally located for a few days of Broadway theatergoing.

**Portland Square,** 132 W. 47th St., New York, NY 10036
**cross streets:** between Avenue of the Americas and Seventh Avenue
**phone:** (212) 382-0600, (800) 388-8988
**fax:** (212) 382-0684
**email:** portlandsq@aol.com
**website:** www.portlandsquarehotel.com
**number of rooms:** 145
**number of floors:** 9 and 7 floors (2 sections)
**smoking policy:** all smoking
**restaurants:** none
**bars:** none
**room service:** none
**hotel amenities:** some shared baths, fitness equipment, laundry
**room amenities:** air-conditioning, safe
**parking:** none
**cancellation:** 6 P.M. day of arrival
**wheelchair accessibility:** public areas — yes, rooms — yes

## **Quality Hotel and Suites Midtown**

| | |
|---|---|
| Extraordinary | $450 and over |
| Excellent | $350–$449 |
| Very Good | $250–$349 |
| **Good** | **$150–$249** |
| Basic | **$75–$149** |
| Poor | under $75 |

There isn't much to this Quality Hotel that makes it distinctive. It's more or less average accommodations with no frills. Fortunately, the price is right.

Avert your eyes as you make your way down the guest room hallways — there's some seriously bad, white light grimming down the proceedings. Guest rooms are done in traditional ho-hum design. There are one-line phones with dataport and voice mail, clock radio, safe, iron and ironing board, hair dryer and coffee maker. Bedding is variable — none of the mattresses seemed to match the hotel name, though. Windows are double-paned, water pressure wasn't strong when we tested it and we have our doubts about it during the morning shower rush hour. Some rooms are dark.

A small business center, operated with your credit card, has a computer, printer, copier, fax and Internet access. The fitness room has a half dozen aerobics machines. A complimentary continental breakfast adds to the value of the Quality.

**Quality Hotel and Suites Midtown,** 59 W. 46th St., New York, NY 10036
**cross streets:** between Fifth Avenue and Avenue of the Americas
**phone:** (212) 719-2300, (800) 848-0020
**reservations fax:** (212) 790-2760, guest fax: (212) 768-3477
**email:** neal@applecorehotels.com
**website:** www.applecorehotels.com
**number of rooms:** 193 (includes 24 suites)
**number of floors:** 12
**smoking policy:** designated nonsmoking rooms
**restaurants:** none
**bars:** none
**room service:** none
**hotel amenities:** fitness equipment, laundry and dry cleaning, business center
**room amenities:** air-conditioning, VCR on request, modem line, safe
**parking:** none
**cancellation:** 3 P.M. 1 day prior to arrival
**wheelchair accessibility:** public areas — yes, rooms — yes. ADA compliant

## Radio City Apartments

| Extraordinary | $450 and over |
|---|---|
| Excellent | $350–$449 |
| Very Good | $250–$349 |
| Good | $150–$249 |
| **Basic** | **$75–$149** |
| Poor | under $75 |

Radio City is all about glitz and glamour, but the Radio City Apartments are far more utilitarian. The prices are on the lower end in the New York market, and for that you get an agreeable amount of space that includes a full kitchen.

There are compromises along the way; mattresses seem not to be of quality and water pressure ranges from fair to poor. Amenities are few. These include a clock radio and one-line phone. Windows are double-paned, and many closets are a rack in the room. The kitchens, though, come with a refrigerator, coffee maker, microwave, kettle, pots and pans and silverware. This gives guests a good way to save money — eating in the room rather than in a restaurant. The hotel says many guests are from Brazil and Argentina. "They love to shop, so they come with one suitcase and leave with five." Staying at the Radio City Apartments could save them enough money to help fund their spree.

**Radio City Apartments,** 142 W. 49th St., New York, NY 10019
**cross streets:** between Avenue of the Americas and Seventh Avenue
**phone:** (212) 730-0728, (877) 921-9321
**fax:** (212) 921-0572
**email:** none
**website:** none
**number of rooms:** 87 (all suites)
**number of floors:** 12
**smoking policy:** all smoking
**restaurants:** none
**bars:** none
**room service:** none
**hotel amenities:** laundry
**room amenities:** air-conditioning, kitchen
**parking:** none
**cancellation:** noon 2 days prior to arrival
**wheelchair accessibility:** public areas — no, rooms — no

## Renaissance New York Hotel

| | |
|---|---|
| Extraordinary | $450 and over |
| Excellent | **$350–$449** |
| **Very Good** | $250–$349 |
| Good | $150–$249 |
| Basic | $75–$149 |
| Poor | under $75 |

This trapezoidal-shaped hotel, straddling the break between Broadway and 7th Avenue in the theater district, opened in 1992 — a new building from top to bottom.

The lobby proper is on the third floor. This separation makes the hotel feel disconnected from the city, but it also enhances security. In the lobby is the Clefs d'Or concierge Christine Spencer, who was voted (along with a concierge from the Waldorf) Chef Concierge of the Year for New York.

The elevators drop you off on handsome and well-lit guest room hallways. The classic contemporary-styled rooms feature wonderful beds (the mattresses score well on our sit-and-bounce test), double-paned windows and a host of amenities. These include clock radio, coffeepot and coffee, iron and board, safe, hair dryer, phone in the bathroom, Bath and Body Works products. The two-line phones have a dataport, direct inward dial and voice mail. The biggest drawback we noticed were low ceilings.

The fitness room has a handful of cardio machines and some free weights. There is no business center, but the hotel does offer a few business services. The restaurant, Foley's Fish House, is glass-enclosed and perched over 47th Street facing south to Times Square. It is a memorable view.

In 1998, Marriott took over the management of the hotel, but you won't find their name embossed on much of anything here. It's a world away (though only two blocks) from the Marriott Marquis — the Renaissance impresses quietly.

**Renaissance New York Hotel,** 714 Seventh Ave., New York, NY 10036
**cross streets:** between W. 47th and W. 48th Streets
**phone:** (212) 765-7676, (800) 468-3571 (HOTELS1)
**reservations fax:** (212) 261-5167, guest fax: (212) 765-1962
**email:** none
**website:** www.renaissancehotels.com
**number of rooms:** 305 (includes 10 suites)
**number of floors:** 26
**smoking policy:** designated nonsmoking rooms
**restaurants:** yes
**bars:** 2
**room service:** yes, 24 hours
**hotel amenities:** fitness center, business services, meeting rooms, laundry and dry cleaning

**room amenities:** air-conditioning, VCR on request, safe, fax on request, modem line, mini-bar
**parking:** valet
**cancellation:** 4 P.M. 1 day prior to arrival
**wheelchair accessibility:** public areas — yes, rooms — yes

## RIHGA Royal

| | |
|---|---|
| Extraordinary | **$450 and over** |
| **Excellent** | $350–$449 |
| Very Good | $250–$349 |
| Good | $150–$249 |
| Basic | $75–$149 |
| Poor | under $75 |

New York plays host to plenty of celebrities, tycoons, and movers and shakers who need comfort, luxury, privacy and security. The RIHGA Royal is one of the city's hotels that caters to the above.

Each of the 500 rooms is a suite, done in classic contemporary style; the most demanding should be at least content with the amenities of the standard accommodations, delighted with their "Pinnacle," top-of-the-line suites. The standard room amenities include a fax machine, two televisions, VCR, three two-line phones, dataport, clock radio, and safe. Quality bedding, double-paned windows and strong water pressure means the basics are well covered, too.

It's the Pinnacle Suites, though, that are the hotel's pride. These are on the hotel's highest floors (better views) and include a plain paper fax/printer/copier, CD player, Aveda bath products, voice mail with pager, town car service to and from the airports, business cards with your private number, and in-suite check-in. A complimentary cell phone loaner is yours for the asking. Hotel calls can be forwarded to it. Some suites have small kitchenettes, and the top suites also have sauna and whirlpool.

The fitness center has Stairmasters, Cybex, treadmills, free weights, men's and women's saunas and an instructor during peak hours. It's open 24 hours a day, to guests only. The 24-hour business center has Internet access, fax, copier, typing and other services. Two of the five concierges at the hotel have the Clefs d'Or designation. Guests concerned about security should note that the RIHGA has a small lobby, which helps keep an eye on who's coming and going; guest floors have only 13 rooms each off short, straight hallways.

**RIHGA Royal,** 151 W. 54th St., New York, NY 10019
**cross streets:** between Avenue of the Americas and Seventh Avenue
**phone:** (212) 307-5000, (800) 937-5454
**fax:** (212) 765-6530
**email:** none
**website:** www.rihga.com

**number of rooms:** 500 (all suites)
**number of floors:** 54
**smoking policy:** designated nonsmoking rooms
**restaurants:** yes
**bars:** yes
**room service:** yes, 24 hours
**hotel amenities:** health club, concierge, laundry and dry cleaning, business center, meeting and function rooms
**room amenities:** air-conditioning, mini-bar, VCR, fax, modem
line, safe
**parking:** none
**cancellation:** 3 P.M. 1 day prior to arrival
**wheelchair accessibility:** public areas — yes, rooms — yes.
ADA compliant

# Royalton

| | |
|---|---|
| Extraordinary | $450 and over |
| **Excellent** | **$350–$449** |
| Very Good | $250–$349 |
| Good | $150–$249 |
| Basic | $75–$149 |
| Poor | under $75 |

Some hotels are a brown tweed jacket, some a dark business
suit, others a well-worn housecoat. The Royalton is a slinky
black cocktail dress. It's the city's most strikingly designed hotel
and, not incidentally, the sexiest.

The sensual aesthetic permeates every aspect of this Ian
Schrager-owned, Philippe Starck-designed hotel. Look at the
long runner carpet in the lobby, somewhere between azure and
sapphire blue, the bow-legged tables and the white, slip-covered
chairs, the tusk-like sconces, the deftly flattering lighting. In the
guest-room hallways, it is always midnight.

Behind the closed doors, ultra-modern guest rooms are not
spatially endowed, but compensate in a number of ways. The
most noticeable is that the furniture is low to the ground — the
room is built, in a sense, horizontally rather vertically. Grays and
whites predominate with contrast from dark wood. The effect is
cool and uncluttered. The beds and the bedding are exceptionally comfortable, closets adequate, and room amenities include
an iron and ironing board, two-line phones, a VCR and a flower.
Many rooms have an "under desk," which rolls out from the
main desk, on which you can eat or work. Forty suites have
working fireplaces and even the fireplace poker has a delightful
and distinctive Starck design.

In the bathroom, it's pretty but petite: the conical Starck sink,
a candle and a flower, Kiehl's products, glassed-in shower and,
in some rooms, large, round tubs. The water pressure is excellent.

Guests have use of a small fitness room, a concierge, the
restaurant 44 and the hidden Round Bar just to the right after

you enter the hotel. The Round Bar walls and banquettes have had a makeover and are now dressed in a luscious caramel leather. Guests may have to share space with New Yorkers; this is one of the few lobbies where natives like to spend time.

In each guest room's mini-bar, there are Dean and Deluca nibbles, a disposable camera and an "Intimacy Kit," which includes condoms and lubricant. We know of no other hotel in the city that offers one like it.

"We sell sex," says a Royalton rep. Does Mayor Giuliani know about this?

**Royalton,** 44 W. 44th St., New York, NY 10036
**cross streets:** between Fifth Avenue and Avenue of the Americas
**phone:** (212) 869-4400, (800) 635-9013
**fax:** (212) 869-8965
**email:** none
**website:** none
**number of rooms:** 169 (includes 24 suites)
**number of floors:** 12
**smoking policy:** designated nonsmoking rooms
**restaurants:** yes
**bars:** yes
**room service:** yes
**hotel amenities:** fitness equipment, concierge, business services
**room amenities:** air-conditioning, mini-bar, VCR, modem line
**parking:** valet
**cancellation:** 3 P.M. 1 day prior to arrival
**wheelchair accessibility:** public areas — no, rooms — no

# St. Moritz

| | |
|---|---|
| Extraordinary | $450 and over |
| Excellent | $350–$449 |
| Very Good | **$250–$349** |
| **Good** | **$150–$249** |
| Basic | $75–$149 |
| Poor | under $75 |

This hotel's current appeal can be summed up in two words: Central Park. Situated at the south end of the park, many guest rooms have glorious views of Manhattan's pride and joy. For the moment, though, the hotel has yet to shrug off its seen-better-days mien.

The St. Moritz was for sale in 1998, and it looked for a time as though real estate developer Donald Trump would convert it into condominiums. In the end, hotelier Ian Schrager bought it and plans to turn the hotel into his flagship.

When Schrager and company took over, there was a quick cosmetic fix. But designer Philippe Starck is back at his drawing board, wrestling with what must by now seem like a familiar challenge: how to turn gentle neglect into high style, how to fit flourishes into smallish rooms and how to do anything with bathrooms that are large enough for dental floss but not much else.

That's the future. The present state of affairs is standard-looking, traditional rooms, energy-saving lights that are good for the environment but hard on the eye and large closets (floral bedspreads, fluorescent lights and roomy closets in a Schrager hotel!). The rooms have double-paned windows, a two-line phone, a clock radio and mattresses that could use an update. Bathrooms look good, but are ready for a Starck makeover. A first-class spa is still to come.

When all is said and done, the St. Moritz may be one of the more desirable hotels in the city. Stay tuned.

**St. Moritz,** 50 Central Park South, New York, NY 10019
**cross streets:** at Avenue of the Americas
**phone:** (212) 752-7760, (800) 444-4786
**reservations fax:** (212) 688-6619, guest fax: (212) 688-6380
**email:** stmoritzny@aol.com
**website:** www.stmoritzonthepark.com
**number of rooms:** 660 (includes 84 suites)
**number of floors:** 33
**smoking policy:** designated nonsmoking rooms
**restaurants:** yes
**bars:** yes
**room service:** none
**hotel amenities:** concierge, business services, meeting and function rooms
**room amenities:** air-conditioning, kitchen, mini-fridge on request
**parking:** none
**cancellation:** 3 P.M. 1 day prior to arrival
**wheelchair accessibility:** public areas — yes, rooms — yes

## Salisbury Hotel

| | |
|---|---|
| Extraordinary | $450 and over |
| Excellent | $350–$449 |
| Very Good | $250–$349 |
| **Good** | **$150–$249** |
| Basic | $75–$149 |
| Poor | under $75 |

The Salisbury follows the current trend in which old-timer hotels get rejuvenated by the energy of the current hotel market in New York.

Bright hallways lead to guest rooms with their steel-blue doors. Inside, traditional American design, with olive green carpets, dark woods and floral print bedspreads. The bedding checks out well, and each room contains a clock radio, safe, iron and ironing board and hair dryer. Phones in standard rooms have not been brought up to millennial standards — there is voice mail but only one line and no dataport. Most rooms have a small pantry area with an unstocked mini-fridge, microwave, coffeepot and coffee. Closet space is generous. Standard bath amenities include Lord and Mayfair products.

About 40 percent of the Salisbury is made up of suites. These have large desks, dataport, and two-line phones. Sofabeds are in each suite as well. Bathrooms in this category of room are larger and feature additional Lord and Mayfair amenities.

The hotel doesn't have a fitness room, but guests can work out for $10 a day at the NY Health and Racquet at 56th between 6th and 7th Avenues or for $10 a day at the NY Sports Club at 63rd and Broadway. There is a concierge desk.

The 57th Street location of the Salisbury, the large rooms and the moderate rates make it an attractive hotel on many counts.

**Salisbury Hotel,** 123 W. 57th St., New York, NY 10019
**cross streets:** between Avenue of the Americas and Seventh Avenue
**phone:** (212) 246-1300, (888) 692-5757
**fax:** (212) 977-7752
**email:** nycsalisbury@worldnet.att.net
**website:** www.nycsalisbury.com
**number of rooms:** 196 (includes 80 suites)
**number of floors:** 17
**smoking policy:** designated nonsmoking rooms
**restaurants:** none
**bars:** none
**room service:** none
**hotel amenities:** concierge, laundry and dry cleaning, business services
**room amenities:** air-conditioning, modem line, safe
**parking:** none
**cancellation:** 6 P.M. 1 day prior to arrival
**wheelchair accessibility:** public areas — yes, rooms — yes

## Sheraton Manhattan

| | |
|---|---|
| Extraordinary | $450 and over |
| Excellent | $350–$449 |
| **Very Good** | $250–$349 |
| Good | **$150–$249** |
| Basic | $75–$149 |
| Poor | under $75 |

## Sheraton New York Hotel and Towers

| | |
|---|---|
| Extraordinary | $450 and over |
| Excellent | $350–$449 |
| **Very Good** | **$250–$349** |
| Good | **$150–$249** |
| Basic | $75–$149 |
| Poor | under $75 |

The Sheraton Manhattan and the Sheraton New York are located catty-corner across the street from each other. Even so, it makes sense to think of them as one mega property.

The Sheraton Manhattan is big, the New York bigger. Rooms,

however, are tight squeezes. The look is standard — mostly light goldish walls, browns, greens and rusts — earth tones, attractive even if ceilings are low. In standard rooms, phones are one-line with dataport and voice mail. The majority have king beds. Amenities include clock radio, safe, iron and ironing board, hair dryer and makeup mirror. Coffeepots come with Starbucks coffee packets. Windows are double-paned, the water pressure throughout is excellent and there are sprinklers and smoke alarms in all rooms. There is video checkout. The Manhattan has standard and club levels. The New York has three levels of rooms: standard, club and towers. Room size and decor remain essentially the same.

Club-level rooms, located on higher floors, are more oriented to the business traveler. Additional amenities include a fax/printer/copier (this actually crowds the room somewhat), two-line phones, bathroom scale, Bose radio and separate check-in. This takes place in the club lounge, which boasts views over Times Square, the Hudson and north to Central Park. Complimentary continental breakfast is served here as well as hors d'oeuvres in the evening. Club guests also have access to their own business center, a small room with two PCs, printer and typewriter. At this level, there is no charge for access to the health club. Night turndown is available on request. These rooms cost $25–$35 above standard rack.

The tower-level, the Sheraton's top of the line, is available only at the New York property. It has its own check-in, a more elegant and smaller version of the club lounge on a still higher floor. Rooms are substantially similar to those of other levels. You get all of the concierge-level amenities, plus more luxurious bedding, bathmat, potpourri, slippers, chocolate with the automatic night turndown and Crabtree and Evelyn bath products. You can have breakfast in either of the lounges, in your room or in any of the hotel's restaurants. They'll do a complimentary press of two clothing items and shoeshine. It is service that is emphasized on the tower-level — sew a button, arrange tickets or reservations. Rates are $20–$45 above the club-level rack.

The health club is especially pleasant. It's available at no charge to concierge- and tower-level guests, at a fee to guests in standard rooms (and open to outside memberships). Though located below ground level, a curving window bank lets in light. There is a full range of equipment, steam and sauna, and personal trainers are available. It's open 24 hours a day, 7 days a week. The general business center (as opposed to the small one reserved for club-level guests) is open 24 hours during the week, open on the weekend, but not all night. It is full service: copying, faxing, secretarial services, overhead transparencies, cell phone rental and customized name tags and business cards. At the Manhattan, there is a pleasant pool with a sundeck.

The meeting facility at the New York, located below ground, is as handsome as they come. Wood paneling, marble, carpeting, its own concierge desk and state-of-the-art meeting rooms.

**Sheraton Manhattan,** 790 Seventh Ave., New York, NY 10019
**cross streets:** at W. 51st Street
**phone:** (212) 581-3300, (800) 325-3535
**reservations fax:** (212) 315-4265, guest fax: (212) 541-9219
**email:** none
**website:** www.sheraton.com
**number of rooms:** 650 (includes 8 suites)
**number of floors:** 22
**smoking policy:** designated nonsmoking floors
**restaurants:** yes
**bars:** yes
**room service:** yes, 24 hours
**hotel amenities:** fitness equipment, swimming pool, laundry
and dry cleaning, business services, concierge
**room amenities:** air-conditioning, mini-bar, VCR on request,
fax, modem line, safe
**parking:** yes
**cancellation:** 4 P.M. day of arrival
**wheelchair accessibility:** public areas — yes, rooms — yes.
ADA compliant

**Sheraton New York Hotel and Towers,** 811 Seventh Ave., New
York, NY 10019
**cross streets:** between W. 52nd and W. 53rd Streets
**phone:** (212) 581-1000, (800) 325-3535
**reservations fax:** (212) 841-6491, guest fax: (212) 262-4410
**email:** none
**website:** www.sheratonnyc.com
**number of rooms:** 1750 (includes 51 suites)
**number of floors:** 50
**smoking policy:** designated nonsmoking rooms
**restaurants:** 2
**bars:** 2
**room service:** yes, 24 hours
**hotel amenities:** health club, concierge, laundry and dry cleaning, business center, meeting and function rooms
**room amenities:** air-conditioning, mini-bar, VCR on request,
fax, modem line, safe
**parking:** yes
**cancellation:** 4 P.M. day of arrival
**wheelchair accessibility:** public areas — yes, rooms — yes.
ADA compliant

# The Shoreham

| Extraordinary | $450 and over |
|---|---|
| Excellent | $350–$449 |
| **Very Good** | **$250–$349** |
| Good | $150–$249 |
| Basic | $75–$149 |
| Poor | under $75 |

Media and fashion people are particularly attracted to The Shoreham, and it's easy to see why. It is good-looking and has most of what you need for a pleasant night's sleep in Manhattan.

The style is contemporary — modern torch sconces in the hallways, lots of taupe, grays and beige in the rooms, velveteen sofabeds, steel headboards, not much on the walls. The room amenities include a VCR, a CD player, a mini-fridge with complimentary spring water, a clock radio, voice mail, a hair dryer and Neutrogena bath products. The closets are lined with cedar, and the bed linens are Belgian cotton. Windows are double-paned.

The only serious drawbacks are one-line phones (two-line phones are said to be on the way), bathrooms that are small and have sluggish water pressure, and some rooms that have far more atmosphere than actual light.

A real plus is room-service dinner, provided by the adjacent, three-star restaurant La Caravelle, one of the city's top French restaurants.

In 1999, the hotel will more than double in size, adding 90 rooms by expanding to an adjacent lot. The current lobby, not much to speak of, will get a complete overhaul. It's likely to make the Shoreham an even more appealing hotel, though next-door construction could, in fact, temporarily disrupt the pleasure of your stay.

**The Shoreham,** 33 W. 55th St., New York, NY 10019
**cross streets:** between Fifth Avenue and Avenue of the Americas
**phone:** (212) 247-6700, (800) 553-3347, (877) 847-4444
**fax:** (212) 765-9741
**email:** none
**website:** www.uniquehotels.com
**number of rooms:** 176 (includes 34 suites)
**number of floors:** 11
**smoking policy:** designated nonsmoking floors
**restaurants:** opening in 1999
**bars:** opening in 1999
**room service:** yes
**hotel amenities:** laundry and dry cleaning, business services
**room amenities:** air-conditioning, VCR, modem line, safe
**parking:** valet
**cancellation:** 1 day prior to arrival
**wheelchair accessibility:** public areas — yes, rooms — yes.
ADA compliant

## Skyline Hotel

| | |
|---|---|
| Extraordinary | $450 and over |
| Excellent | $350–$449 |
| Very Good | $250–$349 |
| Good | $150–$249 |
| **Basic** | **$75–$149** |
| Poor | under $75 |

With only a little work, the Skyline could easily jump a rating category. Were they to replace the mattresses, which are mostly poor, replace the bedspreads and curtains, which are mostly bargain basement, and add a few more room amenities, they'd really have something.

As it is, one-line phones with voice mail, TV and soap are about all you should expect in the amenity department. The water pressure is good, and there's an indoor pool on the top floor, with limited hours of access. Parking is complimentary, unless you take your car in and out during your stay. We hope the management continues upward with the good work they've done in the lobby, so that the guest rooms improve in comfort and looks.

**Skyline Hotel,** 725 Tenth Ave., New York, NY 10019
**cross streets:** at W. 49th Street
**phone:** (212) 586-3400, (800) 433-1982
**fax:** (212) 582-4604
**email:** skylinehot@aol.com
**website:** www.skylineny.com
**number of rooms:** 230 (includes 12 suites)
**number of floors:** 2 buildings 8 and 5 floors
**smoking policy:** designated nonsmoking floor
**restaurants:** yes
**bars:** yes
**room service:** yes
**hotel amenities:** business services, swimming pool, meeting and function rooms, concierge, dry cleaning
**room amenities:** air-conditioning, mini-fridge on request
**parking:** yes
**cancellation:** 4 P.M. day of arrival
**wheelchair accessibility:** public areas — yes, rooms — yes. ADA compliant

## Southgate Tower

| Extraordinary | $450 and over |
|---|---|
| Excellent | $350–$449 |
| Very Good | **$250–$349** |
| **Good** | $150–$249 |
| Basic | $75–$149 |
| Poor | under $75 |

The Southgate Tower is one of ten hotels in the Manhattan East Suite Hotels chain. The group shares a number of features. Not only are they all-suites hotels, each offers somewhat-spacious-to-very-spacious accommodations, kitchen or kitchenette, fitness room and a fair number of amenities. They divide things up as studio suites (which are the smallest and really like a standard hotel room), junior suites, one-bedroom suites and two-bedroom suites. None is a design award-winner, but they are quality hotels at a fair price.

The Southgate is being renovated throughout 1999. For those seeking lodging near Penn Station or Madison Square Garden, the renovated rooms make this a good choice.

The lobby area has been extensively redone, and you are likely to experience a pleasant surprise when you come off the street into the attractive lobby. There are six passenger elevators and three service elevators so you aren't likely to wait for a ride. Guest room hallways are wide, if not exactly cheery.

Rooms are pleasing in a quiet way, with red drapes and olive carpets. The mattresses in the renovated rooms are good. There are one-line phones with dataport and voice mail, individually controlled AC and heat, on command movies, iron and ironing board, and clock radio. Each room has a fully functional kitchen. The bathrooms of course are fully functional — for one person at a time.

The fitness room contains several stairsteppers, bikes, treadmills, some weight resistance machines, a multifunction machine, and free weights. In the concierge department, one of the staff has the Clefs d'Or designation.

One other note: The building was built in 1929, and there are wonderful period details — be sure to note the lobby ceiling, the elevator doors and the beautiful old clock.

**Southgate Tower,** 371 Seventh Ave., New York, NY 10001
**cross streets:** at W. 31st Street
**phone:** (212) 563-1800, (800) 637-8483 (MESUITE)
**fax:** (212) 643-8028
**email:** info@mesuite.com
**website:** www.mesuite.com
**number of rooms:** 523 (all suites)
**number of floors:** 28
**smoking policy:** designated nonsmoking floors
**restaurants:** 2
**bars:** yes
**room service:** yes

**hotel amenities:** fitness equipment, concierge, laundry and dry cleaning, business services, meeting and function rooms
**room amenities:** air-conditioning, kitchen
**parking:** valet
**cancellation:** 3 P.M. day of arrival
**wheelchair accessibility:** public areas — yes, rooms — yes. ADA compliant

## Stanford Hotel

| | |
|---|---|
| Extraordinary | $450 and over |
| Excellent | $350–$449 |
| Very Good | $250–$349 |
| **Good** | $150–$249 |
| Basic | **$75–$149** |
| Poor | under $75 |

This Korean-owned-and-operated hotel, in the heart of Little Korea, has lots of Asian and European guests, many of whom are doing business in the area. As hotels lobbies go, this one hasn't got much going for it; it's sterile-looking, with hard surfaces and a lurking security guard.

Price is certainly a draw here since rooms tend to run under $150. Most rooms are quite dark; the little natural light that makes its way in is soaked up by the dark woods and blues in the design.

Rooms and bathrooms are clean, water pressure is good. Windows are single-glazed. If "suite" means more than one room to you, ask when you book. The suite we saw was a larger room with a separate sitting area.

The Stanford isn't especially distinctive, but the price is right.

**Stanford Hotel,** 43 W. 32nd St., New York, NY 10001
**cross streets:** between Fifth Avenue and Broadway
**phone:** (212) 563-1500, (800) 365-1114
**reservations fax:**(212) 643-0157, guest fax: (212) 629-0043
**email:** stanfordny@aol.com
**website:** none
**number of rooms:** 121 (includes 21 suites)
**number of floors:** 12
**smoking policy:** all smoking
**restaurants:** yes
**bars:** yes
**room service:** none
**hotel amenities:** laundry and dry cleaning
**room amenities:** air-conditioning, modem line
**parking:** yes
**cancellation:** 6 P.M. 1 day prior to arrival
**wheelchair accessibility:** public areas — no, rooms — no

## The Time

| | |
|---|---|
| Extraordinary | $450 and over |
| Excellent | $350–$449 |
| **Very Good** | **$250–$349** |
| Good | **$150–$249** |
| Basic | $75–$149 |
| Poor | under $75 |

You might just want a room for the night. A good hot shower, a comfortable bed, silence. Or, you might want to stay at the latest of New York's dream parks.

Whether or not you want to decipher the concept of time at the Time (there are Roman numerals from 1-12 on the hallway floors) or the Time's relationship to Times Square (the bar is called Times²), you may be roped into the Time's other concept, which has nothing to do with time. That has to do with color.

With us so far? Concept one, time. Concept two, color. Concept one, not so clear. Concept two, red, yellow, blue. Which color room would you like? Request a blue room, the bed cover will be in _____. Correct. There will be a piece of fruit or something else to eat that is the color _____. Correct. There will be a scent bottle you can open that is "color"-inspired. Blue rooms will not smell like _____ or _____ rooms. If you answered red and yellow, you are correct.

The Time can be measured in Ians. The hotelier Ian Schrager, who has imitators all over town nipping at his heels, must be getting tired of so much flattery. It is hard to look at the Time and not count the number of Ian touches, but let's look at what designer Adam Tihany has come up with, partnered with young (age 27) hotelier Vikram Chatwal.

You take a glass elevator to the second floor, where the check-in desks have laptops, no big, unaesthetic computer monitors. That sort of attention to detail is evident throughout. Nothing about the Time is plush — it is all clean lines and stripped down. Most of the colors are black, beige and gray, accented by the previously noted primary colors. The hotel has laid the amenities on thick. Each guest room has three phones, two-lines, dataport and voice mail, desk, fax, TV Internet browser, Bose radio, iron and ironing board, safe, hair dryer, safe, coffee maker, and robe. VCR and mobile phones are available on request. The suites have Jacuzzis. There are window scrims that are back lit — it is a theater technique used to good effect.

The hotel has focused on fundamentals such as plumbing, so the water pressure is good, as are mattresses. While the windows are double-paned, they don't fully eliminate noise from the street. Closets are something of a drawback, they're small and some are simply an area separated by a drape. There is night turndown.

The Time has a concierge and an exercise room (not equipped when we visited). It also has the restaurant Palladin, run by Jean-Louis Palladin, a well-known chef.

We visited the hotel about two weeks prior to its opening, and there was still construction under way. Nevertheless, in spite of the plywood and some conceptual goofiness, the Time looks to be a modern beauty, a new hit in the theater district.

**The Time,** 224 W 49th St., New York NY. 10019
**cross streets:** between Broadway and Eighth Avenue
**phone:** (212) 246-5252, (877) 846-3692 (TIMENYC)
**fax:** (212) 245-2305
**email:** none
**website:** www.thetimeny.com
**number of rooms:** 193 (includes 30 suites)
**number of floors:** 16
**smoking policy:** designated nonsmoking rooms
**restaurants:** yes
**bars:** 2
**room service:** yes
**hotel amenities:** exercise room, meeting rooms, concierge
**room amenities:** air-conditioning, VCR on request, safe, fax, modem line, mini-bar, coffee maker, TV Internet browser, Bose Wave Radio, mobile phone (on request), iron and board, bathrobe
**parking:** valet
**cancellation:** 4 P.M. 1 day prior to arrival
**wheelchair accessibility:** public areas — yes, rooms — yes. ADA compliant

## Travel Inn Hotel

| | |
|---|---|
| Extraordinary | $450 and over |
| Excellent | $350–$449 |
| Very Good | $250–$349 |
| **Good** | **$150–$249** |
| Basic | $75–$149 |
| Poor | under $75 |

The Travel Inn may be the closest thing to Miami in town. That's because of its outdoor pool located in a central court, surrounded by '60's architecture of guest rooms with balconies. No palm trees, though.

Many of its guests are in town for a convention at the Javits Center, a few blocks away. They're probably not here for an aesthetic hotel experience, and the Travel Inn doesn't offer one. It's pinkish brown guest room doors didn't come from the Ralph Lauren line of paints. Still, the guest rooms are perfectly adequate, having undergone renovations in 1999. Mattresses are firm (some perhaps too firm — there isn't much give), there are one-line phones with voice mail, a clock radio, iron and ironing board and a hair dryer. Bathrooms are small and water pressure is only fair. The coffee shop next to the hotel will deliver up room service, but there are a wealth of nearby restaurant choices on Ninth Avenue.

The pool, open only to guests, has plenty of lounge chairs and a small fitness room next to it. There's also a goldfish pond, which, if you look behind it off into the distance, has the Empire State Building as a backdrop. You won't find that in Miami.

**Travel Inn Hotel,** 515 W. 42d St., New York, NY 10036
**cross streets:** between Tenth and Eleventh Avenues
**phone:** (212) 695-7171, (800) 869-4630
**reservations fax:** (212) 967-5025, guest fax: (212) 268-3542
**email:** travel@superlink.net
**website:** www.newyorkhotel.com
**number of rooms:** 160 (includes 1 suite)
**number of floors:** 6 and 7 floors (2 buildings)
**smoking policy:** designated nonsmoking floors
**restaurants:** yes
**bars:** none
**room service:** yes
**hotel amenities:** outdoor swimming pool, fitness equipment
**room amenities:** air-conditioning, mini-fridge on request
**parking:** yes
**cancellation:** 5 P.M. 1 day prior to arrival
**wheelchair accessibility:** public areas — yes, rooms — no

## The Warwick

| | |
|---|---|
| Extraordinary | $450 and over |
| Excellent | $350–$449 |
| **Very Good** | **$250–$349** |
| Good | $150–$249 |
| Basic | $75–$149 |
| Poor | under $75 |

Frankly, we loved the *old* Warwick. It was on the dowdy side, but the rooms were large and you could have one for $99 a night; and that was just in 1993. Now the Warwick's gone all fussy, with renovated rooms, marble and palms in the lobby (though the chandeliers are unsparkly, a nod to the Warwick of old).

The hotel was built in 1927 by William Randolph Hearst for his mistress Marion Davies, which may account for the liberally-sized rooms (for non-New Yorkers, keep in mind that room size is a relative concept). Still, how many New York hotels have closets that were built to be large enough to hold steamer trunks? There are marble bathrooms (with slightly under-pressured water), windows are double-glazed and some rooms have fax machines. The decor is traditional, and the roomy, old-style hallways give the impression of an intimate hotel.

Some suites and regular rooms have balconies, but the hotel management doesn't advertise that since they "don't want people requesting them all the time." The hotel says they have mostly domestic business travelers, but hiding an asset like balconies is an odd concept for a service business. That said, there's no denying that this hotel has good bones.

**The Warwick,** 65 W. 54th St., New York, NY 10019
**cross streets:** at Avenue of the Americas
**phone:** (212) 247-2700, (800) 223-4099
**reservations fax:** (212) 713-1751, guest fax: 957-8915
**email:** none
**website:** www.warwickhotels.com
**number of rooms:** 422 (includes 70 suites)
**number of floors:** 33
**smoking policy:** designated nonsmoking rooms
**restaurants:** yes
**bars:** yes
**room service:** yes
**hotel amenities:** meeting and function rooms, laundry and dry cleaning, business services
**room amenities:** air-conditioning, mini-bar, fax, modem line, safe
**parking:** none
**cancellation:** 4 P.M. day of arrival
**wheelchair accessibility:** public areas — yes, rooms — yes

## Washington Jefferson Hotel

| | |
|---|---|
| Extraordinary | $450 and over |
| Excellent | $350–$449 |
| Very Good | $250–$349 |
| Good | $150–$249 |
| **Basic** | **$75–$149** |
| Poor | under $75 |

The Washington Jefferson looks like a rooming house and in many ways is. There are over 100 permanent residents mixed in with transient guests. Starting in 1997, the hotel has been upgraded, with new wallpaper and black-and-white photos in the hallways and a bit of polish added to guest rooms.

The rooms are small and have a clock radio, cable TV, one-line phones with dataport and voice mail as well as air-conditioning. Microwave and mini-fridge are available on request. Windows are double-paned, but noise from the street can still drift in. Most rooms do not have a bath en suite. While the shared baths have old fixtures, they are very clean. Those without a private bath have a small sink in the room. Water pressure is fair. Bedding seems acceptable for this level of accommodation.

Europeans generally have less resistance to shared baths, so they may be drawn to the Washington Jefferson, particularly European theater buffs, since the hotel is no more than a few minute's walk to any Broadway theater.

**Washington Jefferson Hotel,** 318 W. 51st St., New York, NY 10019
**cross streets:** between Eighth and Ninth Avenues
**phone:** (212) 246-7550, (888) 567-7550
**reservations fax:** (212) 246-7550, guest fax: (212) 246-7622
**email:** blindenbau@aol.com

**website:** www.washingtonjeff.citysearch.com
**number of rooms:** 260 (including 10 suites)
**number of floors:** 6
**smoking policy:** nonsmoking floors
**restaurants:** none
**bars:** none
**room service:** none
**hotel amenities:** meeting room, some shared baths
**room amenities:** air-conditioning, modem line
**parking:** none
**cancellation:** 3 P.M. 1 day prior to arrival
**wheelchair accessibility:** public areas — no, rooms — yes

## Wellington Hotel

| | |
|---|---|
| Extraordinary | $450 and over |
| Excellent | $350–$449 |
| Very Good | $250–$349 |
| Good | **$150–$249** |
| **Basic** | $75–$149 |
| Poor | under $75 |

Much about the Wellington has improved of late. There has been an ongoing renovation since 1997 of the lobby, hallways and guest rooms, which are done in classic contemporary style with beige and rust colors much in evidence.

The hotel still attracts large groups, and when they pull in, the lobby can get seriously congested — throngs of people spilling over mounds of luggage. There aren't many seats to make the wait to check in or out comfortable.

Most rooms are quite small with double-paned windows, one-line phones and voice mail, plenty of closet space and decent water pressure. Even though there are few room amenities, the price is commensurately low. We'd feel more kindly disposed toward the Wellington if the mattresses were comfortable, but they're inconsistent. Many were flabby, and one we tested had a pronounced sag.

Some of the Wellington's "tower" rooms are one category up. They don't have additional amenities, but they're slightly larger rooms, some have serving pantries, views down Seventh Avenue and/or terraces.

There was a time when we wouldn't have dreamed of recommending the Wellington, but it is making strides. More than anything, we wish they'd replace the mattresses. We could recommend the hotel with a clearer conscience.

**Wellington Hotel,** 871 Seventh Ave., New York, NY 10019
**cross streets:** at W. 55th Street
**phone:** (212) 247-3900, (800) 652-1212
**fax:** (212) 581-1719
**email:** wellingtonhotel@erols.com
**website:** www.wellingtonhotel.com
**number of rooms:** 617 (includes 130 suites)

**number of floors:** 27
**smoking policy:** designated nonsmoking rooms
**restaurants:** 2
**bars:** yes
**room service:** yes
**hotel amenities:** laundry and dry cleaning
**room amenities:** air-conditioning
**parking:** valet
**cancellation:** 4 P.M. 1 day prior to arrival
**wheelchair accessibility:** public areas — no, rooms — no

## Westpark

| | |
|---|---|
| Extraordinary | $450 and over |
| Excellent | $350–$449 |
| Very Good | $250–$349 |
| Good | $150–$249 |
| **Basic** | **$75–$149** |
| Poor | under $75 |

A reasonable choice for budget travelers. The downscale traditional
rooms won't enhance your enjoyment of New York, but they are
on the lower end of what you pay in this city for a night's sleep.
The Westpark's location, a block from Columbus Circle and the
southwest end of Central Park, means you're well located for most
purposes. Columbus Circle is also a nexus for many subway lines.

As for the rooms, there isn't much to report — one-line phones,
variable bedding, double-paned windows, acceptable water pressure. There are real wood hangers in the closets and a generous
number of them. Rooms in the back are quieter, darker and $20
cheaper. There's no restaurant in the hotel but you won't miss it.
Just walk down Ninth Avenue from the hotel and the blocks from
the '40's to the '50's are full of quite good, inexpensive restaurants.

**Westpark,** 308 W. 58th St., New York, NY 10019
**cross streets:** between Eighth and Ninth Avenues
**phone:** (212) 246-6440, (800) 248-6440
**fax:** (212) 246-3131
**email:** westparkny@aol.com
**website:** none
**number of rooms:** 88 (includes 5 suites)
**number of floors:** 10
**smoking policy:** all smoking
**restaurants:** none
**bars:** none
**room service:** none
**hotel amenities:** none
**room amenities:** air-conditioning
**parking:** none
**cancellation:** 1 day prior to arrival
**wheelchair accessibility:** public areas — no, rooms — no

## Wyndham

| | |
|---|---|
| Extraordinary | $450 and over |
| Excellent | $350–$449 |
| **Very Good** | $250–$349 |
| Good | **$150–$249** |
| Basic | $75–$149 |
| Poor | under $75 |

A stay at the Wyndham is like submitting to the charms and ministrations of a beloved, if slightly dotty, aunt.

The rooms are oversized and underpriced, which means they are a favorite of, among others, theater and film people in town for a Broadway run or a film shoot. A bit over $200 gets you a suite with enough room to rehearse your lines, reasonably good bedding, double-paned windows and a small pantry with a fridge and sink. Phones are one-line. Closets are large enough for the regular traveler and for the performer with their share of bugle beads. The rooms have a feminine touch, with pink or soft blue carpets and many floral motifs.

Many hotels, *most* hotels, have far more amenities, but we can't help loving the Wyndham. Guests who demand standardization won't like it — all the rooms are different, and the place is full of quirks. Most hotels in the city with comparable room sizes, though, would be charging twice the rates. The Wyndham is very much its own person and, anyway, when you visit your aunt, she doesn't have a fax machine either.

**Wyndham,** 42 W. 58th St., New York, NY 10019
**cross streets:** between Fifth Avenue and Avenue of the Americas
**phone:** (212) 753-3500, (800) 257-1111
**fax:** (212) 754-5638
**email:** none
**website:** none
**number of rooms:** 212 (includes 60 suites)
**number of floors:** 17
**smoking policy:** all smoking
**restaurants:** none
**bars:** none
**room service:** none
**hotel amenities:** laundry and dry cleaning
**room amenities:** air-conditioning, VCR on request
**parking:** none
**cancellation:** 2 days prior to arrival
**wheelchair accessibility:** public areas — yes, rooms — yes. ADA compliant

# MIDTOWN EAST

| Hotel | Price Range | Rating |
|-------|-------------|--------|
| Beekman Tower Hotel | $250–$449 | Very Good |
| The Benjamin | $250–$449 | Excellent |
| The Box Tree | $150–$349 | Poor |
| Crowne Plaza Hotel at the U.N. | $150–$349 | Very Good |
| The Fitzpatrick Grand Central Hotel | $150–$349 | Very Good |
| The Fitzpatrick Manhattan Hotel | $150–$349 | Good |
| The Four Seasons | $450 and over | Extraordinary |
| Grand Hyatt New York | $250–$349 | Very Good |
| Habitat Hotel | $75–$149 | Basic |
| The Helmsley Middletowne | $150–$349 | Good |
| Hospitality House | $150–$249 | Very Good |
| Hotel Delmonico | $350–$449 | Very Good |
| Hotel Elysée | $250–$349 | Good |
| Hotel Inter-Continental | $250–$449 | Very Good |
| Hotel Lexington | $150–$349 | Basic |
| Kimberly Hotel | $150–$349 | Very Good |
| Loews New York Hotel | $150–$349 | Good |
| The Lombardy | $250–$349 | Excellent |
| Lyden House | $150–$349 | Very Good |
| Midtown East Courtyard by Marriott | $150–$249 | Very Good |
| New York Marriott East Side | $150–$349 | Very Good |
| The New York Palace Hotel | $450 and over | Excellent |
| Omni Berkshire Place | $250–$449 | Excellent |
| Pickwick Arms Hotel | $75–$149 | Basic |
| The Pierre | $450 and over | Excellent |
| Plaza Fifty | $250–$449 | Very Good |
| Regal United Nations Plaza | $250–$449 | Excellent |
| The Roger Smith Hotel | $250–$349 | Good |
| Roosevelt Hotel | $150–$349 | Good |
| The St. Regis | $450 and over | Extraordinary |
| San Carlos Hotel | $150–$249 | Good |
| The Sutton | $150–$349 | Excellent |
| Swissotel New York — The Drake | $250–$349 | Excellent |
| Vanderbilt YMCA | $75–$149 | Basic |
| W New York | $250–$449 | Good |
| The Waldorf=Astoria | $250–$449 | Excellent |

## BOUNDARIES

South — E. 42nd Street, West — Fifth Avenue, North — E. 59th Street, North — FDR Drive

## ABOUT THE NEIGHBORHOOD

Midtown East is one of the prime business centers of the city and, as such, has something of an all work and no play reputation. For business travellers, this area makes good sense as a place to stay. For shoppers, there's no shortage of big name retailers and deluxe boutiques. While this area doesn't have the lion's share of museums or theatres it is near to many of them. Nightlife, generally speaking, is elsewhere. Many visitors, nevertheless, are most familiar with this area and wouldn't think of staying anywhere else.

## TRANSPORTATION

The 4 and 5 trains run express and the 6 train is a local along Lexington Ave. Stations are located at E. 51st St. and E. 59th St.

## LANDMARKS

Major landmarks are located here, including the United Nations (don't miss the pleasant park behind it) on First Ave. between 41st and 48th Sts. 963-1234. Grand Central has recently gotten a spectacular make-over, Park Ave at 42nd St. 340-3000. You can drop into St. Patrick's Cathedral, Fifth Ave. at 51st St. 753-2261. The flat-topped MetLife Building, Lexington and 45th, the angle-topped Citicorp Building, Lexington and 53rd, and the steeple-topped Chrysler Building, Lexington and 42nd, are here as well. The Chrysler is a favorite of most New Yorkers (you can't tour the inside, though). Walking along 57th Street offers a chance to do some serious shopping as well as catch up on the art world via the many galleries in the neighborhood.

## SHOPPING

Those in town to shop New York are drawn to Saks, 611 Fifth Ave. 753-4000, Tiffany and Co., 727 Fifth Ave. 755-8000, Cartier, 153 E. 53rd St. 446-3459, Brooks Brothers, 346 Madison Ave. 682-8800, Chanel, 15 E. 57th St. 355-5050, Burberry, 9 E. 57th St. 371-5010. Fine leather goods and luggage are available at Coach, 595 Madison Ave. 754-0041, Louis Vuitton, 49 E. 57th St. 371-6111, and Hermes, 11 E. 57th St. 751-3181. You can spiff up your table settings at Baccarat, 625 Madison Ave. 826-4100 and Takashimaya, 693 Fifth Ave. 350-0100. The sports-minded will want to stop in the huge Niketown, 6 E. 57th St. 891-6453, and the NBA Store on 666 Fifth Ave. 515-6221, as well as Richard Metz Golf on 425 Madison Ave. 759-6940. Bridge Kitchenware, 214 E. 52nd St. 688-4220, is a must for the home chef. Don't miss the wonderful chocolate shop, Richart Design et Chocolat, 7 E. 55th St. 371-9369.

## EATING AND DRINKING

Those who like to eat have plenty to choose from in the area. Top picks include high level versions of Indian cuisine at Dawat, 210 E. 58th St. 355-7555, and Italian at Felidia, 243 E. 58th St. 758-1479. Other luxe meals are dished up at Caviarteria, 502 Park Ave. 759-7410, the Four Seasons, 99 E. 52nd St. 754-9494 and Lutèce, 249 E. 50th St. 752-2225. There's good seafood at Oceana, 55 E. 54th St. 759-5941. Peacock Alley, 301 Park Ave. 872-4895, inside the Waldorf=Astoria serves first-rate French food and there's delicious Mexican at Rosa Mexicano, 1063 First Ave. 753-7407. Scarabée, 230 E. 51st St. 758-6633, goes French Mediterranean and Vong, 200 E. 54th St. 486-9592, uses Thai influences. Some of the hotel bars in the area are especially notable. The King Cole Bar at the St. Regis, 2 E. 55th St. 339-6721, is a delightful room to sit in. The Monkey Bar at the Hotel Elysée, 60 E. 54th St. 838-2600, is often a hopping spot. Le Bateaux Ivres in the Pickwick Arms Hotel, 230 W. 51st St. 583-0579, is a wine bar.

For information on new hotels, ongoing updates, and directions to each hotel by car or mass transit, check online at New York Today, www.nytoday.com/hotels.

## THE HOTELS

### Beekman Tower Hotel

| | |
|---|---|
| Extraordinary | $450 and over |
| Excellent | **$350–$449** |
| **Very Good** | **$250–$349** |
| Good | $150–$249 |
| Basic | $75–$149 |
| Poor | under $75 |

The Beekman Tower is one of ten hotels in the Manhattan East Suite Hotels chain. The properties have a number of features in common. Not only are they all-suites hotels, but each also offers somewhat-spacious-to-very-spacious accommodations, kitchens or kitchenettes, fitness rooms and a fair number of amenities. They classify rooms as studio suites (which are the smallest and really like a standard hotel room), junior suites, one-bedroom suites and two-bedroom suites. None of the hotels in the chain have award-winning design but they are quality hotels at a fair price.

What's nicest about the Beekman Tower is the amount of space you get. We would be happier if they loosened up the design a bit: it's "traditional hotel" — unmemorable and not especially cheery, with olive green carpets, lots of wood, plaid sofas and floral prints. Given the building's and the lobby's Deco design, it might have made sense to incorporate that look into the rooms or move to something more contemporary. At least the rooms are uncluttered.

In any case, the basics of the suites are covered: good bedding, double-paned windows, clock radio, full-length mirror, safe and wood hangers. The suites have full kitchens, which include fridge, dishwasher, range, microwave, toaster, coffee maker, pots and pans and silverware. The hotel also offers a grocery shopping service. The sofa in each suite folds out to a bed. All of this makes it a good choice for corporate relocation.

There is a fitness center with a stairstepper, treadmill, bike, multifunction machine, and free weights, as well as his and hers saunas. The Top of the Tower restaurant and bar offers drinks, dinner and views. It has not, in our memory, ever been particularly elegant up there, nor is the food top drawer — unlike the views — but it is user friendly. That could be said of the entire hotel.

**Beekman Tower Hotel,** 3 Mitchell Place, New York, NY 10017
**cross streets:** at E. 49th Street and First Avenue
**phone:** (212) 355-7300, (800) 637-8483
**fax:** (212) 753-9366
**email:** info@mesuite.com
**website:** www.mesuite.com
**number of rooms:** 174 (all suites)
**number of floors:** 26
**smoking policy:** designated nonsmoking rooms
**restaurants:** 2
**bars:** yes
**room service:** yes
**hotel amenities:** health club, concierge, laundry and dry cleaning, business services, meeting and function room
**room amenities:** air-conditioning, VCR, fax, modem line, safe
**parking:** valet
**cancellation:** 3 P.M. day of arrival
**wheelchair accessibility:** public areas — yes, rooms — yes

# The Benjamin

| | |
|---|---|
| Extraordinary | $450 and over |
| **Excellent** | **$350–$449** |
| Very Good | **$250–$349** |
| Good | $150–$249 |
| Basic | $75–$149 |
| Poor | under $75 |

What would make the Waldorf=Astoria  nervous?

The Benjamin, holding a slingshot toward the Goliath.

This hotel, built in 1927, designed by Emery Roth, has been operating as the undistinguished Hotel Beverly for many years until it was purchased in 1997 by the Manhattan East Suite chain. The $30 million restoration, applied to 209 rooms, was completed in April, 1999, yielding a distinguished and delightful hotel. It is named for the founder of the hotel chain, Benjamin Denihan, Sr.

A word about the Denihans. During most of our site inspections of the 250 properties we visited, we would ask the staff member how long they had been with the hotel. Answers generally ranged from one week to a couple of years. That's par for the course in the hotel industry, where employees check in and out almost as frequently as guests. In the case of the Manhattan East Suite employees, the pattern is entirely different. Six years, ten years, fourteen years were far more typical responses. More than one offered an impromptu and heartfelt speech about their loyalty to the Denihan family and the company. This attitude surely affects how guests are treated and we consider it a major asset of the chain.

The Benjamin is their 10th New York property, and while it has some of the hallmarks of their other hotels, it really should be considered separately. Geared to the executive business traveler, the hotel has been wired like an office building, so that guests have high-speed Internet access in their rooms and the hotel is as ready as it can be for whatever technology throws its way. The look of the rooms is contemporary, in a soft and pleasing way, as if someone took the family living room and made improvements, replacing the fabrics with mohair, linen and chenille. The walls and carpeting are a light beige and earth tones dominate throughout.

As is typical for this hotel chain, the fundamentals are well covered. The Serta mattresses are especially comfortable, and the hotel had a wonderful idea with its pillow menu. There are eleven types, including down, foam, hypo-allergenic gel-filled, buckwheat-filled, water-filled, one that offers "magnetic therapy," and a five-foot body cushion pregnant women often find helpful. The water pressure seems fine, and crucially, given the noisy Lexington Avenue address, the rooms are quiet. That's because the windows are not only double-paned, they're injected with argon gas. All guest rooms have a smoke alarm and sprinkler system.

There are amenities galore. Two-lines phones, dataport with high speed Internet access, direct inward dial and voice mail, a fax/scanner/printer/copier, safe (large enough for a laptop and thoughtfully on a table in the closet rather than on the floor), iron and ironing board, Frette bed linen and bathrobe, Bose radio, movies on command, TV Web browser, individual temperature control, video checkout, fresh flowers, and CD and tape player (the latter in the one-bedroom suites). The white marble bathrooms have a phone, makeup mirror and hair dryer. They also have a "shower caddy," which hangs on the wall and gives you a mirror to shave by as well as a convenient place to stash shampoo and other items. You'll also get Judith Jackson aromatherapy bath products. Visitors who are in town on business will not only appreciate the Internet access but the large desk on wheels and the ergonomically designed swivel chair. The desk doubles as a dining room table. The galley kitchen with coffeepot, microwave, and mini-fridge is another useful amenity. The suites with terraces may not be useful, but they certainly are pleasant.

You could place yourself under house arrest here and live well. Larry Forgione's restaurant An American Place has relocated from 32nd Street to the ground floor of the hotel; there is a Woodstock spa on the premises (most treatments can also be done in your room), and a small, 24-hour fitness facility with treadmills, bikes, stairsteppers and free weights. A concierge staff can offer the usual assistance. The hotel chain is committed to operating in an environmentally friendly way, participating in an extensive recycling program and offering guests the option not to have fresh linen or towels daily.

When the owners installed all the fancy wiring, they must have wanted the Benjamin to be a hotel of the future. It's certainly a nice thought.

**The Benjamin,** 125 E. 50th Street, New York, NY 10022
**cross streets:** at Lexington Avenue
**phone:** (212) 715-2500, (800) 637-8483
**fax:** (212) 715-2525
**email:** info@mesuite.com
**website:** www.thebenjamin.com
**number of rooms:** 209 (includes 97 suites)
**number of floors:** 26
**smoking policy:** designated nonsmoking rooms
**restaurants:** An American Place
**bars:** yes
**room service:** yes
**hotel amenities:** health club, concierge, laundry and dry cleaning, meeting rooms
**room amenities:** air-conditioning, modem line, fax/scanner/printer/copier, safe, kitchenette
**parking:** none
**cancellation:** 3 P.M. day of arrival
**wheelchair accessibility:** public areas — yes, rooms — yes. ADA compliant

# The Box Tree

| Extraordinary | $450 and over |
| Excellent | $350–$449 |
| Very Good | **$250–$349** |
| Good | **$150–$249** |
| Basic | $75–$149 |
| **Poor** | under $75 |

No matter how opulent the room, regardless of the bed linen's thread count, however spectacular the view, irrespective of the talents of the chef in the kitchen or the connections of the concierge, a hotel is judged first and foremost on its hospitality. It is on this fundamental that the Box Tree fails.

The Box Tree's horror vacui style of decorating could work well — anyone who has been to Sharrow Bay in England's Lake District knows that. But Sharrow Bay's famously over-the-top design has an equally famous commitment to cosseting its guests. When we arrive at the Box Tree's front door, the greeting is virtually hostile. Announcing our purpose doesn't change that. If a hotel inspection doesn't have the staff on their best behavior we have zero confidence that most guests will be well treated.

After the reception at the front door, we are introduced to our tour guide, whose arm is wrapped in a bandage, a detail we include because it is in keeping with the combative way she shows the hotel to us. Of all the visits we have made to hotels in this city, this is by far the strangest and most gothic.

What is that used for, we ask of one room. "It was a restaurant. We don't use it anymore. Sometimes things don't work out the way we expect them to," she says ominously. Supply your own dark shadows, organ music or clap of thunder.

The rooms are overdone, but lack taste, restraint and freshness. The mattresses are lumpy. You get noise from 49th Street in some rooms. Most of the ceilings are low, and the bathrooms are minuscule. There are fake flowers everywhere, no elevator (you may have to walk four flights to your room), the fireplaces are non-working, the hall carpets threadbare.

Some people call the Box Tree romantic. It is, if your name is Havisham.

**The Box Tree,** 250 E. 49th Street, New York, NY 10017
**cross streets:** between Second and Third Avenues
**phone:** (212) 758-8320
**fax:** (212) 308-3899
**email:** none
**website:** none
**number of rooms:** 13
**number of floors:** 4
**smoking policy:** designated nonsmoking rooms
**restaurants:** yes
**bars:** yes

**room service:** none
**hotel amenities:** meeting and function rooms
**room amenities:** air-conditioning, modem line, safe, VCR
**parking:** none
**cancellation:** 5 days prior to arrival
**wheelchair accessibility:** public areas — no, rooms — no

## Crowne Plaza Hotel at the United Nations

| | |
|---|---|
| Extraordinary | $450 and over |
| Excellent | $350–$449 |
| **Very Good** | **$250–$349** |
| Good | **$150–$249** |
| Basic | $75–$149 |
| Poor | under $75 |

What was once the Tudor Hotel became the Crowne Plaza in 1997. It looks to us as though the new owners are concentrating on the fundamentals, which is a good sign.

The best evidence of this new focus is the new windows that were being installed as of March, 1999, which give guests triple-paned protection from city noise. Guest rooms have traditional decor and an array of amenities: clock radio, trouser press, two-line phone with dataport, safe, iron and ironing board, coffee maker, makeup mirror, full-length mirror, hair dryer, phone in the bathroom and Institute Swiss bath products. Ceilings can be low in guest rooms and hallways, but the lighting is good throughout. Twenty of the rooms have private terraces.

Also offered are concierge-level guest rooms throughout the hotel rather than on a dedicated floor. They offer continental breakfast, use of a lounge and access to a shared computer and fax. A small fitness center has a couple of treadmills, stairsteppers and bikes, as well as free weights and saunas. The business center has a typewriter (when did you last see one of those?), a computer, a printer and copy machines.

This hotel's location on the far eastern side of midtown makes the Crowne Plaza convenient to the United Nations. It also makes sense for visitors who want to be near midtown, but not in the thick of it.

**Crowne Plaza Hotel at the United Nations,** 304 E. 42nd St., New York, NY 10017
**cross streets:** between First and Second Avenues
**phone:** (212) 986-8800, (800) 227-6963
**reservations fax:** (212) 297-3440, guest fax: (212) 986-1758
**email:** cpunres@aol.com
**website:** www.crowneplaza-un.com
**number of rooms:** 300 (including 14 suites)
**number of floors:** 20
**smoking policy:** designated nonsmoking rooms
**restaurants:** yes

**bars:** yes
**room service:** yes, 24 hours
**hotel amenities:** fitness equipment, concierge, laundry and dry cleaning, business center, meeting and function rooms
**room amenities:** air-conditioning, mini-bar, modem line, safe
**parking:** valet
**cancellation:** 6 P.M. day of arrival
**wheelchair accessibility:** public areas — yes, rooms — yes. ADA compliant

## The Fitzpatrick Grand Central Hotel

| | |
|---|---|
| Extraordinary | $450 and over |
| Excellent | $350–$449 |
| **Very Good** | **$250–$349** |
| Good | **$150–$249** |
| Basic | $75–$149 |
| Poor | under $75 |

This Irish-owned hotel is the sister property to the Fitzpatrick Manhattan, and it is a wee bit younger and a wee bit shinier.

The emerald-aisled hallways are bright and pleasant, as are the rooms. Most are king- and queen-bedded, (at the Fitzpatrick Manhattan, most are suites) the mattress quality is good, and many have canopies. There are two-line phones with dataport and voice mail, fax, clock radio, bathrobe, iron and ironing board, hair dryer, coffee maker, and makeup mirror. VCRs are available on request along with complimentary Irish and kid's movies. Night turndown service is standard.

Hotel amenities include a concierge, afternoon tea, 24-hour room service, Irish breakfast until 10:30 P.M., complimentary *Wall Street Journal* and complimentary daily membership at the New York Sports Club, the nearest of which is three blocks away.

The Fitzpatrick Grand Central may have more polish than the Fitzpatrick Manhattan but both are notable for their warm hospitality. With places like this, it's getting harder and harder for New York to keep its tough-guy image.

**The Fitzpatrick Grand Central Hotel,** 141 E. 44th St., New York, NY 10017
**cross streets:** between Lexington and Third Avenues
**phone:** (212) 351-6800, (800) 367-7701
**reservations fax:** (212) 308-5166, guest fax: (212) 818-1747
**email:** fitzusa@aol.com
**website:** www.fitzpatrickhotels.com
**number of rooms:** 155 (includes 8 suites)
**number of floors:** 10
**smoking policy:** designated nonsmoking rooms
**restaurants:** yes
**bars:** yes
**room service:** yes, 24 hours

**hotel amenities:** concierge, laundry and dry cleaning
**room amenities:** air-conditioning, mini-fridge, fax machine, modem line
**parking:** valet
**cancellation:** 3 P.M. 1 day prior to arrival
**wheelchair accessibility:** public areas — yes, rooms — yes. ADA compliant

## The Fitzpatrick Manhattan Hotel

| | |
|---|---|
| Extraordinary | $450 and over |
| Excellent | $350–$449 |
| Very Good | **$250–$349** |
| **Good** | **$150–$249** |
| Basic | $75–$149 |
| Poor | under $75 |

This cheerful bit of the Emerald Isle in midtown boasts real hospitality. You can get a fine pint of Guinness in the bar and Irish breakfasts are served until 10 P.M. Room decor is traditional, with plenty of dark woods, Bombay Company-style furniture and rose — or emerald-colored carpets.

Easy-going, yes. Impeccable, no. You might find a burned-out bulb here or a cigarette burn on the tub there. People don't stay at the Fitzpatrick for perfection, but for the Irish ambience (each day, the carpet on the floor of the elevator is changed to spell out the day of the week in Gaelic) and for the employees, some of whom are Irish and have worked at the Fitzpatrick family hotels in Ireland. The Fitzpatrick does its bit to warm up the city.

**The Fitzpatrick Manhattan Hotel,** 687 Lexington Ave., New York, NY 10022
**cross streets:** between E. 56th and E. 57th Streets
**phone:** (212) 355-0100, (800) 367-7701
**fax:** (212) 355-1371
**email:** fitzusa@aol.com
**website:** www.fitzpatrickhotels.com
**number of rooms:** 92 (includes 52 suites)
**number of floors:** 16
**smoking policy:** designated nonsmoking floors
**restaurants:** yes
**bars:** yes
**room service:** yes, 24 hours
**hotel amenities:** concierge, laundry and dry cleaning, business services
**room amenities:** air-conditioning, mini-fridge, fax, safe, modem line
**parking:** valet
**cancellation:** 3 P.M. day of arrival
**wheelchair accessibility:** public areas — yes, rooms — yes

## The Four Seasons

| Extraordinary | $450 and over |
|---|---|
| Excellent | $350–$449 |
| Very Good | $250–$349 |
| Good | $150–$249 |
| Basic | $75–$149 |
| Poor | under $75 |

At most hotels, you get out of the taxi, go through the doors, walk to the front desk, and pull out a credit card. You don't just go into I.M. Pei's Four Seasons, however. You make an entrance. Rather than reaching for your wallet, you are likely to be gazing up at the geometric, soaring expanse of the lobby; instead of the mundane concerns of checking in, you are almost compelled to make conclusions about space and scale and comfort. We find it vastly preferable to the timid or the overly familiar, and the stouthearted may find the scale amusing even as it arm wrestles them to the ground in easy domination.

We find sitting in the lobby lounge (for tea or a drink) soothing, since it offers our greatest luxury in abundance: space. It's the tallest hotel in New York and also one of the city's very best. Pei's 52-floor, 1930's Hollywood version of Manhattan is sleek, glamorous and modern. Warm and fuzzy it is not. Nearly everything in the guest rooms is light: light English sycamore paneling, light carpeting, lots of daylight.

The size of the guest rooms are larger than most in town — about 600 square feet is the average and they are lovely and quiet. There are three two-line phones with dataport, bathrobes, slippers, an umbrella, and a safe. Other amenities that you might want in your home are dressing rooms, tubs that fill in 60 seconds, Frette linens and window shades that raise or lower at the touch of a button. The Sealy PostureLux mattresses are so good that many guests have actually purchased them from the hotel.

The views from many of the rooms are nothing short of spectacular (the rooms toward the top of the hotel tend to be smaller but have better views). For $10,000 a night, though, the penthouse gives you plenty of room (3000 square feet), a terrace and 360-degree views of the city, all to yourself.

Twelve concierges (two have the Clef d'Or designation) are on staff and the hotel's three-star restaurant boasts chef Susan Weaver. The combination of high-service standards, for which the Four Seasons hotels are renowned, and the stunning public and private spaces, creates an extraordinary hotel.

**The Four Seasons,** 57 E. 57th St., New York, NY 10022
**cross streets:** between Park and Madison Avenues
**phone:** (212) 758-5700, (800) 332-3442
**reservations fax:** (212) 758-5711, guest fax: (212) 350-6678
**email:** none
**website:** www.fourseasons.com
**number of rooms:** 370 (includes 72 suites)
**number of floors:** 52
**smoking policy:** designated nonsmoking rooms

**restaurants:** Fifty Seven Fifty Seven
**bars:** yes
**room service:** yes, 24 hours
**hotel amenities:** concierge, laundry and dry cleaning, health club, business center, meeting rooms
**room amenities:** air-conditioning, mini-bar, VCR on request, fax on request, modem line, safe
**parking:** valet
**cancellation:** 6 P.M. day of arrival
**wheelchair accessibility:** public areas — yes, rooms — yes. ADA compliant

## Grand Hyatt New York

| | |
|---|---|
| Extraordinary | $450 and over |
| Excellent | $350–$449 |
| **Very Good** | **$250–$349** |
| Good | $150–$249 |
| Basic | $75–$149 |
| Poor | under $75 |

The lobby of the Grand Hyatt, next door to Grand Central, is its most memorable feature — a 1970's-style four-storied fantasia (the former Commodore became the Hyatt in 1980) of waterfall fountains, greenery, reflecting surfaces and cascading space. The enormous lobby strikes us as a guilty pleasure. Pretty? No. Sophisticated? No. Garishly alluring? Yes.

The classic contemporary rooms of this large hotel are comfortable enough but low on both amenities and light. Standard are two-line phones with dataport and voice mail, clock radio, iron and ironing board. As a result of the hotel's tight fit with adjacent buildings, most rooms get little sunlight. Closet space is adequate, water pressure variable. The hotel says work is ongoing in this regard.

For an additional $20, you can be on one of the "Business Plan" floors where you get a fax machine in the room, a daily copy of *USA Today*, free local calls and the use of a small workroom on the floor with desks and a copier (but BYO computer). For an additional $40, guests can stay on one of the two "Regency Club" floors, accessible only by special elevator key. These rooms also have a dedicated concierge and lounge. Both plans include complimentary continental breakfast.

The hotel also has a concierge desk, a fitness room with several pieces of aerobics equipment and free weights, and offers 24-hour room service.

Now that Grand Central has been restored to full glory, maybe the Grand Hyatt will follow the same tracks.

**Grand Hyatt New York,** Park Ave. at Grand Central Terminal, New York, NY 10017
**cross streets:** between Park and Lexington Avenues
**phone:** (212) 883-1234, (800) 233-1234
**reservations fax:** (212) 661-8256, guest fax: (212) 697-3772

**email:** none
**website:** none
**number of rooms:** 1,347 (includes 63 suites)
**number of floors:** 35
**smoking policy:** designated nonsmoking floors
**restaurants:** 3
**bars:** 2
**room service:** yes, 24 hours
**hotel amenities:** fitness equipment, concierge, laundry and dry cleaning, business center, meeting and function rooms
**room amenities:** air-conditioning, VCR on request, modem line
**parking:** valet
**cancellation:** 6 P.M. 1 day prior to arrival
**wheelchair accessibility:** public areas — yes, rooms — yes. ADA compliant

## Habitat Hotel

| | |
|---|---|
| Extraordinary | $450 and over |
| Excellent | $350–$449 |
| Very Good | $250–$349 |
| Good | $150–$249 |
| **Basic** | **$75–$149** |
| Poor | under $75 |

The Habitat was undergoing renovations when we visited but it's clear what direction the hotel, formerly a women's residence, is taking. It offers the bare necessities at low prices in a swanky neighborhood.

Bathrooms are shared — a key piece of information for many visitors. If you're game for that, you'll find they are clean. Showers are located in separate rooms. The plain but tidy bedrooms are small, with enough space for a trundle bed; that is, a single bed that pulls out to make a double. Once you've snapped the second part of the bed into place, there is virtually no room to move around. Windows are double-glazed, the room amenity is a TV — that's about it. You get a closet or dresser, but not both.

The Habitat may not be the best choice for a long stay — if you are here for a while, you'll save money but will have to make ingenious use of the cramped quarters. In that sense, you'll be living like a real New Yorker.

**Habitat Hotel,** 130 E. 57th St., New York, NY 10022
**cross streets:** at Lexington Avenue
**phone:** (212) 753-8841, (800) 255-0482
**fax:** (212) 829-9605
**email:** info@stayinny.com
**website:** www.stayinny.com
**number of rooms:** 207
**number of floors:** 17
**smoking policy:** designated nonsmoking rooms

**restaurants:** none
**bars:** none
**room service:** none
**hotel amenities:** some shared baths
**room amenities:** air-conditioning
**parking:** none
**cancellation:** 1 day prior to arrival
**wheelchair accessibility:** public areas — no, rooms — no

## The Helmsley Middletowne

| | |
|---|---|
| Extraordinary | $450 and over |
| Excellent | $350–$449 |
| Very Good | **$250–$349** |
| **Good** | **$150–$249** |
| Basic | $75–$149 |
| Poor | under $75 |

The Middletowne seems correctly named — this Helmsley offers middle-of-the-road lodging at middle-of-the-road prices.

The lobby is small, with oriental rugs, marble walls and a residential feel. Guest rooms are comfortably-sized, beige and rose or beige and blue is about as far as design goes, except for the floral print bedspreads and framed floral prints on the walls. Mattresses are variable in quality — the ones we tested on the 4th floor were of high quality. Those on the 8th floor seemed markedly less good. Amenities include three two-line phones, dataport, clock radio, hair dryer, makeup mirror, bathroom phone, and Neutrogena bath products. Windows are double-paned and water pressure is strong. There is plenty of closet space for an average visit. There is no health club, no business center and no room service per se, though the hotel supplies menus from neighborhood restaurants that will deliver.

For visitors who don't need a wide array of services, the Helmsley Middletowne offers an unassuming place to rest your head in midtown.

**The Helmsley Middletowne,** 148 E. 48th St., New York, NY 10017
**cross streets:** between Lexington and Third Avenues
**phone:** (212) 755-3000, (800) 221-4982
**fax:** (212) 832-0261
**email:** none
**website:** none
**number of rooms:** 192 (includes 42 suites)
**number of floors:** 16
**smoking policy:** designated nonsmoking floors
**restaurants:** none
**bars:** none
**room service:** none
**hotel amenities:** laundry and dry cleaning, meeting room
**room amenities:** air-conditioning, modem line

**parking:** valet
**cancellation:** 4 P.M. day of arrival
**wheelchair accessibility:** public areas — yes, rooms — yes.
ADA compliant

## Hospitality House

| | |
|---|---|
| Extraordinary | $450 and over |
| Excellent | $350–$449 |
| **Very Good** | $250–$349 |
| Good | **$150–$249** |
| Basic | $75–$149 |
| Poor | under $75 |

For visitors to New York staying more than a few days, Hospitality House is one of the city's better deals. You get a fully outfitted apartment which, if you're staying for a month, works out to about $111 a day. That's a good price, especially for the East Side location, but it's even sweeter when you consider you don't pay any hotel tax.

What's the down side? The only one we can find is no maid service — you'll have to pick up after yourself. While the digs are in no way fancy, hardwood floors and a well-chosen color of paint on the wall (green, taupe or blue) make for pleasant surroundings. The kitchens have a range, microwave, dishwasher, coffee maker, toaster, and service for six (dishes and silverware plus pots and pans). For those staying for shorter periods (not a month, say), you get breakfast foods: muffins, cereal, coffee and juice. Longer stays can get you a better rate, they drop the breakfast foods, and you have to pay for utilities.

Each unit comes with TV and VCR, clock radio, iron and ironing board, and hair dryer. You can do laundry in the basement. The phone is two-line with a dataport and there's an answering machine. Local calls are free.

Hospitality House doesn't earn its "very good" rating for looks — on that basis, it probably belongs in the "good" category. For value, though, Hospitality House is tough to beat.

**Hospitality House,** 145 E. 49th St., New York, NY 10017
**cross streets:** between Third and Lexington Avenues
**phone:** (212) 965-1102, (800) 987-1235
**fax:** (212) 965-1149
**email:** info@hospitalitycompany.com
**website:** www.hospitalitycompany.com
**number of rooms:** 36 (all apartments)
**number of floors:** 10
**smoking policy:** all smoking
**restaurants:** none
**bars:** none
**room service:** none
**hotel amenities:** laundry

**room amenities:** air-conditioning, kitchen, VCR
**parking:** none
**cancellation:** $25 cancellation fee. If within 4 days of arrival, forfeit 1 night's rent.
**wheelchair accessibility:** public areas — yes, rooms — yes

## Hotel Delmonico

| | |
|---|---|
| Extraordinary | $450 and over |
| Excellent | **$350–$449** |
| **Very Good** | $250–$349 |
| Good | $150–$249 |
| Basic | $75–$149 |
| Poor | under $75 |

The Delmonico turned into an all-suites hotel in 1991 after a major renovation. The traditionally designed suites give you a fair amount of room and the feel of an apartment as much as a hotel.

Each suite has a kitchen with a refrigerator (some small, some full-size), microwave, dishwasher, cookware and some even have ovens. Rooms come with fax machines, voice mail, thick, old walls (some of which are a bit scuffed) and large-to-very-large closets. Fifteen guest rooms have terraces. Guests have complimentary use of the adjacent New York Sports Club — the excellent facility is certainly an added value.

Over the years, many notables have stayed here (it was a hotel, then an apartment house, then a hotel again). The Beatles were guests before an appearance on *The Ed Sullivan Show,* and the Delmonico is a favorite of South American celebrities, including Fernanda Montenegro, the exceptional Brazilian actress from the film *Central Station.*

One of the notable features of this hotel is the Lighthouse Suite. It is designed for the needs of a blind or partially sighted visitor to New York. This includes special furniture, colors that emphasize contrast, lighting that reduces glare, large-print books, a large-dial telephone, a large-face clock and many other carefully handled details.

Given the hotel's prime location, the large guest rooms and the relatively moderate rates, the Delmonico is a hotel that can be recommended with enthusiasm.

**Hotel Delmonico,** 502 Park Ave., New York, NY 10022
**cross streets:** at E. 59th Street
**phone:** (212) 355-2500, (800) 821-3842
**reservations fax:** (212) 755-3779, guest fax: (212) 421-4768
**email:** none
**website:** www.srs-worldhotels.com
**number of rooms:** 157 (all suites)
**number of floors:** 30
**smoking policy:** designated nonsmoking rooms

**restaurants:** none
**bars:** yes
**room service:** none
**hotel amenities:** concierge, laundry and dry cleaning, business center
**room amenities:** air-conditioning, kitchen, VCR on request, modem line, safe
**parking:** valet
**cancellation:** 1 day prior to arrival
**wheelchair accessibility:** public areas — yes, rooms — no

# Hotel Elysée

| | |
|---|---|
| Extraordinary | $450 and over |
| Excellent | $350–$449 |
| Very Good | **$250–$349** |
| **Good** | $150–$249 |
| Basic | $75–$149 |
| Poor | under $75 |

Mel Marvin, at the piano of the hotel's Monkey Bar before its renovation in 1994, used to crack jokes about the hotel, referring to it as the Hotel Easylay. No more jokes, no more Mel.

The Elysée is now a small boutique hotel with charm but not pretension. The traditional rooms are done in pale gray and blue tones. A few rooms have sun-room sitting areas, while others have terraces. Amenities include a complimentary breakfast as well as tea, coffee and cookies served in the afternoon and hors d'oeuvres in the evening. Newspapers are also available in the Club Room.

While the Elysée has an appealing, cosmopolitan New York feel, there are some drawbacks: noise can be a problem (request a quieter, but darker, room at the back). Not many of the rooms have two-line phones and, while there are mini-bars, they're not stocked. While the hotel designates some rooms as nonsmoking, it still places ashtrays in all of them. Go figure. What Hotel Elysée comes down to is a few-frills boutique hotel with friendly service in a good location.

**Hotel Elysée,** 60 E. 54th St., New York, NY 10022
**cross streets:** between Park and Madison Avenues
**phone:** (212) 753-1066, (800) 535-9733
**fax:** (212) 980-9278
**email:** elysee99@aol.com
**website:** http://members.aol.com/elysee99
**number of rooms:** 99 (includes 11 suites)
**number of floors:** 15
**smoking policy:** designated nonsmoking rooms
**restaurants:** Monkey Bar
**bars:** yes
**room service:** yes

**hotel amenities:** meeting room, laundry and dry cleaning
**room amenities:** air-conditioning, VCR, modem line, mini-fridge
**parking:** valet
**cancellation:** 1 day prior to arrival
**wheelchair accessibility:** public areas — yes, rooms — yes

## Hotel Inter-Continental

| | |
|---|---|
| Extraordinary | $450 and over |
| Excellent | **$350–$449** |
| **Very Good** | **$250–$349** |
| Good | $150–$249 |
| Basic | $75–$149 |
| Poor | under $75 |

The Inter-Continental has much potential, but much of it is unrealized. The once-moribund lobby has been redesigned, making it livelier than before. Renovation of the meeting rooms and guest room suites is continuing with a major overhaul of the hotel scheduled for 2001. These changes are needed. The neo-Federalist look of the guest rooms seems to be left over from Zachary Taylor's administration and gives the accommodations a decidedly dowdy atmosphere.

Amenities include two-line phones with dataport, voice mail and in-room video checkout. The bedding is adequate, and windows are double-paned. The Inter-Continental is proud of its international staff, and of Abby Newman, an award-winning concierge. There are meeting and function rooms and a well-equipped fitness center.

You could say that the Inter-Continental is unobjectionable, but it needs to find a compelling reason for visitors to choose it.

**Hotel Inter-Continental,** 111 E. 48th St., New York, NY 10017
**cross streets:** between Lexington and Park Avenues
**phone:** (212) 755-5900, (800) 327-0200
**fax:** (212) 644-0079
**email:** newyork@interconti.com
**website:** www.new-york.interconti.com
**number of rooms:** 686 (includes 86 suites)
**number of floors:** 14
**smoking policy:** designated nonsmoking rooms
**restaurants:** yes
**bars:** yes
**room service:** yes
**hotel amenities:** fitness equipment, concierge, laundry and dry cleaning, meeting and function rooms, business services
**room amenities:** air-conditioning, mini-bar, modem line, safe
**parking:** valet
**cancellation:** 4 P.M. 1 day prior to arrival
**wheelchair accessibility:** public areas — yes, rooms — yes. ADA compliant

# Hotel Lexington

| | |
|---|---|
| Extraordinary | $450 and over |
| Excellent | $350–$449 |
| Very Good | **$250–$349** |
| Good | **$150–$249** |
| **Basic** | $75–$149 |
| Poor | under $75 |

Not a great deal to recommend at this Golden Tulip chain hotel. The flight crews who make up some of the hotel's guests are usually in and out quickly, so the small, undistinguished rooms may not be too much of a problem for them.

The noise, though, is something else — some rooms have windows that are single-paned and don't do a good job of keeping out the din. The flight crews might not need a lot of closet or drawer space, though you might. Unfortunately, closet and drawer space is in short supply. Room amenities include an unstocked mini-fridge, safe, phone with dataport and voice mail. The very small marble bathrooms have basic features.

There is a concierge desk and a small exercise room, but these don't offset the hotel's drawbacks.

**Hotel Lexington,** 511 Lexington Ave., New York, NY 10017
**cross streets:** at E. 48th Street
**phone:** (212) 755-4400, (800) 448-4471
**fax:** (212) 751-4091
**email:** sales@hotellexington.com
**website:** www.hotellexington.com
**number of rooms:** 700 (includes 37 suites)
**number of floors:** 28
**smoking policy:** designated nonsmoking rooms
**restaurants:** 2
**bars:** yes
**room service:** yes
**hotel amenities:** fitness equipment, concierge, laundry and dry cleaning, business center
**room amenities:** air-conditioning, mini-fridge, modem line, safe
**parking:** none
**cancellation:** 1 day prior to arrival
**wheelchair accessibility:** public areas — yes, rooms — yes

# Kimberly Hotel

| | |
|---|---|
| Extraordinary | $450 and over |
| Excellent | $350–$449 |
| **Very Good** | **$250–$349** |
| Good | **$150–$249** |
| Basic | $75–$149 |
| Poor | under $75 |

The Kimberly was conceived in the mid-1980's as an apartment building but, during construction, was reconceived as a hotel. The practical effect of this is plenty of room for guests. One-bedroom suites run about 600 square feet, two-bedroom suites about 1200 square feet. Not bad.

The style throughout the hotel is consistent — tasteful enough, but standard issue. Floral prints, rose, blue, maroon, wood side tables are nothing you haven't seen before. In addition to plenty of space in each room, suites include full kitchens, an iron and ironing board, a clock radio, a bathrobe and goose-down pillows.

Suites (which make up most of the rooms) also have a two-line phone, a scale, a hair dryer, ample closet space, Neutrogena bath products, a fax machine and a pull-out couch (in addition to the beds). When you reserve, you can request a firmer or softer mattress. Most rooms have balconies, some with views of the Chrysler Building. Two of the three concierges have the Clefs d'Or designation.

The Kimberly is associated with the New York Health and Racquet Club. By staying at the hotel, you get a free pass to any of the clubs. There is one within a few blocks and a large one located a bit farther away at 25 East 50th Street. 151, a nightclub, is on the hotel premises.

**Kimberly Hotel,** 145 E. 50th St., New York, NY 10022
**cross streets:** between Lexington and Third Avenues
**phone:** (212) 755-0400, (800) 683-0400
**fax:** (212) 486-6915
**email:** info@kimberlyhotel.com
**website:** www.kimberlyhotel.com
**number of rooms:** 186 (includes 154 suites)
**number of floors:** 31
**smoking policy:** designated nonsmoking rooms
**restaurants:** 2
**bars:** 2
**room service:** yes
**hotel amenities:** concierge, laundry and dry cleaning, meeting room
**room amenities:** air-conditioning, mini-bar, VCR on request, fax, modem line, kitchen
**parking:** valet
**cancellation:** 1 day prior to arrival
**wheelchair accessibility:** public areas — yes, rooms — yes

# Loews New York Hotel

| | |
|---|---|
| Extraordinary | $450 and over |
| Excellent | $350–$449 |
| Very Good | **$250–$349** |
| **Good** | **$150–$249** |
| Basic | $75–$149 |
| Poor | under $75 |

There are no city buses in this hotel's lobby, but otherwise it does a fair impression of congested Lexington Avenue outside its door. Long check-in lines can form in this hectic space filled with airline flight crews on their way in and out, and people entering and leaving a bar that is so close to the check-in area that it seems the bartender could take your order while you're waiting for your room key.

Hallways aren't always perfectly clean (with paper on the floor), but how could they be with this much traffic? Rooms are small, done in tones of brown, beige and rust. Windows are also small so there isn't a great deal of light. Since some of these windows are single-paned, you are almost certain to get noise from the street.

Amenities include safes, hair dryers, irons and ironing boards and mini-fridges. There is also in-room checkout. Loews has a full fitness center and a business center, as well as upgraded rooms on their "VIP floors" that include use of a lounge.

The hotel competition has intensified in New York in the last few years, and visitors have more choices. It's not clear why you'd choose to stay here.

**Loews New York Hotel,** 569 Lexington Ave., New York, NY 10022
**cross streets:** at E. 51st Street
**phone:** (212) 752-7000, (800) 836-6471
**reservations fax:** (212) 752-3817, guest fax: (212) 758-6311
**email:** loewsnewyork@loewshotels.com
**website:** www.loewshotels.com
**number of rooms:** 722 (includes 38 suites)
**number of floors:** 20
**smoking policy:** designated nonsmoking rooms
**restaurants:** yes
**bars:** yes
**room service:** yes
**hotel amenities:** fitness equipment, concierge, laundry and dry cleaning, business center, meeting and function rooms
**room amenities:** air-conditioning, modem line, safe, mini-fridge
**parking:** none
**cancellation:** 4 P.M. day of arrival
**wheelchair accessibility:** public areas — yes, rooms — yes

# The Lombardy

| | |
|---|---|
| Extraordinary | $450 and over |
| **Excellent** | $350–$449 |
| Very Good | **$250–$349** |
| Good | $150–$249 |
| Basic | $75–$149 |
| Poor | under $75 |

The Lombardy is somewhat inconsistent. The better rooms are beautifully done — but since each of the guest quarters is privately and separately owned — decor varies considerably, though the standards throughout are high. The one — and two-bedrooms are beauties, more attractive by far than the run-of-the-hotel-mill singles.

Standard in all rooms are two-line phones with dataport, voice mail, clock radio, most have VCRs, some have a pants press. The water pressure is good. The marble bathrooms are pleasant but, as always, not large. Closets, on the other hand, are roomy and have plenty of shelves and hangers. In most cases, there are kitchens with stove, toaster, microwave, fridge, plates, silverware and pots and pans.

The fitness room isn't much — some inexpensive-looking treadmills, bike, stairstepper and free weights. A much more exciting hotel perk is Soma Park restaurant, with chef Gary Robins at the helm. Soma Park provides room service as well.

William Randolph Hearst built the hotel in 1926, and one has the sense that old W. R. would like what he found here, not least the solicitous staff. The rating here is really a split decision — 'excellent' for the one and two bedrooms, 'very good' for the rest.

**The Lombardy,** 111 E. 56th St., New York, NY 10022
**cross streets:** between Park and Lexington Avenues
**phone:** (212) 753-8600, (800) 223-5254
**fax:** (212) 754-5683
**email:** none
**website:** www.lombardyhotel.com
**number of rooms:** 125 (includes 70 suites)
**number of floors:** 14
**smoking policy:** all smoking rooms
**restaurants:** Soma Park
**bars:** 1
**room service:** yes
**hotel amenities:** fitness equipment, function rooms, concierge, laundry and dry cleaning
**room amenities:** air-conditioning, kitchen, fax on request, modem line
**parking:** valet
**cancellation:** 2 P.M. day of arrival
**wheelchair accessibility:** public areas — yes, rooms — yes. ADA compliant

# Lyden House

| | |
|---|---|
| Extraordinary | $450 and over |
| Excellent | $350–$449 |
| **Very Good** | **$250–$349** |
| Good | **$150–$249** |
| Basic | $75–$149 |
| Poor | under $75 |

The Lyden House is one of ten hotels in the Manhattan East Suite Hotels chain. The group shares a number of features in common. Not only are they all-suites hotels, each offers somewhat-spacious-to-very-spacious accommodations, kitchen or kitchenette, fitness room, and a good number of amenities. They divide things up as studio suites (which are the smallest and really like a standard hotel room), junior suites, one-bedroom suites, and two-bedroom suites. None is a design award-winner (with the exception of their flagship, the newly opened Benjamin) but they are quality hotels at a fair price.

In the Manhattan East portfolio, the Lyden House is one of the nicest properties. One-bedroom suites are the most common accommodation here, but all come complete with kitchen, two-line phones and dataport and voice mail. Also standard are a clock radio, iron and ironing board, hair dryer and movies on command. There are some distinctive suites here, too — one on the ground floor has a Jacuzzi, a small patio and a circular, glass-enclosed dining room. The four penthouse suites have terraces to enjoy the views of the Empire State Building, the Chrysler Building and a sliver of the East River.

There is a laundromat in the basement, particularly helpful for longer stays. The Lyden House has no food and beverage service, but they will do grocery shopping for you to stock up the kitchen.

Another winner from this hotel chain.

**Lyden House,** 320 E. 53rd St., New York, NY 10022
**cross streets:** between First and Second Avenues
**phone:** (212) 888-6070, (800) 637-8483
**fax:** (212) 935-7690
**email:** info@mesuite.com
**website:** www.mesuite.com
**number of rooms:** 80 (all suites)
**number of floors:** 11
**smoking policy:** designated nonsmoking rooms
**restaurants:** none
**bars:** none
**room service:** none
**hotel amenities:** laundry and dry cleaning
**room amenities:** air-conditioning, kitchen
**parking:** none
**cancellation:** 3 P.M. 1 day prior to arrival
**wheelchair accessibility:** public areas — yes, rooms — yes. ADA compliant

## Midtown East Courtyard by Marriott

| | |
|---|---|
| Extraordinary | $450 and over |
| Excellent | $350–$449 |
| **Very Good** | $250–$349 |
| Good | **$150–$249** |
| Basic | $75–$149 |
| Poor | under $75 |

This new Courtyard by Marriott (it opened in November, 1998) on Third Avenue in midtown offers an alternative to the other midtown Courtyard, located just south of Times Square. The two hotels are roughly comparable, though this location has larger rooms.

Its lobby, though, looks like the office building it was. The fake plants and acoustical tile ceiling don't help. Fortunately, the rooms are much better, if you can find yours. The hallways zigzag, and there are few directional signs. The majority of rooms, done in green and purple tones, have ample space (by New York standards) and very large windows. This keeps the accommodations, which have a slightly sterile feel to them, from any kind of gloominess. Since the guest rooms start at the 14th floor, you're likely to get light and a feeling of openness, not to mention, in some cases, a bird's-eye view of the Lipstick Building, so-called because of its similarity to a lipstick tube. In spite of the large windows and busy Third Avenue, the rooms are quiet.

Amenities include two-line phones with dataport and voice mail, clock radio, safe, iron and ironing board, hair dryer, and coffee maker. Mattresses are foam, as is typical at Marriott, water pressure is fine and there are smoke alarms and sprinklers. Many have a separate vanity sink outside of the toilet and shower. White, yellow, and business pages are thoughtfully included. Room service is offered until midnight.

King-bedded rooms are the majority here. Most double doubles and suites have sofa beds. The suites, $60 above standard rack, also have a microwave and mini-fridge. There is a 24-hour exercise room, full of light, with a couple of treadmills, stairsteppers, bikes and resistance machines. No free weights, though.

A stay at this hotel would be enhanced if you get a room on the 04 line. It has wonderful East River views. It's a comfortable perch in midtown.

**Midtown East Courtyard by Marriott,** 866 Third Ave., New York, NY 10022
**cross streets:** at E. 53rd Street
**phone:** (212) 644-9600, (800) 321-2211
**fax:** (212) 813-1945
**email:** none
**website:** none
**number of rooms:** 306 (includes 8 suites)
**number of floors:** 18
**smoking policy:** designated nonsmoking rooms

**restaurants:** yes
**bars:** yes
**room service:** yes
**hotel amenities:** fitness equipment, meeting rooms, laundry and dry cleaning, concierge
**room amenities:** air-conditioning, multiline phones, voice mail, modem line, safe, iron and ironing board
**parking:** valet
**cancellation:** 6 P.M. day of arrival
**wheelchair accessibility:** public areas — yes, rooms — yes. ADA compliant

## New York Marriott East Side

| | |
|---|---|
| Extraordinary | $450 and over |
| Excellent | $350–$449 |
| **Very Good** | **$250–$349** |
| Good | **$150–$249** |
| Basic | $75–$149 |
| Poor | under $75 |

When it opened in 1924, the 24-story Shelton Towers, as this hotel was then known, was the largest in the world. Its developer was James T. Lee, Jackie Onassis's grandfather, and the architect was Arthur Loomis Harmon, best known for his later project, the Empire State Building. If you compare the two buildings, you can see a similar shape.

Throughout the years, the Shelton has had other laurels. Georgia O'Keeffe lived at the hotel for a time and painted two well-known works, "The Shelton with Sunspots" and "View of the East River from The Shelton." The famous Olympic swimming star, Buster Crabbe, taught swimming lessons in the basement pool, and Houdini escaped from a locked, chained box, also in the pool.

This sort of long history makes the hotel atypical for Marriott (the hotel is actually owned by the Chicago company Strategic Hotels and managed by Marriott). The guest rooms, too, are distinctive. They tend not to be large, but are snappily contemporary, with beige and camel colors predominating.

Amenities include two-line phones, dataport, voice mail, clock radio, iron and ironing board, hair dryer, a phone in the bathroom, and a Shower Massage. The hotel is on a "four-pipe system" (the majority of hotels in the city are "two-pipe"). The advantage to the four-pipe is you can have heat or air-conditioning at any time of the year and guests have their own climate control. Our tests of water pressure, though, showed the building's age — pressure isn't strong.

The Marriott offers a "concierge" level, which means you get use of a special lounge, upgraded amenities, a room on a higher floor, continental breakfast and an honor bar. All guests have access to the hotel's concierge. There is a business center with a computer, copier, fax and typing services available. The fitness center has aerobic and resistance machines and free weights.

The Marriott Marquis over in Times Square is best suited for large groups. The Marriott East Side comes with more panache.

**New York Marriott East Side,** 525 Lexington Ave., New York, NY 10017
**cross streets:** at E. 49th St.
**phone:** (212) 755-4000, (800) 242-8684
**reservations fax:** (212) 980-7625, guest fax: (212) 751-3440
**email:** none
**website:** none
**number of rooms:** 643 (includes 5 suites)
**number of floors:** 33
**smoking policy:** designated nonsmoking rooms
**restaurants:** yes
**bars:** yes
**room service:** yes
**hotel amenities:** fitness center, business center, concierge, meeting and function rooms, laundry and dry cleaning
**room amenities:** air-conditioning, modem line, mini-bar
**parking:** valet
**cancellation:** 6 P.M. day of arrival
**wheelchair accessibility:** public areas — yes, rooms — yes. ADA compliant

## The New York Palace Hotel

| | |
|---|---|
| Extraordinary | **$450 and over** |
| **Excellent** | $350–$449 |
| Very Good | $250–$349 |
| Good | $150–$249 |
| Basic | $75–$149 |
| Poor | under $75 |

Two hundred and twenty-seven staff members — close to 25 percent of the Palace's employees — have been with the hotel for 15 years or more. That's one of the best indicators of the quality of service in this well-run, near-the-top-of-the-market hotel.

Built by the Helmsleys over the beautiful and historic Villard Houses, the Palace is now owned by the Sultan of Brunei, who has done a mostly superior job with renovations that were completed in 1997. The four-star restaurant, Le Cirque 2000, is on the grounds, giving the compound enormous cachet.

There are essentially three levels of service and amenities. There are the standard rooms, nine executive floors geared to the business traveler, and the Towers, virtually a boutique hotel in its own right. The rooms in the Towers are done in either classic or modern design (the modern is really modern Deco), room service is available from Le Cirque, and amenities, such as customized business cards and stationery, are provided for every Towers guest.

You don't have to be in the Towers, though, to benefit from spectacular views (if views are important, avoid floors nine through the mid-teens facing east). The Palace has a complimentary, well-outfitted health club (where you can gaze at St. Patrick's Cathedral while you're on the Stairmaster).

**The New York Palace Hotel,** 455 Madison Ave., New York, NY 10022
**cross streets:** between E. 50th and E. 51st Streets
**phone:** (212) 888-7000, (800) 697-2522
**fax:** (212) 303-6000
**email:** none
**website:** www.newyorkpalace.com
**number of rooms:** 900 (includes 110 suites)
**number of floors:** 54
**smoking policy:** designated nonsmoking rooms
**restaurants:** Le Cirque 2000
**bars:** 2
**room service:** yes, 24 hours
**hotel amenities:** concierge, business center, meeting and function rooms, health club, laundry and dry cleaning
**room amenities:** air-conditioning, mini-bar, VCR on request, fax, modem line, safe
**parking:** valet
**cancellation:** 2 P.M. day of arrival
**wheelchair accessibility:** public areas — yes, rooms — yes. ADA compliant

## Omni Berkshire Place

| | |
|---|---|
| Extraordinary | $450 and over |
| **Excellent** | **$350–$449** |
| Very Good | **$250–$349** |
| Good | $150–$249 |
| Basic | $75–$149 |
| Poor | under $75 |

The Omni does seem to have it all: comfortable, quiet rooms with plenty of amenities.

The building was built in 1926 by the well-known architectural firm Warren and Wetmore. More than 70 years, many owners, and a 1995 $70 million renovation later, you won't find much of the roaring '20's left. Rooms are done in classic contemporary style with pale yellows and greens. Next to the exceptionally comfortable bedding is a superphone — besides two lines, dataport and voice mail, it also controls the light, temperature, TV, music and gives you the time around the world. The double-paned windows open, but the rooms are reasonably quiet, especially considering the prime location. Amenities include clock radio, fax, safe, umbrella, bathrobe, iron and ironing board, wood and padded hangers, hair dryer, makeup mirror, phone in the bathroom, and Institute Swiss bath products. The marble bathrooms have good water pressure, though, as usual, it's weaker on the upper floors. There is night turndown service and 24-hour room service from the restaurant Kokachin, which serves contemporary continental and American food.

The hotel has a concierge staff, one of whom has the Clefs d'Or designation. The business center has three computers, printer, fax, typewriter, copier and a small conference room. The fitness room on the 17th floor, only for hotel guests, is light and pleasant and it's got all the basics. There are 18 handicapped access rooms — the hotel does an especially good job in this area.

Omni may not have as high a profile as some hotels in the city, but we imagine Omni's guests are content just the way things are.

**Omni Berkshire Place,** 21 E. 52nd St., New York, NY 10022
**cross streets:** between Madison and Fifth Avenues
**phone:** (212) 753-5800, (800) 843-6664 (THE OMNI)
**reservations fax:** (212) 754-5020, guest fax: (212) 754-5018
**email:** none
**website:** www.omnihotels.com
**number of rooms:** 396 (includes 47 suites)
**number of floors:** 21
**smoking policy:** designated nonsmoking rooms
**restaurants:** yes
**bars:** yes
**room service:** yes, 24 hours
**hotel amenities:** fitness center, concierge, business center, meeting and function rooms, laundry and dry cleaning
**room amenities:** air-conditioning, mini-bar, VCR, fax, modem line, safe, multiline phones
**parking:** valet
**cancellation:** 4 P.M. 1 day prior to arrival
**wheelchair accessibility:** public areas — yes, rooms — yes. ADA compliant

## Pickwick Arms Hotel

| Extraordinary | $450 and over |
|---|---|
| Excellent | $350–$449 |
| Very Good | $250–$349 |
| Good | $150–$249 |
| **Basic** | **$75–$149** |
| Poor | under $75 |

It's not easy to sleep in midtown Manhattan for $65 a night, but it's possible at the Pickwick Arms, if you're by yourself and are willing to use a hall bath.

No one, it's safe to say, is staying at the Pickwick because the rooms are so beautiful. They're tiny and plain as can be. The Pickwick is always busy because the rates are low. Most of the rooms here are singles; about one-third of the accommodations do not have a private bath. Bathrooms can be private, in the hall or shared with one other room. Every room has a sink. Mattresses are adequate but, it hardly needs saying, not top-of-the-line. There are one-line phones in the room, a TV and a desk. The bathrooms are also pint-sized, and there is much fluorescent lighting. The hallways were renovated in the first third of 1999 and are considerably more appealing than they used to be.

There are two terrific spots on the ground floor, independently operated. The modest Le Bateaux Ivres is a wine bar; Scarabée is a wonderful (moderately expensive) restaurant serving Mediterranean food. What you save upstairs could be put toward a memorable meal downstairs.

**Pickwick Arms Hotel,** 230 E. 51st St., New York, NY 10022
**cross streets:** between Second and Third Avenues
**phone:** (212) 355-0300, (800) 742-5945
**fax:** (212) 755-5029
**email:** none
**website:** none
**number of rooms:** 330
**number of floors:** 13
**smoking policy:** all smoking rooms
**restaurants:** Scarabée
**bars:** yes
**room service:** none
**hotel amenities:** some shared baths
**room amenities:** air-conditioning
**parking:** none
**cancellation:** 1 day prior to arrival
**wheelchair accessibility:** public areas — yes, rooms — no

# The Pierre

| | |
|---|---|
| Extraordinary | **$450 and over** |
| **Excellent** | $350–$449 |
| Very Good | $250–$349 |
| Good | $150–$249 |
| Basic | $75–$149 |
| Poor | under $75 |

The Pierre not only has elevator operators (one of the few remaining hotels in the city that does), but they wear white gloves. That tells you much of what you need to know about the Pierre. It is old-world, well-mannered and enormously appealing. After a night at this hotel, stepping out onto the hurly-burly of New York's streets can be a difficult adjustment.

The style of the rooms is traditional — dark woods, chintzes and prints — and everything is done in good taste. Ceilings are high, which means that even the smaller rooms feel airy. It is easy to get comfortable here very quickly. The amenities do not include a large number of electronics and gadgets (things like VCRs and fax machines are mostly on request), but you can leave your shoes outside your door for an overnight shine and there are superb mattresses, a tie rack in the closet and even a small humidifier. While the water pressure is good, many of the bathrooms we visited were not especially spacious. The most memorable rooms are the ones with views west over Central Park and north over Manhattan.

This is not a business-oriented hotel, so the business facility is one desk with a computer, but most of the business services you need can be arranged by the concierge staff, several of whom have the Clefs d'Or designation. There is a fitness facility (open to hotel guests only) and you can take tea in the distinctive Rotunda room, with its trompe l'oeil murals by artist Edward Melcarth.

It's a white-glove operation from top to bottom, penthouse to lobby.

**The Pierre,** 2 E. 61st St., New York, NY 10021
**cross streets:** between Fifth and Madison Avenues
**phone:** (212) 838-8000, (800) 332-3442
**reservations fax:** (212) 758-1615, guest fax: (212) 940-8109
**email:** none
**website:** www.fourseasons.com
**number of rooms:** 202 (includes 52 suites)
**number of floors:** 39
**smoking policy:** designated nonsmoking rooms
**restaurants:** 2
**bars:** yes
**room service:** yes, 24 hours
**hotel amenities:** fitness equipment, concierge, laundry and dry cleaning, business services, meeting and function rooms

**room amenities:** air-conditioning, mini-bar, VCR on request, fax on request, modem line, safe
**parking:** valet
**cancellation:** 6 P.M. day of arrival
**wheelchair accessibility:** public areas — yes, rooms — yes. ADA compliant

## Plaza Fifty

| | |
|---|---|
| Extraordinary | $450 and over |
| Excellent | **$350–$449** |
| **Very Good** | **$250–$349** |
| Good | $150–$249 |
| Basic | $75–$149 |
| Poor | under $75 |

The Plaza Fifty is one of ten hotels in the Manhattan East Suite Hotels chain. The group shares a number of features in common. Not only are they all-suites hotels, each offers somewhat-spacious-to-very-spacious accommodations, kitchen or kitchenette, fitness room, and a good number of amenities. They divide things up as studio suites (which are the smallest and really like a standard hotel room), junior suites, one-bedroom suites, and two-bedroom suites. The Plaza Fifty isn't a design award-winner, but it is a quality hotel at a fair price.

You may find yourself thinking about doctors and dentists at the Plaza Fifty. The lobby looks like a doctor's reception area, minus the well-thumbed magazines, and the guest room hallways have a bland, gray hospital look to them, minus the gurneys.

The guest rooms, true to Manhattan East form, are considerably more appealing — they tend to be spacious, even in the basic accommodation. The traditional design scheme features beige walls, camel-colored drapes, and dark blue carpeting. Amenities include clock radio, safe, iron and ironing board, one-line phones with dataport and voice mail. The kitchens or kitchenettes have a microwave, mini-fridge, toaster, coffee maker and plates and silverware.

The small, plain bathrooms have a hair dryer, middling water pressure and Shower Massages. The closets are quite good and stocked with wooden hangers. There are twelve deluxe one-bedrooms, and all but one have balconies as well as a more contemporary look, VCR, larger size and plenty of light.

The Plaza Fifty may not have much of a lobby, but you could always stay here and hang out at the Waldorf.

**Plaza Fifty,** 155 E. 50th St., New York, NY 10022
**cross streets:** between Lexington and Third Avenues
**phone:** (212) 751-5710, (800) 637-8483
**fax:** (212) 753-1468
**email:** info@mesuite.com
**website:** www.mesuite.com

**number of rooms:** 129 (all suites)
**number of floors:** 22
**smoking policy:** designated nonsmoking rooms
**restaurants:** none
**bars:** none
**room service:** yes
**hotel amenities:** health club, laundry and dry cleaning, business services, meeting and function rooms
**room amenities:** air-conditioning, kitchen, safe
**parking:** valet
**cancellation:** 3 P.M. 1 day prior to arrival
**wheelchair accessibility:** public areas — yes, rooms — yes

## Regal United Nations Plaza

| | |
|---|---|
| Extraordinary | $450 and over |
| **Excellent** | **$350–$449** |
| Very Good | **$250–$349** |
| Good | $150–$249 |
| Basic | $75–$149 |
| Poor | under $75 |

What is now the Regal U.N. Plaza was built in 1977 to house diplomats. There have been various owners throughout its relatively short life as a hotel. In its current state, the hotel rooms are quite pleasant and comfortable, boasting views of the east side of Manhattan and of Queens. The lobby, on the other hand, could use a thorough de-80's-ification (design themes like glitzy rings of ceiling lights and lots of reflecting surfaces).

One of the most distinctive features of the hotel is its collection of tapestries, batiks, silks and brocades, which adorns hallways and some guest rooms. They are donations of United Nations members (the U.N. is across the street). The beige, hand-woven bedspreads from India are a pleasant change from the usual floral prints.

In addition to enchanting views, guests will find many things to like about their rooms. They are particularly quiet, the bedding is good, there are two-line phones, clock radios, irons and ironing boards, bathrobes, Gilchrist and Soames bath products and fax machines.

Tennis players will love the single court at the top of the building — it's the only hotel in the city with an indoor court. It feels very secluded up there, a rare commodity in Manhattan. The health club is small but adequate. Its views, though, to the north and east, are dazzling. The heated swimming pool, with views east and south, is equally arresting.

The tennis, the vistas and the quiet, comfortable rooms offer a diplomatic immunity to the city clamor down below.

**Regal United Nations Plaza,** 1 United Nations Plaza at E. 44th St., New York, NY 10017
**cross streets:** between First and Second Avenues

**phone:** (212) 758-1234, (800) 222-8888
**fax:** (212) 702-5051
**email:** none
**website:** www.regal-hotels.com
**number of rooms:** 427 (includes 45 suites)
**number of floors:** 13
**smoking policy:** designated nonsmoking rooms
**restaurants:** yes
**bars:** yes
**room service:** yes, 24 hours
**hotel amenities:** health club, indoor tennis court, swimming pool, concierge, laundry and dry cleaning, meeting and function rooms
**room amenities:** air-conditioning, mini-bar, VCR on request, fax, modem line, safe, multiline phones
**parking:** valet
**cancellation:** 4 P.M. 2 days prior to arrival
**wheelchair accessibility:** public areas — yes, rooms — yes. ADA compliant

## The Roger Smith Hotel

| | |
|---|---|
| Extraordinary | $450 and over |
| Excellent | $350–$449 |
| Very Good | **$250–$349** |
| **Good** | $150–$249 |
| Basic | $75–$149 |
| Poor | under $75 |

Frumpy, eccentric and hip, pretty much at the same time. The hotel attracts a sizeable number of rock performers and groups (Barenaked Ladies, Jewel, Sheryl Crow) as guests, who take in stride that the rooms have more character than charm.

In some rooms the smell test has competing claims from mildew, room deodorant and smoke. Windows are single-paned, and the hotel is on Lexington Avenue, so you're bound to get street noise. There are, however, a fair number of amenities for the price range: voice mail, iron and ironing board, hair dryer, coffee maker, unstocked mini-fridge and continental breakfast.

The hotel is run by artist/sculptor James Knowles, which helps explain the hotel's adjacent art gallery, the art exhibits throughout the property and the colorful, abstract murals in the restaurant. They were painted, the hotel says, by Mr. Knowles in the course of one frenzied day. While we have to caution that the polish level at the Roger Smith isn't high, it has personality, which is no small feat.

**The Roger Smith Hotel,** 501 Lexington Ave., New York, NY 10017
**cross streets:** between E. 47th and E. 48th Streets
**phone:** (212) 755-1400, (800) 445-0277
**fax:** (212) 319-9130
**email:** reservations@rogersmith.com

**website:** www.rogersmith.com
**number of rooms:** 136 (includes 26 suites)
**number of floors:** 16
**smoking policy:** designated nonsmoking rooms
**restaurants:** yes
**bars:** yes
**room service:** none
**hotel amenities:** laundry and dry cleaning, business services, meeting rooms
**room amenities:** air-conditioning, mini-fridge, VCR, modem line
**parking:** valet
**cancellation:** 4 P.M. 1 day prior to arrival
**wheelchair accessibility:** public areas — yes, rooms — no

## Roosevelt Hotel

| | |
|---|---|
| Extraordinary | $450 and over |
| Excellent | $350–$449 |
| Very Good | **$250–$349** |
| **Good** | **$150–$249** |
| Basic | $75–$149 |
| Poor | under $75 |

The Roosevelt's proximity to Grand Central Terminal was surely a prime asset when the hotel was built in 1924. There was even an underground passage (now closed) that connected the two buildings. Unfortunately, with fewer visitors arriving by train, the Roosevelt seemed to coast through the last couple of decades.

Now, however, the hotel has emerged from a two-and-a-half-year, $65 million, top-to-bottom renovation in 1997, and it is possible to imagine Teddy Roosevelt, for whom the hotel is named, striding through the bustling, old-fashioned lobby, nodding approval and shouting "Bully!"

The traditionally-styled rooms are spotless, if not overflowing with personality. Mattresses are good, and windows are double-glazed, though you may get some traffic noise on the lower floors over Madison Avenue. Closets and bathrooms can be small, but water pressure and cleanliness are fine. All rooms have a full run of amenities. Hallways are roomy and pleasant even if the lighting is harsh. The business center and fitness center are both adequate, if small. The Roosevelt is a large hotel (there are over 1,000 rooms) offering straightforward, reliable lodging, perfectly in keeping with its namesake.

**Roosevelt Hotel,** 45 E. 45th St., New York, NY 10017
**cross streets:** at Madison Avenue
**phone:** (212) 661-9600, (888) 833-3969 (TEDDYNY)
**reservations fax:** (212) 885-6168, guest fax: (212) 885-6161
**email:** nyrsales@attmail.com
**website:** www.therooseveltel.com
**number of rooms:** 1,013 (includes 34 suites)

**number of floors:** 18
**smoking policy:** designated nonsmoking rooms
**restaurants:** yes
**bars:** yes
**room service:** yes
**hotel amenities:** fitness equipment, concierge, laundry and dry cleaning, business center, meeting and function rooms
**room amenities:** air-conditioning, fax, modem line, safe, iron and board
**parking:** valet
**cancellation:** 4 P.M. 1 day prior to arrival
**wheelchair accessibility:** public areas — yes, rooms — yes. ADA compliant

## The St. Regis

| **Extraordinary** | **$450 and over** |
| --- | --- |
| Excellent | $350–$449 |
| Very Good | $250–$349 |
| Good | $150–$249 |
| Basic | $75–$149 |
| Poor | under $75 |

The industrialist John Jacob Astor commissioned the St. Regis Hotel, purchasing the land in 1891 (the hotel was completed in 1904). Today, its Beaux-Arts design and Gilded Age aura remain vibrant pieces of social history, linking the 19th century with the new millennium.

A major renovation in 1991 insured thoroughly modern conveniences, but in terms of style, it's old world all the way. After checking in, guests are escorted to their floor, where they are greeted by a butler. If you don't have a butler in your everyday life, you will get used to it easily. The rooms are little laps of luxury: high ceilings, silk wall coverings, perfect beds, 300-thread count Egyptian cotton sheets, a console on the telephone that controls the lights, temperature and television. There's also a portable phone. Most bathrooms have two sinks, bathrobes, a scale, a makeup mirror and a hair dryer.

The St. Regis is home to one of the city's few four-star restaurants, Lespinasse. The restaurant had originally been awarded four stars by then *Times* critic, Ruth Reichl, for chef Gray Kunz's fusion cuisine. Christian Delouvrier took over the kitchen in 1998, tilting the cuisine back toward more classical French cooking. Mr. Delouvrier earned four stars on his own from Reichl in 1998.

The hotel has a number of other noteworthy features: concierges who have the Clef d'Or designation; a small, comfortable fitness center; the King Cole Bar with its Maxfield Parrish mural, and the St. Regis Rooftop, one of the most sought-after spaces in the city for weddings and other events.

There may be hotels in town with more gadgets and better views, but none match the St. Regis for grace and civility.

**The St. Regis,** 2 E. 55th St., New York, NY 10022
**cross streets:** between Fifth and Madison Avenues
**phone:** (212) 753-4500, (800) 759-7550
**reservations fax:** (212) 350-6900, guest fax: (212) 787-3447
**email:** res081_stregisnyc@sheraton.com
**website:** www.luxurycollection.com
**number of rooms:** 314 (includes 91 suites)
**number of floors:** 20
**smoking policy:** designated nonsmoking rooms
**restaurants:** Lespinasse
**bars:** yes
**room service:** yes, 24 hours
**hotel amenities:** health club, concierge, laundry and dry cleaning, business center, meeting and function rooms
**room amenities:** air-conditioning, mini-bar, modem line, safe
**parking:** valet
**cancellation:** 3 P.M. 1 day prior to arrival
**wheelchair accessibility:** public areas — yes, rooms — yes. ADA compliant

## San Carlos Hotel

| | |
|---|---|
| Extraordinary | $450 and over |
| Excellent | $350–$449 |
| Very Good | $250–$349 |
| **Good** | **$150–$249** |
| Basic | $75–$149 |
| Poor | under $75 |

Talk about low profiles! It would be surprising if the San Carlos has come up in many conversations around town for, oh, the last several decades. It's nice that way. Many of the staff have been with the hotel for many years; Gabriel, the front desk manager, has been there for 22 years and he's a favorite of kids, for whom he does magic tricks. Many of the hotel's guests have themselves been coming back to the San Carlos for a long time, attracted by the reasonable prices and the spacious rooms.

The lobby is attractively old-fashioned in a wood-paneled way, consisting of the front desk and a small sitting area. You would think most hotels would have fresh flowers, but most small hotels, anyway, do not. Here, two vases cheer up the proceedings. As befits its 1950's aura, many of the hallways and guest-room walls are beige ("the owner likes beige," the hotel rep tells us) though some of the recently repainted hallways have made it up to yellow. Accommodations aren't chic, but what you give up in style you gain in space; for the money, it's one of the roomiest hotels in the city.

This is one hotel where you will almost certainly have more closet space than you can use. Rooms are clean, windows double-glazed, and mattresses can be a bit bouncy. Bathrooms are old-fashioned-looking, but the water pressure is good. The bathrooms that have not yet been renovated may be scuffed up a bit (enamel coming off a bathtub).

Most rooms have kitchenettes with microwave, toaster, coffee maker and coffee, a pot or two and cups and plates. On the "01" line up to 1201, there are extra windows, which is nice because some of the other rooms can be dark. The San Carlos hasn't got the latest whiz-bang technology or sleek lines, but it's as appealing as a pair of fluffy slippers on a winter night.

**San Carlos Hotel,** 150 E. 50th St., New York, NY 10022
**cross streets:** between Lexington and Third Avenues
**phone:** (212) 755-1800, (800) 722-2012
**fax:** (212) 688-9778
**email:** sancarlos@pobox.com
**website:** www.sancarloshotel.com
**number of rooms:** 146 (including 75 suites)
**number of floors:** 18
**smoking policy:** designated nonsmoking rooms
**restaurants:** none
**bars:** none
**room service:** yes
**hotel amenities:** concierge, laundry and dry cleaning
**room amenities:** air-conditioning, modem line
**parking:** valet
**cancellation:** 11 A.M. 1 day prior to arrival
**wheelchair accessibility:** public areas — no, rooms — no

## The Sutton

| | |
|---|---|
| Extraordinary | $450 and over |
| **Excellent** | $350–$449 |
| Very Good | **$250–$349*** |
| Good | **$150–$249*** |
| Basic | $75–$149 |
| Poor | under $75 |

The Sutton is designed for people who need accommodations for an extended period — the minimum stay is one month. The lobby is wood-paneled and marble-floored — it looks less like a hotel lobby and more like the entrance to a handsome apartment building, which, in some ways, it is.

Rooms are furnished apartments with traditional décor; a few have solariums, and some have a terrace or sun deck. Even the studios tend to have good light. The ceilings, though, are low. Each unit has a fully-equipped and quite attractive kitchen: stove, full-size refrigerator, dishwasher, pots, pans, dishes, silverware, coffee maker and microwave. TV with cable, VCR, stereo and two-line phones are standard, but there are no fax machines in the rooms.

Daily maid service is included. There is a fitness center, open only to residents, that boasts a terrific lap pool, a small collection of machines and a sauna. The washer and dryer in the basement are provided at no extra charge.

The Sutton appeals to executives relocating to the city, movie stars on film shoots, people associated with the United Nations, and hospital outpatients and their families. They are attracted by the privacy and quiet of the Sutton as well as its full range of amenities.

**The Sutton,** 330 E. 56th St., New York, NY 10022
**cross streets:** between First and Second Avenues
**phone:** (212) 752-8888
**fax:** (212) 752-2605
**email:** none
**website:** www.thesutton.com
**number of rooms:** 84 (all suites)
**number of floors:** 17
**smoking policy:** all smoking rooms
**restaurants:** yes
**bars:** yes
**room service:** none
**hotel amenities:** health club, swimming pool, laundry and dry cleaning
**room amenities:** air-conditioning, kitchen, VCR, modem line, safe
**parking:** none
**cancellation:** nonrefundable lease
**wheelchair accessibility:** public areas — yes, rooms — yes. ADA compliant
**\*notes:** 30 day minimum stay

## Swissotel New York — The Drake

| | |
|---|---|
| Extraordinary | $450 and over |
| **Excellent** | $350–$449 |
| Very Good | **$250–$349** |
| Good | $150–$249 |
| Basic | $75–$149 |
| Poor | under $75 |

After a bumpy patch, the Drake seems back in form. This Swissotel on Park Avenue, largely geared toward the corporate traveler, had had inconsistent service in recent years, fueled by persistent staff turnover. The hotel says that the situation has stabilized, and from all appearances, you get the feeling that order, so dear to the Swiss heart, has been restored.

The rooms and amenities as well as the hotel facilities, are certainly impressive. Guests will walk into a handsome, classic contemporary-styled room that is most pleasing to the eye. The furniture is modern and elegant, and walls have a white/off-white stripe. Windows are triple-paned, and they open. There are three phones per room with two lines, dataport and voice mail. A fax/copier/printer, clock radio, coffeepot and coffee, mini-bar and movies on command are all standard. In the closets you'll find wood hangers, an umbrella, bathrobe, iron and ironing board, and a light that turns on when you open the door.

Bathrooms don't take up much real estate, but they come stocked with hair dryer, phone, makeup mirror, Neutrogena soap and shampoo (how about a few more freebies, though?), cotton balls and swabs.

Room service is 24 hours, and there is night turndown, individual climate control, and a personal, as opposed to computer, wakeup call. One nice touch is the master light switch, located by the door to the hallway. Turn it on or off and all the lights go on or off.

The Drake has three levels of accommodations — superior (standard to you), deluxe, which is larger than a superior, and executive deluxe, which is both larger and has a better location in the building. Many of the Park Avenue Suites have terraces. Other rooms, too, may have terraces but it's the luck of the draw when you check in. The suites have different "soft goods" (bedspreads, curtains, etc.) from standard rooms as well as a CD player and VCR.

Lafayette, which was the hotel's restaurant, had at one time earned four stars from the *Times* when Jean-Georges Vongerichten was in the kitchen but, in the intervening years, had lost much of its luster. In the fall of 1999, it will reopen as Quantum.

The fitness center has not only the requisite aerobics and weight resistance machines, as well as free weights, but a spa center with a variety treatments (facials, hydrotherapy, massage, hand and foot paraffin treatments and aromatherapy.) Steam and sauna use comes with any treatment.

The Drake now seems to be very much in form.

**Swissotel New York — The Drake,** 440 Park Ave., New York, NY 10022
**cross streets:** at E. 56th Street
**phone:** (212) 421-0900, (888) 737-9477 (73SWISS)
**reservations fax:** (312) 565-9930, guest fax: (212) 371-4190
**email:** none
**website:** www.swissotel.com
**number of rooms:** 495 (includes 108 suites)
**number of floors:** 21
**smoking policy:** designated nonsmoking floors
**restaurants:** Quantum
**bars:** yes
**room service:** yes, 24 hours
**hotel amenities:** fitness equipment, concierge, laundry and dry cleaning, business center, meeting and function rooms
**room amenities:** air-conditioning, mini-bar, fax, safe
**parking:** valet
**cancellation:** 4 P.M. 1 day prior to arrival
**wheelchair accessibility:** public areas — yes, rooms — yes. ADA compliant

## Vanderbilt YMCA

| Extraordinary | $450 and over |
| Excellent | $350–$449 |
| Very Good | $250–$349 |
| Good | $150–$249 |
| **Basic** | **$75–$149** |
| Poor | under $75 |

You wouldn't want to spend a few months at the Vanderbilt YMCA — the amenities are too few, the mattresses too iffy, bathrooms are shared and rooms are too small and plain. For a few nights on a restricted budget, a definite maybe.

No visitors are allowed on guest floors. You show your room key to the guard at the desk. There are cameras on each floor to increase security.

Rooms consist of linoleum floors, nothing on the walls, no phones, shared baths, small closet or a rack, three drawers, TV with cable, air-conditioning, a fluorescent overhead light, towel and soap. Some have bunk beds. Windows are single-paned, and mattresses are not good.

The accommodations are not the drawing card of a stay at the Vanderbilt Y. In addition to budget prices, guests have free access to the extensive athletic facilities on site. There are over 135 fitness classes, two swimming pools (one is laps-only), a running track and a full array of aerobics, weight training machines, steam room and sauna.

**Vanderbilt YMCA,** 224 E. 47th St., New York, NY 10017
**cross streets:** between Second and Third Avenues
**phone:** (212) 756-9600
**fax:** (212) 752-0210
**email:** yswaysales@worldnet.att.net
**website:** none
**number of rooms:** 400 (includes 7 suites)
**number of floors:** 7
**smoking policy:** all smoking
**restaurants:** cafe
**bars:** none
**room service:** none
**hotel amenities:** health club, 2 swimming pools, meeting rooms, self-service laundry
**room amenities:** air-conditioning, color cable TV, mini-fridge on request.
**parking:** none
**cancellation:** 11 A.M. 1 day prior to arrival
**wheelchair accessibility:** public areas — yes, rooms — yes
**notes:** no in-room phones

# W New York

| | |
|---|---|
| Extraordinary | $450 and over |
| Excellent | **$350–$449** |
| Very Good | **$250–$349** |
| **Good** | $150–$249 |
| Basic | $75–$149 |
| Poor | under $75 |

There is a great deal to like about the exciting W New York (which opened December, 1998) but there is one mistake so serious that it is hard to believe.

This spa hotel, designed throughout every cubic inch to reflect nature and inspire mind and body relaxation, does not have double-paned windows in every guest room. The guest rooms from the third through twelfth floors do, but the ones from the twelfth through eighteenth floors do not. New York, it should not come as news, is a noisy place, and busy Lexington Avenue, which has its share of traffic and frequent sirens, is especially so. Installing triple-paned windows would not be excessive. If the hotel fixes this serious problem, a "Very Good" rating might be more appropriate than its current rating of "Good."

If a good night's sleep is not a top priority for you, the W offers much else. There are major players involved: The hotel is owned by Starwood Hotels, and was designed by David Rockwell (known for his design of restaurants including Nobu and the Monkey Bar). Restaurateur Drew Nieporent runs the restaurant concession called Heartbeat, and nightclub owner Rande Gerber runs the bar, Whiskey Blue.

David Rockwell has not only had a field day with this property, but a forest, mountain, ocean and desert day, too. The nature theme plays out in many ways, including a repeating pressed leaf motif, rooms with a decorative box of grass and a mat in the elevators that gives the weather forecast. (When we visited, one elevator mat predicted sunny, in another elevator the mat predicted rainy and a third hazarded cloudy.) It is in the use of color that the W differs most from its obvious model, the Schrager hotels (the Royalton, the Paramount and Morgans). They favor grays and beiges while W prefers earth tones. In this way, the W could be considered the anti-Schrager. Schrager hallways are dark and moody; here, color is everywhere, including the lobby, which resembles an inviting ski lodge.

The rooms, closets and bathrooms tend to be on the small side; space may be at a premium, but amenities are plentiful. These include VCR, CD player, iron and ironing board, safe, two-line phones, hair dryer and Aveda bath products. Much attention has been given to the beds, which include feather bedding, 200-thread-count sheets and a down comforter. On the border of the sheets, there are sayings such as "Dance with Abandon" and "Sleep with Angels" (though our preference would be "Sleep with Double-Paned Windows"). A button on the telephone marked "Whatever, whenever" connects you to hotel staffers who provide additional concierge services.

The spa called Away offers massage, facials, wraps and other kinds of treatments in addition to a full range of health-club equipment. The hotel says only a limited number of outside memberships are available. The restaurant, Heartbeat, has a menu oriented toward fresh and healthy eating. Whiskey Blue, the bar, has no such orientation, beyond whatever salubrious effects you ascribe to alcohol.

The W New York is meant to be the launching pad for W hotels around the country. Whether their prospects are sunny, rainy or cloudy may be tied less to the marquee value of the people involved and more to the fundamentals of running a good hotel. At the moment, W New York is a nice place to visit, but we'd think twice about sleeping there.

**W New York,** 541 Lexington Ave., New York, NY 10022
**cross streets:** at E. 49th St.
**phone:** (212) 755-1200, (877) 946-8357 (WHOTELS)
**reservations fax:** (212) 644-0951, guest fax: (212) 319-8344
**email:** none
**website:** www.whotels.com
**number of rooms:** 720 (includes 50 suites)
**number of floors:** 18
**smoking policy:** designated nonsmoking floors
**restaurants:** Heartbeat
**bars:** 2
**room service:** yes, 24 hours
**hotel amenities:** health club, spa, business services, meeting and function rooms, concierge, laundry and dry cleaning
**room amenities:** air-conditioning, VCR, modem line, mini-bar
**parking:** valet
**cancellation:** 4 P.M. day of arrival
**wheelchair accessibility:** public areas — yes, rooms — yes. ADA compliant

## The Waldorf=Astoria

| Extraordinary | $450 and over |
| **Excellent** | **$350–$449** |
| Very Good | **$250–$349** |
| Good | $150–$249 |
| Basic | $75–$149 |
| Poor | under $75 |

From its classic New York Deco lobby, to the top-of-the-line Towers (a hotel-within-a-hotel), the Waldorf has many attractions other hotels can only dream of, and the hotel seems now to be capitalizing on its assets.

The Waldorf has a long and interesting history. In the last decade of the 1800s, William Waldorf Astor hit upon a plan to inconvenience the aunt he didn't like: Mrs. William Astor, the doyenne of New York society. He built a hotel, the Waldorf, in what was then her backyard: 5th Avenue and 33rd Street (where the Empire State Building is now). William won that round: Mrs. Astor moved uptown. Her son, John Jacob Astor IV, who loathed William but couldn't fail to notice the Waldorf's success, began negotiating with him to build a hotel on his mother's former plot of land. The Waldorf (named after the town in Germany where the Astors came from) and the Astoria became one hotel in 1893. Since the hotel was a marriage of convenience, John Jacob and his mother insisted on a clause in the contract that the two hotels maintain at least 30 inches of air space between them, giving John Jacob and his mother the right to seal up the space and break off into a separate hotel, should the need arise. The Waldorf=Astoria used the 'equal' sign between the names as a way of stating that the two entities were equal. It also came to represent the walkway between the two hotels that became known as Peacock Alley.

Peacock Alley got its name because the public area became a hot spot. All day, every day, and late into the night, people (up to 15,000 a day) dressed up (way up), and went to see and be seen. The more passive spectators took positions on the many comfortable chairs and sofas (lounging at the Waldorf) and the more active ones attended functions, ate in the restaurants, and promenaded. Someone is said to have remarked that it looked like an "alley of peacocks" and the name stuck. Catering to the need of the rich and famous was the man known as Oscar of the Waldorf. For many years, he was the public face and style of the hotel. His understanding of social distinctions and his many practical skills imbued him with a kind of power and aura that became legendary.

The hotel made its plans to move to the current and larger uptown site and completed financing just days before the Crash. Construction took two years and the new Waldorf=Astoria opened on October 1, 1931. The new building was built over the tracks now used by Metro-North, so the architects built the structure on stilts to act as a cushion against vibrations. If you look outside at the base, you can see the sidewalk curve up to meet the building.

The new Waldorf remained a vital part of the city's nightlife with the Starlight Roof Supper Club. Everyone played there from Glenn Miller to Ella to Jascha Heifetz. The roof opened and there was dancing under the stars. The hotel closed the roof (not the room) because the air conditioner compressors were placed over that part of the hotel.

No hotel's heyday can last forever, but the Waldorf of late feels like it's back at the top of its form — nearly everything gleams. Hotel management lured chef Laurent Gras, a protégé of Alain Ducasse, to run the restaurant, Peacock Alley. The hotel lobby boasts enormous and absolutely exquisite floral arrangements.

When we visited the Presidential Suite in 1993, the history certainly came through (every president since Hoover has stayed there, and one of J.F.K.'s rocking chairs is still in place) but the decor felt like a politician who'd been in office too long. It has since been refurbished and now feels suitably presidential. Regular rooms are solid on amenities and many have exciting views of midtown. The Waldorf concierge staff is well regarded and guests have use of the PlusOne fitness center on the premises.

One note, though. When we stayed here in 1992, the guestroom showers were a problem. The controls were located at the end of the tub opposite the shower head, requiring frequent trips back and forth to get the right balance between pressure and temperature. We never did manage it. During our most recent visit in 1998, we were told by hotel staff that they have since done work to improve the plumbing.

**The Waldorf-Astoria,** 301 Park Ave., New York, NY 10022
**cross streets:** at E. 50th Street
**phone:** (212) 355-3000, (800) 925-3673
**reservations fax:** (570) 450-1588, guest fax: (212) 872-7272
**email:** none
**website:** www.hilton.com
**number of rooms:** 1,387 (includes 225 suites)
**number of floors:** 42
**smoking policy:** designated nonsmoking floors
**restaurants:** Peacock Alley and three others
**bars:** 4
**room service:** yes, 24 hours
**hotel amenities:** health club, business center, laundry and dry cleaning, meeting and function rooms, concierge
**room amenities:** air-conditioning, mini-bar, VCR on request, fax, modem line
**parking:** valet
**cancellation:** 4 P.M. 1 day prior to arrival. 2 days prior to arrival during peak seasons
**wheelchair accessibility:** public areas — yes, rooms — yes. ADA compliant

# Uptown

## UPPER WEST SIDE

| Hotel | Price Range | Rating |
|---|---|---|
| Amsterdam Inn | $75–$149 | Basic |
| Belleclaire Hotel | $75–$149 | Unrated |
| The Comfort Inn at Central Park West | $75–$149 | Good |
| Country Inn the City | $150–$249 | Very Good |
| The Ellington | $75–$149 | Basic |
| Empire | $150–$249 | Good |
| Excelsior Hotel | $150–$249 | Good |
| Hostelling International — New York | under $75 | Basic |
| Hotel Beacon | $150–$249 | Good |
| Hotel Newton | $75–$149 | Basic |
| Hotel Olcott | $75–$149 | Good |
| Hotel Riverside | $75–$149 | Basic |
| Inn New York City | $350–$449 | Excellent |
| Jazz on the Park | under $75 | Basic |
| Lincoln Square Hotel | under $75 | Poor |
| The Lucerne | $150–$249 | Basic |
| Malibu Hotel | $75–$149 | Basic |
| Mayflower Hotel on the Park | $150–$249 | Good |
| The Milburn Hotel | $150–$249 | Basic |
| On The Ave | $150–$249 | Very Good |
| Park West Studios | under $75 | Poor |
| The Phillips Club (extended stay) | $150–$249 | Very Good |
| The Phillips Club (nightly) | $450 and over | Very Good |
| The Quality Hotel on Broadway | $75–$149 | Good |
| Riverside Tower Hotel | $75–$149 | Basic |
| Trump International Hotel and Tower | $350 and over | Extraordinary |
| West Side Inn | under $75 | Basic |
| West Side YMCA | $75–$149 | Basic |
| Wyman House | $150–$249 | Very Good |

## NEIGHBORHOOD BOUNDARIES

South — W. 59th St., West — Hudson River, North — 125th St., East — Frederick Douglass Blvd./Central Park West

## ABOUT THE NEIGHBORHOOD

The Upper West Side is largely residential. The tall buildings here tend to be apartment houses rather than offices. This means that the streets and avenues are crowded with people running errands, shopping for daily needs rather than luxury goods. Central Park borders the neighborhood on the east edge with easy access to the running track around the Jackie Onassis Reservoir at 86th St. and to the Delacorte Theatre at 81st St. The major and minor performance venues in the neighborhood make it a good choice if you are planning on a heavy dose of concerts, opera or ballet. Columbia University occupies the area just above 114th St. between Amsterdam Ave. and Broadway. Its Miller Theater, located at 116th and Broadway 854-1633, offers music and film programming.

## TRANSPORTATION

The 1/9, 2, and 3 trains run along Broadway. The B and C trains run along Central Park West in this area, but they run less frequently than the 1, 2, 3 lines. Major station stops are located at 59th St. Columbus Circle, W. 72nd St., 96th St., and W. 125th St.

## LANDMARKS

Lincoln Center at Broadway and W. 65th St. 721-6500, draws music and ballet lovers to its grand concert halls. The Merkin Hall, 129 W. 67th St. 501-3330, Symphony Space, 2537 Broadway, 864-5400, and the Beacon Theater, 2124 Broadway 496-7070, present a variety of musical programs, from classical to jazz to popular. The American Museum of Natural History, Central Park West and W. 79th St. 769-5100, is filled with families marveling at the dinosaur skeletons on display, among other things. The Children's Museum of Manhattan, 212 W. 83rd St. 721-1234, is full of interactive exhibitions for young children. The Cathedral of St. John the Divine, 1047 Amsterdam Ave. 316-7540, is well worth a visit.

## SHOPPING

There are not the intense clusters of shops you will find in other neighborhoods but here are some worth looking into. Avventura, 463 Amsterdam Ave. 769-2510, sells beautiful dishes and glassware. Zabar's, 2245 Broadway 787-2000, made its reputation on its wonderful food selection. Upstairs you will find a full housewares selection. Maya Schaper Cheese and Antiques, 106 W. 69th St. 873-2100, is a quirky place devoted to food-related antiques and cheese. If there is a music book you have not been able to locate, stop into the Juilliard Bookstore, Lincoln Center Plaza, 799-5000. Plain Jane, 525 Amsterdam Ave. 595-6916, sells fancifully-designed children's bed linens. Bath Island, 469 Amsterdam Ave. 787-9415, has a good selection of soaps and personal care products.

## EATING AND DRINKING

Picholine, 35 W. 64th St., 724-8585, serves Provençal-inspired food. It's a good, if hectic and expensive, stop before or after an event at Lincoln Center. Barney Greengrass, 541 Amsterdam Ave. 724-4707, is popular for smoked salmon and chicken soup. Gabriel's, 11 W. 60th St., 956-4600, seems to have more than the ordinary number of celebrity sightings and some good Italian food. Alouette, 2588 Broadway 222-6808, serves contemporary French-influenced food in a neighborhood that needs it. Go to Cafe Con Leche, 424 and 726 Amsterdam Ave. 678-7000, for Cuban sandwiches, Popover Cafe, 551 Amsterdam Ave. 595-8555, when you need to soothe the kids. There's good TexMex at Citrus Bar & Grill, 320 Amsterdam Ave. 595-0500, and a bistro-style menu at Savann, 414 Amsterdam Ave. 580-0202. Cafe Luxembourg, 200 W. 70th St. 873-7411, is one of the liveliest places in the neighborhood. Cafe des Artistes, 1 W. 67th St. 877-3500, is a neighborhood institution. Jean Georges, 1 Central Park West 299-3900, is the four-star restaurant of Jean-Georges Vongerichten.

For information on new hotels, ongoing updates, and directions to each hotel by car or mass transit, check online at New York Today, www.nytoday.com/hotels.

## THE HOTELS

### Amsterdam Inn

| | |
|---|---|
| Extraordinary | $450 and over |
| Excellent | $350–$449 |
| Very Good | $250–$349 |
| Good | $150–$249 |
| **Basic** | **$75–$149** |
| Poor | under $75 |

This new inn opened at the beginning of 1999. It is certainly basic but clean and comfortable enough. It is two flights up, no elevator, to reach the front desk. The hotel currently occupies three floors, with a fourth to come. Point number one, be willing and able to carry your luggage. Point two, the rooms. Beds aren't made up of high-quality mattresses, the "closet" is a small rack in the room with four hangers, there are single-line phones, the bathtubs are tiny, there are no bathroom amenities. Windows are double-paned, though, many rooms have good light, there is decent drawer space and the bathrooms are shiny and new. Some rooms share a bath, all have a sink en suite. Point three is the best news — modest prices — visitors can stay on the Upper West Side and not spend a lot of money — a Dutch treat.

**Amsterdam Inn,** 340 Amsterdam Ave., New York, NY 10023
**cross streets:** at W. 76th Street
**phone:** (212) 579-7500
**fax:** (212) 579-6127
**email:** info@amsterdaminn.com
**website:** www.amsterdaminn.com
**number of rooms:** 25
**number of floors:** 4
**smoking policy:** all nonsmoking
**restaurants:** none
**bars:** none
**room service:** none
**hotel amenities:** some shared baths
**room amenities:** air-conditioning, TV, iron on request
**parking:** none
**cancellation:** 1 day prior to arrival
**wheelchair accessibility:** public areas — no, rooms — no
**notes:** does not accept credit cards

## Belleclaire Hotel

| | |
|---|---|
| Extraordinary | $450 and over |
| Excellent | $350–$449 |
| Very Good | $250–$349 |
| Good | $150–$249 |
| Basic | **$75–$149** |
| Poor | under $75 |

The Belleclaire is unrated because it was under renovation when we visited. We did see a couple of model rooms. They're over-sized-for-New York, with a cheerful, warm, orange-yellow coat of paint on the walls. Carpeting is gray with gray bedspreads. It is all a vast improvement over the previous conditions at the hotel. There are two-line phones with dataport, mattresses are new, and in the closet is a small dresser with three drawers. This is a landmarked building, so exterior windows must remain intact — that means single panes, so rooms may be get a fair amount of traffic noise from Broadway. The 06 line are called the Tower rooms. They're a little more expensive, but they have four windows and because of a crook in the road here, you have the sensation of being right over Broadway. It couldn't feel more New York.

**Belleclaire Hotel,** 250 W. 77th St., New York, NY 10024
**cross streets:** at Broadway
**phone:** (212) 362-7700, (877) 468-3522 (HOTELBC)
**fax:** (212) 362-1004
**email:** sjdefazio@aol.com

**website:** www.belleclaire.com
**number of rooms:** 279
**number of floors:** 10
**smoking policy:** designated nonsmoking floors
**restaurants:** none
**bars:** none
**room service:** none
**hotel amenities:** some shared baths
**room amenities:** air-conditioning
**parking:** none
**cancellation:** 6 P.M. day of arrival
**wheelchair accessibility:** public areas — yes, rooms — yes

## The Comfort Inn at Central Park West

| | |
|---|---|
| Extraordinary | $450 and over |
| Excellent | $350–$449 |
| Very Good | $250–$349 |
| **Good** | $150–$249 |
| Basic | **$75–$149** |
| Poor | under $75 |

Before the current owners bought out this hotel, it was the sleepiest backwater of a hotel imaginable. The little old lady who ran it liked it that way, untroubled by recent developments such as the telephone. There was one phone in the hotel — at the front desk. When a guest got a phone call, a message was put into their mailbox. When a guest got an *urgent* call, she put the phone down, rode the elevator to the guest floor and knocked on their door. When the call came with an offer to buy the hotel, the little old lady knew when opportunity had knocked at *her* door and sold.

A renovation is in progress through 1999 and beyond. The upper floors (10-14) will retain their traditional look, while those on 2-9 have been given a Mission-flavored contemporary look. All the rooms are small, so if limited space is a deal-breaker, look elsewhere. Otherwise, the Comfort looks to be a good value for the neighborhood. Rooms come with comfortable mattresses, two-line phones, dataport and voice mail (quite a change), clock radio, double-paned windows, iron and ironing board, hair dryer, and good water pressure.

When we visited, the business and mini-fitness rooms were still under construction, but the fitness room will have a bike and treadmill, the business room will have a computer with Internet access, fax and copier. These will be activated by your room key card and charges will be applied to your hotel bill. A complimentary continental breakfast is more extensive than that usually implies: hot and cold cereals, yogurt, muffins, bagels, Danish, coffee and juice.

The staff here seems winning, and you have the feeling that if there were an urgent message for you, they'd hop on the elevator and knock on your door, too.

**The Comfort Inn at Central Park West,** 31 W. 71st St., New York, NY 10023
**cross streets:** between Columbus Avenue and Central Park West
**phone:** (212) 721-4770, (877)-727-5236 (PARKCEN)
**fax:** (212) 579-8544
**email:** cphw71@aol.com
**website:** none
**number of rooms:** 102
**number of floors:** 14
**smoking policy:** designated nonsmoking floors
**restaurants:** none
**bars:** none
**room service:** none
**hotel amenities:** business center, meeting room, laundry and dry cleaning
**room amenities:** air-conditioning, modem line, mini-fridge on request, iron and ironing board
**parking:** none
**cancellation:** 4 P.M. 1 day prior to arrival
**wheelchair accessibility:** public areas — yes, rooms — yes. ADA compliant

## Country Inn the City

| | |
|---|---|
| Extraordinary | $450 and over |
| Excellent | $350–$449 |
| **Very Good** | $250–$349 |
| Good | **$150–$249** |
| Basic | $75–$149 |
| Poor | under $75 |

A charmer. You enter a small, limestone building (built in 1891) on a residential side street, and walk up the stairs (as many as three flights) to one of the four thoughtfully and attractively outfitted guest rooms.

Creaking wood floors are catnip to us, and Country Inn creaks. Others may enjoy the four-poster beds, the (nonworking) fireplaces, the ceiling fan, or, in one room, the delightful terrace. Each comes with a fully equipped kitchen that the owners stock with coffee, milk, jam and cereal. The kitchens feel lived in — there is a calendar on the wall, cookbooks are piled up on top of the fridge. The bathrooms lack the distinction of the rooms and soap is the only amenity. Each room has a direct inward dial phone with answering machine and a clock radio. Instead of closets, there are armoires, with (whoops) plastic hangers. Nice touches include free local calls, the flagon of brandy (very English country house), the bed tray and the moose head in the hallway.

There is a three-day minimum, they accept no credit cards and smoking is not permitted. It is a small price to pay for the small price you pay. Every neighborhood should have a Country Inn.

**Country Inn the City,** W. 77th St., New York, NY 10024
**cross streets:** between Broadway and West End Avenue
**phone:** (212) 580-4183
**fax:** (212) 874-3981
**email:** ctryinn@aol.com
**website:** www.countryinnthecity.com
**number of rooms:** 4 apartments
**number of floors:** 5
**smoking policy:** all nonsmoking
**restaurants:** none
**bars:** none
**room service:** none
**hotel amenities:** none
**room amenities:** air-conditioning, kitchen
**parking:** none
**cancellation:** 30 days prior to arrival
**wheelchair accessibility:** public areas — no, rooms — no.
**notes:** no children under 12 years of age, maximum 2 people
per apartment, no credit cards, 3 night minimum stay.

## The Ellington

| | |
|---|---|
| Extraordinary | $450 and over |
| Excellent | $350–$449 |
| Very Good | $250–$349 |
| Good | $150–$249 |
| **Basic** | **$75–$149** |
| Poor | under $75 |

Duke Ellington, who lived not far from this hotel, wrote "Take
the A Train," but it's the 1 or 9 train you want to get here. Its
location make it a good choice for friends and family of Columbia students looking for relatively inexpensive lodging. Budget
travelers who want to stay on the Upper West Side should also
like the Ellington.

This former SRO reopened in 1998 with some deft modern
touches by the Amsterdam Hospitality Group hotel chain. Some
of their properties are better maintained than others. The Ellington has a few scuffs and chips, but nothing we saw gave us
cause for concern.

Mattresses, double-paned windows and water pressure,
always our first concern, check out well here. Phones are one
line with dataport, rooms have an air conditioner, hair dryer and
a clock radio. Don't come with a lot of clothes — not if you
want to hang them up. There are three plastic hangers in the
pint-sized closet. Televisions are, relatively speaking, jalopies,
and the breakfast wouldn't pass muster with most nutritionists
— it's coffee and doughnuts only.

**The Ellington,** 610 W. 111th St., New York, NY 10025
**cross streets:** between Broadway and Riverside Drive
**phone:** (212) 864-7500

**fax:** (212) 749-5852
**email:** none
**website:** www.nycityhotels.net
**number of rooms:** 82
**number of floors:** 6
**smoking policy:** designated nonsmoking rooms
**restaurants:** none
**bars:** none
**room service:** none
**hotel amenities:** laundry and dry cleaning
**room amenities:** air-conditioning
**parking:** none
**cancellation:** 3 P.M. 1 day prior to arrival
**wheelchair accessibility:** public areas — no, rooms — no

## Empire

| | |
|---|---|
| Extraordinary | $450 and over |
| Excellent | $350–$449 |
| Very Good | $250–$349 |
| **Good** | **$150–$249** |
| Basic | $75–$149 |
| Poor | under $75 |

You would never know the Empire, a former Radisson, is owned
by Ian Schrager, the hotelier known for such high-style hotels as
the Delano in Miami and the Royalton in New York.

This hotel, though, is still Radisson through and through,
with pink-striped hallways, apron-plaid curtains and furniture
with no sharp edges. Situated across from Lincoln Center, the
hotel hasn't relied on its location alone. The rooms are in good
shape now and will get a few cosmetic nips and tucks in 1999.

The standard rooms are quite small, suitable for one person
or two people who are very well acquainted. The bathrooms can
also require some shuffling — doors open inward — but once in
the shower, you'll appreciate the strong water pressure. Closets
are on the small side. Plenty of amenities, though: mini-bar, CD
and tape deck, clock radio, makeup mirror and hair dryer.
Guests can borrow from a CD library.

The rooms facing Lincoln Center have the most interesting
views. On the second floor of the hotel is the West 63rd St.
Steakhouse, which also has some prime seats facing Lincoln
Center. Iridium, the popular jazz club and bar, is just outside the
hotel's front door.

**Empire,** 44 W. 63rd, New York, NY 10023
**cross streets:** between Broadway and Columbus Avenue
**phone:** (212) 265-7400, (888) 822-3555
**fax:** (212) 245-3382
**email:** empirerqst@aol.com
**website:** www.empirehotel.com

**number of rooms:** 381 (includes 28 suites)
**number of floors:** 11
**smoking policy:** designated nonsmoking rooms
**restaurants:** yes
**bars:** yes
**room service:** yes
**hotel amenities:** laundry and dry cleaning, meeting rooms, concierge
**room amenities:** air-conditioning, mini-bar, VCR, modem line
**parking:** valet
**cancellation:** September-December, 14 days prior to arrival; January-August, 3 P.M. 1 day prior to arrival
**wheelchair accessibility:** public areas — yes, rooms — yes. ADA Compliant

## Excelsior Hotel

| | |
|---|---|
| Extraordinary | $450 and over |
| Excellent | $350–$449 |
| Very Good | $250–$349 |
| **Good** | **$150–$249** |
| Basic | $75–$149 |
| Poor | under $75 |

Judge Judy might say it this way . . .

"OK, Excelsior, you've messed up in the past. Big time. You got a lot of nice people teed off at you because you overbooked a lot and when people showed up at the hotel, sometimes after an international flight, you didn't lift a finger to "walk" them, as the hotel lingo goes, to another hotel. You got an unsatisfactory rating at the Better Business Bureau. People called to complain at *Manhattan User's Guide.* I take a very dim view of those kind of shenanigans. You with me so far?"

"Now, I believe hotels can change. Your new manager says things *have* changed. You have certainly done an exemplary job of renovating during '97 and '98. The place is unrecognizable. The court notes the good-looking traditional-style hotel rooms. (Did you get a deal with the Bombay company? Talk to me in chambers). I will accept it as prima facie evidence of laudable motives. You put in two-line phones with dataport and voice mail. I see bathrooms have Gilchrist and Soames bath products, a phone and a hair dryer. Even Q-tips and cotton balls. Nice touch. Pants press, iron and ironing board and bathrobe, too. I like the new dining room on the second floor, the breakfast of fruits, cereals, breads, scrambled and hard-boiled eggs. The little writing desk with stationery in the back of the dining room's shrewd, too. Maybe you really have changed.

Listen to me, though. Any recidivist activity and I'll be at your front desk in a New York minute. Next case."

**Excelsior Hotel,** 45 W. 81st St., New York, NY 10024
**cross streets:** between Columbus Avenue and Central Park West
**phone:** (212) 362-9200, (800) 368-4575
**reservations fax:** (212) 580-3872, guest fax: (212) 721-2994
**email:** hotelexcel@aol.com
**website:** www.excelsiorhotel.com
**number of rooms:** 197 (includes 80 suites)
**number of floors:** 16
**smoking policy:** designated nonsmoking rooms
**restaurants:** none
**bars:** none
**room service:** none
**hotel amenities:** concierge, laundry and dry cleaning
**room amenities:** air-conditioning
**parking:** none
**cancellation:** 4 P.M. 1 day prior to arrival
**wheelchair accessibility:** public areas — yes, rooms — no.

## Hostelling International — New York

| | |
|---|---|
| Extraordinary | $450 and over |
| Excellent | $350–$449 |
| Very Good | $250–$349 |
| Good | $150–$249 |
| **Basic** | $75–$149 |
| Poor | **under $75** |

Some hostels are known as party hostels, some have a mellow groove. With 624 beds, Hostelling International New York, is the largest hostel in the country and has a more institutional atmosphere than most. It is located in a former nursing home and run with the precision of the Swiss railroad.

The lobby looks not unlike a regular hotel lobby with five clocks behind the front desk showing the time in various cities around the world. During the afternoons, it can be as crowded, and the lines as long, as some midtown hotels that specialize in large groups. Once check-in is sorted out, everyone gets a key card for access to the rooms.

Hallways are long, clean and wardlike but pleasant enough. Rooms can have as many as twelve beds in them, but there are "family" rooms with a queen bed and at least one bunk. Mattresses are vinyl covered (this is to help against bedbugs — see more in our section on hostels in the introduction), fresh sheets are provided. No sleeping bags are permitted on room floors — again, to help fight infestation. While there are some rooms with private bath, the vast majority are shared. These hall bathrooms are kept impressively clean. Pay phones are located on every hall floor.

No hostel in the city can compete with the array of facilities that this one has. There is a common kitchen, coin-operated laundry, elevator to guest floors, TV room, game room, Internet access, an ATM, a foreign currency machine, a gift shop, and travel agency. In warmer months, hostelers have use of the lovely grounds. Walk outside onto the large, brick-covered patio, with a fountain, tables and chairs, trees for shade, and birds providing background sounds. From there, you can stroll onto the well-maintained lawn. In warm weather months, there are nightly barbecues.

Some other key points: unlike at some other hostels, alcohol is forbidden. Walk-ins are allowed but no tri-state residents (NY, NJ, CT) are permitted to stay. This hostel has wheelchair access.

It cannot be easy to run a ship for 624 hostelers day in and day out. Hostelling International New York does it well.

**Hostelling International — New York,** 891 Amsterdam Ave., New York, NY 10025
**cross streets:** at W. 103rd Street
**phone:** (212) 932-2300, (800) 909-4776, code 01
**fax:** (212) 932-2574
**email:** reserve@hinewyork.org
**website:** www.hinewyork.org
**number of rooms:** 624 beds
**number of floors:** 6
**smoking policy:** all nonsmoking
**restaurants:** cafeteria
**bars:** none
**room service:** none
**hotel amenities:** all shared baths, self-service laundry, common kitchen, lockers
**room amenities:** air-conditioning
**parking:** none
**cancellation:** 6 P.M. 1 day prior to arrival
**wheelchair accessibility:** public areas — yes , rooms — yes. ADA compliant
**notes:** $25 annual worldwide membership fee or you pay additional $3 per night

# Hotel Beacon

| | |
|---|---|
| Extraordinary | $450 and over |
| Excellent | $350–$449 |
| Very Good | $250–$349 |
| **Good** | **$150–$249** |
| Basic | $75–$149 |
| Poor | under $75 |

The Upper West Side is booming these days, and the hotels in the area are rushing to catch up. The Beacon was built in 1929 as an apartment hotel and for many years was primarily residential. Since 1990 it has moved toward becoming a full-fledged hotel. Roomy accommodations have been its draw, but decor left a lot to be desired. The ongoing upgrades, though, are creating a much-improved hotel. Upper West Siders like a good value and the Beacon is one.

In addition to a lot of space, most of the traditionally designed rooms have two comfortable, full-size beds and couches in the suites fold out. All rooms have a small kitchen that includes a mini-fridge, range top (the ovens are being phased out), coffee maker, a few pots and pans, dishes and silverware. Fairway, an excellent market with an emphasis on fruit and vegetables and Citarella, which features fish, are across the street.

Amenities include iron and board, clock radio, hair dryer and Neutrogena products in the bathroom. Some bathrooms are so small you almost have to side step in. Closets, though, are decently sized. Telephones are direct inward dial and have voice mail, though there is only one line. Even though the windows are double-glazed, the noise from Broadway is still audible. We hope the water pressure will be more robust after the plumbing is replaced this year.

The focus at the Beacon isn't on hotel amenities or service but rather on room size and value — on those counts, it scores well.

**Hotel Beacon,** 2130 Broadway, New York, NY 10023
**cross streets:** between W. 74th and W. 75th Streets
**phone:** (212) 787-1100, (800) 572-4969
**reservations fax:** (212) 787-8119, guest fax: (212) 724-0839
**email:** info@beaconhotel.com
**website:** www.beaconhotel.com
**number of rooms:** 230 (includes 105 suites)
**number of floors:** 25
**smoking policy:** designated nonsmoking rooms
**restaurants:** yes
**bars:** none
**room service:** none
**hotel amenities:** concierge, laundry and dry cleaning
**room amenities:** air-conditioning, kitchenette
**parking:** none
**cancellation:** 6 P.M. day of arrival
**wheelchair accessibility:** public areas — yes, rooms — yes.
ADA compliant

# Hotel Newton

| | |
|---|---|
| Extraordinary | $450 and over |
| Excellent | $350–$449 |
| Very Good | $250–$349 |
| Good | $150–$249 |
| **Basic** | **$75–$149** |
| Poor | under $75 |

On upper Broadway, the Hotel Newton offers a less attractive but less expensive alternative to the Quality Hotel on Broadway, located around the corner. Both are convenient enough to midtown — it's two express stops on the subway — offering generally lower prices than comparable lodging in the higher rent districts of midtown.

The Newton has large, plain rooms with high ceilings, outfitted with inexpensive-looking furniture and maroon carpets. Each room has a desk, two-line phones with voice mail, clock radio, iron and ironing board. Most rooms are doubles or double doubles — we wished the mattresses felt better on our sit tests. Lower-quality mattresses invariably make a variety of noises when you sit on them as these do.

There is a reasonable amount of closet and drawer space, double-paned windows (some inevitable noise, though, from Broadway) but curtains are not in every room — some have Venetian blinds only. That's something we'd like to see remedied.

Not much in the way of hotel amenities — no room service, no fitness room. With budget accommodations, something's got to give. For those looking to keep their hotel bill down, the 10 rooms with a shared bath (there are 100 rooms in all) gets you a break on price. So does AAA membership.

**Hotel Newton,** 2528 Broadway, New York, NY 10025
**cross streets:** between W. 94th and W. 95th Streets
**phone:** (212) 678-6500, (888) 468-3558 (HOTEL 58)
**fax:** (212) 678-6758
**email:** travel@superlink.net
**website:** www.newyorkhotel.com
**number of rooms:** 110 (includes 14 suites)
**number of floors:** 9
**smoking policy:** designated nonsmoking rooms
**restaurants:** none
**bars:** none
**room service:** yes
**hotel amenities:** some shared baths
**room amenities:** air-conditioning
**parking:** none
**cancellation:** 4 P.M. 1 day prior to arrival; 2 days prior for weekend stays
**wheelchair accessibility:** public areas — yes, rooms — no

# Hotel Olcott

| | |
|---|---|
| Extraordinary | $450 and over |
| Excellent | $350–$449 |
| Very Good | $250–$349 |
| **Good** | $150–$249 |
| Basic | **$75–$149** |
| Poor | under $75 |

We often ask hotel staffers for the rack rate of the room we're standing in, watching their faces to see if they can say it with a straight face. Usually they manage it.

While you can't talk about glamour in the same sentence with the Olcott, it is generous in terms of space and gentle on your wallet. A stay at this partially residential hotel, located a few doors from the Dakota on the Upper West Side, for example, would only cost $200 a night for four people. This would get them a two-bedroom, two-bath suite. The rooms are clean, mattresses are firm, windows are double-paned, but amenities are generally low-tech (no fax machines, multiline phones, modem lines, etc). Instead, roomy closets, kitchens with a hot plate, mini-fridge, toaster, pots and pans, plates and glasses. The suites feel more like an apartment than a hotel room. What we like least about the Olcott is the awful fluorescent lighting in the rooms and in the hallways. The unrenovated hallways are a gray, sclerotic eyesore but some have already been redone with more appealing wallpaper and carpet. The rating, in this case, is based on the value that the Olcott offers — not at all on looks.

**Hotel Olcott,** 27 W. 72nd St., New York, NY 10023
**cross streets:** between Central Park West and Columbus Avenue
**phone:** (212) 877-4200
**fax:** (212) 580-0511
**email:** none
**website:** none
**number of rooms:** 150 (includes 110 suites)
**number of floors:** 16
**smoking policy:** all smoking rooms
**restaurants:** yes
**bars:** yes
**room service:** none
**hotel amenities:** none
**room amenities:** air-conditioning, kitchens
**parking:** none
**cancellation:** 1 week prior to arrival
**wheelchair accessibility:** public areas — yes, rooms — yes

# Hotel Riverside

| | |
|---|---|
| Extraordinary | $450 and over |
| Excellent | $350–$449 |
| Very Good | $250–$349 |
| Good | $150–$249 |
| **Basic** | **$75–$149** |
| Poor | under $75 |

This former ladies' residence still houses some longtime tenants, but there are 55 transient rooms available. The Riverside, though, doesn't exactly make a compelling case for itself. Hallways don't pass the smell test — it's hard to say exactly what it is, but floral it's not. The plain guest rooms contain a bed (decent mattress) and a desk with tiny closets. There are one-line phones, Gilchrist and Soames soap and shampoo, Venetian blinds with no curtains. The rooms with shared baths are a way to save money, and the hall baths are in good shape — in stark contrast to the hall baths used by the residents. Some rooms have small views of Riverside Park and the Hudson. There is a guest laundry in the basement and common kitchens throughout, but the latter are considered for permanent tenant use. You may be told so in no uncertain terms if you try to cook. We wouldn't mess with these ladies.

**Hotel Riverside,** 350 W. 88th St., New York, NY 10024
**cross streets:** between West End Avenue and Riverside Drive
**phone:** (212) 724-6100, (888) 468-3558 (HOTEL 58)
**fax:** (212) 873-5808
**email:** riverside@newyorkhotel.com
**website:** www.newyorkhotel.com
**number of rooms:** 170
**number of floors:** 8
**smoking policy:** designated nonsmoking rooms
**restaurants:** none
**bars:** none
**room service:** none
**hotel amenities:** some shared baths, self-service laundry
**room amenities:** air-conditioning, TV, telephone
**parking:** none
**cancellation:** 6 P.M. 1 day prior to arrival
**wheelchair accessibility:** public areas — no, rooms — no

## Inn New York City

| Extraordinary | $450 and over |
| **Excellent** | **$350–$449** |
| Very Good | $250–$349 |
| Good | $150–$249 |
| Basic | $75–$149 |
| Poor | under $75 |

Everything about this four-room inn is immensely charming and special. It is the very antithesis of cookie-cutter, corporate lodging and the Manhattan apotheosis of individual hospitality. As such, it isn't for everybody — places this distinctive never are.

On a quiet block just east of West End Avenue lies a brownstone with virtually no marking. On entering, you find a small hallway and a staircase — there is no front desk, no concierge, no lobby, no meeting rooms, no health club, no restaurant, no bar. There's no common area to speak of, all the space goes into the rooms. It's pure lodging.

And what lodging! Everything you can think of has been thought of and then some; each suite has a unique flavor and features. There is the Opera, the Library, the Spa, and the Vermont suites.

All the rooms have one-line phones with dataport and voice mail, CD player, VCR, fresh flowers, washer and dryer (except the Opera Suite — the staff will do your laundry for you in that instance), iron and ironing board, bathrobe and hair dryer.

Before you arrive, your kitchen will get stocked on some variation of this theme: muffins, bagels, brioche, perhaps some slices of a rich cake, jams, syrup, pancake mix, milk, juice, cream cheese, butter, dried fruits, figs, dates, fresh ground coffee, mineral water and wine. After that, they keep an eye on what guests are eating — not to bill you, only to replenish the supply.

The Opera suite features books on opera, opera CDs — naturally — 12-foot ceilings, a fireplace (used with a Duraflame log only), a baby grand piano, a Jacuzzi tub, a charming outdoor terrace, and a full kitchen: stove, refrigerator, dishwasher, toaster oven, and a full set of pots, pans, dishes and silverware. The opera lover (and any guest in this room) will be tempted to shout bravas to the innkeepers.

The Library Suite is the largest of the inn's four accommodations. There are floor-to-14-foot ceiling bookshelves, a working fireplace, a large Chesterfield sofa, two leaded-glass skylights. You can read anything from Dickens to Saul Bellow. Mid-suite is a full kitchen with a good-sized dining room table. Warning: staying here may be as addictive as a page turner.

New England temperament is in evidence in the Vermont Suite. You get a private entrance, lots of pine and oak, a full kitchen to whip up some chowder, and a spiral staircase that leads to a below ground bedroom — even more privacy — with a quilt-topped bed. This suite is rented out on a monthly basis only. A month here might beat a month of great runs on slopes with perfect powder.

The centerpiece of the Spa Suite is a large Jacuzzi, a shower behind glass brick, items such as a razor, toothbrush, body gels, loofa and body brush. After your Jacuzzi, you could spend some time in the sauna or stretch out on the chaise longue and read a book. Who needs Canyon Ranch?

You should also know that there is a two-night minimum except in the Vermont Suite, which has a one-month minimum. There is no smoking allowed and there are a total of three floors plus the outside steps. Inn New York City is expensive, but sometimes the best things in life are.

**Inn New York City,** W. 71 St., New York, NY 10023
**cross streets:** between Broadway and West End Avenue
**phone:** (212) 580-1900
**fax:** (212) 580-4437
**email:** none
**website:** www.innnewyorkcity.com
**number of rooms:** 4 (all suites)
**number of floors:** 4
**smoking policy:** all nonsmoking
**restaurants:** none
**bars:** none
**room service:** none
**hotel amenities:** business services, laundry room
**room amenities:** air-conditioning, stocked kitchens, VCR, Jacuzzi, modem line
**parking:** none
**cancellation:** 14 days prior to arrival, forfeit $50 for cancellation.
**wheelchair accessibility:** public areas — no, rooms — no
**notes:** two-night minimum stay, no children under 12 years of age

## Jazz on the Park

| Extraordinary | $450 and over |
| Excellent | $350–$449 |
| Very Good | $250–$349 |
| Good | $150–$249 |
| **Basic** | $75–$149 |
| Poor | **under $75** |

Jazz Jordan. The name is euphony itself. Mr. Jordon turns out to be a 29-year-old, self-described army brat, son of a Nigerian father and an Alabamian mother. He always loved hostelling and worked in the neighborhood at Hostelling International — New York. When the owners of Jazz on the Park offered him the chance to run his own hostel, he took the gig, which put him on the street where Duke Ellington lived. His middle name really is Jazz.

When you walk up the steps into the hostel, you find the check-in to the right. Straight ahead is an appealingly funky cafe called the Java Joint; if it were located on an East Village side street, it would be mobbed. As it is, when we visit on a muggy day, a few people are hanging out, writing postcards, talking, listening to the music that's playing at the perfect decibel level. The dreadlocked postman hangs out for a minute, snapping his fingers to the beat.

The hostel has key cards for access to the five guest room floors (no elevator). The rooms themselves aren't much to speak of, as is generally the case with hostels. Vinyl-covered mattresses are a good thing (this helps prevent bedbug infestation) and you get sheets and a towel. There is air-conditioning throughout and ceiling fans as well.

Complimentary breakfast is offered in the Java Joint, consisting of cereal, yogurt, croissant, bagel, coffee and juice. In the basement, there's a lounge and a stage where musicians perform in the evenings. Pleasant sundecks on the second and fourth floors overlook the now-closed Towers Nursing Home, infamous for its deplorable conditions and closed in the 1970's. Conditions at Jazz's place are much more buoyant. As he says, "there aren't a lot of rules — but no excess."

**Jazz on the Park,** 36 W. 106th St., New York, NY 10025
**cross streets:** at Central Park West
**phone:** (212) 932-1600
**fax:** (212) 932-1700
**email:** jazzonpark@aol.com
**website:** www.jazzhostel.com
**number of rooms:** 218 beds in dormitory-style rooms
**number of floors:** 5
**smoking policy:** designated nonsmoking rooms
**restaurants:** none
**bars:** none
**room service:** none
**hotel amenities:** laundry and dry cleaning, all shared baths
**room amenities:** air-conditioning
**parking:** none

**cancellation:** 6 P.M. day of arrival
**wheelchair accessibility:** public areas — no, rooms — no

## Lincoln Square Hotel

| | |
|---|---|
| Extraordinary | $450 and over |
| Excellent | $350–$449 |
| Very Good | $250–$349 |
| Good | $150–$249 |
| Basic | $75–$149 |
| **Poor** | **under $75** |

Too grim. Fluorescent lighting, a small metal utility closet for your clothes, single-paned windows, a mini-fridge, and a bed (the bed's not too terrible). You are in a nice neighborhood, just not a nice hotel.

**Lincoln Square Hotel,** 166 W. 75th St., New York, NY 10023
**cross streets:** between Columbus and Amsterdam Avenues
**phone:** (212) 873-3000
**fax:** (212) 873-6912
**email:** none
**website:** none
**smoking policy:** designated nonsmoking rooms
**restaurants:** none
**bars:** none
**room service:** none
**parking:** none
**cancellation:** 1 day prior to arrival
**wheelchair accessibility:** public areas — no, rooms — no

## The Lucerne

| | |
|---|---|
| Extraordinary | $450 and over |
| Excellent | $350–$449 |
| Very Good | $250–$349 |
| Good | **$150–$249** |
| **Basic** | $75–$149 |
| Poor | under $75 |

In terms of accommodations, the Upper West Side has been underserved for quite a while, so the 1996 renovation of this 1903 building is welcome. The rooms aren't especially attractive, sporting standard-issue dusty rose and eggplant colors, and simple, conventional furniture. It has also the overly deodorized smell that some hotels can't seem to do without. Windows are single-glazed, and the mattresses are a bit squishy. Small touches, an iron and ironing board, are welcome, but we'd warm up to the Lucerne more if the rates dropped a bit.

**The Lucerne,** 201 W. 79th St., New York, NY 10024
**cross streets:** at Amsterdam Avenue
**phone:** (212) 875-1000, (800) 492-8122
**reservations fax:** (212) 721-1179, guest fax: (212) 362-7251

**email:** travel@superlink.net
**website:** www.newyorkhotel.com
**number of rooms:** 250 (includes 40 suites)
**number of floors:** 12
**smoking policy:** designated nonsmoking rooms
**restaurants:** yes
**bars:** yes
**room service:** yes
**hotel amenities:** fitness equipment, business services, meeting room
**room amenities:** air-conditioning, modem line, VCR on request
**parking:** none
**cancellation:** 4 P.M. day of arrival
**wheelchair accessibility:** public areas — no, rooms — no

## Malibu Hotel

| | |
|---|---|
| Extraordinary | $450 and over |
| Excellent | $350–$449 |
| Very Good | $250–$349 |
| Good | $150–$249 |
| **Basic** | **$75–$149** |
| Poor | under $75 |

For those not familiar with New York, 2688 Broadway, where the Malibu is located, is "way up west" — the neighborhood is fine, but it's about 60 blocks to Times Square. If the location isn't an issue for you (and it is an easy subway ride to get to midtown), this former hostel offers clean, inexpensive lodging. For friends and relatives of Columbia students, it makes especially good sense.

There's not much to the rooms — they're done in black and white decorated with black-and-white photos of contemporary and old New York. Most have high ceilings. Over 80 percent have private baths. The beds are acceptable, there are no closets (just a rack in the room), a clock radio and cable television are about the only amenities, unless you count soap in the bathroom. All rooms have steam heat and air conditioners. The only phones for guests are pay phones in the lobby. No elevators, either — it's five floors in all.

**Malibu Hotel,** 2688 Broadway, New York, NY 10025
**cross streets:** between W. 102nd and W. 103rd Streets
**phone:** (212) 222-2954, (800) 647-2227
**fax:** (212) 678-6842
**email:** rooms@malibuhotelnyc.com
**website:** www.malibuhotelnyc.com
**number of rooms:** 150
**number of floors:** 4
**smoking policy:** all smoking rooms
**restaurants:** none
**bars:** none
**room service:** none

**hotel amenities:** none
**room amenities:** air-conditioning, some shared baths
**parking:** none
**cancellation:** 3 days prior to arrival
**wheelchair accessibility:** public areas — no, rooms — no

## The Mayflower Hotel on the Park

| | |
|---|---|
| Extraordinary | $450 and over |
| Excellent | $350–$449 |
| Very Good | $250–$349 |
| **Good** | **$150–$249** |
| Basic | $75–$149 |
| Poor | under $75 |

A Central Park view for about $200 is one of the compelling reasons to stay at the Mayflower. The thrill of the park's beauty and the satisfaction of a bargain could be considered a quintessential New York moment. The hotel has a lived-in feel to it, rooms with room to breathe, large closets and not-overcrowded bathrooms. While most have pantries and mini-fridges, no cooking is allowed. Amenities are limited in scope: there are hair dryers in all rooms and movies on demand, but only one-line phones, no VCRs, fax machines, or iron and board. The fitness room has a few machines — treadmill, bike, Stairmaster — but no multi-function machine or free weights. The Mayflower hasn't been cutting edge in over 70 years — but it's got that front row seat on the park that's as comfortable as a BarcaLounger.

**The Mayflower Hotel on the Park,** 15 Central Park West, New York, NY 10023
**cross streets:** between W. 61st and W. 62nd Streets
**phone:** (212) 265-0060, (800) 223-4164
**reservations fax:** (212) 265-0227, guest fax: (212) 265-5098
**email:** none
**website:** www.mayflowerhotel.com
**number of rooms:** 365 (includes 180 suites)
**number of floors:** 17
**smoking policy:** designated nonsmoking rooms
**restaurants:** yes
**bars:** yes
**room service:** yes
**hotel amenities:** fitness equipment, laundry and dry cleaning, meeting and function rooms
**room amenities:** air-conditioning, mini-fridge
**parking:** valet
**cancellation:** 4 P.M. day of arrival
**wheelchair accessibility:** public areas — yes, rooms — no

# The Milburn Hotel

| | |
|---|---|
| Extraordinary | $450 and over |
| Excellent | $350–$449 |
| Very Good | $250–$349 |
| Good | **$150–$249** |
| **Basic** | $75–$149 |
| Poor | under $75 |

Perhaps it's not right to say the rooms at the Milburn are just plain ugly, but they are just plain. There are a number of amenities: two-line phones, safe, iron and board, clock radio, hair dryer, Caswell-Massey products and a phone in the bathroom. Each room has a kitchenette with range and fridge (there are excellent markets within a couple of blocks), microwave, coffeepot, and coffee. Pots and pans are available on request.

Some mattresses are a little saggy, and smoking is permitted in all rooms. On the higher floors, pressure is less strong, as usual, than on the lower floors. Rooms and closets tend to be at least adequate in size. Even if the design is drab, the rooms are clean and moderately priced. The Upper West Side location is a plus for many visitors.

The Milburn is clearly trying hard, offering a fair number of amenities (a new exercise room has two treadmills and a bike). If ambience is not paramount for you, the Milburn may be a reasonable choice.

**The Milburn Hotel,** 242 W. 76th St., New York, NY 10023
**cross streets:** between Broadway and West End Ave.
**phone:** (212) 362-1006, (800) 833-9622
**fax:** (212) 721-5476
**email:** milburn@milburnhotel.com
**website:** www.milburnhotel.com
**number of rooms:** 111 (includes 56 suites)
**number of floors:** 15
**smoking policy:** all smoking rooms
**restaurants:** none
**bars:** none
**room service:** none
**hotel amenities:** self-service laundry room, meeting or function room
**room amenities:** air-conditioning, kitchen, modem line, safe
**parking:** none
**cancellation:** 2 P.M. 3 days prior to arrival for stays of a week or more; 2 P.M. 1 day prior to arrival for stays under a week
**wheelchair accessibility:** public areas — yes, rooms — yes

## On The Ave

| | |
|---|---|
| Extraordinary | $450 and over |
| Excellent | $350–$449 |
| **Very Good** | $250–$349 |
| Good | **$150–$249** |
| Basic | $75–$149 |
| Poor | under $75 |

Ever since a roach divebombed us from the ceiling, we avoided the hotel that was previously on this site, and we weren't thrilled about coming back for a look. A few minutes into our visit, however, it became quite clear that this is no longer a roach hotel. In fact, it is an extremely attractive hotel and the most stylish place to stay in the area.

When we visited, the renovation wasn't complete — many rooms are waiting for their makeover and the lobby is temporary. From what we saw, however, Warren Bohn and Associates has done a lovely job of creating serene contemporary rooms where Upper West Siders will be happy to stash friends and relatives, and said friends and relatives should find quite satisfactory (unless contemporary isn't their thing).

Rooms come in three sizes: standard, then the larger superior, then deluxe. For $175, even a standard feels roomy. One of the more distinctive features is the "floating bed" about which designer Kelly Woodruff says, "The concept for the room was to create a clean, almost a Zen, environment. They have an element of engulfing you, protecting and calming." The earth tones are even extended to the ecru-colored sheets. You know when a hotel is paying this much attention to the beds that they're on the right track.

There are one-line phones with dataport and voice mail, clock radio, a bedtray (also good for laptops), hair dryer, Gilchrist and Soames bath products, iron and ironing board. The bathrooms are marble with slate floors and custom-designed stainless sinks. Some of them have a window from which you have Upper West Side views. Not all have tub and shower — some are shower only, so specify if you have a preference.

About the name — it may take a moment for locals to get — our first thought was *What* avenue? Broadway may be an avenue in the sense that it runs, sort of, north and south, but nobody thinks of it as an avenue, it's just Broadway.

**On the Ave,** 2178 Broadway, New York, NY 10024
**cross streets:** at W. 77th Street
**phone:** (212) 362-1100
**fax:** (212) 787-9521
**email:** ontheave@stayinny.com
**website:** www.stayinny.com
**number of rooms:** 250 (includes 15 suites)
**number of floors:** 15

**smoking policy:** designated nonsmoking floors
**restaurants:** none
**bars:** none
**room service:** yes, 24 hours
**hotel amenities:** laundry and dry cleaning
**room amenities:** air-conditioning, modem line, mini-fridge on request
**parking:** none
**cancellation:** 4 P.M. 1 day prior to arrival
**wheelchair accessibility:** public areas — yes, rooms — yes

## Park West Studios

| | |
|---|---|
| Extraordinary | $450 and over |
| Excellent | $350–$449 |
| Very Good | $250–$349 |
| Good | $150–$249 |
| Basic | $75–$149 |
| **Poor** | **under $75** |

This old and worn out hotel on the upper reaches of Central Park West was about to be closed for renovations. Not a moment too soon. As it is, one creaky elevator (painted hot pink inside), dark guest room hallways, unadorned rooms with an old TV, sink, single-paned windows, fluorescent lighting and shared baths. Radiators are peeling and stained. The Park West, in this condition, is not recommended. If and when the renovation is complete, it may well be worth a second look.

**Park West Studios,** 465 Central Park West, New York, NY 10025
**cross streets:** between W. 106th and W. 107th Streets
**phone:** (212) 866-1880
**fax:** (212) 316-9555
**email:** spstudios@aol.com
**website:** none
**number of rooms:** 60
**number of floors:** 7
**smoking policy:** designated nonsmoking floors
**restaurants:** none
**bars:** none
**room service:** none
**hotel amenities:** laundry, all shared baths
**room amenities:** TV
**parking:** none
**cancellation:** noon 1 day prior to arrival
**wheelchair accessibility:** public areas — yes, rooms — yes

## The Phillips Club

| | |
|---|---|
| Extraordinary | **$450 and over*** |
| Excellent | $350–$449 |
| **Very Good** | $250–$349 |
| Good | **$150–$249**** |
| Basic | $75–$149 |
| Poor | under $75 |

There would be no horseracing if everyone agreed on everything, so it's perfectly possible that you will like the Phillips Club more than we do. This extended stay property opened in 1996, and while extended stay properties are needed on the West Side (there are more on the other side of town), the Phillips thinks small.

A little desk has been jerryrigged for Phillips Club guests into the back corner of a condominium lobby. It is the first clue that space is at a premium here. Your first impression of the guest rooms may be favorable — they are done in sleek, modern style, gray, black, white and brown. Your second impression may be less favorable — the living room is small, the bedroom is small, the bathroom is smaller. Comparable properties on the East Side, such as the Bristol Plaza, have far more room in their rooms.

The amenity list is good: two-line phones with dataport and voice mail, clock radio, CD, VCR, iron and ironing board, safe, and hair dryer. A kitchen comes fully outfitted with range, refrigerator, microwave, toaster, pots and pans, silverware, even dish towels. Neutrogena products are in the bathroom, which may be small enough to make the Neutrogena soap bar look like a brick.

Daily maid service is standard, and there is a washer and dryer on each floor. There is no business center (the front desk will handle simple services such as faxing and copying) and no fitness center. Guests do get a break at the nearby Reebok Club — it's $90 for two weeks — a fair price for the excellent, though otherwise expensive, facility. Gas and electricity are included in the rate, but there is a charge for local and long distance calls.

The closets have cheap doors and shelving, and not enough hangers. One closet door couldn't open all the way because it would have hit the bed. In another, it would have been impossible to hang much of anything because a dresser was in it.

When you need an extended stay hotel on the West Side, the Phillips Club is fine, unless you need to spread out.

**The Phillips Club,** 155 W. 66th Street, New York, NY 10023
**cross streets:** at Broadway
**phone:** (212) 835-8800, (877) 854-8800
**fax:** (212) 835-8850
**email:** concierge@phillipsclub.com
**website:** www.phillipsclub.com
**number of rooms:** 96 (all apartments)
**number of floors:** 4
**smoking policy:** all smoking
**restaurants:** none

**bars:** none
**room service:** none
**hotel amenities:** self-serve laundry, dry cleaning
**room amenities:** air-conditioning, kitchens, VCR, fax, modem line, safe
**parking:** none
**cancellation:** 6 P.M. 1 day prior to arrival for nightly rooms. Extended stay guests sign a lease.
**wheelchair accessibility:** public areas — yes rooms — yes. ADA compliant
**notes:** * nightly rate; ** extended-stay rate, 30-day minimum stay

## The Quality Hotel on Broadway

| | |
|---|---|
| Extraordinary | $450 and over |
| Excellent | $350–$449 |
| Very Good | $250–$349 |
| **Good** | $150–$249 |
| Basic | **$75–$149** |
| Poor | under $75 |

This 1915 building had a top to bottom renovation that began in 1998 and was finishing up when we visited. The Upper West Side is finally starting to get a number of hotels and the Quality is a welcome addition. Its location at 94th and Broadway may seem out of the way for visitors not overly familiar with the city, but it's right by a subway entrance and only two express stops to Times Square.

Red-carpeted hallways have a crisp confidence to them, with prints on the walls, mostly of French Impressionist works. The majority of the traditionally designed rooms are king-bedded, and the Simmons mattresses they have chosen are quite good. Amenities include a clock radio, one-line phone with dataport, but no voice mail. Windows are single-paned, there is a desk and swivel chair, three drawer dressers for clothing and a clothesline over the bathtub. You'll also find a coffeepot and coffee, hair dryer, phone and makeup mirror in the bathroom, though only shampoo and soap for bath products. There are sprinklers, smoke detectors, and electronic locks. Iron and ironing board are available on request.

Closets are average size, and rooms are acceptable in terms of space, but the ceilings are low. There is no room service, no fitness room (though one is planned), and noise may be audible in the rooms from Broadway. While there are dataports in the rooms, one guest asked the front desk when we were there if there was a way the hotel could check their E-mail for them. No. When the guests asked where the nearest place to do that was, they were told Kinko's at 120th and Broadway. If there is really nothing closer within 26 blocks, the hotel should accommodate guests in some way.

**The Quality Hotel on Broadway,** 215 W. 94th St., New York, NY 10025
**cross streets:** between Broadway and Amsterdam Avenue
**phone:** (212) 866-6400, (800) 834-2972
**fax:** (212) 866-1357
**email:** none
**website:** www.bestnyhotels.com
**number of rooms:** 348 (includes 6 suites)
**number of floors:** 14
**smoking policy:** designated nonsmoking rooms
**restaurants:** none
**bars:** none
**room service:** none
**hotel amenities:** fitness center
**room amenities:** air-conditioning
**parking:** none
**cancellation:** 4 P.M. 1 day prior to arrival
**wheelchair accessibility:** public areas — yes, rooms — yes

## Riverside Tower Hotel

| | |
|---|---|
| Extraordinary | $450 and over |
| Excellent | $350–$449 |
| Very Good | $250–$349 |
| Good | $150–$249 |
| **Basic** | **$75–$149** |
| Poor | under $75 |

In spite of the owner's assertion that the Riverside is a good value, we don't agree.

Demerits for a surly front desk, dark hallways with stained carpets and luggage-bruised walls, cramped rooms with noise from the West Side Highway, old everything — mattresses, TV, furniture — and virtually no hotel amenities. The pistachio-colored walls seem like a graphic representation of nausea. In the rooms are a mini-fridge, one-line phone and a desk. The water pressure is acceptable. On the plus side, some rooms have an engaging view of Riverside Park and the Hudson.

The hotel claims to be on the Hudson River but is no such thing. And plenty of hotels have a view of the river. Let's be plain: at $50 it would be a bargain, at $100, it's a dump.

**Riverside Tower Hotel,** 80 Riverside Dr., New York, NY 10024
**cross streets:** at W. 80th Street
**phone:** (212) 877-5200, (800) 724-3136
**fax:** (212) 873-1400
**email:** none
**website:** www.travelweb.com
**number of rooms:** 75 (includes 45 suites)
**number of floors:** 16
**smoking policy:** designated nonsmoking rooms
**restaurants:** none
**bars:** none

**room service:** none
**hotel amenities:** laundry
**room amenities:** air-conditioning
**parking:** none
**cancellation:** 11 P.M. 1 day prior arrival
**wheelchair accessibility:** public areas — yes, rooms — yes

## Trump International Hotel and Tower

| **Extraordinary** | **$450 and over** |
|---|---|
| Excellent | **$350–$449** |
| Very Good | $250–$349 |
| Good | $150–$249 |
| Basic | $75–$149 |
| Poor | under $75 |

Old joke:

"The Plotnick diamond comes with a curse."

"What's the curse?"

"*Mister* Plotnick."

The Trump International may be considered a diamond with a curse — controversial Donald Trump is, we think it's fair to say, not universally beloved by New Yorkers. He's the Plotnick part. Even so, it is hard to imagine any New Yorker (or, more to the point) any visitor, finding fault with the diamond-of-a-hotel that bears his name. It is simply beautiful.

Rooms with a view over Central Park are the most prized. You can gaze at the panorama of the park or, as each room comes with a small telescope, focus on a single leaf. Those rooms with a "city view" over Broadway lose some of the magic.

They retain their luxuriousness, though. Designed by Costas Kondylis (Philip Johnson did the exterior makeover of what was the Gulf and Western building), the rooms are restrained sumptuousness, contemporary but timeless-looking, with warm, soft beiges and honey colors predominating.

The hotel is located at a busy crossroads of New York, just above Columbus Circle, in between Broadway and Central Park West. Yet the rooms are quiet enough for meditation. They're roomy, too: the smallest are about 400 square feet. Closets are generous enough to recall the golden days of travel when that meant steamer trunks, rather than carry-on.

You wouldn't need, however, to brink a trunk of amenities. Rooms are outfitted with TV, VCR, Nintendo, CD player, fax, clock radio, two-line phones with dataport, direct-in dial, voice mail, umbrella, garment bag, Frette bathrobes, slippers, safe, clothes steamer, iron and board. Beds have Frette linen.

The bathrooms are Italian marble and come with a Jacuzzi. The majority of the rooms have kitchens — range top, dishwasher, Limoges china.

This last note about the kitchens is important, even if you

have no intention of scrambling an egg. The four-star restaurant Jean Georges is part of the hotel, and if you don't feel like eating in the dining room, one of the sous-chefs of the restaurant will come up to your room and prepare a meal for you. No hotel in town has anything like a similar perk.

The impressive health club is open to hotel guests and condo residents only. In addition to all the machines you want, there is a lap pool, steam and sauna. Two of the three concierges on staff have the Clefs d'Or designation. There is no business center to speak of, but business services are available. At the Trump, that could mean a complimentary laptop for your room if you need it.

The Trump is a small hotel (167 rooms), which means it has time to do the little things right, too. Night turndown service includes a silver tray on your bed with a rose, an apple and de Granvelle chocolate. That should make for sweet dreams.

**Trump International Hotel & Tower,** 1 Central Park West, New York, NY 10023
**cross streets:** between Columbus Circle and W. 61st Street
**phone:** (212) 299-1000, (888) 448-7867
**fax:** (212) 299-1150
**email:** chamaty@trumpintl.com
**website:** www.trumpintl.com
**number of rooms:** 167 (includes 128 suites)
**number of floors:** building has 52 floors, hotel rooms are on floors 3-17
**smoking policy:** designated nonsmoking rooms
**restaurants:** Jean Georges
**bars:** yes
**room service:** yes, 24 hours
**hotel amenities:** health club, swimming pool, concierge, laundry and dry cleaning, business center, meeting and function rooms
**room amenities:** air-conditioning, kitchen, mini-bar, VCR, Jacuzzi, modem line, safe
**parking:** valet
**cancellation:** 4 P.M. 1 day prior to arrival
**wheelchair accessibility:** public areas — yes, rooms — yes. ADA compliant

## West Side Inn

| | |
|---|---|
| Extraordinary | $450 and over |
| Excellent | $350–$449 |
| Very Good | $250–$349 |
| Good | $150–$249 |
| **Basic** | $75–$149 |
| Poor | **under $75** |

Each room has a bright color of paint but is otherwise the most basic of basic accommodations. Those looking for cheap sleeps near Columbia may find the West Side Inn just right. It's clean and the staff seems friendly. For about $50, you'll get a room with a bed, sink, mini-fridge, a rack in the room for a closet, some with an air conditioner. Three or four rooms share a bath. There's an Internet kiosk in the lobby.

**West Side Inn,** 237 W. 107th St., New York, NY 10025
**cross streets:** between Amsterdam Avenue and Broadway
**phone:** (212) 866-0061
**fax:** (212) 866-0062
**email:** westsideinn@hotmail.com
**website:** none
**number of rooms:** 105
**number of floors:** 6
**smoking policy:** designated nonsmoking rooms
**restaurants:** none
**bars:** none
**room service:** none
**hotel amenities:** laundry
**room amenities:** kitchenettes (not equipped), TV
**parking:** none
**cancellation:** noon 1 day prior to arrival
**wheelchair accessibility:** public areas — no, rooms — no

## West Side YMCA

| | |
|---|---|
| Extraordinary | $450 and over |
| Excellent | $350–$449 |
| Very Good | $250–$349 |
| Good | $150–$249 |
| **Basic** | **$75–$149** |
| Poor | under $75 |

Plain, simple, clean rooms for not much money have long been the Y's stock-in-trade, lodging-wise. At this location, most have shared baths and few have phones. Those that do can only receive calls. The design scheme is linoleum floors, a dresser with three drawers, desk, a bunk or single bed, cable TV, a coat of white paint on the walls, air-conditioning, one overhead light and single-paned windows.

Closets have a half dozen or so hangers and perhaps two shelves. Towels are provided. The vast majority of the rooms do not have baths en suite. For security, the women's bathrooms have a key code you have to punch for entry.

As is generally the case with the Ys, a big perk is the free use of their gym. The one here is enormous — including a pool — with virtually any kind of workout possible, from medicine ball to the latest cardio machine. Shuttles leave from the Y's front door to all three area airports.

**West Side YMCA,** 5 W. 63rd St., New York, NY 10023
**cross streets:** between Central Park West and Broadway
**phone:** (212) 875-4273, (800) 348-9622
**fax:** (212) 875-1334
**email:** none
**website:** www.ymcanyc.org
**number of rooms:** 500
**number of floors:** 8
**smoking policy:** all nonsmoking rooms
**restaurants:** yes
**bars:** none
**room service:** yes
**hotel amenities:** some shared baths, health club, two swimming pools, steam room, saunas, laundry
**room amenities:** air-conditioning
**parking:** none
**cancellation:** 3 days prior to arrival
**wheelchair accessibility:** public areas — yes, rooms — yes, ADA compliant
**notes:** no children under 10 years of age

# Wyman House

| | |
|---|---|
| Extraordinary | $450 and over |
| Excellent | $350–$449 |
| **Very Good** | $250–$349 |
| Good | **$150–$249\*** |
| Basic | $75–$149 |
| Poor | under $75 |

This 1886 house on Riverside Drive has been tenderly cared for, so you get rooms with character and some remarkable details — the carved alabaster fireplace comes to mind. There's a Victorian feel to some of the rooms, but it's not overdone — there's a light touch at work. Modern amenities come in the form of AC (except in one room), clock radio, hair dryer, iron and ironing board, answering machine and a full kitchen. The kitchen consists of a stove, toaster oven, coffee maker and most everything else you'd need in that department. Guests receive a start-up basket consisting of muffins, jam, yogurt, orange juice and coffee. We particularly like the views of the Hudson from the penthouse terrace.

You should know that Wyman House has a three-night minimum, doesn't take kids under 10 or pets and there's no smoking allowed. Maid service is provided after three nights.

A lovely way to experience the Upper West Side and New York.

**Wyman House,** Riverside Dr., New York, NY 10023
**cross streets:** at W. 75th Street
**phone:** (212) 472-2000, (800) 835-8880
**fax:** none
**email:** none
**website:** www.abodenyc.com
**number of rooms:** 6
**number of floors:** 4
**smoking policy:** all nonsmoking rooms
**restaurants:** none
**bars:** none
**room service:** none
**hotel amenities:** kitchen (equipped)
**room amenities:** air-conditioning
**parking:** none
**cancellation:** 14 days prior to arrival
**wheelchair accessibility:** public areas — no, rooms — no
**note:** \*three-night minimum stay

# UPPER EAST SIDE

| Hotel | Price Range | Rating |
|---|---|---|
| Barbizon | $250–$449 | Very Good |
| The Bentley | $250–$349 | Very Good |
| The Bridge Suite Apartments | $75–$149 | Good |
| Bristol Plaza | $150–$249 | Excellent |
| The Carlyle | $350 and over | Extraordinary |
| Carnegie Hill Suites | $150–$249 | Good |
| De Hirsch at the 92nd St Y | under $75 | Basic |
| The Franklin | $150–$249 | Good |
| The Gracie Inn | $150–$349 | Good |
| The Helmsley Carlton Hotel | $450 and over | Very Good |
| Hotel Wales | $150–$249 | Very Good |
| The Lowell | $350–$449 | Excellent |
| Lyden Gardens | $250–$349 | Good |
| The Mark | $450 and over | Excellent |
| The Marmara-Manhattan | $150–$249 | Excellent |
| Plaza Athénée | $250–$449 | Very Good |
| The Regency, A Loews Hotel | $350–$449 | Excellent |
| The Sherry-Netherland | $350 and over | Excellent |
| The Stanhope | $350–$449 | Excellent |
| Surrey Hotel | $350–$449 | Very Good |

## NEIGHBORHOOD BOUNDARIES

South — E. 59th St., West — Fifth Ave., North — E. 96th St.,
East — East River

## ABOUT THE NEIGHBORHOOD

Commercial at the southern end, the Upper East Side becomes
increasingly residential as you go north. The apartments and
brownstones on Park and Fifth Avenues are some of the most
desirable in the city. Madison Ave. from 59th St. on up is loaded
with shopping and Fifth Ave. is bordered by Central Park from
59th St. to 110th St. The neighborhood called Carnegie Hill
which runs, roughly, from 86th to 96th between Fifth Ave. and
Lexington Ave. is one of the highest points on the island. Shade
trees and the sidewalk benches provided by neighborhood mer-
chants make it feel like an oasis from urban pressures.

## TRANSPORTATION

The 4, 5, and 6 trains run along Lexington Ave. with stops at E.
59th St., E. 68th St., E. 77th St. E. 86th St and E. 96th St.

## LANDMARKS

Museum Mile is the name given to the part of Fifth Ave. that contains, among other institutions, The Metropolitan Museum of Art at 82nd St. 879-5500, the Solomon R. Guggenheim Museum between 88th and 89th 423-3500, the Cooper-Hewitt Museum at 91st St. 860-6868, the Jewish Museum at 92nd St. 423-3230, and the International Center for Photography's uptown exhibition space at 94th St. 860-1777. The Whitney Museum of American Art is located on Madison Ave. at 75th St. 570-3676. On Park Avenue you will find the Asia Society at 70th St. 288-6400. The very special Frick Collection, with its choice selection of European masterpieces, is located at 1 E. 70th St. 288-0700. Gracie Mansion, the official residence of the mayor of New York, is located in Carl Schurz Park at 88th St and East End Ave. 570-4751. It can be visited by guided tour once a week. If a person could be considered a landmark, that person would have to be Bobby Short, who has been performing at the Cafe Carlyle, 35 E. 76th St. 744-1600, for more than 30 years now.

## SHOPPING

Bloomingdale's, Lexington and 59th St. 705-2000, Barneys NY at Madison and 61st St. 826-8900, and Crate and Barrel at Madison and 59th 308-0011, are within a few blocks of one another. The shops along Madison Avenue are an encyclopedia of clothing designers. You will find stores from Calvin Klein, 645 Madison 292-9000, Giorgio Armani, 760 Madison 988-9191, Prada, 28 E. 70th 327-4200, Ralph Lauren, 867 Madison 606-2100, Valentino, 747 Madison 772-6969, Krizia, 769 Madison 879-1211, BCBG, 770 Madison 717-4225, Nicole Miller, 780 Madison 288-9779, Emanuel Ungaro, 792 Madison 249-4090, Moschino, 803 Madison 639-9600, Kenzo 805 Madison 717-0101, Dolce & Gabbana, 825 Madison 249-4100, Sonia Rykiel, 849 Madison 396-3060, Yves St. Laurent, 855 Madison 988-3821, and others. There are also fancy linens at Leron, 750 Madison 249-3188 and Frette, 799 Madison 988-5221, leather goods at Dooney & Bourke, 759 Madison 439-1657 and Coach, 710 Madison 319-1772, interesting table settings at MacKenzie-Childs, 824 Madison 570-6050, and Pierre Deux, 870 Madison 570-9343, and fine gifts at Adrien Linford, 927 Madison 628-4500. Don't miss the display of new and vintage wrist watches at Time Will Tell, 962 Madison 861-2663.

## EATING AND DRINKING

Cafe Crocodile, 354 E. 74th St. 249-6619, is a charming restaurant set into a town house serving Mediterranean-inspired French food. Sarabeth's, inside both the Hotel Wales, 410-7335, and the Whitney Museum, 570-3670, serves good breakfasts and brunches. Butterfield 81, 170 E. 81st 288-2700, and La Fourchette, 1608 1st Ave. 249-5924, are for fine dining without a lot of fuss. The Lobster Club, 24 E. 80th 249-6500, features creative riffs on home cooking by chef Anne Rosenzweig. Park View at the Boathouse, Central Park Lake 517-2233, is best for drinking in the view over the lake. Payard Pâtisserie, 1032 Lexington 717-5252, brings the French pastry shop window to New York — and a well-liked restaurant, to boot. Daniel, 60 E. 65th St. 288-0033, just keeps getting rave reviews. Park Ave. Cafe, 100 E. 63rd St. 644-1900, is an enjoyable, if noisy, place for grownups and Serendipity 3, 225 E. 60th St. 838-3531, is where the sweet sixteeners, and everyone else, goes for their frozen hot chocolates.

For information on new hotels, ongoing updates, and directions to each hotel by car or mass transit, check online at New York Today, www.nytoday.com/hotels.

# THE HOTELS

## Barbizon

| | |
|---|---|
| Extraordinary | $450 and over |
| Excellent | **$350–$449** |
| **Very Good** | **$250–$349** |
| Good | $150–$249 |
| Basic | $75–$149 |
| Poor | under $75 |

The Barbizon opened in 1927 as a hotel for women. With the Barbizon's purchase by hotelier Ian Schrager (Royalton, Paramount) and the presence of the stylish gym Equinox on the ground floor, the Barbizon seems to have relinquished its past for a leap into the future. Its location, at the southern end of the Upper East Side, remains a prime asset.

There is a substantial "but." Over one-third of the hotel has rooms that are 10 feet by 12 feet. This would be fine if you slept vertically, but a queen-sized bed, which most of these rooms have, means you have just enough room to sleep but no room to gather your thoughts.

It's the other two-thirds of the hotel that we can recommend with enthusiasm. The property completed a renovation in November, 1998 but they were initiated by the company that owned the hotel before Mr. Schrager. Don't expect his ultra-contemporary style. The rooms are contemporary looking, but not in a high concept way — peach, dusty rose, and celadon are featured in the palette and there are white shutters where there would be cabinet doors and in front of the double-paned windows.

Amenities include two-line phones with dataport and voice mail, mini-fridge, clock radio, safe, hair dryer and makeup mirror. There is also a CD player — if you haven't brought any, look through their menu of CDs, call housekeeping, and they'll bring one to your room. Bathrooms have an extra square foot or two, compared to the average in town, but they're still likely to seem small to visitors. The asset of the Lexington Avenue location can be considered a drawback when it comes to noise — light sleepers may have some difficulties.

Guests get complimentary use of the Equinox health club on the ground floor. This large, full-service club has everything you could want in the way of machines as well as a pool, Jacuzzi, steam, sauna and spa.

As with most hotels, there are a number of levels of accommodations, beginning with standard, then superior, deluxe, executive suites, one-bedroom suites and the top-of-the-line tower suites. These tower suites are worth a special note. Located from the 18th to the 22nd floors, the Moorish influence of the hotel's design is in evidence, particularly the arched forms of the terraces. The penthouse suite is also a knockout. In it, there is a loft area library and writing desk. From that desk, you can look out the large windows and get a view of Central Park. There isn't a better place to write a letter in New York. You might even find yourself writing home about the Barbizon.

**Barbizon,** 140 E. 63rd St., New York, NY 10021
**cross streets:** at Lexington Avenue
**phone:** (212) 838-5700, (800) 223-1020
**reservations fax:** (212) 223-3287, guest fax: (212) 888-4271
**email:** none
**website:** none
**number of rooms:** 306 (includes 27 suites)
**number of floors:** 22
**smoking policy:** designated nonsmoking rooms
**restaurants:** none
**bars:** none
**room service:** yes
**hotel amenities:** concierge, laundry and dry cleaning
**room amenities:** air-conditioning, mini-bar, modem line, safe
**parking:** valet
**cancellation:** 4 P.M. day of arrival
**wheelchair accessibility:** public areas — yes, rooms — yes. ADA compliant

# The Bentley

| | |
|---|---|
| Extraordinary | $450 and over |
| Excellent | $350–$449 |
| **Very Good** | **$250–$349** |
| Good | $150–$249 |
| Basic | $75–$149 |
| Poor | under $75 |

Hoteliers put hotels where they think people will stay. York and 62nd Street wouldn't be the first area to come to *our* mind in Manhattan, or the twentieth either. It's not at all a bad area, it just feels far from what's at the top of most visitors' lists. Walking east and downhill from more familiar pedestrian zones, even then you may look twice at the building that has the address of your hotel. It looks like an office building; in fact, it was.

Once you're inside, though, the Bentley reveals itself to be a very pleasant surprise. The lobby is strikingly stylish — a space with high ceilings, with an ultra contemporary design in moss and beige tones as well as lots of black and white, a huge floral display, billowy curtains, stocked bookshelves and a 24-hour espresso/cappuccino machine. Most New Yorkers would probably have a hard time describing the gist of York Avenue in the 60s but this would certainly not be it.

This is the flagship property in the hotel chain called the Amsterdam Hospitality Group. While we have concerns about maintenance in some of their other properties, the Bentley, which opened early in 1998, looks quite spiffy. The rooms are clean and comfortable, if somewhat spare-looking. Bedding is new and seems to be of good quality, there are one-line phones with dataport and voice mail. Amenities include iron and ironing board, clock radio, CD player, Nintendo, hair dryer and a phone in the bathroom. Water pressure checks out well. There are only single-paned windows — a drawback — but the rooms seem fairly quiet anyway. Closets can be very small.

Given the hotel's offbeat location, it has some unusual city views. There are invigorating, if not beautiful, views facing west to the East Side, and even more compelling is the up-close look at the 59th Street Bridge. The Bentley offers a complimentary continental breakfast in its rooftop restaurant (there's an outdoor roof terrace) which strikes us as a goldmine in waiting.

It's a pleasant surprise when you walk in here and it's surely an equally pleasant surprise when you leave: rates are generally modest.

**The Bentley,** 500 E. 62nd St., New York, NY 10021
**cross streets:** at York Avenue
**phone:** (212) 644-6000, (800) 664-6835 (66HOTEL)
**reservations fax:** (212) 751-7868, guest fax: (212) 207-4800
**email:** none
**website:** www.nychotel.com
**number of rooms:** 197 (includes 21 suites)
**number of floors:** 21

**smoking policy:** designated nonsmoking rooms
**restaurants:** yes
**bars:** yes
**room service:** yes
**hotel amenities:** laundry and dry cleaning, meeting and function room
**room amenities:** air-conditioning, VCR on request, modem line
**parking:** yes
**cancellation:** 3 P.M. 1 day prior to arrival
**wheelchair accessibility:** public areas — no, rooms — no

## The Bridge Suite Apartments

| | |
|---|---|
| Extraordinary | $450 and over |
| Excellent | $350–$449 |
| Very Good | $250–$349 |
| **Good** | $150–$249 |
| Basic | **$75–$149*** |
| Poor | under $75 |

Most of the extended stay hotels in the city emphasize their luxury amenities. Bridge Suite is more modest and commensurately less expensive. The bridge referred to is the 59th Street Bridge, which means the location is far east at 59th Street. This makes it particularly convenient for those who need access to the East Side hospitals or the U.N. but makes it less so for those in town on the more conventional sightseeing route.

Bridge Suite is made up of several former apartment buildings. The style of the accommodations would be familiar to many New York apartment dwellers: hardwood floors, white walls and a brick wall, and (not separate) kitchen. The kitchen includes a stove, refrigerator, pots and pans, and dishes. Amenities include a clock radio and hair dryer. A coin-op laundry is located on the ground floor — there is no maid service. Mattresses are adequate, windows are double-paned, phones are one-line with voice mail. A pleasant courtyard with plants and flowers has a table and chairs where you could enjoy your morning paper.

**The Bridge Suite Apartments,** 351 E. 60th St., New York, NY 10022
**cross streets:** at First Avenue
**phone:** (212) 221-8300
**fax:** (212) 704-0915
**email:** bridgeste@aol.com
**website:** www.bridgesuites.com
**number of rooms:** 100 (all apartments)
**number of floors:** 5
**smoking policy:** all smoking rooms
**restaurants:** yes
**bars:** none

**room service:** none
**hotel amenities:** concierge, laundry
**room amenities:** air-conditioning, kitchens (equipped)
**parking:** none
**cancellation:** forfeit 1 month's rent upon cancellation
**wheelchair accessibility:** public areas — no, rooms — no
**\*notes:** minimum stay 30 days

## Bristol Plaza

| | |
|---|---|
| Extraordinary | $450 and over |
| **Excellent** | $350–$449 |
| Very Good | $250–$349 |
| Good | **$150–$249\*** |
| Basic | $75–$149 |
| Poor | under $75 |

The Bristol Plaza is an extended stay apartment building (one-month minimum) that is so appealing that you may easily want to extend your extended stay as long as possible.

Traditionally decorated apartments have a generous number of windows, a three-line phone with direct inward dial, dataport, voice mail, clock radio, VCR, safe, iron and ironing board and marble bathrooms. Kitchens include refrigerator, range, microwave, dishwasher, coffee maker, pots and pans and utensils. There is daily maid service and a coin-operated washer and dryer on each floor. The basics are well covered, too: bedding is comfortable, water pressure is good, and windows are double-paned, though you may get some street noise. Electricity is billed separately.

Other assets include complimentary use of a most attractive, glass-enclosed heated pool, small but adequate health club and an outside terrace for sunbathing. There is steam and sauna in the men's locker room, a sauna in the ladies' locker room and a masseur on call. The health club and pool are open only to extended stay guests and adjacent condo residents. On-site parking is available for an additional charge.

The Bristol attracts a wide variety of guests, actors shooting a movie, those affiliated with the U.N. and people receiving medical treatment from nearby hospitals. It looks as though it would serve them all well.

**Bristol Plaza,** 210 E. 65th St., New York, NY 10021
**cross streets:** at Third Avenue
**phone:** (212) 753-7900
**reservations fax:** (212) 753-7905, guest fax: (212) 980-3457
**email:** none
**website:** none
**number of rooms:** 167 (all apartments)
**number of floors:** 22
**smoking policy:** all smoking
**restaurants:** none

**bars:** none
**room service:** none
**hotel amenities:** health club, swimming pool, laundry and dry cleaning
**room amenities:** air-conditioning, kitchen, VCR, safe, fax on request, modem line
**parking:** yes
**cancellation:** 30 days prior to arrival
**wheelchair accessibility:** public areas — yes, rooms — yes
**\*notes:** minimum stay 30 days

## The Carlyle

| **Extraordinary** | **$450 and over** |
|---|---|
| Excellent | **$350–$449** |
| Very Good | $250–$349 |
| Good | $150–$249 |
| Basic | $75–$149 |
| Poor | under $75 |

Baden-Baden isn't a jogging sort of town. Germany's famous spa center is stately and elegant. The historic city's Brenner's Park Hotel is quintessential Baden-Baden: it is a hotel that keeps time not by check-in and check-out but in markers of decades and generations. The Carlyle is New York's answer to Brenner's Park, discreet and glamorous.

About half of the Carlyle is comprised of permanent residents and that is reflected in its distinctly un-public lobby. Though it doesn't invite you to park on a pouf for a few hours, the subdued lobby has a shiny black marble floor, soft light and an unmistakable aura of glamour. You aren't likely to see many joggers traipsing through the place. Fifty years ago you would have seen the delightful bell captain, Michael O'Connell, and the same was true when we last visited. As with Brenner's Park, the Carlyle is about continuity.

It is also about discretion, and it is that discretion which draws the moneyed, the power brokers and the well-known. The rooms were originally designed by Dorothy Draper and more recently by Mark Hampton. Understated, traditional elegance and little frippery gives the rooms a timeless feel. You'll find chintz coverlets, satin-covered chairs and most have wooden floors with a large area rug, imparting a character that wall-to-wall does not. A full roster of amenities includes Scalamandré bedspreads, VCR, CD player, tape deck, umbrella, fax, safe, hair dryer and scale. There are also, however, room amenities here that you won't find most places: several types of hangers (skirts, pants), a tie rack and bed tray. Many prefer the rooms on the higher floors, in the tower. They're not large, but the light and the views, particularly those overlooking Central Park, are enthralling.

The fully-equipped gym, open only to hotel guests, is especially attractive. For the more sedentary, Bobby Short and Barbara Cook perform regularly in Cafe Carlyle while Barbara Carroll entertains in Bemelman's Bar with its famously charming murals. Even Brenner's Park can't top that mix of continuity and star power.

**The Carlyle,** 35 E. 76th St., New York, NY 10021
**cross streets:** at Madison Avenue
**phone:** (212) 744-1600, (800) 227-5737
**fax:** (212) 717-4682
**email:** none
**website:** none
**number of rooms:** 190 (including 52 suites)
**number of floors:** 34
**smoking policy:** all smoking rooms
**restaurants:** 2
**bars:** 2
**room service:** yes, 24 hours
**hotel amenities:** health club, concierge, laundry and dry cleaning, business services, meeting and function rooms
**room amenities:** air-conditioning, mini-bar, VCR, fax, modem line, safe
**parking:** valet
**cancellation:** 6 P.M. day prior to arrival
**wheelchair accessibility:** public areas — yes, rooms — yes

## Carnegie Hill Suites

| | |
|---|---|
| Extraordinary | $450 and over |
| Excellent | $350–$449 |
| Very Good | $250–$349 |
| **Good** | **$150–$249** |
| Basic | $75–$149 |
| Poor | under $75 |

If you've been to New York but haven't discovered the Carnegie Hill neighborhood, you're in for a treat. A good way to get a feel for it is by staying at either the Hotel Wales or here. The Carnegie Hill isn't a bed and breakfast or a hotel — it's an oddity — but it has some appealing features. Rooms are large, there is a one-line phone and answering machine, CD player, clock radio, nonworking fireplaces, microwave and coffeepot, pants press, iron and ironing board. Some of the rooms have a full, serious desktop computer up and running for you. You won't find that everywhere. In fact, you won't find that anywhere else in New York. Maintenance isn't perfect here — scuffs and stains — so the Carnegie feels lived in, it's not pristine. There are no elevators and no hotel amenities, but the aforementioned may suit certain needs well.

**Carnegie Hill Suites,** E. 93rd St., New York, NY 10128
**cross streets:** between Madison and Fifth Aves.
**phone:** (212) 472-2000, (800) 835-8880
**fax:** none

**email:** none
**website:** www.abodenyc.com
**number of rooms:** 3
**number of floors:** 4
**smoking policy:** all nonsmoking rooms
**restaurants:** none
**bars:** none
**room service:** none
**hotel amenities:** kitchenette
**room amenities:** air-conditioning, desktop computer, modem line
**parking:** none
**cancellation:** 14 days prior to arrival
**wheelchair accessibility:** public areas — no, rooms — no

## De Hirsch Residence at the 92nd St Y

| | |
|---|---|
| Extraordinary | $450 and over |
| Excellent | $350–$449 |
| Very Good | $250–$349 |
| Good | $150–$249 |
| **Basic** | $75–$149 |
| Poor | **under $75*** |

The accommodations at the De Hirsch may be basic, but for the many N.Y.U. and Columbia students who can't find other housing, they're a godsend. Budget-minded travelers have also discovered the benefits of a stay here.

It's not the charm of the rooms — they're small, plain and dormlike, with a twin bed or two, desk, dresser and a closet just big enough to suffice for longer stays. Windows are double-glazed and there is central air-conditioning. There's no phone in the room (pay phones are on every floor) but there are jacks, so if you are staying for a few weeks, you can get a phone installed. Bathrooms are shared, and each floor has a common kitchen area, washer-dryer and an ironing board (but no iron). It's BYOT—bring your own towels. There is daily maid service, and the whole residential area is spotless because the place is cleaned twice every 24 hours.

The real perks of staying here are the facilities, lectures and performances offered by the 92nd Street Y. This Y is known for its cultural programming. In addition, there is a first-rate health club to which De Hirsch residents have free access, with facilities including aerobic equipment, squash courts, swimming pool, steam room, sauna, Jacuzzi and a program of classes. Did you miss last night's 92nd Street Y concert or lecture? It has been taped so that you can watch it from your personal TV attached to your treadmill or stair-stepper.

The De Hirsch takes the issue of safety seriously, so you can't just show up here and expect to get a room — you need to apply in advance and there is a three-day minimum stay. Everyone gets a picture ID that's needed to enter the residential area.

There are surveillance cameras as well. It's much more like staying in a dorm than staying in a hotel, but the De Hirsch offers a lot for little money.

**DeHirsch Residence at the 92nd St. Y,** 1395 Lexington Ave., New York, NY 10128
**cross streets:** between E. 91st and E. 92nd Streets
**phone:** (212) 415-5650, (800) 858-4692
**fax:** (212) 415-5578
**email:** dehirsch@92ndsty.org
**website:** www.92ndsty.org
**number of rooms:** 300
**number of floors:** 11
**smoking policy:** all smoking
**restaurants:** none
**bars:** none
**room service:** none
**hotel amenities:** health club, swimming pool, Jacuzzi, laundry, meeting and function rooms, communal kitchen
**room amenities:** air-conditioning
**parking:** none
**cancellation:** 3 days prior to arrival
**wheelchair accessibility:** public areas — yes, rooms — yes. ADA compliant
**\*notes:** minimum stay of 3 days, must be 18 years of age

## The Franklin

| | |
|---|---|
| Extraordinary | $450 and over |
| Excellent | $350–$449 |
| Very Good | $250–$349 |
| **Good** | **$150–$249** |
| Basic | $75–$149 |
| Poor | under $75 |

A silk purse from a sow's ear. The sow is the building as it was — a wreck — until Bernard Goldberg, who developed the Franklin before selling to Unique Hotels, transformed it with good fabrics and colors, if no actual silk. The look is modern: blacks, whites, beiges, with white swag canopies and bright white sheets with no bedspread. If you like that look, and we do, it's inviting.

Everything is mini here. Mini-rooms, mini-bathrooms, mini-closets. The in-room safe is mini — too small for a laptop. Standard rooms, the miniest of all, have full-size beds and a sink in the room instead of in the mini-bathroom. These rooms face the back. Superior rooms have queen-size beds, are somewhat more spacious, and face the front. The "one" line of superior rooms are especially popular — the closets are cedar and they're the largest in the hotel — the room configuration may also be the most comfortable. Amenities include a CD player (there's a complimentary CD library downstairs), VCR (a VCR library, too), one-line phone with dataport and voice mail, Neutrogena bath

products, complimentary bottled water. Water pressure is good,
mattresses are adequate, but the bedding looked better to us
(those white sheets) than the mattress felt.

There are no hotel amenities — no restaurant, concierge, fitness or business room. The Franklin may not be a silk purse
after all. Think of it as a mini silk clutch.

**The Franklin,** 164 E. 87th St., New York, NY 10128
**cross streets:** between Lexington and Third Avenues
**phone:** (212) 369-1000, (877) 847-4444
**fax:** (212) 369-8000
**email:** none
**website:** www.uniquehotels.com
**number of rooms:** 53
**number of floors:** 9
**smoking policy:** designated nonsmoking floors
**restaurants:** none
**bars:** none
**room service:** none
**hotel amenities:** dry cleaning
**room amenities:** air-conditioning, VCR, CD player
**parking:** valet
**cancellation:** 1 day prior to arrival
**wheelchair accessibility:** public areas — no, rooms — no

## The Gracie Inn

| | |
|---|---|
| Extraordinary | $450 and over |
| Excellent | $350–$449 |
| Very Good | **$250–$349** |
| **Good** | **$150–$249** |
| Basic | $75–$149 |
| Poor | under $75 |

As New York moves into the new millennium, one of the most
striking changes recently has been what some have called the
"mallification" of the city — the decline of the mom and pop,
the idiosyncratic and the personal in favor of the mega, the
bland and the electronic. While the Gracie Inn isn't centrally
located (it's way east on the Upper East Side), it offers a very
personal experience. It is a virtue not to be taken lightly.

The manager, Daniel Chappuis, says, "There's no checkout
time. I don't want to force people to go. I have 12 rooms and
one cleaning person. It all works out." It is not hotel chain
thinking. Neither are the rooms. They are simply but cheerfully
furnished, with stenciled walls, dried flowers and quilts, giving a
homey feel. Windows are double-paned and the mattresses are
good. There aren't many amenities besides a TV, VCR, and complimentary Evian and Perrier, but each room has a full kitchen,
so you can further the illusion of a home in the city (some people do rent a room for an extended stay). The bathrooms are
small but in fine shape and include a Shower Massage shower
head. The penthouse has two water beds and a Jacuzzi. Break-

fast is different every day of the week. There is always coffee and juice, but one day it's a croissant, another day muesli, etc. It's delivered to your room on a silver tray.

That may not feel exactly like home, but it's a nice thought.

**The Gracie Inn,** 502 E. 81st St., New York, NY 10028
**cross streets:** between York and East End Avenues
**phone:** (212) 628-1700, (800) 404-2252
**fax:** (212) 628-6420
**email:** none
**website:** none
**number of rooms:** 12 (all apartments)
**number of floors:** 5
**smoking policy:** designated nonsmoking rooms
**restaurants:** none
**bars:** none
**room service:** none
**hotel amenities:** laundry and dry cleaning
**room amenities:** air-conditioning, kitchen
**parking:** none
**cancellation:** 1-2 weeks prior to arrival depending on season
**wheelchair accessibility:** public areas — no, rooms — no

## The Helmsley Carlton Hotel

| | |
|---|---|
| Extraordinary | **$450 and over** |
| Excellent | **$350–$449** |
| **Very Good** | $250–$349 |
| Good | $150–$249 |
| Basic | $75–$149 |
| Poor | under $75 |

"This is the best place," volunteers one chic young woman (on the elevator with us at the Helmsley Carlton) after she notices our clipboard. In its low key way, the hotel wins us over, too.

The small lobby, with its black-and-white marble floors and fresh flowers, feels cozily residential, an oasis off bustling Madison Avenue. You feel well-protected, too — there are two doormen and two elevator attendants. Before you call, though, you need to know that the odds of getting a room are against you.

The building was built in 1950 as permanent residences by the Astor family, but the Helmsleys bought it before it opened. It is still mostly residential. There are only four transient rooms, although occasionally permanent residents rent out when they're away.

Should you get a room, you'll find traditional-style, absolutely quiet rooms, with plenty of light. Each has a full kitchen with old-fashioned everything. There are no microwaves, which would seem too fashion forward. There aren't many amenities besides a clock radio, two-line phones and Neutrogena products in the sweetly old-style bathrooms. Even though the restaurant Maxim's is downstairs, there is no room service available.

If you're seeking a quiet, low-profile, private spot on the Upper East Side, you could have the same reaction as the women in the elevator.

**The Helmsley Carlton Hotel,** 680 Madison Ave., New York, NY 10021
**cross streets:** between E. 61st and E. 62nd Streets
**phone:** (212) 838-3000
**fax:** (212) 753-8575
**email:** none
**website:** www.helmsleyhotels.com
**number of rooms:** 4
**number of floors:** 17
**smoking policy:** none
**restaurants:** yes
**bars:** yes
**room service:** none
**hotel amenities:** laundry and dry cleaning
**room amenities:** air-conditioning, kitchen
**parking:** valet
**cancellation:** 2 days prior to arrival
**wheelchair accessibility:** public areas — yes, rooms — yes. ADA compliant

# Hotel Wales

| | |
|---|---|
| Extraordinary | $450 and over |
| Excellent | $350–$449 |
| **Very Good** | $250–$349 |
| Good | **$150–$249** |
| Basic | $75–$149 |
| Poor | under $75 |

Carnegie Hill, where the Hotel Wales is located, is one of New York's more attractive neighborhoods and the hotel is at home there. On Sunday afternoons, the hotel hosts concerts of Juilliard music students, which people from the neighborhood like to attend. It's a civilized neighborhood and a civilized hotel.

The design mixes contemporary lines and colors with warm details such as wood door mouldings. Guest rooms aren't large, but they're outfitted with comfy bedding, crisp white sheets, two-line phones with dataport and voice mail, clock radio, VCR and CD player (there's a complimentary VCR and CD library), complimentary mineral water, hair dryer, tie rack and Neutrogena bath products. Water pressure is sluggish. You may get some noise from Madison Avenue (windows are double-paned), but this is a relatively quiet part of town.

Breakfast, at which a harpist plays, is included in the rate. It consists of muffins, rolls, cereal, and hard-boiled eggs. Guests can work off the muffins in the fitness room, where there are a couple of treadmills, a bike and free weights. Room service is available from Sarabeth's — a popular restaurant best known for its brunch.

Some rooms on the "22" line have a partial view of the reservoir in Central Park. A stay at the Wales and a walk around the reservoir could further undermine the city's reputation as tough and edgy.

**Hotel Wales,** 1295 Madison Ave., New York, NY 10128
**cross streets:** between E. 92nd and E. 93rd Streets
**phone:** (212) 876-6000, (877) 847-4444
**fax:** (212) 860-7000
**email:** wales@uniquehotels.com
**website:** www.uniquehotels.com
**number of rooms:** 87 (includes 40 suites)
**number of floors:** 10
**smoking policy:** designated nonsmoking floor
**restaurants:** Sarabeth's
**bars:** none
**room service:** yes
**hotel amenities:** laundry and dry cleaning
**room amenities:** air-conditioning, VCR, modem line, safe
**parking:** valet
**cancellation:** 1 day prior to arrival
**wheelchair accessibility:** public areas — no, rooms — no

# The Lowell

| | |
|---|---|
| Extraordinary | $450 and over |
| **Excellent** | **$350–$449** |
| Very Good | $250–$349 |
| Good | $150–$249 |
| Basic | $75–$149 |
| Poor | under $75 |

The Lowell is among the very best "boutique" hotels in New York. Small, quiet, private, elegant, and service-oriented, the Lowell is a place you know about because a trusted friend has told you about it. Even though it's well located at the midtown end of the Upper East Side, it feels like a hideaway.

You won't be hanging out in the lobby any time soon — there are only a couple of seats — and the front desk is right by the elevators, which helps insure privacy and security. While the setup might suggest a certain hauteur from the staff, warmth is the order of the day.

Standard guest rooms have plenty of everything to keep you cosseted. Good beds, clock radio, VCR, fax, bathrobe, umbrella, tie rack, shoe horn, makeup mirror, scale, two-line phones with dataport, direct inward dial and voice mail. There is night turndown. Bathrooms tend to be small, and water pressure is acceptable but not strong.

Staying at the Lowell in a standard room would be very nice. Staying in one of the suites would be a joy. There are 46 of them and 33 have wood-burning fireplaces. Wood is included. All the suites have small kitchens variously outfitted. The Lowell Suites, chintzed to the max, are just right for honeymoons and special occasions (they're also used for interviews by Barbara Walters and Dateline NBC). The Gym Suite came about because Madonna was staying for a longer period at the hotel, ordered gym equipment in and it stayed. It's the only hotel room in town with a ballet barre. The Hollywood Suite has a 41-inch TV, a stack of videos of Hollywood classics and movie paraphernalia. The Garden Suite, with two terraces, is an absolute delight.

The hotel has a snappy fitness room with brand new Cybex and Trotter equipment, the Pembroke Room is lovely for breakfast or tea, and the Post House, a steak house, does room service.

A stay at the Lowell would make a visit to New York especially memorable, but it's such a good hotel that if it were located in Hartford or Cleveland, it could make those cities memorable too.

**The Lowell,** 28 E. 63rd St., New York, NY 10021
**cross streets:** between Madison and Park Avenues
**phone:** (212) 838-1400, (800) 221-4444
**reservations fax:** (212) 605-6808, guest fax: (212) 319-4230
**email:** lowellhtl@aol.com
**website:** www.preferredhotels.com
**number of rooms:** 67 (includes 46 suites)
**number of floors:** 17
**smoking policy:** designated nonsmoking rooms
**restaurants:** Post House
**bars:** 2
**room service:** yes
**hotel amenities:** fitness center, concierge, laundry and dry cleaning, meeting and function rooms
**room amenities:** air-conditioning, VCR, fax, modem line
**parking:** valet
**cancellation:** 2 days prior to arrival
**wheelchair accessibility:** public areas — yes, rooms — yes

# Lyden Gardens

| | |
|---|---|
| Extraordinary | $450 and over |
| Excellent | $350–$449 |
| Very Good | **$250–$349** |
| **Good** | $150–$249 |
| Basic | $75–$149 |
| Poor | under $75 |

The Lyden Gardens is one of ten hotels in the Manhattan East Suite Hotels chain. The group shares a number of features. Not only are they all-suites hotels, each offers somewhat-spacious-to-very-spacious accommodations, kitchen or kitchenette, fitness room, and a good number of amenities. They divide things up as junior suites, one-bedroom suites, and two-bedroom suites. None is a design award-winner (with the exception of their flagship — and newest — property, the Benjamin) but they are quality hotels at a fair price.

This hotel was the first of the chain, opening in 1965, but looks robust — the last renovation was in 1995. The contemporary-styled lobby doesn't seem much like a hotel — there's a front desk and a curved banquette and not much else. Rooms aren't similarly contemporary-looking. They're more traditional (down to the framed riding prints on the walls), with plenty of room, plenty of light and little noise from the street. In short, a good hotel room.

Amenities include a clock radio, iron and ironing board, hair dryer, one-line phone with dataport and voice mail. There are in-room safes but they are not large enough to hold a laptop. Kitchens have everything you'd need: refrigerator, range, microwave, toaster, coffee makers, pots, pans, dishes and silverware. The hotel has a shopping service to stock you up when you don't have time. Coin-operated washers and dryers are available on premises, and the Lyden Gardens has a fitness room with a handful of aerobics machines, free weights and television.

Some ground floor rooms have terraces (they're in the back, so they're quiet), as do some suites on the 11th and 12th floors and the penthouse. They would enhance a stay here but, terrace or not, the Lyden Gardens is commendable.

**Lyden Gardens,** 215 E. 64th St., New York, NY 10021
**cross streets:** between Second and Third Avenues
**phone:** (212) 355-1230, (800) 637-8483
**reservations fax:** (212) 465-3697, guest fax: (212) 758-7858
**email:** info@mesuite.com
**website:** www.mesuites.com
**number of rooms:** 130 (all suites)
**number of floors:** 13
**smoking policy:** designated nonsmoking floors
**restaurants:** none
**bars:** none

**room service:** yes
**hotel amenities:** fitness equipment, laundry and dry cleaning
**room amenities:** air-conditioning, kitchen, safe
**parking:** valet
**cancellation:** 4 P.M. day prior to arrival
**wheelchair accessibility:** public areas — yes, rooms — yes.
ADA complaint

# The Mark

| | |
|---|---|
| Extraordinary | **$450 and over** |
| **Excellent** | $350–$449 |
| Very Good | $250–$349 |
| Good | $150–$249 |
| Basic | $75–$149 |
| Poor | under $75 |

Watch the body language. You can tell a lot about a hotel by spending some time seeing how the staff interacts with a variety of people — guests, other staff members, service providers. On the day we visited, the mailman was in the hotel for all of 30 seconds, but the kindness accorded him seems typical of this staff and their exceptional hotel. It is the mark of distinction.

The doormen are white-gloved. The lobby is bright, with black-and-white marble floors, creamy white molded walls, with oil paintings, and an old-fashioned front desk — trim, elegant, understated. The concierge desk is along the opposite wall, and the head concierge wears the golden keys on his lapel — he holds the Clefs d'Or designation.

Guest rooms are a comfortable design mix of traditional and contemporary that fit as comfortably as the doorman's glove. The first thing we notice is a phone on either side of the king-size bed — you don't have to plan your sleeping arrangements around the phone. They have two lines, dataport and voice mail. Cell phones are available at no charge, except for usage — $1.75 a minute incoming or outgoing to anywhere in the world. Those beds are luxurious, too — Frette bed linens on top of cushiony mattresses. Kitchens or kitchenettes are in three-quarters of the guest rooms and come in a number of configurations. Those that do not have either have a mini-bar.

You'll also find a clock radio, fax machine, video cassette player, a bathrobe, tie rack, and safe (though it's too small for a laptop). Bathrooms at the Mark tend to be larger than in other New York hotels. We especially like the ones with black and white tiles. Most bathrooms have separate tub and shower. There are heated towel bars, hair dryer and Molton Brown bath products, though no makeup mirror. The hotel offers a shuttle to Wall Street and the theater district at certain hours.

**The Mark,** 25 E. 77th St., New York, NY 10021
**cross streets:** at Madison Avenue
**phone:** (212) 744-4300, (800) 843-6275 (THE MARK)
**reservations fax:** (212) 472-5714, guest fax: (212) 744-2749

**email:** reservations@themarknyc.com
**website:** www.themarkhotel.com
**number of rooms:** 180 (includes 60 suites)
**number of floors:** 15
**smoking policy:** designated nonsmoking floors
**restaurants:** yes
**bars:** yes
**room service:** yes, 24 hours
**hotel amenities:** fitness equipment, concierge, laundry and dry cleaning, complimentary Wall St. shuttle, meeting and function rooms
**room amenities:** air-conditioning, kitchen, mini-bar, VCR, CD player, fax, modem line, safe
**parking:** valet
**cancellation:** 4 P.M. day of arrival
**wheelchair accessibility:** public areas — yes, rooms — yes. ADA compliant

## The Marmara-Manhattan

| | |
|---|---|
| Extraordinary | $450 and over |
| **Excellent** | $350–$449 |
| Very Good | $250–$349 |
| Good | **$150–$249\*** |
| Basic | $75–$149 |
| Poor | under $75 |

Most people who stay at the Marmara are there for R & R — relocation or renovation. There are a handful of luxury extended stay hotels in the city (thirty day minimums are the rule of thumb) and the Marmara is the most northerly of them. Since it is located uptown, without highrises crowding it at every angle, it enjoys that precious commodity in New York — rooms with a lot of light. It also has a great deal more to offer.

Guest quarters are either done in modern Scandinavian style or contemporary American. They're a touch on the plain side but pleasant, with two-line phones, dataport, direct inward dial and voice mail, comfortable bedding, fax/scanner/copier, washer and dryer (in many suites), CD player, TV Internet browser, safe, umbrella, iron and ironing board. Each has a full service kitchen down to the box of Cascade. Closets are plentiful if not particularly elegant: plastic hangers and "California" racks. The bathroom (suites have more than one) has good water pressure, a hair dryer, makeup mirror and ProTerra bath products. Jacuzzis are in the larger suites. Utilities are included in the monthly rent. There are, though, additional per-call phone charges.

A number of features further distinguish the Marmara. It offers three-bedroom suites — something in short supply around the city. There is an exercise room with a small number of machines and free weights. For guests who want a full service gym, there are complimentary passes to the 92nd Street Y. The roof club on the 32nd floor serves a full buffet breakfast ($15). It has relatively unobstructed 360-degree views that include the Triborough Bridge and the Empire State Building. The lobby has a green, shady atrium off it and, near the front desk, a birdcage with several birds. They seem as happy to be there as we expect you will be.

**The Marmara-Manhattan,** 301 E. 94th St., New York, NY 10128
**cross streets:** at Second Ave.
**phone:** (212) 427-3100, (800) 621-9029
**fax:** (212) 427-3042
**email:** info@marmara-manhattan.com
**website:** www.marmara-manhattan.com
**number of rooms:** 107 (all suites)
**number of floors:** 32
**smoking policy:** designated nonsmoking floors
**restaurants:** none
**bars:** none
**room service:** none
**hotel amenities:** fitness equipment, laundry and dry cleaning, meeting and function rooms
**room amenities:** TV Internet browser, air-conditioning, kitchen, VCR, safe, fax/scanner/copier, modem lines, laundry
**parking:** none
**cancellation:** must sign lease, with substantial penalties for cancellation
**wheelchair accessibility:** public areas — yes, rooms — no
**\*notes:** minimum stay 30 days

## Plaza Athénée

| | |
|---|---|
| Extraordinary | **$450 and over** |
| Excellent | $350–$449 |
| **Very Good** | $250–$349 |
| Good | $150–$249 |
| Basic | $75–$149 |
| Poor | under $75 |

The decor is French, all right, but there is no longer any connection between this hotel and the Paris hotel of the same name. In fact, the owner is a Thai corporation, the chef is from Vancouver, the room chocolates are from Belgium.

The Plaza Athénée is regularly cited in magazine articles and travel books as a top New York hotel, but we think since rates here are often in the $500 a night neighborhood, you have a right to expect double-paned windows (they're not). What you may not expect are somewhat flaccid mattresses, small, dark rooms, low ceilings, tiny bathtubs, and no-name bathroom amenities. Some rooms have considerably more charm than others, certainly, and there is a fair roster of room amenities, including several types of hangers, tie rack, makeup mirror, bathrobe, clock radio, and hair dryer. The larger rooms and suites are richly and attractively furnished. The fitness room has fewer than a dozen machines; there is no business center.

The Plaza Athénée is not a bad hotel, by any means, but it has some formidable competition at this price level. It is hard to say exactly what you're getting for your money.

**Plaza Athénée,** 37 E. 64th St., New York, NY 10021
**cross streets:** between Park and Madison Avenues
**phone:** (212) 734-9100, (800) 447-8800
**fax:** (212) 772-0958
**email:** kgoldberg@plaza-athenee.com
**website:** www.plaza-athenee.com
**number of rooms:** 152 (includes 36 suites)
**number of floors:** 17
**smoking policy:** designated nonsmoking floors
**restaurants:** yes
**bars:** yes
**room service:** yes, 24 hours
**hotel amenities:** fitness equipment, concierge, laundry and dry cleaning, business services, meeting and function rooms
**room amenities:** air-conditioning, mini-bar, fax on request, modem line, safe
**parking:** valet
**cancellation:** 1-3 days prior to arrival depending on season
**wheelchair accessibility:** public areas — yes, rooms — yes. ADA compliant

## The Regency, A Loews Hotel

| | |
|---|---|
| Extraordinary | $450 and over |
| **Excellent** | **$350–$449** |
| Very Good | $250–$349 |
| Good | $150–$249 |
| Basic | $75–$149 |
| Poor | under $75 |

The Regency has new polish, grace and flair following a major renovation. Connie Beale was the designer, and she has done fine work enriching the rooms with silks, velvets, leather and mahogany. The look is contemporary, with pale gray walls, gold and wood accents. The newly redone lobby and the lovely hallways, too, now live up to the Park Avenue address. It is all seductively plush.

The guest rooms have a strong lineup of amenities: firm mattresses, fax machines, safe, two-line phones, dataport, voice mail and a spacious desk area. Most closets are spacious. Bathrooms come equipped with a small TV, hair dryer, bathrobe and scale. Those bathrooms, though, are something of a drawback — many of them are quite small. For these prices, how about Teuscher instead of Lindt chocolates? Room service is available 24 hours.

The hotel has a well-outfitted fitness center that includes a full range of equipment: treadmill, stairsteppers, cycles, free weights and a sauna. The hotel has concierge services, and overnight shoeshine, and guests can observe one of the city's most serious "power breakfasts" in the hotel's restaurant.

**The Regency, A Loews Hotel,** 540 Park Ave., New York, NY 10021
**cross streets:** at E. 61st Street
**phone:** (212) 759-4100, (800) 233-2356
**reservations fax:** (212) 688-2898, guest fax: (212) 826-5674
**email:** regency@loewshotels.com
**website:** www.loewshotels.com
**number of rooms:** 351 (includes 86 suites)
**number of floors:** 21
**smoking policy:** designated nonsmoking floors
**restaurants:** yes
**bars:** yes
**room service:** yes
**hotel amenities:** fitness center, concierge, laundry and dry cleaning, business center, meeting and function rooms
**room amenities:** air-conditioning, mini-bar, VCR, modem line, safe
**parking:** valet
**cancellation:** 1 day prior to arrival
**wheelchair accessibility:** public areas — yes, rooms — yes. ADA compliant

## The Sherry-Netherland

| | |
|---|---|
| Extraordinary | **$450 and over** |
| **Excellent** | **$350–$449** |
| Very Good | $250–$349 |
| Good | $150–$249 |
| Basic | $75–$149 |
| Poor | under $75 |

Eloise may have been a child at the Plaza but, when she grew up, we think she would have moved across Fifth Avenue to the Sherry-Netherland.

Named for ice cream maker Louis Sherry, on the site of the New Netherlands hotel, the Sherry has had, since its opening in 1927, a mix of permanent residents and hotel accommodations. It has successfully created a nether-nether world within its confines quite unlike the one on its doorstep.

This world is a mix of New England pragmatism (befitting Sherry's Vermont upbringing) running through its comfortable but understated rooms, and allusions to grandeur, including the friezes from the razed Vanderbilt mansion and the lobby's Vatican Library design. The Sherry has never been a part of any chain, and its distinctiveness shows.

On the ride up in the white-gloved, 24-hour-attended elevators, you'll note the wood in the elevators and painted panels, again salvaged from the Vanderbilts. Guest rooms vary consider-

ably in decor, but all are traditional (you were expecting
Anouska Hempel?), and you won't feel the walls are closing in
on you. Those walls are thick, and doors close with a deep thud.
There are one-line phones with dataport and voice mail, a mini-
bar, VCR, and a copy of every Academy Award-winning movie to
borrow from downstairs. They also stock *New York Times* best-
sellers to borrow. Other amenities include a clock radio, fax
machine, bathrobe, Godiva chocolates and fresh flowers. The
marble bathrooms have a makeup mirror and Caswell-Massey
bath products. The water pressure has a Yankee thriftiness.

The Sherry is also permanent home to many New Yorkers
and they obviously prefer a quiet lobby over an array of amenities. There is a fitness room with a multifunction machine, bike,
stairstepper, treadmill and a few free weights. Breakfast and
room service are provided by Cipriani.

Some people might stay at the Sherry for its great views over
Central Park (and also of the Plaza). Others might like the fact
that, unlike the Plaza, you won't ever find movie crews between
you and where you want to walk. If Eloise were to move in,
she'd like the fact that the staff-to-guest ratio is 2:1, that they'd
buy a Christmas tree for her if she wanted that (as they did for
one guest) and decorate it, too.

**The Sherry-Netherland,** 781 Fifth Ave., New York, NY 10022
**cross streets:** between E. 59th and E. 60th Streets
**phone:** (212) 355-2800, (800) 247-4377
**fax:** (212) 319-4306
**email:** none
**website:** www.sherrynetherland.com
**number of rooms:** 150 (including 75 suites)
**number of floors:** 37
**smoking policy:** designated nonsmoking rooms
**restaurants:** yes
**bars:** yes
**room service:** yes, 24 hours
**hotel amenities:** fitness equipment, laundry and dry cleaning,
meeting and function room
**room amenities:** air-conditioning, kitchen, VCR, fax, modem
line
**parking:** valet
**cancellation:** 3 P.M. 1 day prior to arrival
**wheelchair accessibility:** public areas — yes, rooms — yes.
ADA compliant

# The Stanhope

| Extraordinary | $450 and over |
| **Excellent** | **$350–$449** |
| Very Good | $250–$349 |
| Good | $150–$249 |
| Basic | $75–$149 |
| Poor | under $75 |

Guests of the Stanhope have the Metropolitan Museum of Art across the street, the Frick, the Guggenheim, and the Whitney in easy walking distance, as well as the elegant charms of the Upper East Side at hand. That might be enough reason to stay at the Stanhope, but the hotel offers many additional incentives.

Primary among these might be privacy and security. The lobby is small, with only a couple of chairs, and everyone entering necessarily attracts attention. Trying to get to a guest floor? The only way is with a floor key given to guests. Another attraction is the room design, done in peach and gold French Empire ("one of those Louis," says our guide), accented with Chinoiserie. The list of room amenities is also impressive: two-line phones with dataport and voice mail, fax, CD player, clock radio, safe, umbrella, bathrobe, slippers. Bathrooms can be small but are stocked with hair dryer, makeup mirror, scale, phone and Floris bath products.

Many rooms get a lot of light. This is nice during the day but we wish the hotel had blackout curtains. The oatmeal cookie the hotel gives you at night turndown should help get you off to sleep. While there are double-paned windows, light sleepers may still hear some street noise.

Hotel amenities include a concierge staff, one of whom has the Clefs d'Or designation. There is a workout room with aerobics machines, free weights and a sauna. Guests can enjoy the restaurant Cafe M. Matthew Kenney is the well known executive chef, Jeremy Griffiths is the chef de cuisine. There is a nice little bar just off the lobby but, when weather permits, most guests very sensibly sit at the outdoor cafe called The Terrace, where the people watching is superb. It is a quintessential New York view, courtesy of a quintessential New York hotel.

**The Stanhope,** 995 Fifth Ave., New York, NY 10028
**cross streets:** at E. 81st St.
**phone:** (212) 288-5800, (800) 828-1123
**reservations fax:** (212) 650-4705, guest fax: (212) 517-0088
**email:** reservations@thestanhope.com
**website:** www.thestanhope.com
**number of rooms:** 187 (includes 61 suites)
**number of floors:** 16
**smoking policy:** designated nonsmoking floors
**restaurants:** Cafe M
**bars:** yes
**room service:** yes

**hotel amenities:** fitness equipment, concierge, laundry and dry cleaning, business services, meeting and function rooms
**room amenities:** air-conditioning, mini-bar, VCR on request, fax, modem line, safe
**parking:** valet
**cancellation:** 6 P.M. 1 day prior to arrival
**wheelchair accessibility:** public areas — yes, rooms — yes. ADA compliant
**notes:** small pets allowed with advance approval.

## Surrey Hotel

| | |
|---|---|
| Extraordinary | $450 and over |
| Excellent | **$350–$449** |
| **Very Good** | $250–$349 |
| Good | $150–$249 |
| Basic | $75–$149 |
| Poor | under $75 |

Room service from Daniel Boulud (Cafe Boulud) isn't the only good reason to stay at the Surrey, but what could be better than that?

The lobby has a slightly faded air, the hallways upstairs could do with some gentler lighting. The studio and one-bedroom suites are solid, old-fashioned New York hotel rooms. They have thick walls, roomy bedrooms and closets, a pink and green design thing going (a cosmetic makeover is due, perhaps overdue, in 2000), black and white tiled bathrooms. All rooms have kitchens, with gas ovens, refrigerator, toaster, microwave, coffee maker, pots and pans. The hotel will do grocery shopping for you. The basics at the Surrey check out well — firm mattresses, double-glazed windows, iron and board, voice mail, clock radio, Caswell-Massey products in the bathroom, a room with a few workout machines and a professional staff. The Upper East Side location is attractive to many leisure travelers, and the hotel's rates, while not exactly bargain, aren't staggering either. Order up Mr. Boulud's bass and you could be very happy at the Surrey.

**Surrey Hotel,** 20 E. 76th St., New York, NY 10021
**cross streets:** between Fifth and Madison Avenues
**phone:** (212) 288-3700, (800) 637-8483
**reservations fax:** (212) 465-3697, guest fax: (212) 628-1549
**email:** info@mesuite.com
**website:** www.mesuite.com
**number of rooms:** 131 (all suites)
**number of floors:** 16
**smoking policy:** designated nonsmoking floors
**restaurants:** yes
**bars:** yes
**room service:** yes

**hotel amenities:** concierge, fitness equipment, laundry and dry cleaning, business services, meeting room, function room
**room amenities:** air-conditioning, kitchen, refrigerator, VCR, modem line, safe
**parking:** valet
**cancellation:** 4 P.M. day of arrival
**wheelchair accessibility:** public areas — yes, rooms — yes. ADA compliant

# Harlem

| Hotel | Price Range | Rating |
|---|---|---|
| Blue Rabbit International House | under $75 | Basic |
| Sugar Hill International House | under $75 | Basic |
| Urban Jem Guest House | $75–$149 | Good |

## NEIGHBORHOOD BOUNDARIES

South — E. 96th St., West — Central Park West/Frederick Douglass Blvd. to 125th St. then west on 125th St to the Hudson River, North — 155th St., East — East River

## ABOUT THE NEIGHBORHOOD

A large African-American community is at home in an area on its way back economically. The sometimes stunningly beautiful domestic architecture is, in some places, being restored. The residences along Strivers' Row, 138th and 139th Streets between Adam Clayton Powell Jr. Blvd. and Frederick Douglass Blvd., were built for residents keeping a horse and carriage. You can still see signs saying Walk Your Horses on some of the gates. The number of churches and jazz clubs make it a Saturday night, Sunday morning neighborhood for many visitors.

## TRANSPORTATION

The major stations in Harlem are 125th St., 135th St., 145th St. and 155th St., served by the 1, 2, 3, 9, 4, 5, 6, A, B, C and D lines. You will find few, if any, yellow cabs in the area.

## LANDMARKS

The Morris-Jumel Mansion, 65 Jumel Terrace 923-8008, is a Colonial period house with an historical connection to Aaron Burr. The corner of 155th St and Broadway is the location of Audubon Terrace, site of the Hispanic Society of America, 690-0743, filled with Spanish master paintings and a terra cotta courtyard. John James Audubon is buried in the graveyard behind the Church of the Intercession across Broadway. Visit the exhibition space at the Schomburg Center, 515 Lenox Ave. 491-2200 and see the Studio Museum in Harlem, 144 W. 125th St. 864-4500.

## SHOPPING

Books about African-American history and culture can be bought at the gift shops at the Studio Museum of Harlem and the Schomburg Center. The main shopping thoroughfare is 125th Street.

## EATING AND DRINKING

Chicken and waffles are a specialty dish in Harlem. Tasty examples can be found at Londel's of Strivers Row, 2620 Frederick Douglass Blvd. 234-6114. Sylvia's, 328 Lenox Ave. 996-0660, is a soul-food magnet for the entire city. Copeland's, 547 W. 145th St. 234-2357, serves dinner and a gospel brunch on Sunday mornings. On Monday night at Well's, 2247-49 7th Ave. 234-0700, you can dine while listening to the Harlem Renaissance Orchestra.

For information on new hotels, ongoing updates, and directions to each hotel by car or mass transit, check online at New York Today, www.nytoday.com/hotels.

## THE HOTELS

### Blue Rabbit International House

| Extraordinary | $450 and over |
|---|---|
| Excellent | $350–$449 |
| Very Good | $250–$349 |
| Good | $150–$249 |
| **Basic** | $75–$149 |
| Poor | **under $75** |

### Sugar Hill International House

| Extraordinary | $450 and over |
|---|---|
| Excellent | $350–$449 |
| Very Good | $250–$349 |
| Good | $150–$249 |
| **Basic** | $75–$149 |
| Poor | **under $75** |

Blue Rabbit and Sugar Hill are run as essentially one hostel by Jim Williams, who wrote the book on hostelling, or at least one of them. His two neighbor hostels appear to be well run, and they have something of the ambience of a bed and breakfast, since the owners live on site. The 1888 building is now holding up well, after some surgery.

As hostels go, it's definitely on the quiet side — partyers should look elsewhere. Mattresses are foam (to help fight bed-bug infestation), there are ceiling fans, no closets, shared baths, and a common area with a kitchen. There are sprinklers and a

smoke alarm — more evidence that you're in good hands here.
A passport is required for ID.

In addition to inexpensive lodging, staying at one of these
two hostels puts you in Harlem, with its fascinating history and
great eats.

**Blue Rabbit International House,** 730 St. Nicholas Ave.,
New York, NY 10031
**cross streets:** at W. 147th Street
**phone:** (212) 491-3892
**fax:** (212) 283-0108
**email:** bluerabbit@hostelhandbook.com
**website:** www.hostelhandbook.com/bluerabbit
**number of rooms:** 5
**number of floors:** 4
**smoking policy:** all nonsmoking
**restaurants:** none
**bars:** none
**room service:** none
**hotel amenities:** shared kitchen
**room amenities:** all shared baths
**parking:** none
**cancellation:** 1 day prior to arrival
**wheelchair accessibility:** public areas — no, rooms — no
**notes:** valid passport required, reconfirm reservations 1 day
prior to arrival, reservations taken only before 4 P.M.

**Sugar Hill International House,** 722 St. Nicholas Avenue,
New York, NY 10031
**cross streets:** at W. 146th Street
**phone:** (212) 926-7030
**fax:** (212) 283-0108
**email:** sugarhill@hostelhandbook.com
**website:** www.hostelhandbook.com/sugarhill
**number of rooms:** 20 beds in 5 dormitory-style rooms
**number of floors:** 4
**smoking policy:** all nonsmoking
**restaurants:** none
**bars:** none
**room service:** none
**hotel amenities:** shared kitchen, shared baths
**room amenities:** none
**parking:** none
**cancellation:** 1 day prior to arrival
**wheelchair accessibility:** public areas — no, rooms — no

## Urban Jem Guest House

| | |
|---|---|
| Extraordinary | $450 and over |
| Excellent | $350–$449 |
| Very Good | $250–$349 |
| **Good** | $150–$249 |
| Basic | **$75–$149** |
| Poor | under $75 |

As Harlem burgeons, people from New York and around the world have begun to rediscover its many appeals, from its rich historical, cultural, and artistic history to its rich and delicious food, to a jazz scene that swings into the night. Not every corner is well manicured — far from it — but the rewards for the curious visitor are many.

Its location, near to subways, and just off 125th Street, a well-trafficked thoroughfare, makes the Urban Jem an ideal base for exploring Harlem and indeed the rest of the city.

It is run by Jane Alex Mendelson, who gave up corporate life to open this urban gem. She found this 1878 townhouse and did extensive renovations, opening her doors in 1998. When you open her door, you walk into an enchanting parlor, with high ceilings, gorgeous woodwork and a marble fireplace. There are books and magazines to while away some time and games such as Scrabble. Off the parlor is the kitchen area with a large dining room table, where guests gather for continental breakfast, juice and coffee, perhaps biscuits, doughnuts, fruit and cheese. Off the kitchen is a deck where guests can sit with their morning coffee.

Up the narrow staircase are two floors of rooms, two per floor, that are simply decorated, comfortable, and not midtown cramped. All have air-conditioning, double-paned windows, one-line phones, clock radio, microwave, toaster and TV. Two have a private bath and kitchen, the top floor rooms share kitchen and bath, which makes them well-suited for a family. A washer and dryer is available for a small fee.

Outside the guest house, Harlem is at your feet. Dinner at Sylvia's or Copeland's is invariably delicious. You could spend the evening in the neighborhood, dropping in to one of the thriving jazz clubs.

However much time you spend in Harlem (and we recommend you do), Urban Jem provides a delightful alternative to impersonal lodging, a delightful alternative to the usual location and a fresh way to see New York.

**Urban Jem Guest House,** 2005 Fifth Avenue, New York, NY 10035
**cross streets:** between E. 124th and E. 125th Streets
**phone:** (212) 831-6029
**fax:** (212) 831-6940
**email:** JMendel760@aol.com
**website:** www.urbanjem.com

**number of rooms:** 4
**number of floors:** 2
**smoking policy:** all nonsmoking
**restaurants:** none
**bars:** none
**room service:** none
**hotel amenities:** laundry
**room amenities:** some shared baths, air-conditioning, kitchen
**parking:** none
**cancellation:** 25 percent nonrefundable deposit required
**wheelchair accessibility:** public areas — no, rooms — no

# Outer Boroughs and the Airports

| Hotel Name | Price Range | Rating | Location |
| --- | --- | --- | --- |
| Akwaaba Mansion Bed & Breakfast | $75–$149 | Very Good | Brooklyn |
| Bed and Breakfast on the Park | $150–$249 | Very Good | Brooklyn |
| New York Marriott Brooklyn | $150–$249 | Very Good | Brooklyn |
| Best Western City View | $75–$149 | Good | Queens |
| Ramada Inn Adria | $75–$149 | Good | Queens |
| Sheraton La Guardia East | $150–$249 | Very Good | Queens |
| Le Refuge Inn Bed & Breakfast | $75–$149 | Very Good | Bronx |
| Harbor House Bed & Breakfast | under $75 | Good | Staten Island |
| Staten Island Hotel | $75–$149 | Good | Staten Island |
| Airway Motor Inn at La Guardia | $75–$149 | Basic | La Guardia Airport |
| Crowne Plaza Hotel La Guardia | $75–$249 | Very Good | La Guardia Airport |
| La Guardia Courtyard by Marriott | $75–$149 | Good | La Guardia Airport |
| La Guardia Marriott | $150–$249 | Very Good | La Guardia Airport |
| Wyndham Garden Hotel La Guardia | $75–$149 | Good | La Guardia Airport |
| Hilton J. F. K. Airport | $75–$249 | Good | J.F.K. Airport |
| Holiday Inn at J. F. K. Airport | $150–$249 | Very Good | J.F.K. Airport |
| Radisson Hotel J. F. K. Airport | $150–$249 | Good | J.F.K. Airport |
| Ramada Plaza J. F. K. Airport | $150–$249 | Good | J.F.K. Airport |
| Newark Airport Marriott | $75–$249 | Very Good | Newark (NJ) Airport |

# BROOKLYN

Brooklyn covers a lot of territory, over 80 square miles, so you
are unlikely to see more than the highlights in a short visit. The
Brooklyn Museum, 200 Eastern Pkwy. (718) 638-5000, in a
McKim, Mead & White building, has a collection of American
and European paintings and a special collection of Rodin sculptures. It's located at the edge of the Brooklyn Botanic Garden,
Eastern Pkwy. (718) 622-4433, which is worth a visit at any time
of the year. Brooklyn's Prospect Park was designed by Olmsted
and Vaux, who also did Central Park. The aptly named Park
Slope neighborhood is found along the northwest edge of
Prospect Park. The mostly residential streets are intersected by
commercial avenues in a quieter version of a Manhattan neighborhood like the Upper East Side. Paris's Arc de Triomphe was
the inspiration for Grand Army Plaza located at the point where
Flatbush Ave. and Prospect Park West meet. The Soldier's and
Sailor's Memorial Arch located there is dedicated to those who
perished on the side of the Union in the Civil War. A walk along
the Brooklyn Promenade, looking across to the skyline of Manhattan, is one of the most romantic sights in the entire city. Head
inland to see the brownstone and brick buildings on Pierrepont
and Montague Streets in Brooklyn Heights. Take in a chamber
concert at Bargemusic, Fulton Ferry Landing, (718) 624-4061,
which is an actual barge tied up under the Brooklyn Bridge. The
Brooklyn Academy of Music, 30 Lafayette Ave. (718) 636-4100,
brings in the new in music, dance and theater in their yearly
Next Wave Festival.

Two restaurants that deserve special mention are The River
Cafe, 1 Water St. (718) 522-5200 with its spectacular view and
Cucina, 256 Fifth Ave. (718) 230-0711, which serves Italian food
that anyone would be proud of.

For information on new hotels, ongoing updates and directions to each hotel by car or mass transit, check online at New
York Today, www.nytoday.com/hotels.

## Akwaaba Mansion Bed and Breakfast

| | |
|---|---|
| Extraordinary | $450 and over |
| Excellent | $350–$449 |
| **Very Good** | $250–$349 |
| Good | $150–$249 |
| Basic | **$75–$149** |
| Poor | under $75 |

The outside of Akwaaba doesn't give much away. Located in Bedford-Stuyvesant, the name of the place means "welcome" in Ghana. The house is from the 1860s and is made up of 18 rooms. It opened for guests in 1995.

Many memorable details distinguish Akwaaba. There are period details such as a 'bun warmer' built into the dining room radiator and many Afrocentric textiles, artifacts and furnishings.

Each suite has a different theme including the "Jumping the Broom" suite, which is the charming honeymoon suite and a Black memorabilia suite. Amenities include a clock radio, two rooms with Jacuzzis, as well as a library and a small television room. Iron and ironing board are available and guests share a portable phone. A full Southern-style breakfast is served in the dining room. You might get fried apples, pancakes, sausage, eggs and grits. Tea is served at 4 P.M., and the Akwaaba Cafe is located nearby.

Akwaaba isn't centrally located for typical sightseeing but it offers many delightful reasons to stay there.

**Akwaaba Mansion Bed and Breakfast,** 347 MacDonough St., Brooklyn, NY 11233
**cross streets:** between Stuyvesant and Lewis Avenues
**phone:** (718) 455-5958
**fax:** (718) 774-1744
**email:** akwaaba@aol.com
**website:** www.akwaaba.com
**number of rooms:** 4
**number of floors:** 2
**smoking policy:** all nonsmoking rooms
**restaurants:** yes
**bars:** none
**room service:** none
**hotel amenities:** library, TV and game room
**room amenities:** air-conditioning
**parking:** none
**cancellation:** 4 P.M. 2 weeks prior to arrival or forfeit 50 percent of entire stay
**wheelchair accessibility:** public areas — no, rooms — no

## Bed and Breakfast on the Park

| | |
|---|---|
| Extraordinary | $450 and over |
| Excellent | $350–$449 |
| **Very Good** | $250–$349 |
| Good | **$150–$249** |
| Basic | $75–$149 |
| Poor | under $75 |

At the great travel agency in the sky, Queen Victoria wades up to the agent's desk in her dark silk dress and books two weeks in New York (flying Virgin's upper class). "Should one stay at the St. Regis," she demands. "The W?" "No, mum, I think you would be most comfortable at Bed and Breakfast on the Park."

Two weeks later, the Queen returns to report that she had a wonderful time. "Yes, child, you were exactly right. I felt right at home. The lovely building was put up in 1895, right across from that lovely Prospect Park in a place called Brooklyn. The house was enchantingly fitted out with furniture that the proprietress kept referring to as antiques, but they certainly seemed current to me. Lovely oriental rugs, oil painting, stained glass. Just lovely. Pity the fireplace wasn't working. There was a telephone in the room and something called a modem line. When I asked for eggs at breakfast, the proprietress said with a twinkle, 'We don't do anything as mundane as eggs.' I must say the breakfast was vast and satisfying. I should like to go back."

**Bed and Breakfast on the Park,** 113 Prospect Park West, Brooklyn, NY 11215
**cross streets:** between 6th and 7th Streets
**phone:** (718) 499-6115
**fax:** (718) 499-1385
**email:** none
**website:** www.bbnyc.com
**number of rooms:** 7
**number of floors:** 4
**smoking policy:** all nonsmoking rooms
**restaurants:** none
**bars:** none
**room service:** none
**hotel amenities:** none
**room amenities:** air-conditioning, modem line
**parking:** none
**cancellation:** 10 days prior to arrival; $25 cancellation fee
**wheelchair accessibility:** public areas — no, rooms — no

## New York Marriott Brooklyn

| Extraordinary | $450 and over |
|---|---|
| Excellent | $350–$449 |
| **Very Good** | $250–$349 |
| Good | **$150–$249** |
| Basic | $75–$149 |
| Poor | under $75 |

When Marriott went into Times Square in the 1980s, there wasn't even a whisper of the transformation that the area has since undergone in the '90s. It does everything a hotel can do to disguise its location to guests once they have breached the ramparts. To borrow George W. S. Trow's phrase, it is within the context of no context. As a result, that property seems itself a sad relic — a hotel as fortress against the big, bad city.

The good news is that Marriott didn't make the same mistake in Brooklyn. The hotel, which opened in July, 1998, is seven floors of a big office tower, and it seems pleased to be right where it is. It's the first full-service hotel the borough has had in over 50 years. Brooklyn feels part of it, and vice versa, in a number of ways. The lobby isn't eight floors off the ground as it is in Times Square; it's on the second floor, and there are windows that make the space feel a part of its surroundings. As you ride up the escalator, your eye is drawn upward to a trompe l'oeil cupola on the ceiling. Your are looking up through the dome and out to the "sky". It's an attractive work and contextual as well: it imitates the conservatory dome at the Brooklyn Botanic Garden.

A mural of the Brooklyn Bridge is behind the front desk, throughout the hotel artwork and photos of Brooklyn or by Brooklyn artists adorn the walls. Books by or about its famous natives or about the city itself line the walls of the lounge. The Brooklyn Historical Society has filled several glass showcases with Brooklyn memorabilia and artifacts. Park Slope pils is on tap in the bar (though a few more Brooklyn ales and lagers wouldn't hurt).

Should all this Brooklyniana cause you concern, the Marriott has installed its usual pink and green carpets in the wide hallways and when you've reached your room, it's strictly Marriott. All the basics are well covered. There are two-line phones with dataport and voice mail, clock radio, coffeepot and coffee, minibar, safe (large enough to hold a laptop), iron and ironing board and hair dryer. Each room has individually controlled heat and air-conditioning. *USA Today* gets delivered to every guest.

Closets are roomy enough, water pressure solid, and the bedding is comfortable (some, though not all, of the beds have foam mattresses). One thing you notice right away: even though the hotel is built over busy Adams Street, the rooms are tranquil. Concierge Level accommodations include a bathrobe as well as access to a special lounge where a complimentary continental breakfast is served.

The hotel has a fitness center, open to outside membership,

with roughly 10 Cybex resistance machines as well as treadmills, stairsteppers and bikes. A 75-foot lap pool and a whirlpool are adjacent in a light and pleasant space.

In the lobby, you'll find a concierge desk, an ATM, and a small business center with copier, one computer, printer, fax, and Internet access. Many of the guests of the hotel are from Washington D.C., making it a home base to the nearby government offices in downtown Brooklyn. Quite a few subway lines converge in this area, so access citywide is easy. We think that even for visitors to New York used to staying in Manhattan, the Marriott Brooklyn could be a refreshing and comfortable change.

**New York Marriott Brooklyn**, 333 Adams St., Brooklyn, NY 11201
**cross streets:** between Tillary and Willoughby Streets
**phone:** (718) 246-7000, (888) 436-3759
**fax:** (718) 246-0563
**email:** none
**website:** www.marriotthotels.com
**number of rooms:** 376 (includes 21 suites)
**number of floors:** 7
**smoking policy:** designated nonsmoking rooms
**restaurants:** yes
**bars:** yes
**room service:** yes
**hotel amenities:** health club, lap pool, business center, meeting and function rooms, concierge, laundry and dry cleaning
**room amenities:** air-conditioning, safe, modem line, multiline phones, mini-bar
**parking:** valet
**cancellation:** 6 P.M. day of arrival
**wheelchair accessibility:** public areas — yes, rooms — yes. ADA compliant


# QUEENS

The city's largest borough is also its most diverse. Immigrants have flooded into Queens from dozens of countries in both hemispheres. Within a few blocks of the intersection of Roosevelt Ave. and Broadway you can find businesses and restaurants run by Indians, Pakistanis, Argentinians, Koreans, Chinese, Mexicans, and Uruguayans. Downtown Flushing, as the area around Northern Blvd. and Main St. is called, is a haven of Asian restaurants and food shops. It also contains Flushing Town Hall, 137-35 Northern Blvd. (718) 463-7700, a lovely building that hosts a series of classical and jazz concerts. Flushing Meadows Corona Park was built as the site for the 1939 World's Fair. The 1964 Fair was also held there, and some remains of both can still be seen. Shea Stadium, (718) 507-8499, and Arthur

Ashe Stadium (home of the U.S. Open tennis tournament) at the USTA Tennis Center, (718) 592-8927, are located at the Shea Stadium-Willets Point stop on the 7 train. For those who like to go off the beaten path on their travels, a ride on this elevated (in Queens) subway train will take them through a variety of neighborhoods and cuisines. P.S. 1, 22-25 Jackson Avenue at 46th St. (718) 784-2084, in Long Island City is a site for cutting-edge contemporary art exhibitions and performances.

For information on new hotels, ongoing updates, and directions to each hotel by car or mass transit, check online at New York Today, *www.*nytoday.com/hotels.

## Best Western City View

| | |
|---|---|
| Extraordinary | $450 and over |
| Excellent | $350–$449 |
| Very Good | $250–$349 |
| **Good** | $150–$249 |
| Basic | **$75–$149** |
| Poor | under $75 |

A former school building located across from the Calvary Cemetery, the City View feels both close to the city (it does have views of Manhattan) and at a definite remove, even though you're only a few minutes drive from it.

Rooms are familiar-looking, with comfortable new mattresses, two-line phones and dataport but no voice mail. There is a VCR in each room and a video rental machine in the lobby. Parking is complimentary, and the hotel offers a free shuttle to La Guardia, subways, and to any restaurant in the area. Breakfast is included in the room rate (cereals, fruit, bagels, muffins, doughnuts, coffee and juice). About two-thirds of the rooms here have an exercise bike in them. The best rooms, we think, are the ones with the eponymous city views. You can see the World Trade Center, the Empire State Building, the Chrysler Building — the whole nine yards.

**Best Western City View,** 33-17 Greenpoint Ave., Long Island City, NY 11101
**cross streets:** between Bradley and Gale Avenues
**phone:** (718) 392-8400, (800) 248-9843
**fax:** (718) 392-2110
**email:** none
**website:** www.bestwestern.com
**number of rooms:** 71
**number of floors:** 5
**smoking policy:** designated nonsmoking rooms
**restaurants:** none
**bars:** none
**room service:** none

**hotel amenities:** meeting rooms, laundry and dry cleaning, free transportation to La Guardia
**room amenities:** air-conditioning, modem line, VCR, mini-fridge on request, multiline phone, exercise bike
**parking:** free
**cancellation:** 4 P.M. 1 day prior to arrival
**wheelchair accessibility:** public areas — no, rooms — no

## Ramada Inn Adria

| | |
|---|---|
| Extraordinary | $450 and over |
| Excellent | $350–$449 |
| Very Good | $250–$349 |
| **Good** | $150–$249 |
| Basic | **$75–$149** |
| Poor | under $75 |

Two hotels, the Ramada Inn and the Adria, are virtually next door to each other, under the same ownership, and essentially considered one hotel. Nothing fancy here, nor especially pleasing to the eye, but the rooms are modestly comfortable and rates are reasonable.

There are one-line phones with voice mail, most rooms have dataport, clock radio, iron and ironing board, and hair dryer. None of the soft goods — bedspreads, curtains, etc. — look fresh but at least everything is clean. Mattresses vary from quite firm to not quite so firm. Closets are a long open rack, with plenty of room to hang lots of clothes. We prefer the Adria building for two reasons. The first is that all rooms have double-paned windows — helpful since Northern Boulevard is a busy thoroughfare. Second, there is a generous complimentary continental breakfast. At the Ramada, because of chain policy, a full breakfast is offered but it's not free.

Some of the rooms at the back have a definite suburban feel — you overlook people's green back yards; there are trees as far as the eye can see and a peek of blue water, the Bayside Marina.

**Ramada Inn Adria,** 220-33 Northern Blvd., Bayside, NY 11361
**cross streets:** between 221st Street and Northern Boulevard
**phone:** (718) 631-5900, (800) 272-3742
**Adria fax:** (718) 279-9080, Ramada fax: (718) 631-7501
**email:** none
**website:** none
**number of rooms:** 105
**number of floors:** 4
**smoking policy:** designated nonsmoking rooms
**restaurants:** yes
**bars:** yes
**room service:** yes
**hotel amenities:** meeting rooms, function rooms, dry cleaning, guests have access to Bell Plaza Health Club (15 minute walk from hotel)

**room amenities:** air-conditioning
**parking:** free
**cancellation:** 4 P.M. day of arrival
**wheelchair accessibility:** public areas — yes, rooms — yes

## Sheraton La Guardia East

| | |
|---|---|
| Extraordinary | $450 and over |
| Excellent | $350–$449 |
| **Very Good** | $250–$349 |
| Good | **$150–$249** |
| Basic | $75–$149 |
| Poor | under $75 |

The best reason to stay at this Sheraton from our point of view is its location in downtown Flushing. What that means is it's a short walk to wonderful food: Chinese, Korean, Japanese, Vietnamese, Malaysian, among other cuisines represented. Savvy New Yorkers know that it's possible to eat well in Manhattan's Chinatown; in Flushing, it's hard not to eat well.

This hotel, built in 1992, is in fine shape. The guest rooms are a little more roomy than they would be in Manhattan. There are light woods and a fair amount of natural light, so they feel even more expansive. Phones are one-line with dataport and voice mail. Amenities include a clock radio, iron and ironing board, coffee maker, hair dryer, and Avalon & Gray bath products. Planes do fly over the hotel as they approach the runway, and it's not completely inaudible, but neither is it particularly noticeable. The Sheraton offers a couple of pieces of fruit in the room to new arrivals and *USA Today* or the *World Journal* (a Chinese paper) every morning. A small execise room includes a stairstepper, treadmill, bike, and multifunction machine.

On the 16th floor of the hotel are the Executive Level rooms, available for $10 over the rack rate. You get a marble bathroom, bathrobe in the room, and use of a lounge on the floor. In that lounge, a complimentary continental breakfast is served with hors d'oeuvres in the evening. The room also has a desk and fax machine.

This Sheraton isn't right at the airport, but it's close by (they do not have an airline monitor). The amenities within, and Flushing's many restaurants, make it a smart choice.

**Sheraton La Guardia East,** 135-20 39th Ave, Flushing, NY 11354
**cross streets:** at Main Street
**phone:** (718) 460-6666, (800) 325-3535
**fax:** (718) 445-2655
**email:** none
**website:** www.sheraton.com
**number of rooms:** 173 (includes 8 suites)
**number of floors:** 8
**smoking policy:** designated nonsmoking floors

**restaurants:** yes
**bars:** yes
**room service:** yes
**hotel amenities:** fitness equipment, meeting and function
rooms, laundry and dry cleaning
**room amenities:** air-conditioning, modem line, mini-bar
**parking:** valet
**cancellation:** 4 P.M. day of arrival
**wheelchair accessibility:** public areas — yes, rooms — yes.
ADA compliant

# BRONX

For most New Yorkers, the Bronx is synonymous with the zoo.
The officials there may have added the words Wildlife Conserva-
tion to the name, but when you hear people talking about the
zoo this is the one they mean. If you have the time, you can get
there via the 2 and 5 trains. Bronx River Parkway at Fordham
Rd. (718) 367-1010. Nearby, is the New York Botanical Garden,
200th St. at Southern Blvd. (718) 817-8700, easily reached by
Metro-North trains. The extensive gardens provide great wander-
ing and birdwatching and the Enid A. Haupt Conservatory is a
showstopper. The Bronx has its own version of Down East ambience on City Island, located off to the northeast and accesible by
bridge. It's a place to go to rent small boats, to fish and to eat
seafood at dockside picnic tables.

For information on new hotels, ongoing updates, and directions
to each hotel by car or mass transit, check online at New York
Today, www.nytoday.com/hotels.

## Le Refuge Inn Bed and Breakfast

| | |
|---|---|
| Extraordinary | $450 and over |
| Excellent | $350–$449 |
| **Very Good** | $250–$349 |
| Good | $150–$249 |
| Basic | **$75–$149** |
| Poor | under $75 |

The warmth of the welcome, the pleasant old sea captain's
house on the main strip of City Island, and the chamber concerts on Sundays are the best reasons to visits Pierre Saint-Denis'
inn in the far reaches of the Bronx. M. Saint-Denis is also the
proprietor of the delightful Le Refuge restaurant on the Upper
East Side. Though we have stayed at the inn, we have not tried
the prix fixe dinner here. We expect it is up to M. Saint Denis's
high standards.

For us, City Island allows you to feel far removed from many aspects of city life, yet you can stand at the water's edge and see the twin towers on the far horizon. The island is often described as a bit of New England in New York, a description that may be stretching a point.

**Le Refuge Inn Bed and Breakfast,** 620 City Island Ave., Bronx NY 10464
**cross streets:** between Sutherland and Cross Streets
**phone:** (718) 885-2478
**fax:** (718) 885-1519
**email:** none
**website:** www.cityisland.com/lerefuge
**number of rooms:** 9 (includes 2 suites)
**number of floors:** 3
**smoking policy:** designated nonsmoking rooms
**restaurants:** yes
**bars:** none
**room service:** yes
**hotel amenities:** some shared baths
**room amenities:** air-conditioning, TV, phone in suites only, refrigerator on request
**parking:** yes
**cancellation:** noon 2 days prior to arrival
**wheelchair accessibility:** public areas — no, rooms — no
**notes:** chamber music concert every Sunday

# STATEN ISLAND

After the bracing (and free) ride to the island on the ferry, there are some sights you may want to see. The Sailors Snug Harbor Cultural Center, 1000 Richmond Terrace (718) 448-2500, hosts concerts and site-specific art installations. The Alice Austin House, 2 Hylan Park Blvd. (718) 816-4506, offers great harbor views, a rolling lawn in summer time, and a look at the works of this early photographer. A collection of Tibetan art can be seen at the Jacques Marchais Center of Tibetan Art, 338 Lighthouse Ave. (718) 987-3500.

For information on new hotels, ongoing updates, and directions to each hotel by car or mass transit, check online at New York Today, www.nytoday.com/hotels.

## Harbor House Bed and Breakfast

| Extraordinary | $450 and over |
| Excellent | $350–$449 |
| Very Good | $250–$349 |
| **Good** | $150–$249 |
| Basic | $75–$149 |
| Poor | **under $75** |

Next door to the charming Alice Austin House is the Harbor House, built in 1890, which has its own charms. It's not luxurious in any way, but it does have views over the harbor to Manhattan. One smart man rented the whole place for the Fourth of July and had his family there to watch the fireworks. The Harbor House feels more like a beach house than anything else, and you can lie in bed and look out to the water. It is distinctly un-New York in feel. Rooms tend to be large, with a clock radio, TV, dresser, armoire, ceiling fan, but there are no phones in the rooms. A good-size continental breakfast is offered. Having your morning coffee on the porch would be a treat. The house is far enough east that you don't see the less attractive parts of Staten Island — it's the water, the Verrazano Bridge, the Statue of Liberty, Manhattan, and it feels like it's all yours.

**Harbor House Bed and Breakfast,** 1 Hylan Boulevard., Staten Island, NY 10305
**cross streets:** at Edgewater Street
**phone:** (718) 876-0056, (800) 626-8096
**fax:** (718) 983-7768
**email:** skyline@erols.com
**website:** www.nyharborhouse.com
**number of rooms:** 11 (includes 3 suites)
**number of floors:** 3
**smoking policy:** all nonsmoking rooms
**restaurants:** none
**bars:** none
**room service:** none
**hotel amenities:** some shared baths
**room amenities:** air-conditioning, VCR on request, iron and board
**parking:** free
**cancellation:** 10 days prior to arrival
**wheelchair accessibility:** public areas — no, rooms — no
**notes:** pets permitted with advance approval

## Staten Island Hotel

| | |
|---|---|
| Extraordinary | $450 and over |
| Excellent | $350–$449 |
| Very Good | $250–$349 |
| **Good** | $150–$249 |
| Basic | **$75–$149** |
| Poor | under $75 |

There was a time when the Staten Island Hotel had a bad rep, but since new owners took over in 1995, it's been onward and upward.

It's now a comfortable, full-service hotel. If you're looking for something near the ferry, this isn't the hotel for you (though it's a quick car ride). Traditional guest rooms, Americana-style, have two-line phones, dataport, voice mail, clock radio, hair dryer, pay-per-view, Nintendo and coffee maker. A safe would hold smaller laptops. Bedding checks out well and in spite of its proximity to a highway, it's reasonably quiet. A good night's sleep should be possible. The closet is an open rack. Some guest rooms have a balcony. Copies of *USA Today* are left by the elevator banks. The hotel has a restaurant, lounge and room service. A pool lies dormant, awaiting repairs. Meantime, if you want some exercise, there are free guest passes to a Bally gym about half a mile away. There is a coin-op laundry and guests are offered a number of freebies for people who have forgotten to pack something — left your toothbrush at home? They'll give you one at no charge.

That's the kind of hospitality we like to see and it seems par for the course here. It's heartening that a once down-on-its-luck hotel has turned things around.

**Staten Island Hotel,** 1415 Richmond Avenue, Staten Island, NY 10314
**cross streets:** between Christopher Lane and Akron Street (off I 278 expressway)
**phone:** (718) 698-5000, (800) 532-3532
**fax:** (718) 354-7071
**email:** none
**website:** www.statenislandhotel.com
**number of rooms:** 187 (includes 3 suites)
**number of floors:** 9
**smoking policy:** designated nonsmoking floors
**restaurants:** yes
**bars:** yes
**room service:** yes
**hotel amenities:** business services, meeting rooms, laundry and dry cleaning
**room amenities:** air-conditioning, safe, modem line, iron and board
**parking:** free
**cancellation:** 6 P.M. 1 day prior to arrival
**wheelchair accessibility:** public areas — yes, rooms — yes

# LA GUARDIA AIRPORT

## Airway Motor Inn at La Guardia

| | |
|---|---|
| Extraordinary | $450 and over |
| Excellent | $350–$449 |
| Very Good | $250–$349 |
| Good | $150–$249 |
| **Basic** | **$75–$149** |
| Poor | under $75 |

A budget choice near La Guardia though not much to look at. The red and brown rooms are pretty drab, if that isn't oxymoronic, the mattresses have no give, and the whoosh of planes can be easily heard. You hang your clothes on a small open rack in the room. Nevertheless, the rooms are clean, not cramped, the water pressure is good and there is a VCR. You can rent videos from a machine in the lobby. It's near to the airport but far from the nicest accommodations in the area.

**Airway Motor Inn at La Guardia,** 82-20 Astoria Blvd., E. Elmhurst, NY 11370
**cross streets:** between 82nd and 83rd Streets
**phone:** (718) 565-5100, (800) 356-0250
**fax:** (718) 565-5194
**email:** none
**website:** none
**number of rooms:** 58
**number of floors:** 6
**smoking policy:** designated nonsmoking rooms
**restaurants:** none
**bars:** none
**room service:** none
**hotel amenities:** none
**room amenities:** air-conditioning, VCR
**parking:** free
**cancellation:** 6 P.M. 1 day prior to arrival
**wheelchair accessibility:** public areas — no, rooms — no

## Crowne Plaza Hotel La Guardia

| | |
|---|---|
| Extraordinary | $450 and over |
| Excellent | $350–$449 |
| **Very Good** | $250–$349 |
| Good | **$150–$249** |
| Basic | **$75–$149** |
| Poor | under $75 |

A renovation in 1998 has left the Crowne Plaza in fighting form. Classic contemporary rooms have two-line phones with dataport and voice mail, *USA Today*, coffee maker, hair dryer, makeup mirror and Institute Swiss bath products. Closets aren't large, and ceilings are low but, crucially, the soundproofing is very good. For $20 over the rack rate, guests get access to the executive level lounge which has a full American breakfast buffet, hors d'oeuvres in the evening and enhanced rooms (brass bed, VCR, scale, bottled water and other items). A pleasant indoor pool with a sun deck, Jacuzzi, sauna, and a room with free weights and aerobics equipment are pluses here. There is an airline screen with up-to-date flight information as you'd expect, and a chef who makes amazing chocolate sculptures — you probably weren't expecting that.

**Crowne Plaza Hotel La Guardia,** 104-04 Ditmars Blvd., E. Elmhurst, NY 11369
**cross streets:** at 23rd Ave.
**phone:** (718) 457-6300, (800) 692-5429
**fax:** (718) 899-9768
**email:** none
**website:** www.crowneplazalaguardia.citysearch.com
**number of rooms:** 358 (includes 23 suites)
**number of floors:** 7
**smoking policy:** designated nonsmoking rooms
**restaurants:** yes
**bars:** yes
**room service:** yes, 24 hour
**hotel amenities:** health club, business services, swimming pool, meeting rooms, concierge, laundry and dry cleaning
**room amenities:** air-conditioning, VCR on request, modem line, mini-fridge on request
**parking:** yes
**cancellation:** 6 P.M. day of arrival
**wheelchair accessibility:** public areas — yes, rooms — yes. ADA compliant

## La Guardia Courtyard by Marriott

| | |
|---|---|
| Extraordinary | $450 and over |
| Excellent | $350–$449 |
| Very Good | $250–$349 |
| **Good** | $150–$249 |
| Basic | **$75–$149** |
| Poor | under $75 |

Marriott has two hotels near each other at La Guardia. The Courtyard doesn't offer as many services, but it has a few strong pluses: the first is quiet — the rooms are very well sound-proofed. The second is an outdoor pool. The pool area is quite pleasant, including a small gazebo. It would be possible to forget you're near an airport if you were wearing headphones, and if you didn't stand up. When you stand, you can see planes land through the hedges.

As for guest rooms, standard issue Courtyard setup. Function is prized over form — it's not pretty but it does work. There are one-line phones with dataport (you'd expect two lines to be a brand standard) and voice mail. Other true-to-forms are foam mattresses, low ceilings, complimentary *USA Today*, hair dryer, coffee maker, iron and ironing board.

There is a fitness room next to the pool with a handful of aer-obics machines and a whirlpool. Parking is complimentary. There is no airline monitor. The hotel offers a shuttle to the air-port every fifteen minutes or on request. The staffer giving us a tour talked about how friendly the staff is. But when we were leaving we asked to be dropped off at the other Marriott. "I haven't got time," snapped a driver. "You can walk." That's not our idea of friendly.

**La Guardia Courtyard by Marriott,** 90-10 Grand Central Pkwy., E. Elmhurst, NY 11369
**cross streets:** at 94th Street
**phone:** (718) 446-4800, (800) 321-2211
**fax:** (718) 446-5733
**email:** none
**website:** none
**number of rooms:** 286
**number of floors:** 6
**smoking policy:** designated nonsmoking rooms
**restaurants:** yes
**bars:** yes
**room service:** yes
**hotel amenities:** health club, outdoor swimming pool, Jacuzzi, business center, meeting rooms, laundry and dry cleaning
**room amenities:** air-conditioning, modem line, mini-fridge on request, multiple phone lines, iron and board
**parking:** free
**cancellation:** 4 P.M. day of arrival
**wheelchair accessibility:** public areas — yes, rooms — yes. ADA compliant

# La Guardia Marriott

| | |
|---|---|
| Extraordinary | $450 and over |
| Excellent | $350–$449 |
| **Very Good** | $250–$349 |
| Good | **$150–$249** |
| Basic | $75–$149 |
| Poor | under $75 |

Competent, comfortable, if not colorful lodging near to La Guardia's terminal. That it's positioned near the terminal, rather than a runway, helps keep the noise down in the room. If you're sensitive to noise, though, ask for a room facing away from the airport.

Familiar Marriott trappings. Foam mattresses, two-line phones with voice mail, low ceilings, clock radio, iron and iron-ing board, hair dryer and coffee maker. Ask for one of the "rooms that work" and you'll get, at the same rate as a room that doesn't work (that's not right, but it sounds good), a pull-out under desk, swivel chair, and a dataport located in the desk lamp base. For $20 over the rack rate, guests are upgraded to the Concierge level — which entitles you to use of a lounge with a concierge, continental breakfast, checkout service. This lounge is closed weekends.

There is a business center with Internet access, fax, printer, and copier. They've also included a pencil sharpener and stapler — details often left out of other business centers. The hotel has a whirlpool, a 50-foot pool, sauna, 24-hour gym with decent, basic equipment and an airline monitor. There is also a strip of grass outside that is one of our favorite hotel quirks in the city. Green, green grass, reclining sunbathing chairs, a bright white fence. Just on the other side of the fence, the Grand Central Parkway.

**La Guardia Marriott Hotel,** 102-05 Ditmars Blvd., E. Elmhurst, NY 11369
**cross streets:** at 23rd Avenue
**phone:** (718) 565-8900, (800) 228-9290
**reservations fax:** (718) 533-3001, guest fax: (718) 898-4955
**email:** none
**website:** www.marriott.com
**number of rooms:** 436 (includes 3 suites)
**number of floors:** 9
**smoking policy:** designated nonsmoking floors
**restaurants:** yes
**bars:** yes
**room service:** yes
**hotel amenities:** health club, business center, swimming pool, dry cleaning, meeting and function rooms
**room amenities:** air-conditioning, iron and board, VCR on request, modem line
**parking:** free
**cancellation:** 6 P.M. day of arrival
**wheelchair accessibility:** public areas — yes, rooms — yes. ADA compliant

# Wyndham Garden Hotel La Guardia Airport

| Extraordinary | $450 and over |
| Excellent | $350–$449 |
| Very Good | $250–$349 |
| **Good** | $150–$249 |
| Basic | **$75–$149** |
| Poor | under $75 |

This is the octagonal-shaped hotel you see when you're on the Grand Central Parkway. It's two connected buildings, one regular-shaped, the other is the octagonal "tower," as the staff refers to it. The hotel was closed for over two years, reopening in 1997 after a $17 million renovation.

In spite of the unconventional design outside, it's straight-ahead inside. Two-line phones with voice mail, clock radio, iron and ironing board, coffee maker, a reclining chair, a small rack in the room for a closet, and Bath and Body Works bath products. Two bathroom problems: water pressure isn't as strong as we'd like, and bathtubs have peeling enamel. The hotel says there are plans to remedy the tubs. The "tower" rooms have, as you'd expect, a pleasing curve to them. You do get some traffic and plane noise from front rooms. There are no dataports and no airline monitors.

Wyndham Garden offers a complimentary full breakfast buffet and free parking — two perks. A fitness rooms contains two stairsteppers, a bike and treadmills. Their Park and Fly package consists of a one-night stay at the hotel and up to seven nights parking at no charge. A small library and sitting area in the lobby makes a comfortable place to hang out and read a book. Our guide says, "We replace the books quite often."

**Wyndham Garden Hotel at La Guardia Airport,** 100-15 Ditmars Blvd., E. Elmhurst, NY 11369
**cross streets:** at 23rd Avenue
**phone:** (718) 426-1500, (800) 457-2230 (WYNDHAM)
**fax:** (718) 205-5853
**email:** none
**website:** www.wyndham.com
**number of rooms:** 229
**number of floors:** 8
**smoking policy:** designated nonsmoking rooms
**restaurants:** yes
**bars:** yes
**room service:** yes
**hotel amenities:** fitness equipment, meeting rooms, function rooms, laundry and dry cleaning
**room amenities:** air-conditioning, VCR on request, modem line, coffee maker with coffee, iron and board
**parking:** free
**cancellation:** 4 P.M. day of arrival
**wheelchair accessibility:** public areas — yes, rooms — yes. ADA compliant

# J. F. K. AIRPORT

## Hilton J. F. K. Airport

| | |
|---|---|
| Extraordinary | $450 and over |
| Excellent | $350–$449 |
| Very Good | $250–$349 |
| **Good** | **$150–$249** |
| Basic | **$75–$149** |
| Poor | under $75 |

This low-slung Hilton that hugs the edge of the Belt Parkway isn't one of the chain's more fetching properties. If it were quieter in the guest rooms, we'd think more of it, but its perch over the highway is a problem not solved — the Holiday Inn, two doors down, has done a much better job of filtering out noise. For an airport hotel, we would have thought that a high priority.

The rooms themselves are perfectly acceptable. Two-line phones, dataport, voice mail, mini-bar with a safe large enough for a laptop. Also standard are a clock radio, iron and ironing board, hair dryer, scale and coffee maker. Room size is comfortable, but bathrooms and closets are extremely small.

Room service is available until midnight. During the wee hours, you can still get food, but the menu is more limited.

Executive level rooms are essentially the same size, but on higher floors and with additional amenities: water, chips and chocolate, bathrobe, razor and shaving cream, and use of the executive lounge off the lobby. There's a fairly extensive complimentary breakfast in a light and airy room, a complimentary cocktail and hors d'oeuvres in the evening.

Concierge services are available in the morning and in the early evening. One nice hotel feature is that check-in can be done on the shuttle bus from the terminal, so you get off the bus and go straight to your room — no waiting on line. There is a fitness room with a half dozen or so aerobic machines, a Universal-type machine, but no free weights. A vague sort of business center is at the desk in the executive lounge — a fax, computer and Internet access are offered at no charge. The Park and Fly package is $195. It includes parking for up to 7 days and one night at the hotel. The deal at the Holiday Inn is up to 14 days for the same price. The Hilton runs a shuttle service to the airports every 30 minutes in the morning and every hour after 1 P.M. Given the hotel's location, it's hard to understand why there is no flight information available in the hotel.

**Hilton J. F. K. Airport,** 138-10 135th Ave., Jamaica, NY 11436
**cross streets:** at North Conduit Avenue
**phone:** (718) 322-8700, (800) 445-8667 (HILTONS)
**fax:** (718) 529-0749
**email:** none
**website:** www.hhctownsquare.hilton.com
**number of rooms:** 330 (includes 10 suites)

**number of floors:** 9
**smoking policy:** designated nonsmoking floors
**restaurants:** yes
**bars:** yes
**room service:** yes
**hotel amenities:** fitness equipment, business center, meeting and function rooms, concierge, laundry and dry cleaning
**room amenities:** air-conditioning, mini-bar, safe, iron and board, coffee maker
**parking:** yes
**cancellation:** 4 P.M. day of arrival
**wheelchair accessibility:** public areas — yes, rooms — yes
**notes:** pets allowed in kennel; park and fly package offered

## Holiday Inn J. F. K. Airport

| | |
|---|---|
| Extraordinary | $450 and over |
| Excellent | $350–$449 |
| **Very Good** | $250–$349 |
| Good | **$150–$249** |
| Basic | $75–$149 |
| Poor | under $75 |

J. F. K. may conjure up lines, crowds and boarding announcements. The Holiday Inn, on the airport's periphery, actually offers some serenity. It has quiet rooms, a pleasant pool and even a Japanese garden. In fact, if you have a room facing away from the airport, it would be possible not to know you were anywhere near an airport.

This hotel had a complete renovation in 1998, and even if the rooms aren't bursts of charm, they are clean, comfortable and decently-sized. There are two-line phones with dataport and voice mail, clock radio, iron and ironing board, hair dryer, and coffee maker. Mini-fridges are in the suites. Bedding is quite comfortable, closets are small, bathrooms are plain but adequate. Smoke detectors and sprinklers are installed throughout the hotel.

Besides the Japanese garden that can be seen from one of the restaurants and from the lobby, the Holiday Inn offers some other helpful and popular amenities. One is the up-to-date airline schedules, available at a kiosk in the lobby. Another is a selection of fairly new movies and, while you're watching, you can order up a pint of ice cream. The hotel has a pool that, in warm weather, has a roof that retracts. There is an exercise room with eight or so aerobics machines, free weights and a Universal-type machine. After your workout, you can relax in the sauna or in the whirlpool next to the pool. A business center in the lobby has an ATM machine, computer, Internet access, printer, fax and copier.

The hotel offers a complimentary shuttle every half hour to J. F. K., and three morning shuttles to La Guardia as well as one to the Green Acres mall. The Park and Fly at the Holiday Inn is worth knowing about, too. You can stay one night, leave your car for up to 14 days, for $199. If you just need long-term parking, it's $8 a day at J. F. K., but it doesn't, needless to say, come with a night in a hotel.

**Holiday Inn J. F. K. Airport,** 144-02 135th Ave., Jamaica, NY 11436
**cross streets:** off exit 2 of the Van Wyck Expressway
**phone:** (718) 659-0200, (800) 692-5350
**reservations fax:** (718) 322-5769, guest fax: (718) 322-2533
**email:** holidayinnjfk@holidayinnjfk.com
**website:** www.holidayinnjfk.com
**number of rooms:** 360 (includes 11 suites)
**number of floors:** 12
**smoking policy:** designated nonsmoking rooms
**restaurants:** 2
**bars:** yes
**room service:** yes
**hotel amenities:** health club, business center, swimming pool, meeting function, laundry and dry cleaning
**room amenities:** air-conditioning, multiline phones, modem lines
**parking:** yes
**cancellation:** 6 P.M. day of arrival
**wheelchair accessibility:** public areas — yes, rooms — yes

## Radisson Hotel J. F. K. Airport

| | |
|---|---|
| Extraordinary | $450 and over |
| Excellent | $350–$449 |
| Very Good | $250–$349 |
| **Good** | **$150–$249** |
| Basic | $75–$149 |
| Poor | under $75 |

The newest of the airport hotels, this Radisson opened in 1998 — there was an abandoned hotel on this site when Radisson bought it and renovated to the tune of $30 million.

Greens and rust are used heavily in the traditionally designed rooms. There are two-line phones with dataport and voice mail, a clock radio, iron and ironing board, hair dryer and coffee maker. The desk, which is arranged so that the long end extends into the room, seems well suited to working, and the dataport is located in the desk lamp. Mattresses are good, but your sleep may be undermined by noise from the Belt Parkway just outside. Closets are acceptably large, bathrooms small and ceilings quite low. All rooms have smoke alarm and sprinklers.

The Radisson is the only one of the four hotels in the area to have a 24-hour restaurant and room service. The hotel offers complimentary shuttle service to J. F. K. and the Green Acres mall. The lobby has an ATM, a flight information kiosk, a business room with fax machine, Internet access, copier and printer.

The fitness room is spacious, with bike, stairsteppers, treadmills, free weights, lockers and showers. It's the only place we know of in New York where you can work out while watching planes land.

**Radisson Hotel J. F. K. Airport,** 135-30 140th St., Jamaica, NY 11436
**cross streets:** at 140th Street
**phone:** (718) 322-2300, (800) 333-3333
**fax:** (718) 322-6894
**email:** none
**website:** www.radisson.com
**number of rooms:** 386
**number of floors:** 12
**smoking policy:** designated nonsmoking floors
**restaurants:** yes
**bars:** yes
**room service:** yes, 24 hours
**hotel amenities:** fitness equipment, business center, meeting and function rooms, laundry and dry cleaning
**room amenities:** air-conditioning, modem line, mini-fridge on request, multiline phone
**parking:** free
**cancellation:** 4 P.M. day of arrival
**wheelchair accessibility:** public areas — yes, rooms — yes

## Ramada Plaza J. F. K. Airport

| | |
|---|---|
| Extraordinary | $450 and over |
| Excellent | $350–$449 |
| Very Good | $250–$349 |
| **Good** | **$150–$249** |
| Basic | $75–$149 |
| Poor | under $75 |

If they could just move the hotel a little to the left. That way, when all those planes are in their final approach, their very final approach, right over the hotel onto the runway, you wouldn't feel inclined to duck your head every few minutes.

Rooms are unremarkable-looking, but they're maintained well and are quiet (except when planes are landing). Amenities include one-line phones with dataport and voice mail, clock radio, iron and ironing board, coffee maker, and most have a mini-fridge. We wish the mattresses were more consistent — some are fresh, others well worn (the king size mattresses are more consistently new). Bathrooms are quite small and come with few bath products but good water pressure. Closets consist of a rack in the room. All rooms have smoke alarms and sprinklers. The floor designated "Business Level" has somewhat upgraded furniture, marble bathrooms and two phones in the room.

There is 24-hour food service though it's not a full menu late at night. The hotel is a Pizza Hut franchise, so you can order up a pizza. A business center has a credit card-activated copier, fax machine and computer with Internet access. It's the only business center we can recall with a pencil sharpener and calculator. A fitness room has two treadmills, two bikes, a rower, two stairsteppers and a cross-country machine. At the bar area, a pool table, pinball machine, video game and outdoor area. At night, complimentary hors d'oeuvres are served. Parking is free while you're staying at the hotel. There is an airline monitor and shuttle service to the terminals. You can also do a Park and Fly here: $175 includes one night at the hotel and up to two weeks parking.

The Ramada is the only hotel actually on J. F. K. property. The other hotels are nearby, but their location means they don't have much land. This hotel actually has two picnic tables underneath trees on a grassy lawn. True, you're watching the entrance road to the airport. And every few minutes, watch your head.

**Ramada Plaza Hotel J. F. K. Airport,** J. F. K. Airport, Van Wyck Expressway, Jamaica, NY 11430
**cross streets:** 1st building on airport property
**phone:** (718) 995-9000, (888)-535-7262 (JFK RAMADA)
**reservations fax:** (718) 244-8962, guest fax (718) 995-9075
**email:** reservations@ramadajfk.com
**website:** www.ramadajfk.com
**number of rooms:** 476 (includes 4 suites)
**number of floors:** 6
**smoking policy:** designated nonsmoking rooms
**restaurants:** yes
**bars:** yes
**room service:** yes
**hotel amenities:** exercise room, business center, meeting rooms, function room, laundry and dry cleaning
**room amenities:** air-conditioning, VCR on request, fax on request
**parking:** free
**cancellation:** 6 P.M. day of arrival
**wheelchair accessibility:** public areas — yes, rooms — yes

# NEWARK INTERNATIONAL AIRPORT, Newark, NJ

## Newark Airport Marriott

| | |
|---|---|
| Extraordinary | $450 and over |
| Excellent | $350–$449 |
| **Very Good** | $250–$349 |
| Good | **$150–$249** |
| Basic | **$75–$149** |
| Poor | under $75 |

The only hotel on Newark Airport property, this Marriott, which opened in 1985, has the company's familiar combination of comforts and corporate traveler amenities. They got a key ingredient right, too. The windows offer virtually complete soundproofing against airplane noise.

Rooms aren't particularly spacious, but they're adequate, done in the familiar Marriott pinks, greens and floral prints. Mattresses are foam; there are one-line phones, dataport and voice mail, clock radio, iron and ironing board and coffee maker. Individual temperature control, sprinklers and a smoke alarm are in all rooms. Concierge level rooms, $20 over the standard rack rate, have two-line phones, upgraded bathroom products and use of a separate lounge. It serves continental breakfast, evening hors d'oeuvres, and there are views over the airport. A telescope helps you keep track of the air traffic, and an airline monitor in the lobby helps you keep track of flight schedules.

The hotel has a concierge desk, a business center with the usual faxing, copying and secretarial services plus a number of office supplies for sale. A fitness room is open 24 hours. There is a pool that gets a lot of natural light, whirlpool and sauna. There are several dining options, including 24-hour room service and a bar with a pool table and outdoor patio. You can take a hotel van directly to your airline at no charge.

If your travel agent books you into the Newark Marriott as a leisure destination, get a new travel agent. For those stuck at the airport or who need to hold a meeting or interviews at Newark, the Marriott is fine.

**Newark Airport Marriott,** Newark International Airport, Newark, NJ 07114
**cross streets:** center of airport
**phone:** (973) 623-0006, (800) 882-1037
**fax:** (973) 623-7618
**email:** none
**website:** www.marriotthotels.com/ewrap
**number of rooms:** 610 (includes 6 suites)
**number of floors:** 10
**smoking policy:** designated nonsmoking floors
**restaurants:** 2
**bars:** yes
**room service:** yes, 24 hours

**hotel amenities:** health club, swimming pool, business center, meeting rooms, function room, concierge, 24 hour shuttle to all terminals, laundry and dry cleaning
**room amenities:** air-conditioning, VCR on request, mini-fridge on request
**parking:** free
**cancellation:** 6 P.M. 1 day prior to arrival
**wheelchair accessibility:** public areas — yes, rooms — yes

# Indexes

## ADA (Americans with Disabilities Act) Compliant

The Algonquin
The Avalon
Belvedere Hotel
The Benjamin
Best Western President
Best Western Seaport
Central Park Inter-Continental NY
The Chelsea Hotel
Comfort Inn at Central Park West
Courtyard by Marriott Times Square South
Crowne Plaza Hotel at the U.N.
Crowne Plaza Hotel La Guardia
Crowne Plaza Manhattan
Days Hotel
De Hirsch Residence at the 92nd St. Y
Doubletree Guest Suites
Dumont Plaza
Eastgate Tower
Empire
Essex House, A Westin Hotel
The Fitzpatrick Grand Central Hotel
The Four Seasons
The Gorham New York
Gramercy Park Hotel
Grand Hyatt New York
The Helmsley Carlton
The Helmsley Middletowne
Holiday Inn Broadway
Holiday Inn Wall Street
Hostelling International — New York
Hotel Beacon
Hotel Casablanca
Hotel Inter-Continental
Hotel Pennsylvania
Howard Johnson Plaza Hotel
The Iroquois New York
Kitano New York
La Guardia Courtyard by Marriott
La Guardia Marriott Hotel
The Lombardy

## Bed and Breakfasts

Akwaaba Mansion Bed and Breakfast
Bed and Breakfast on the Park
Harbor House Bed and Breakfast
The Inn on 23rd Street
Le Refuge Inn Bed and Breakfast
SoHo Bed and Breakfast

## Business Oriented

Millenium Hilton
Millennium Broadway
Millennium Premier
The Regency, A Loews Hotel
Regent Wall Street
RIHGA Royal
Sheraton New York Hotel and Towers
Swissotel New York — The Drake

## Extended Stay

The Bridge Suite Apartments
Bristol Plaza
DeHirsch Residence at the 92nd St. Y
The Envoy Club
The Marmara-Manhattan
The Phillips Club
Rooms to Let
The Sutton

## Good Deals

Hospitality House
Hotel Bedford
Hotel Olcott
The Inn on 23rd Street
Larchmont Hotel
Mayfair New York
The Mayflower Hotel on the Park
Wyndham

## Gay Friendly

Abingdon Guest House
Chelsea Pines Inn
Incentra Village House

## Health Club

Barbizon
The Carlyle
Crowne Plaza Manhattan
De Hirsch Residence at the 92nd St. Y
The New York Palace Hotel
Le Parker Meridien
The Peninsula
RIHGA Royal
Sheraton New York Hotel and Towers
Trump International Hotel and Tower
Vanderbilt YMCA
W New York
The Waldorf=Astoria
West Side YMCA

## Historic

The Algonquin
The Chelsea Hotel
Essex House, A Westin Hotel
The Plaza
The Sherry-Netherland
The Waldorf=Astoria

## Hostels

Big Apple Hostel
Blue Rabbit International House
Chelsea International Hostel
Hostelling International — New York
Jazz on the Park
Sugar Hill International House

## Kitchen(ettes)

Bed and Breakfast on the Park
Blue Rabbit International House
The Bridge Suite Apartments
Bristol Plaza
Chelsea Inn
Country Inn the City
De Hirsch Residence at the 92nd St. Y
Dumont Plaza
Eastgate Tower
Flatotel
The Gorham New York
The Gracie Inn
The Helmsley Carlton
Hospitality House
Hostelling International — New York
Hotel Beacon
Hotel Bedford
Hotel Delmonico
Hotel Olcott
Hotel Riverside
Inn New York City
Kimberly Hotel
The Lombardy
The Lowell
Lyden Gardens
Lyden House
The Mark
The Marmara-Manhattan
Murray Hill East Suites
Murray Hill Suites
Off SoHo Suites Hotel
The Phillips Club
Plaza Fifty
Radio City Apartments
Shelburne Murray Hill
The Sherry-Netherland
SoHo Bed and Breakfast
Southgate Tower
Sugar Hill International House
The Surrey Hotel
The Sutton
Trump International Hotel and Tower
Urban Jem Guest House
Wyman House

## Major Restaurants

### Hotel

The Avalon
The Benjamin
Dumont Plaza
Four Seasons
Kitano New York
NY Marriott Financial Center
Mercer Hotel
Morgans
The New York Palace Hotel
Pickwick Arms Hotel
Regent Wall Street
The St. Regis
The Shoreham
The Surrey Hotel
Trump International Hotel and Tower
The Waldorf=Astoria

### Restaurant

The Coach House
An American Place
Sonia Rose
Fifty Seven Fifty Seven
Nadaman Hakubai
Roy's New York
The Mercer Kitchen
Asia De Cuba
Le Cirque 2000
Scarabée
55 Wall St.
Lespinasse
La Caravelle
Cafe Boulud
Jean Georges
Peacock Alley

### Romantic

Akwaaba Mansion Bed and Breakfast
Bed and Breakfast on the Park
Harbor House Bed and Breakfast
The Inn at Irving Place
Inn New York City
Le Refuge Inn Bed and Breakfast
The Lowell
The Mark
Wyman House

### Spa Services

The Benjamin
Essex House, A Westin Hotel
The Four Seasons
The Peninsula
Regent Wall Street
W New York

### Suites (All or Mostly)

Beekman Tower Hotel
Dumont Plaza
Eastgate Tower
The Helmsley Carlton
Hospitality House
Hotel Delmonico
Inn New York City
Kimberly Hotel
Lyden Gardens
Lyden House
Murray Hill East Suites
Plaza Fifty
Radio City Apartments
Shelburne Murray Hill
Southgate Tower
The Sutton

### Swimming Pool

Barbizon
Bristol Plaza
Crowne Plaza Hotel La Guardia

Crowne Plaza Manhattan
De Hirsch Residence at the 92nd St. Y
Holiday Inn at J.F.K. Airport
Holiday Inn Midtown
La Guardia Courtyard by Marriott
La Guardia Marriott Hotel
Millenium Hilton
New York Marriott Brooklyn
New York Marriott Financial Center
New York Marriott World Trade Center
Newark Airport Marriott
Le Parker Meridien
The Peninsula
Regal United Nations Plaza
Sheraton Manhattan
Skyline Hotel
The Sutton
Travel Inn Hotel
Trump International Hotel and Tower
Vanderbilt YMCA
West Side YMCA

## Technology Oriented

The Benjamin
Fulton Plaza
Holiday Inn Wall Street
The Marmara-Manhattan
Regent Wall Street
Swissotel New York — The Drake
The Time

## 24-Hour Room Service

Central Park Inter-Continental
Crowne Plaza Hotel at the U.N.
Crowne Plaza Manhattan
Essex House, A Westin Hotel
The Fitzpatrick Grand Central Hotel
The Fitzpatrick Manhattan Hotel
The Four Seasons
Grand Hyatt New York
The Iroquois New York
The Mark
The Michelangelo
Millennium Broadway
Millennium Premier
New York Marriott Marquis
The New York Palace Hotel
New York Marriott World Trade Center
Omni Berkshire Place
Paramount
Le Parker Meridien
The Pierre
The Plaza
Plaza Athénée
Regal United Nations Plaza
Regent Wall Street
Renaissance New York Hotel
RIHGA Royal
The St. Regis
Sheraton Manhattan

| Alphabetical | Location | Rating | Price | Page |
|---|---|---|---|---|
| Abingdon Guest House | West Village | Good | $150–$249 | 27 |
| Airway Motor Inn at La Guardia | La Guardia Airport | Basic | $75–$149 | 294 |
| Akwaaba Mansion | Brooklyn | Very Good | $75–$149 | 283 |
| Aladdin Hotel | Midtown West | Basic | $75–$149 | 90 |
| The Algonquin | Midtown West | Very Good | $250–$349 | 91 |
| Americana Inn | Midtown West | Basic | $75–$149 | 92 |
| Ameritania | Midtown West | Good | $150–$249 | 93 |
| Amsterdam Court Hotel | Midtown West | Basic | $150–$249 | 94 |
| Amsterdam Inn | Upper West Side | Basic | $75–$149 | 219 |
| Arlington Hotel | Flatiron/ Gramercy | Basic | $75–$149 | 45 |
| The Avalon | Murray Hill | Good | $150–$349 | 58 |
| Barbizon | Upper East Side | Very Good | $250–$449 | 251 |
| Bed and Breakfast on the Park | Brooklyn | Very Good | $150–$249 | 284 |
| Beekman Tower Hotel | Midtown East | Very Good | $250–$449 | 174 |
| Belleclaire Hotel | Upper West Side | Unrated | $75–$149 | 220 |
| Belvedere Hotel | Midtown West | Basic | $150–$249 | 95 |
| The Benjamin | Midtown East | Excellent | $250–$449 | 176 |
| The Bentley | Upper East Side | Very Good | $250–$349 | 253 |
| Best Western Ambassador | Midtown West | Good | $150–$249 | 96 |
| Best Western City View | Queens | Good | $75–$149 | 287 |
| Best Western Manhattan | Midtown West | Good | $75–$249 | 97 |

| Alphabetical | Location | Rating | Price | Page |
|---|---|---|---|---|
| Best Western President | Midtown West | Good | $75–$249 | 98 |
| Best Western Seaport Inn | Lower Manhattan | Good | $150–$249 | 3 |
| Best Western Woodward | Midtown West | Good | $150–$349 | 99 |
| Big Apple Hostel | Midtown West | Basic | under $75 | 100 |
| Blue Rabbit International House | Harlem | Basic | under $75 | 276 |
| The Box Tree | Midtown East | Poor | $150–$349 | 178 |
| The Bridge Suite Apartments | Upper East Side | Good | $75–$149 | 254 |
| Bristol Plaza | Upper East Side | Excellent | $150–$249 | 255 |
| Broadway Inn | Midtown West | Good | $75–$149 | 101 |
| Carlton Arms Hotel | Flatiron/ Gramercy | Basic | $75–$149 | 46 |
| The Carlton Hotel | Murray Hill | Good | $150–$249 | 59 |
| The Carlyle | Upper East Side | Extra-ordinary | $350 and over | 256 |
| Carnegie Hill Suites | Upper East Side | Good | $150–$249 | 257 |
| Carnegie Hotel | Midtown West | Good | $250–$349 | 102 |
| Central Park NY Inter-Continental | Midtown West | Excellent | $350 and over | 103 |
| The Chelsea Hotel | Chelsea | Good | $150–$349 | 37 |
| Chelsea Inn | Flatiron/ Gramercy | Good | $150–$249 | 47 |
| Chelsea International Hostel | Chelsea | Basic | under $75 | 38 |
| Chelsea Pines Inn | Chelsea | Good | $75–$149 | 39 |
| Chelsea Savoy Hotel | Chelsea | Good | $75–$149 | 40 |
| Clarion Fifth Avenue | Murray Hill | Good | $150–$249 | 60 |
| Comfort Inn at Central Park West | Upper West Side | Good | $75–$149 | 221 |
| Comfort Inn Manhattan | Midtown West | Good | $75–$249 | 104 |
| Comfort Inn Midtown | Midtown West | Good | $75–$249 | 105 |
| Cosmopolitan Hotel | TriBeCa | Basic | $75–$149 | 18 |
| Country Inn the City | Upper West Side | Very Good | $150–$249 | 222 |
| Courtyard by Marriott Times Square | Midtown West | Good | $150–$349 | 106 |
| Crowne Plaza Hotel . at the U.N | Midtown East | Very Good | $150–$349 | 179 |
| Crowne Plaza Hotel La Guardia | La Guardia Airport | Very Good | $75–$249 | 295 |
| Crowne Plaza Manhattan | Midtown West | Very Good | $250–$449 | 107 |
| Days Hotel | Midtown West | Good | $150–$249 | 108 |
| De Hirsch Residence at the 92nd St. Y | Upper East Side | Basic | under $75 | 258 |
| Deauville Hotel | Murray Hill | Basic | $75–$149 | 61 |
| Doral Park Avenue | Murray Hill | Good | $250–$449 | 62 |